# COUNTRY

# BAKING

ALSO BY THE AUTHOR

*Home for the Holidays*
*Country Breakfasts*

# COUNTRY

# BAKING

*Simple Home Baking with Wholesome Grains*
*and the Pick of the Harvest*

# KEN HAEDRICH

BANTAM BOOKS

NEW YORK · TORONTO · LONDON · SYDNEY · AUCKLAND

COUNTRY BAKING
A Bantam Book

PUBLISHING HISTORY
Bantam hardcover edition / December 1990
Bantam trade paperback edition / October 1994

ISBN 0-553-37414-1

*Published simultaneously in the United States and Canada*

Bantam Books are published by Bantam Books, a division of Bantam Doubleday
Dell Publishing Group, Inc. Its trademark, consisting of the words "Bantam
Books" and the portrayal of a rooster, is Registered in U.S. Patent and Trademark
Office and in other countries. Marca Registrada. Bantam Books, 1540 Broadway,
New York, New York 10036.

PRINTED IN THE UNITED STATES OF AMERICA

FFG   0 9 8 7 6 5 4 3 2 1

*This book is dedicated,*
*with affection,*
*to Karen.*

# Contents

# Contents

# Acknowledgments

Acknowledgments are like a personal "Who's Who," of interest—theoretically, at least—only to the people included; everyone else has to suffer through the gushing, private jokes, and words of gratitude. Here's mine:

I would like to thank Coleen O'Shea at Bantam for her part in this and my editor, Fran McCullough, for her guidance in applying the polish. Also, thanks to Chris Benton, my copy editor, for ironing out the many wrinkles. And a big squeeze to my agent, "Mega" Meg Ruley, for bringing us together.

Over the years I have had the opportunity to work with some of the most wonderful and professional editors in magazine publishing, especially Patty McWilliams, Paul Schullery, Fred Schultz, and Susan McInerney at *Country Journal*; Pamela Mitchell and Tina Ujlaki at *Food & Wine*; David Sleeper, Wanda Shipman, and Lisa Furgatch at *Vermont* magazine; and John Barstow, wherever you are today. Many thanks also to food writer Richard Sax, who wrote a lot of nice things about me in a *Yankee* magazine article, some of them even true; and to Marion Cunningham, for the many conversations—and too few meals—we've shared over the years.

On the home front, thanks to all my gardening friends who have been so generous: Michael and Nancy Phillips; crazy Chris Owens; Vid, Annie, and Vincent Valdmanis; Sandy and Daniel Dunfey; Barb Delzio; and Elzey and Melanie Burkham. And to Andy Johnson, our cranberry connection.

A special thanks to Cindy Collea, for just about everything, and Sam Johnson, for the same, not to mention his good—if often skewed—sense of humor.

To my parents—Warren and Muriel—I wish you all the love in the world (you'll be happy to know I'm still wiping the ketchup lid before I put the bottle away, Mom). And to my brothers and sisters—Joe, Barb, Tom, Will, Joanne, and Mary—thanks for keeping in touch when I've been so bad at it.

And finally, love and gratitude to my mate, Karen, and our children—Ben, Tess, Ali, and Sam. Without all of you I'd have nothing to write about. ◆

# COUNTRY

# BAKING

# An
# Invitation
# to
# Home Baking

**M**y family and I—four youngsters, two adults, and a dog who thinks she's the reincarnation of Euell Gibbons (see Blueberry Cornmeal Crumb Cake, page 49)—live in central New Hampshire, on a dirt road next to a mountain lake. We aren't back-to-the-landers, but we enjoy our relative seclusion, and we do our best to live a close, simple family life. We read together a lot, take family walks down old logging roads, and somehow manage to subsist on a steady diet of little kid humor ("What's green and really likes to rock and roll?" "Elvis Parsley!").

Central to our life in the country is good, home-cooked food. We love to eat and we especially love to bake, and over the years we've adopted a baking style that's been influenced by several camps. You won't have to read far in this collection to see that there's a strong whole grain influence here. The whole grain baking movement of the sixties was a good one in that it introduced home cooks to the panoply of little-known grains and flours and brought alternative awareness. But it was destined to fade away:

1

compared to the way Americans had traditionally baked, it was too heavy, too uncompromising, and took itself far too seriously.

So it would be a misrepresentation to call this a whole grain baking book. But neither is it what you would call traditional. It's somewhere between the two: laid-back, eclectic, earthy but not heavy; you might say it's baking that speaks the various tongues of a generation that grew up on Betty Crocker, turned hippie, then saw the dawning of the New American Cuisine. It's baking that sees no reason to turn its back on tradition but can't help stepping on tradition's toes in its ongoing search for individual meaning and style. And it's also baking with a strong sense of place, rooted in the local provender. Were I a Californian, you'd probably see recipes here using blood oranges, Meyer lemons, and a lot of other edible California arcana I've only read about. But this is New England, so I bake with lots of apples and cranberries, spuds and winter squashes—the same stuff cooks have baked with around here for a long time. I sometimes think of it as native American baking, with contemporary flair.

It's only fair to mention that I am a self-taught baker, not a professionally trained one. I sometimes joke that a self-taught baker is someone who took 15 years to learn what he could have learned at cooking school in 15 weeks, had he not got sidetracked by life—things like raising a family, rebuilding a tumbledown house, and thawing frozen pipes with a hair dryer in the dead of winter. Self-learning has its downside, the biggest being that there will always be gaps in your bank of knowledge. But the advantage of a continuing home baking education, I've found, is that it gives you a foundation in practical baking and never lets you venture too far toward the very sophisticated or the very involved. As a busy father, I'm happy to get a pie in the oven, but seldom is there time for a lattice top. What I'm getting at is that home life—its demands, the seasons, your family's preferences, and your level of interest—essentially dictates and creates a framework for the home baker, on which you build a repertoire of recipes that suit your tastes and serve your needs. You start with a few basics and branch out from there.

So what you will find on the following pages aren't recipes that have the patina of a professional baking background. Instead of recipes introduced with statements like "I learned this from my mentor, the great pastry chef Jean-Claude Croissant," you're more likely to encounter little slices of domestic life: pies or coffee cakes we make year in and year out from the blackberries we pick; a 60-minute sandwich bread we've come to depend on for school lunches; and unorthodox but useful techniques and advice. This is baking with rough edges, not particularly refined in appearance—pies that occasionally spill over, hot cakes that come to the table in cast-iron skillets, and big, brawny homemade pizzas and calzones and turnovers so irresistibly good that you'll dig in too fast and probably burn your mouth; don't say I didn't warn you.

You may wonder why I call this a *country* baking book. What does it really mean to be a country baker? Is it a function of place? My brother lives on five acres abutting a wildlife preserve, and deer visit his pond daily. But he lives only minutes from New York City. Can his wife's baking qualify as country? Or is it a specific style? A friend who lives farther back in the sticks than I do bakes from box mixes. Is *that* country baking?

Hard times beg for easy answers, so it's no wonder *country* has fallen into heavy use. *Country* has become an advertising panacea, a feel-good word that dodges the issue of substance and goes right for the emotional jugular with pretty slices of Americana: fresh cream on the table, antiques in the parlor, and chickens in the coop. We think of simpler times, safer times, a time of fewer worries and obligations.

Those of us who live here know another side of country life, one that's seldom as facile or picturesque as the popular images. You can no more reduce country living to isolated frames of the simple life than you can capture the complexity of family by showing the old family slides. Country is an intricate weave and country life a daily paradox of extremes: small-town pettiness and boundless community spirit; poverty in the midst of earth's majesty; illiteracy surrounded by the poetry and eloquence of nature, predictable only in its unpredictability. Country is a home, a place that you grow to love and care for in spite of, or perhaps because of, the hardships. Some, the fortunate, come to the country because this is their playground, a second-home retreat. But they see country in another light; when the country is your mistress, and not your mate, the blossom may never fall off the rose.

The ones who stay and make it here—the natives, the misfits, the city refugees—learn a little piece of country wisdom: that survival hinges on creative involvement with one's reality. You can't change the reality of country life, but you can learn to dance with it, to be a willing subject of its demands and a witness to its beauty. Palatability, one learns, is seasoned with acceptance: of the people, the geography, and the fact that out here you may always paddle around in the eddies of life's uncertainties without ever letting your boat drift into the mainstream.

By extension, the underlying theme of country baking is creative involvement with one's resources. Country baking isn't just a look, a recipe, or an ingredient. If anything, it's a joyful dance with the seasons, a reflection of a specific time, place, mood, or economic condition. Country baking is an intricate fabric, woven by cooks who speak a common, earthy dialect. Country baking is frugal, for the most part, true to the native economy; efficient, for the sake of simplicity; it admires craft but doesn't bother with excessive decoration, lest one shortchange other obligations.

Not that country baking doesn't believe in beauty. But beauty, it believes, is manifest in the effort, in the appreciation, and in the subtle way a homemade pie or cake or bread provides some of the connective tissue for a people who hunger for closeness. The voice of country baking speaks with an eloquence that's only confused by the hype.

Of course, not everyone lives—or desires to live—in the country. But no matter where your home is you can capture the spirit of country baking by using the freshest, top-grade ingredients available. In major cities, and in the suburbs, you are likely to find markets where seasonal organic produce, fresh eggs, and pure maple syrup are sold. Seek these markets out, go there, and strike up conversations with the folks who grow and sell farm products. Also, inquire at your local health food store for sources of fresh foods. They often stock such products. And even if you live in a city apartment, you can grow fresh herbs and tomatoes in old coffee cans, and incorporate your small harvest into your baking. The point is to get involved; you'll be able to taste the difference.

I hope this book, these recipes, will inspire you to bake. Furthermore, I hope this book helps you understand that baking is more than mere mechanics, mixing this and that and putting it in the oven. I hope these recipes and reflections illuminate for you the ways in which home baking is part of a continuum, a small link in the chain that unites us as human beings. When you bake, you reestablish your connection with the earth and the farmer who put the grain there. When you bake, you have the opportunity to fill an artistic void. When you bake, you sow the seeds of brotherhood; what is better therapy for the soul than sitting down to a homemade pie, to share coffee and conversation with close friends and family? What better way to spend a few minutes with your kids than cutting out cookies?

Finally, I hope reading this book is as much a pleasure for you as writing it has been for me. ♦

# Getting Organized

As the former King of Clutter, I can assure you that the greatest impediment to home baking is disorganization. What motivation is there to knock out a pie or a tray of cookies if you can't find the flour, the cinnamon tin is empty, or the baking sheet is buried beneath an ocean of grocery sacks, whisk brooms, and overdue parking tickets?

If this sounds familiar, one of the first things to do is designate a portion of your kitchen—commensurate with your ambitions as a baker and the amount of baking equipment you own—as your baking area. This might encompass a counter space, an entire cabinet or portion of one, and an open shelf for ingredients you always need: baking powder, salt, flour, and the like.

One of the problems all bakers face is how to store cookie sheets and assorted pans, usually in a limited amount of space. This dilemma often takes on towering proportions: everything gets stacked on top of everything else until someone opens the cabinet door, only to be met by an avalanche of metal. I solved this problem, quite cleverly if I might say so, by designing one long shelf with a series of 3/8-inch dowels running the length of it; the dowels support

all my pans on edge, to save room, and nothing gets stacked on anything else. I planned the spacing between the dowels to coincide with the height of specific pans. If a pie pan was, say, 2 inches high, I made a slot 2 1/4 inches wide to accommodate it.

Beneath that shelf I have an open shelf, 12 inches deep, for odd and fat pans, like my kugelhopf pan, pudding molds, and some of my bread pans. Ten or so of my favorite cookbooks are supported by another dowel on one end of the shelf.

Right below that is a 4-inch-wide shelf where I put all sorts of baking odds and ends, from leavenings to spices and biscuit cutters. I like a narrow shelf for oft-used things because it reminds me to put stuff back in the same location after I use it, so I know where it is the next time I need it; on a wider shelf everything would scatter.

Below my maple work counter is a large cabinet with a big drawer for rolling pins, wax paper, plastic wrap, and foil. And beneath that are two oversize sliding shelves that hold my flour bins. Sliding shelves are one of the greatest inventions since the wheel, because without them you tend to let the back area of the cabinet turn into a baking dungeon, the contents of which are soon forgotten. On the upper slider I have two big bins, one each for whole wheat and unbleached flour. Keeping flours you use often in bins is a good idea because all bags have narrow openings, making them hard to get into. And then flour gets all over the tops of the bags, and when you open them it flies all over the place.

There's a second, smaller cabinet to the right of these shelves, where I keep things like honey, molasses, sugars, vanilla, and cocoa powder on another slide-out tray. This entire baking area measures only 5 feet by 30 inches, but because it was designed specifically for me and the type of baking I do, virtually all of my baking needs fit into that area.

In addition to any ideas you might glean from the description of my baking area, here are a few other tips.

♦ *Many cabinet companies manufacture cabinets made specifically for storing baking sheets on edge. Keep that in mind if you happen to remodel or want to add on to an existing group of cabinets.*

♦ *The same goes for slide-out trays. You can order them for standard-size cabinets from most building/home centers.*

♦ *Use cup hooks to hang things on. Screw them underneath open shelves and cabinets. Hanging tools—measuring spoons, pastry blender, beaters—is a good discipline because it keeps things in their own place; you know where to reach for them.* ♦

# Ingredients

## Flour

The bulk of my baking involves two kinds of flour: unbleached flour (also known as unbleached all-purpose flour) and whole wheat flour.

*Unbleached flour* is wheat flour from which the bran and wheat germ have been extracted and that has not been bleached with chemical whiteners—including chlorine and benzoyl peroxide. Bleaching flour is mainly a cosmetic procedure, harking back to a time when white flour was associated with affluence; bleaching also tends to weaken the flour's protein—allowing less volume with yeast breads—and destroys vitamin E. For my money, the consistently good King Arthur unbleached flour, widely available in the Northeast, is the best value. King Arthur is also the only unbleached flour brand I'm aware of that uses no potassium bromate, an oxidizing agent that allows the flour to be used immediately instead of being aged naturally.

My predilection for *whole wheat flour* in baking stems more from gastronomic than health convictions, though there's no doubt that whole wheat flour—which contains both the outer bran and the oil-rich germ—is nutritionally superior. Even a small amount of whole wheat flour added to your baked goods gives them a rustic look and a rich, earthy flavor. For a number of years I ground my own whole wheat flour, from wheat berries I would buy in 50-pound bags, but eventually I found that my desire to bake outweighed my ambition to grind. I've since switched to King Arthur whole wheat.

In certain cakes and quick breads I prefer to use *whole wheat pastry flour,* different from regular whole wheat flour in that it is made from a softer strain of wheat. By soft I mean lower in gluten, the protein in wheat that gives baked goods their elastic structure. The extra softness can be an asset if you want a slightly higher rise and a more tender—though often more crumbly too—product.

I use *stone-ground yellow cornmeal* purchased from the local health food store, where they grind their own every week. The mass-market cornmeal you find in supermarkets has generally had the germ removed, and consequently it tastes flat and unexciting (though I do use it for sprinkling

9

on my baking sheets when I bake bread; it is less expensive and, without the germ, smokes less in the oven). So for baking purposes, look for cornmeal that says *undegermed* and *stone-ground*. Some supermarkets carry stone-ground cornmeal. Stone grinding—as opposed to high-speed steel roller grinding—is the preferred method, because it does not subject the oily germ to heat that might otherwise cause the cornmeal to turn rancid prematurely. For the same reason, stone-ground whole wheat flour is best.

The health food store is also a good source for many of the specialty flours and grains I use in my baking, including *rye, barley, buckwheat, whole millet* or *millet flour,* and *rolled oats* and *oat flour*. Unless you are a prolific whole grain baker, I suggest buying only small amounts of these flours and grains for specific recipes, and then storing the remainder, tightly sealed, in your freezer for optimum life.

Flour storage, in general, should be tied to your frequency of use. I keep my unbleached and whole wheat flours at room temperature, but I often go through pounds of both each week; there's little chance of spoilage. If you are only an occasional baker, store whole wheat flour in either the fridge or freezer—especially in the summer—in an airtight container or plastic bag (but bring it to room temperature when you're baking yeast bread, or the cold will inhibit the action of the yeast). ♦

## Sweeteners

I like to use a variety of sweeteners in my baking—*granulated white sugar* when I simply want to sweeten something, without flavoring it; *light brown sugar* when a slight caramel flavor is appropriate; *honey, molasses,* or *maple syrup* if I'm looking for a more assertive flavor and a bit of extra moisture, for good keeping. These liquid sweeteners can be stored at room temperature, which is just the right temperature when you are creaming them with butter.

I have no brand preference for either white or brown sugar (which is just white sugar with molasses added); I usually just buy the least expensive I can find, often the store brand. For ease of handling (measuring), I like to keep the sugars in tightly closed containers with wide openings, for hassle-free scooping. White sugar is essentially self-packing, but brown sugar should always be packed when it's measured.

I used to experiment in my baking with different honeys, many of them dark-colored and exotic, only to find I actually prefer the least expensive and lightest-colored honey I can find, simply because light honey doesn't dominate the flavor of baked goods. Orange blossom and clover honey, if indeed there's even a variety listed on the label, fall into this category. Try to keep your honey in a warmish spot, so it's easy to pour and measure. Also, keep the container clean; even small dribbles of honey can attract ants from out of state.

Molasses adds color and a bittersweet quality to baked goods. My preference is for unsulphured molasses, not the very dark blackstrap variety, which is too strong for my liking. Both honey and molasses will keep indefinitely, stored in a cupboard.

Because I live in the heart of maple country, I know many producers, and without exception they are a hardworking breed who care enormously about the quality of their product. Real maple syrup—not the ersatz pancake syrup that's seldom more than 3 percent of the real McCoy—has become quite expensive of late. Nonetheless, dedicated cooks will always want to bake with it. I try to use it in baking only when there's a definite maple flavor payoff. For baking purposes most cooks I know prefer one of the lower grades—Grade A, dark amber, or perhaps Grade B (which is sometimes called Grade C; the grading system is a bit confounding). If at all possible, buy your maple syrup directly from the source; you'll get the best price. Pour several months' supply into a jar and refrigerate it; bottle up the rest in canning jars—leaving a little headroom—and freeze for longer storage. Frozen, it will last indefinitely. ◆

## Fats

The role of fats in baking is to contribute tenderness and, sometimes, flavor. My solid fat of choice is *unsalted butter*; all one need do to appreciate the clean, fresh flavor of unsalted butter is to taste it alongside some salted butter. You'll be amazed at the difference. I use Cabot's butter from Vermont—

as well as Land O'Lakes—but any good AA grade butter will be fine. Unsalted butter is more perishable than salted, though I have never had unsalted butter, which I used by the expiration date stamped on the package, turn rancid on me. When a recipe calls for *softened* butter—and I prefer that term to *room temperature* because our kitchen's climate is never steady, depending on the season and whether or not the woodstoves are cranking out the heat—it means the entire stick should yield to gentle finger pressure, without feeling *squishy*-soft.

*Vegetable oil* doesn't have the flavor of butter, but it is a good choice when you don't need a solid fat and there are other assertive flavors in the recipe (in which case you'd probably miss the butter flavor anyway). I use a basic flavorless vegetable oil; I use olive oil for some Italian-type breads. Some cooks like to use specialty oils—walnut, corn, and the like—to add another layer of flavor to certain breads, but these are expensive and, in my experience, often languish on the shelf if they've been purchased for one specific recipe. Oil can be stored at room temperature if you go through it within several weeks; otherwise, it's better to refrigerate it. ◆

## Olive Oil

A number of the recipes in this book call for olive oil, an incredibly complex subject. (For an excellent overview, refer to *Tastings* [Crown, 1986] by Jennifer Harvey Lang.)

Throughout this book I have recommended using a good quality olive oil, which—as Mrs. Lang points out—is a highly subjective judgment. Some olive oils are fine textured, with a subtle flavor. Others are more robust and fruity. If you're curious, experiment by trying a number of olive oils, to see which characteristics appeal to you. Those labeled "first-pressed" are generally considered very good; these are unrefined oils which taste strongly of olives, especially if they are also unfiltered. The terms "extra virgin" and "virgin" should also tip you off that the oil has a relatively low level of acidity, an indication that the oil will have a good olive flavor. ♦

## Eggs

I use large eggs in baking, out of habit and for the sake of standardization. It makes no difference whether you use brown- or white-shelled eggs, so long as they are fresh and kept under refrigeration. If you can find farm-fresh eggs from a local source, all the better, and you'll notice not just a more vibrant color (from the yolk), but a clearer flavor, especially when used in custard-type pies. ♦

## Chemical Leavenings

When *baking powder* is called for in these recipes, it refers to double-acting baking powder, which to my knowledge is the only kind of powder commercially available these days. Baking powder leavens baked goods by producing carbon dioxide gas, initially in the presence of moisture (when you mix your batter) and then again in the heat of the oven; the words *double-acting* refer to this two-stage leavening. Baking powder can be stored for roughly a year at room temperature, tightly covered. *Baking soda* requires an acid ingredient, such as buttermilk, yogurt, or molasses, to act as a leavening. ♦

## Nuts

The health food store is my nut supplier of choice. Nuts spoil very quickly, so be sure to keep them tightly wrapped in the freezer. ♦

# Picks and Pans

## A Pretty Long Talk About Bakeware

Even if I have a terrible weakness for the shiny new bakeware you have in gourmet shops, I'd be the last person in the world to suggest you go out and spend a lot of money on fancy baking pans. First of all, much of my own stuff is quite old, battered, and grease-stained (and much of it was purchased at yard sales), yet I wouldn't dream of replacing it as long as it still serves its function. And second, a body just doesn't need much equipment to do most baking. Ninety percent of the time you can get by with the Big Three—loaf pan, pie pan, and baking sheet—plus a skillet and a knack for improvisation.

So, my first rule for buying bakeware is simple: buy only what your current level of expertise and interest necessitates. Let your collection of baking equipment grow as you grow as a baker. Don't run out and buy three bundt pans if you've never so much as looked at a recipe for bundt cake. (And besides, I have two for sale if you're interested.) ◆

## The Big Three

For the typical home baker the most important piece of bakeware is probably your *baking sheet.* By baking sheet I mean cookie sheet—usually rimless on the two long sides and having low, sloping edges on each short end. French-style baking sheets generally have a low, continuous rim on all four sides. The reason for low or no sides is to allow oven heat to travel unimpeded across the surface of your cookies or crackers or whatever. The arrangement also allows you to slide off fragile tart shells or tea rings without having to lift them.

You can tell a lot about a baking sheet simply by picking it up. Are you impressed with its weight? You should be, although a good aluminum sheet won't feel as hefty as a steel one the same size. Note the sheet's thickness, or "gauge." If you can flex the sheet easily, it is too thin, liable to encourage burning or buckling, upsetting whatever it supports.

Baking sheets come in both shiny and dark finishes, and both have their advantages. I'll choose a shiny sheet when I'm baking something rich in butter and sweetener, like cookies, because the shininess reflects the oven heat and tempers the too-dark browning you can get with rich baked goods. On the other hand, if I'm baking a lean, free-form bread (one with a minimum of fat), I'm more inclined to select a dark sheet, one that collects the heat quickly and helps give the loaf a nice lift and crusty crust.

Some bakeware starts shiny and turns dark with long-term use. Other bakeware comes with a dark finish, of which there are several types. My top choice in this second category is a material called Bakalon, made by Chicago Metallic. Bakalon is CM's name for a highly durable anodized finish (anodizing is an electrostatic process which actually hardens the aluminum, sealing the surface and making it nonporous). These sheets aren't cheap, but they're guaranteed for five years and could well stand up to a lifetime of home baking use.

There are other black or blue steel sheets too, coatings applied to protect the steel and enhance their heat-absorbing properties. My experience is that the heavy black steel pans tend to hold up better; any of the blue steel stuff I have seems to be quite prone to scratching and rusting.

My first choice for shiny sheets is tinned steel; Chicago Metallic makes good ones.

Generally interchangeable with a cookie sheet is a jelly roll pan. The difference between the two is the jelly roll pan's continuous sides, 1/2 to 3/4 inch high. The sides are there, of course, for containment. They're useful if you're roasting and stirring granola,

need side support for a batch of dinner rolls, or fear something will run onto your oven floor—jelly roll batter, for instance. In theory, jelly roll pans are unsuitable for squat baked goods like cookies and crackers because the side wall interferes with the flow of heat over the pan. Most of the jelly roll pans I know, however, aren't aware of this theory and work just fine for cookies and the like. And you can transform any jelly roll pan into a cookie sheet by turning it over and baking on the bottom.

*Bread pans* come in almost every size and material under the sun. I've collected dozens over the years, but—as with rolling pins—you tend to settle on just a couple for everyday baking. Mine measure 4 1/2 by 8 1/2 inches, one made of tinned steel, the other of anodized aluminum. This size pan gives you a good-size loaf, big enough for sandwiches but not so big you can't fit the slices in a toaster, which happens with bigger pans.

These two pans offer a good lesson in the baking properties of different materials: even though I always start baking loaves in these pans at the same time, the bread in the darker, anodized aluminum pan is always done first. The bread in the tinned steel pan always needs an extra five minutes in the oven, out of the pan.

I have no major complaints about glass loaf pans, but I have noticed more sticking problems with them. I tend to underuse both my glass pan and a very nice ceramic loaf pan just because I don't like to break things.

For batter breads (quick breads), I like to use shiny reflective pans. Dark pans aren't a good match with sweet and buttery breads, because you tend to get excessive browning on all sides.

As for *pie pans,* I'm stuck on the old tin ones that are embossed with the name of the companies that once sold pies in returnable pie plates. Most of mine are called "Table Talk." You can buy these—for a buck or two—in antique shops all over New England, but I'm not sure about their availability in the rest of the country.

I got away from glass pie pans a long time ago because I don't like going from freezer to oven with glass, and I almost always do that with a single-crust pie. Most of the glass bakeware I see today, however, says this quick change in temperature won't break the glass; be sure to read the package.

There seems to be a distinction among manufacturers of pie pans between "deep-dish" and shallower pie pans. I think these must be in-house distinctions, because a real deep-dish pan—or at least what I've always called a deep-dish pie pan—is almost always ceramic and a good deal deeper than the metal ones the manufacturers call deep-dish.

All of the pies in this book call for a 9-inch pie pan, which will yield eight good-size servings. I prefer what manufacturers generally refer to as a "deep-dish" pie pan, or one whose top edge—measured from the flat surface on which the pan sits—measures at least 1¼ inches. With pans much squatter than that, you'll have a hard time fitting in many of the fillings in this book. ◆

# QUICK
# BREADS

*W*hen a bread isn't yeasted, it is usually said to be "quick," meaning leavened with baking powder or baking soda. Muffins are quick breads. So are biscuits, soda breads—the most well known being Irish soda bread—tea breads, like banana bread, and coffee cake. Unlike yeast breads, which develop their wheaty and relatively complex flavor through fermentation, quick breads rely more on the sum of their good ingredients— butter, nuts and dried fruits, sweeteners—for their flavorful payoff.

The "quick" in quick bread also refers to the relatively fast method of combining the ingredients; they either aren't kneaded at all or only very briefly. In fact, the method of mixing quick breads—quickly and with as little handling as possible—is directly opposed to the way yeast breads are mixed; the gluten developed through kneading, which gives yeast breads their elasticity, is anathema to quick breads. That's why recipes for quick breads almost always advise you not to beat but to mix ingredients with a few strokes, just until they're combined.

There's yet a third aspect to the "quick" in quick breads: *when* they should be eaten. Muffins and biscuits should be eaten within minutes of being removed from the oven. Their peak point of enjoyment—when you can crack one open and inhale their steamy, fragrant vapors—lasts only about five minutes. Beyond that, they begin to dry out. (You *can* stall the process by holding muffins in foil in a warm oven, but that doesn't work as well for biscuits, because the interior steam takes the crustiness out of the crust.) So when I tell you in a recipe to put the biscuits or muffins in a cloth-lined basket and serve at once, I mean *at once.*

On the other hand, quick tea breads *shouldn't* be eaten right away, but cooled first and then immediately wrapped to preserve them. Of all the quick breads, quick tea breads—because they contain more fat and sweetener than most—have the longest life.

Once you get in the habit of making quick breads, you will probably take them for granted, as my family does. Rare is the week when we don't make several kinds of muffins or biscuits: berry muffins in summer, squash muffins in the fall, herb biscuits when fresh herbs are abundant. In winter we like plain whole wheat or cheese biscuits. But plain or fancy, they're always made from scratch, and the flavor never lies. ◆

## Cornmeal Molasses Crumb Muffins

*Makes 12 muffins*

These light, grainy, straw-colored muffins with cornmeal/brown sugar topping are perfect at breakfast, accompanied by applesauce and yogurt. If these appeal to you, don't overlook Pecan Streusel Coffee Cake (page 47), a buttery, sweet variation on this theme.

MUFFIN BATTER
*1 cup unbleached flour*
*³/4 cup yellow cornmeal, preferably stone-ground*
*¹/2 cup whole wheat flour*
*2 teaspoons baking powder*
*¹/2 teaspoon salt*
*¹/4 teaspoon ground cinnamon*
*¹/4 teaspoon freshly grated nutmeg*
*¹/4 teaspoon ground ginger*
*1 large egg*
*1 cup milk*
*¹/3 cup flavorless vegetable oil*
*¹/4 cup unsulphured molasses*

CRUMB TOPPING
*2 tablespoons yellow cornmeal, preferably stone-ground*
*1¹/2 tablespoons unbleached flour*
*2 tablespoons packed light brown sugar*
*pinch of salt*
*1 tablespoon cold unsalted butter*

Preheat the oven to 400° and butter 12 muffin cups. To make the muffin batter, stir the unbleached flour, cornmeal, whole wheat flour, baking powder, salt, and spices together in a large mixing bowl. In a separate bowl, beat the egg lightly, then whisk in the milk, oil, and molasses. Set aside.

Make the crumb topping by combining the crumb ingredients in a mixing bowl and then rubbing them between your fingers until you have large, damp crumbs.

Make a well in the dry ingredients, add the liquids, and stir with a few deft strokes, just to blend. Divide the batter evenly among the muffin cups. Sprinkle some of the crumb topping on each muffin and bake for 18 to 20 minutes. When the muffins are done, the topping should be browned lightly and the muffins themselves slightly springy to the touch. Cool the muffins on a rack in the pan for 5 minutes, after which they should lift right out. Serve them hot, storing leftovers in a sealed plastic bag for up to 2 days. To reheat, wrap in foil and place in a hot oven for 5 minutes. ◆

# Banana Blueberry Muffins

*Makes 12 muffins*

We like to eat most of our summer meals out at the picnic table. On a typical morning we're likely to have a basketful of these plump, grainy muffins, made with just-picked berries, and some soft butter or cream cheese to spread on them.

*1 cup (2 large) mashed very ripe banana*
*1 large egg*
*²/₃ cup packed light brown sugar*
*5 tablespoons very soft unsalted butter*
*1 teaspoon vanilla extract*
*1 cup unbleached flour*
*³/₄ cup whole wheat flour*
*¹/₃ cup yellow cornmeal, preferably stone-ground*
*1¹/₂ teaspoons baking powder*
*¹/₂ teaspoon baking soda*
*¹/₄ teaspoon salt*
*¹/₄ teaspoon freshly grated nutmeg*
*1 cup fresh blueberries (frozen will do, if need be)*

Preheat the oven to 400° and butter 12 muffin cups. In a large mixing bowl, beat together the banana, egg, brown sugar, butter, and vanilla. In a separate bowl, stir together the remaining ingredients except the blueberries. Make a well in the dry mixture, add the liquid ingredients, and stir just until blended. On the last few strokes, fold in the blueberries.

Divide the batter evenly among the muffin cups and bake for 10 minutes. Reduce the heat to 375° and bake for another 10 minutes. Let the muffins sit in the pan on a rack for 5 minutes, then remove them and serve warm, from a cloth-lined basket. Store cooled leftovers in a sealed plastic bag for up to 2 days. To reheat, wrap in foil and place in a hot oven for 5 minutes.

VARIATIONS: *Use other berries in place of the blueberries. Also, a small grating of lemon zest gives these a nice lift.* ◆

## Freezing Quick Breads

Many quick breads—in particular muffins and tea breads—can be frozen quite successfully (biscuits and the various soda breads much less so, and I don't encourage it). For best results, if you do plan to freeze them, do it as soon as possible once they have cooled, to prevent them from drying out. For tea breads, you can wrap a loaf whole—in plastic, then foil—and freeze it like that. Or, you can cut and wrap individual slices. The advantage of the latter method is that you can drop a slice right into a lunch bag, and it will thaw in plenty of time for lunch.

Muffins can be wrapped whole, but a lot of people like to split them first, so they're ready to be popped right into the toaster oven without having to cut them while they're still frozen. If you plan to reheat muffins in your regular oven, wrap them individually, in foil, and store them in the freezer. To reheat, put the foil-wrapped muffins in a preheated 400° oven for 10 minutes.

## Oat Bran Banana Muffins

*Makes 12 muffins*

Whether or not you've felt any enthusiasm for the oat bran movement, you'll have a hard time remaining indifferent to these muffins. Besides using oat bran, I've taken further steps to bolster their nutritional profile: adding whole wheat flour, keeping the sugar to a minimum, and using a moderate amount of oil. My only problem with these muffins is that I can't resist spreading them with soft, sweet butter, thus both elevating and lowering my cholesterol level in each bite. More conscientious types might opt for a dab of yogurt, jelly, or honey.

1 cup unbleached flour
³/₄ cup oat bran
¹/₂ cup whole wheat flour
1 tablespoon baking powder
¹/₂ teaspoon salt
¹/₂ cup (1 large) mashed ripe banana
¹/₃ cup flavorless vegetable oil
1 large egg
¹/₂ cup packed light brown sugar
2 tablespoons unsulphured molasses
¹/₂ cup milk

Preheat the oven to 400° and butter 12 muffin cups. In a medium mixing bowl, stir together the unbleached flour, oat bran, whole wheat flour, baking powder, and salt. In a separate bowl, beat the remaining ingredients with an electric mixer. Make a well in the dry ingredients and stir in the liquids with a few deft strokes; do not beat. Spoon the batter into the muffin cups and bake for 10 minutes. Reduce the heat to 375° and bake for another 10 minutes. When done, they'll be nicely browned and springy to the touch. Let the muffins sit in the pan on a rack for 5 minutes before transferring them to a cloth-lined basket. Serve hot. Store completely cooled leftovers in sealed plastic bags.

VARIATIONS: *These are excellent with ¹/₂ cup raisins, chopped dried fruit, or nuts folded in on the last few strokes.* ♦

# Toasted Almond Pear Muffins

*Makes 10 muffins*

Here's a light, elegant muffin for a crisp fall morning.

1/2 cup (2 ounces) shelled almonds
1/2 cup packed light brown sugar
1 2/3 cups unbleached flour
1 tablespoon baking powder
1/2 teaspoon salt
1/4 teaspoon ground ginger
1/4 teaspoon freshly grated nutmeg
1 large egg
3/4 cup milk
1/4 cup unsalted butter, melted and cooled
1 large pear, peeled, cored, and chopped
finely grated zest of 1 lemon

Preheat the oven to 375° and butter 10 muffin cups. Spread the almonds on a baking sheet and roast them in the preheated oven for 8 to 10 minutes, until they become fragrant and darken slightly. Cool them on a plate. When they've cooled, put them in a blender or food processor with the brown sugar and process to a fine meal (a few remaining large almond chunks are fine). Stir the almond mixture with the unbleached flour, baking powder, salt, and spices.

In a separate bowl, beat the egg with the milk. Make a well in the dry ingredients and stir in the liquid ingredients. Before the batter is fully blended, add the butter, pear, and lemon zest. Stir again, just until no traces of dry ingredients are visible.

Divide the batter evenly among the buttered cups and bake for 25 minutes, until the tops are golden brown and spring back to the touch. Cool them briefly in the cups on a rack, then transfer them to a cloth-lined basket and serve hot. Store leftovers in a sealed plastic bag. To reheat, wrap in foil and place in a hot oven for 5 minutes. ◆

## Dried Fruits

Raisins, dates, prunes, cherries—all these dried fruits and others add sparkle, texture, and interesting flavors to home-baked goods.

Your local health food store is likely to be your best source for a variety of dried fruits; what they don't stock, they can probably order for you. The health food store is also the likeliest place to find *unsulphured* dried fruits. Sulphur is a common preservative used in the drying of fruits. Not only are some people allergic to it, but—in my estimation—it can adversely affect the flavor of the fruit.

Many dried fruits can be incorporated into your baking as is; pit dates and prunes, of course, and chop all dried fruits into bite-size pieces. If a fruit seems *too* dry—difficult to cut or chew—a short soaking will rehydrate it, and vastly improve its texture. Simply put the chopped fruit into a small bowl and add enough warm water or fruit juice to cover. Let the fruit soak for at least 10 minutes, then drain and use. If you like, you can use the soaking liquid to replace some of the liquid in the recipe.

# Raspberry Mint Muffins

*Makes 12 muffins*

This is a pretty, festive muffin, splattered with big red berries. It would be a good muffin to help mark a special summer occasion, like Father's Day, the first day of vacation, or the Fourth of July. The yogurt, honey, and berries keep these moist and fresh longer than most. If you grow or can buy fresh lemon thyme, it can replace the mint quite nicely.

*1/2 cup honey*
*1/4 cup unsalted butter*
*1 1/3 cups whole wheat flour*
*1 cup unbleached flour*
*1 teaspoon baking soda*
*1/2 teaspoon salt*
*1/4 teaspoon ground ginger or allspice*
*1 large egg*
*1 cup plain yogurt*
*1/4 to 1/3 cup fresh mint leaves (not packed)*
*1 tablespoon sugar*
*1 1/4 cups fresh raspberries*
*additional sugar for sprinkling tops (optional)*

Preheat the oven to 375° and butter 12 muffin cups. Put the honey and butter in a small saucepan and place over low heat to melt the butter; don't let it boil.

In a medium mixing bowl, mix the flours, baking soda, salt, and ginger or allspice. Set aside. In a separate bowl, beat the egg and yogurt, then whisk in the honey and butter, which should now be melted. Reserve.

Chop the mint leaves coarsely, then sprinkle the tablespoon of sugar over them and mince the leaves until quite fine. In a small bowl, toss this mint sugar with the raspberries.

Make a well in the dry ingredients and stir in the liquid ingredients just to blend. Fold in the raspberries on the last few strokes. Divide the batter evenly among the muffin cups and sprinkle each of the tops, if you wish, with a pinch of sugar. Bake for 20 minutes. Let the pan cool on a rack for 5 minutes, then pop the muffins out and put them in a cloth-lined basket. Serve right away, storing cooled leftovers in a sealed plastic bag. ♦

# Chocolate Almond Cherry Muffins

*Makes 12 muffins*

Sweet and festive, this is more of a holiday or weekend muffin than a workaday one. Over time I've toned down the chocolate to accommodate the cherry purists I live with, but I still hanker for the days when I made these with twice as much.

> 1/4 *cup unsalted butter*
> 1 *ounce unsweetened chocolate*
> 2/3 *cup packed light brown sugar*
> 1 *large egg*
> 1 *cup milk*
> 1 *teaspoon vanilla extract*
> 1 *cup unbleached flour*
> 3/4 *cup whole wheat flour*
> 1/2 *cup (about 2 ounces) finely chopped unblanched almonds*
> 1 *tablespoon baking powder*
> 1/2 *teaspoon salt*
> 1/2 *teaspoon ground cinnamon*
> 1/2 *cup quartered pitted sweet cherries (see note on pitting cherries, page 220)*

Preheat the oven to 375° and butter 12 muffin cups. Over very low heat, start to melt the butter in a small saucepan. Once it covers the bottom of the pan, add the chocolate. Melt the chocolate completely, then remove it from the heat and whisk until smooth.

In a mixing bowl, whisk the melted butter and chocolate with the brown sugar and egg. Blend in the milk and vanilla. In a separate bowl, mix the flours, almonds, baking powder, salt, and cinnamon. Make a well in the dry ingredients, then stir in the liquid ingredients all at once. Stir gently, just until no dry streaks are visible; fold the cherries in on the last few strokes.

Divide the batter evenly among the muffin cups and bake for 20 minutes. Cool them in the pan on a rack for several minutes, then transfer the muffins to a cloth-lined basket and serve right away. Store cooled leftovers in a plastic bag. ◆

## Sam's Carrot and Apple Muffins

*Makes 12 muffins*

*K*aren and I have worked out a loose agreement that goes like this: she carries and delivers the kids, and I, for several weeks postpartum, prepare all her favorite foods. Knowing her weakness for carrot cake, I dreamed these up for her after Sam, our fourth child, arrived. Believe me, they're every bit as good as carrot cake—moist, tender, and rich-tasting.

> 1 cup loosely packed grated carrot
> 1 cup loosely packed grated apple
> 2/3 cup packed light brown sugar
> 1/2 cup raisins, preferably golden
> finely grated zest of 1 lemon
> 1 large egg
> 1/3 cup flavorless vegetable oil
> 3/4 cup milk
> 1 1/4 cups whole wheat flour
> 1 cup unbleached flour
> 2 teaspoons baking powder
> 1 teaspoon baking soda
> 1/2 teaspoon salt
> 1/2 teaspoon ground cinnamon
> 1/2 teaspoon ground allspice

Preheat the oven to 375° and butter 12 muffin cups. Mix the grated carrot, apple, brown sugar, raisins, and lemon zest in a medium mixing bowl. Set aside. In another bowl, beat the egg lightly, then blend in the oil and milk. In yet another, larger bowl, stir together the remaining dry ingredients.

Combine the grated mixture with the liquid ingredients. Make a well in the center of the dry ingredients, then add the wet ingredients and stir just to blend; stop stirring when no dry streaks are visible. Divide the batter evenly among the muffin cups. It will probably almost fill the cups, but that's okay, since I find these dome up quite nicely and don't spill out over the top. Bake for 20 minutes, until browned and the tops are just springy to the touch. Cool the muffins in the cups on a rack for several minutes, then transfer them to a cloth-lined basket and serve hot. Store leftovers in a sealed plastic bag. To reheat, wrap in foil and place in a hot oven for 5 minutes. ◆

# Winter Squash Crumb Muffins

*Makes 12 muffins*

I love crumb toppings, and I think they are an especially welcome attraction on a soft, moist muffin such as this one, made with winter squash. If you would rather skip cooking the squash, you can simply substitute 1 cup canned squash or pumpkin puree.

CRUMB TOPPING

*2 tablespoons yellow cornmeal, preferably stone-ground*
*1¹/₂ tablespoons unbleached flour*
*2 tablespoons packed light brown sugar*
*pinch of salt*
*1 tablespoon cold unsalted butter*

MUFFIN BATTER

*2 cups cubed peeled winter squash or pumpkin (see note above)*
*1¹/₄ cups unbleached flour*
*1 cup whole wheat flour*
*1 tablespoon baking powder*
*³/₄ teaspoon salt*
*¹/₂ teaspoon ground cinnamon*
*¹/₂ teaspoon ground cloves*
*¹/₂ teaspoon freshly grated nutmeg*
*1 large egg*
*³/₄ cup packed light brown sugar*
*¹/₄ cup unsalted butter, melted, or flavorless vegetable oil*
*1 teaspoon vanilla extract*
*¹/₃ cup milk*
*¹/₂ cup dark or golden raisins*

To make the topping, mix the topping ingredients in a small bowl, rubbing them together with your fingers until you have large, damp crumbs. Reserve.

Put the squash cubes in a large saucepan and cover with about 1 quart lightly salted water. Bring to a boil, cover, and reduce heat to a low boil. Cook for about 20 minutes, until very tender and easily pierced with a fork. Drain, and when cool enough to handle, puree the squash in a blender, food processor, or food mill. Preheat the oven to 400°. While the squash is cooling, butter 12 muffin cups and prepare the batter.

In a medium bowl, mix the flours, baking powder, salt, and spices. In a separate bowl, beat the egg lightly, then beat in the cooled squash, brown sugar, melted butter or oil, and vanilla. Stir half of the dry ingredients into the liquid ingredients, followed by the milk, then the rest of the dry ingredients. Fold in the raisins.

Divide the batter evenly among the muffin cups. Sprinkle some of the crumb topping on each muffin and bake for 20 minutes. Cool in the pan on a rack for several minutes, then transfer the muffins to a cloth-lined basket and serve right away. Store leftovers in a sealed plastic bag. To reheat, wrap in foil and place in a hot oven for 5 minutes. ◆

# Double-Corn and Cheese Muffins

*Makes 12 muffins*

Here's a great muffin to make during corn season, with fresh-cut corn kernels. If the corn is tender, you can just fold the uncooked kernels into the batter. If the kernels are on the tough side, they'll benefit from a short boiling first; drain and cool them before proceeding. Out of season, you can substitute thawed frozen kernels, patted dry between paper towels.

These are marvelous with a bowl of chili or just a plate of sliced vine-ripened summer tomatoes.

*1¹/₂ cups unbleached flour*
*²/₃ cup yellow cornmeal, preferably stone-ground*
*2 tablespoons sugar*
*1 tablespoon baking powder*
*1 teaspoon salt*
*2 large eggs*
*1 cup milk*
*5 tablespoons unsalted butter, melted*
*1 cup corn kernels (see note above)*
*1 cup (about 3 ounces) grated cheese, such as Cheddar, Monterey Jack, or Fontina*

Preheat the oven to 400° and butter 12 muffin cups. In a large mixing bowl, combine the flour, cornmeal, sugar, baking powder, and salt. In a separate bowl, beat the eggs lightly, then whisk in the milk and melted butter. Make a well in the dry ingredients, pour in the liquid ingredients, and stir gently, just until combined. Fold in the corn and cheese. Divide the batter among the cups, filling each about three-quarters full.

Bake the muffins for 15 minutes, then reduce the heat to 375° and bake for another 10 minutes. When done, the tops will be golden brown and slightly springy to the touch. Cool the muffins in the pan on a rack for 5 minutes, then transfer them to a cloth-lined basket and serve right away. Store completely cooled leftovers in a sealed plastic bag. ♦

## How to Build the Better Biscuit

Round biscuits are traditional, but have you ever considered *square* biscuits? Not only are they faster to cut, because there's no re-rolling of scraps, but since you aren't using the scraps you don't end up with those three or four slightly tough biscuits (handling the scraps a second time always makes the dough less tender).

To make square biscuits, simply roll or pat the dough to the specified thickness—on a lightly floured surface—into the best square shape you can manage. Then, just cut the dough into squares with a sharp knife—either nine larger or twelve slightly smaller rectangles. Transfer to the baking sheet and bake as directed.

If you like a biscuit that's crusty on all sides, leave at least 3 inches between them. Cluster them close together, about 1/2-inch apart, if you prefer softer sides.

Finally, there are many different sizes of biscuit cutters. The yields of the recipes in this section are based on a 2 1/2-inch diameter cutter. You can increase the yield by about half again if you use a 2-inch cutter. Remember to keep the cuts as close as possible, to minimize the scraps.

# Mashed Potato Parsley Biscuits

*Makes about 18 biscuits*

I think most cooks feel uplifted when they make good use of leftovers, perhaps none more so than New England cooks, who I sometimes imagine were encoded with thrifty-cooking genes since that first hard winter at Plymouth Rock. These biscuits are the essence of thrift, squeezing as many as half a dozen extra biscuits out of a 12-biscuit recipe. The potatoes add moisture and tenderness. If you serve these with plainer foods—like scrambled or fried eggs—you can add a little kick to the biscuits by putting some crumbled feta or kasseri cheese into the batter.

*1 1/2 cups unbleached flour*
*1/2 cup whole wheat flour*
*1 tablespoon baking powder*
*3/4 teaspoon salt*
*several good grinds of pepper*
*1/4 cup cold unsalted butter, cut into 1/4-inch*
  *pieces*
*1 cup leftover mashed potatoes, at room*
  *temperature*
*1/4 to 1/2 cup milk*
*1/4 cup chopped fresh parsley*

Preheat the oven to 425° and lightly butter a large baking sheet. In a medium mixing bowl, mix the flours, baking powder, salt, and pepper. Add the butter and cut it in until the mixture resembles coarse crumbs.

In a separate bowl, stir the mashed potatoes with ¼ cup of the milk. (If the potatoes are cold, heat the milk first.) Make a well in the dry mixture and stir in the potatoes and milk and the parsley. Try to blend the ingredients, but if it becomes apparent you need extra milk, add it. When the dough coheres, shake a little flour on it and knead for 30 seconds on a floured surface.

On a floured surface, roll or pat the dough to a thickness of about ¾ inch. Cut the biscuits (see page 33), then place them on the prepared sheet. Bake them for 15 to 18 minutes, until browned and crusty. Transfer the biscuits to a cloth-lined basket and serve hot. Store leftovers in a sealed plastic bag. ♦

## Crusty Cheddar Biscuits

*Makes 10 to 12 biscuits*

I've put almost every cheese you can imagine into biscuits at one point or another, and some were more successful than others. Like other cheese biscuits, they turn extra-crusty on the bottom, which everybody seems to appreciate. Sometimes I'll use half whole wheat flour. This is the topping for the Apple and Pear Cheddar Cobbler on page 276, which you'll want to try if you like fruit and cheese together.

*2 cups unbleached flour*
*1 tablespoon baking powder*
*1 tablespoon sugar*
*½ teaspoon salt*
*¼ cup cold unsalted butter, cut into ¼-inch pieces*
*1½ cups (¼ pound) grated sharp Cheddar cheese*
*¾ cup milk or light cream*

Preheat the oven to 400°. In a medium bowl, mix the flour, baking powder, sugar, and salt. Add the butter and cut it in until the mixture resembles coarse meal. Mix in the cheese.

Make a well in the dry ingredients and add all the milk or cream. Stir quickly, just until the dough coheres; use a touch more liquid if the dough seems dry in spots. Turn the dough out onto a flour-dusted surface and knead once or twice.

Pat or roll the dough to a thickness of ¾ inch. Cut the biscuits (see page 33), then put them on an ungreased baking sheet. Bake for 12 to 15 minutes, until well browned and crusty. Transfer them to a cloth-lined basket and serve at once. ♦

# 100 Percent Whole Wheat Sour Cream Biscuits

*Makes 12 biscuits*

Home bakers often complain to me that they can't make a light whole wheat biscuit; analogies to hockey pucks and doorstops abound. I usually go over some of the basics with them, and then I give them this recipe, one that uses only whole wheat, except for a tiny bit of unbleached for handling the dough. Almost without fail, I receive glowing reports. To me these are everything you could ask for in a biscuit: light, with soft and tender insides and a full wheaty flavor.

*2 cups whole wheat flour*
*1 tablespoon sugar*
*2 teaspoons baking powder*
*1 teaspoon baking soda*
*1/2 teaspoon salt*
*1/4 cup cold unsalted butter, cut into 1/4-inch*
  *pieces*
*3/4 cup sour cream*
*1/4 cup milk*
*unbleached flour for handling*

Preheat the oven to 425° and lightly oil a heavy medium or large baking sheet. Put the flour, sugar, baking powder, baking soda, and salt in a large mixing bowl. Toss with hands to mix. Add the butter and cut it into the flour until the mixture resembles coarse crumbs.

Measure the sour cream into a glass mea-suring cup. Top it off with the milk to make 1 cup. Stir with a fork to blend. Make a well in the dry mixture and add all the liquid at once. Stir the dough just until it coheres. If it is still dry and clumpy, add a tablespoon or 2 of milk; better at this point for it to be a little tacky than dry.

Dust your hands, the dough, and a kneading surface with a little unbleached flour. Turn the dough out and knead it gently, about 10 times, dusting the surface with a little extra flour if necessary. Roll or pat the dough to a thickness of 1/2 to 3/4 inch. Cut the biscuits (see page 33) and place them on the baking sheet an inch or so apart. Bake for about 13 to 15 minutes, until light golden and crusty. Transfer the biscuits to a cloth-lined basket and serve hot. ♦

# Onion-Flecked Parmesan Biscuits

*Makes 12 biscuits*

It's been my observation that baked goods covered with crisp pieces of half-charred onion have a devoted following. Here's a biscuit that has not only the onions but also cornmeal for texture, Parmesan cheese for deep flavor, and basil for an herbaceous lift. It all adds up to a wonderful flavor scheme, one that's gloriously compatible with Italian and other tomato-based meals. The bottom crust, thanks to the cheese, is particularly crisp.

*1 tablespoon olive oil*

*1 medium-size onion, minced*

*1¹/₂ cups unbleached flour*

*¹/₂ cup yellow cornmeal, preferably stone-ground*

*1 tablespoon baking powder*

*¹/₂ teaspoon salt*

*¹/₄ teaspoon freshly ground black pepper*

*1 tablespoon dried basil*

*¹/₄ cup cold unsalted butter*

*¹/₂ cup (almost 2 ounces) finely grated Parmesan cheese*

*³/₄ cup milk*

In a small skillet, heat the oil and stir in the onions. Cook over medium-high heat, stirring, for only about 3 minutes, then scrape them onto a plate to cool. Preheat the oven to 400° and lightly oil a medium or large baking sheet.

In a large mixing bowl, stir together the flour, cornmeal, baking powder, salt, pepper, and basil. Cut the butter into small pieces and drop it into the dry mixture. With your hands or a pastry blender, cut the butter into the dry ingredients until it is reduced to little pellet-size pieces. Stir in the Parmesan cheese.

Make a well in the dry mixture, then stir in the milk; it should pull together into a somewhat dense but still soft mass. Scrape it out onto a lightly floured surface and knead with floured hands 8 or 10 times. Flour your surface lightly, then roll or pat the dough out to a thickness of about ¹/₂ inch.

Scrape the onions out of the plate and onto the dough, spreading them evenly. Lightly tamp them into the surface with your hands. Cut the biscuits (see page 33), then place them on the baking sheet an inch or so apart. Bake for 15 minutes, until the onions are well colored and the bottoms a deep golden. Transfer the biscuits to a cloth-lined basket and serve them hot.

NOTE: *You can use up to 1 cup of cornmeal here, cutting the flour back to 1 cup; the biscuits will be a little crunchier.* ♦

## Yeasted Buckwheat Biscuits

*Makes 12 to 14 biscuits*

These are light, very tall biscuits, with just enough buckwheat to get the message across. Both the texture of the dough and the finished biscuits are much the same as a yeast bread, these being a sort of hybrid between a quick and yeasted bread.

*¼ cup lukewarm water*
*1¼-ounce package (about 1 tablespoon) active dry yeast*
*¾ cup milk*
*1 tablespoon unsulphured molasses*
*1½ cups unbleached flour*
*½ cup whole wheat flour*
*½ cup buckwheat flour*
*2 teaspoons baking powder*
*1 teaspoon salt*
*5 tablespoons cold unsalted butter, cut into ¼-inch pieces*

Preheat the oven to 425°. Lightly oil a heavy medium or large baking sheet. Pour the lukewarm water into a small bowl and stir in the yeast. As that dissolves, gently heat the milk in a small saucepan, bringing it to body temperature. Pour the milk into a medium mixing bowl; stir in the molasses and dissolved yeast. Set aside.

In a separate bowl, mix the flours, baking powder, and salt. Add the butter and cut it in until the mixture resembles coarse meal. Make a well in the dry ingredients and add the liquid ingredients all at once. Stir until the mixture comes together in a soft, cohesive mass; it will feel softer than other biscuit doughs you are used to.

Sprinkle the dough with several tablespoons of unbleached flour and work it in with the back of a wooden spoon or rubber spatula. When you have a soft, kneadable dough, scrape it out onto a well-floured surface and knead gently for a minute; the dough will become slightly elastic and lose its tackiness. On a floured surface, roll or pat the dough to a thickness of ¾ inch. Cut the biscuits (see page 33) and then transfer them to the prepared sheet. Bake the biscuits for 17 to 20 minutes, until browned and crusty. Transfer them to a cloth-lined basket and serve them hot. ♦

# Blue Cheese Cornmeal Biscuits

*Makes 12 biscuits*

These are fine, sharp-flavored biscuits, shot with blue throughout. They're wonderful with ham and eggs or, for dinner, with a simple soup and coleslaw. If you like these as much as I do, you'll definitely want to try the pear cobbler (page 271) for which this biscuit is the topping.

1²/₃ cups unbleached flour

¹/₃ cup yellow cornmeal, preferably stone-ground

1 tablespoon baking powder

¹/₂ teaspoon salt

pinch of cayenne pepper

3 tablespoons cold unsalted butter, cut into ¹/₄-inch pieces

¹/₂ cup (about 2 ounces) crumbled blue cheese

scant ²/₃ cup milk

Preheat the oven to 425° and lightly oil a medium baking sheet; a dark one is best.

In a large mixing bowl, stir together the flour, cornmeal, baking powder, salt, and cayenne pepper. Add the butter and blue cheese and cut them into the flour until the mixture resembles coarse crumbs; only little pieces of blue cheese and butter should be visible.

Make a well in the dry ingredients, add the milk, and stir until the mixture coheres as a firm, dampish mass. Knead the dough once or twice with floured hands, then roll or pat it to a thickness of ³/₄ inch on a floured surface. Cut the biscuits (see below) and then place them on the prepared sheet. Bake for about 12 minutes, until browned and crusty. Transfer them to a cloth-lined basket and serve them hot.

NOTE: *I've never done this, but I imagine these would look neat made with blue cornmeal instead of yellow.* ◆

---

## Cutting Biscuits

Unlike yeast dough, biscuit dough generally should be handled as little as possible, to prevent the dough from becoming tough. The problem is, once you've rolled your biscuit dough and cut round biscuits, you're always left with scraps that need to be gathered, re-rolled, and cut. This second cutting inevitably leaves you with two or three less-than-tender biscuits.

There is a solution, one that will save you a little time in the bargain: cutting square biscuits. Simply roll or pat the dough into the best square shape you can manage, to the specified thickness. Then cut the dough into squares—usually nine or twelve. Your other option is to roll the dough into a circle and cut it into wedges, pie style. In any case, transfer the biscuits to your baking sheet and bake as usual.

# Dark Yogurt Rye Biscuits

*Makes 12 biscuits*

*Y*ou might envision a rye biscuit as dense and heavy, but these are quite the opposite. The rye flour actually helps to soften this biscuit, and the egg gives the dough a little extra spring in the oven. I love the dark, earthy tone these biscuits have. If you find yourself in need of an eye-appealing centerpiece for a special breakfast, arrange these in a cloth-lined basket with a batch of lighter-colored biscuits. As dinner biscuits, these are great with soups and slices of Swiss cheese.

*1 cup rye flour*

*1 cup unbleached flour*

*2 teaspoons baking powder*

*1 teaspoon baking soda*

*³/4 teaspoon salt*

*1 teaspoon unsweetened cocoa powder or carob powder*

*¹/2 teaspoon caraway seeds*

*¹/4 cup cold unsalted butter, cut into ¹/4-inch pieces*

*²/3 cup plain yogurt*

*1 large egg*

*1 tablespoon unsulphured molasses*

Preheat the oven to 425°. Lightly oil a medium or large baking sheet; a dark one is best.

Sift the dry ingredients into a medium mixing bowl. (Just dump anything that's left behind in the sifter into the bowl.) Add the butter and cut it in until the mixture resembles coarse crumbs. In a smaller bowl, whisk together the yogurt, egg, and molasses. Make a well in the dry ingredients, add the liquid, and stir with a wooden spoon until the dough gathers into a rough, dense, tacky mass. Sprinkle the dough lightly with flour, working it in with the flat part of a rubber spatula or a wooden spoon.

Turn the dough out onto a well-floured surface and knead gently with floured hands for 30 seconds; don't be concerned if it soaks up a bit of flour. Heavily dust a small area of your surface with flour, then roll or pat the dough out on it, ¹/2 to ³/4 inch thick. Cut the dough (see page 33), placing the biscuits no less than 1 inch apart on the prepared baking sheet. Bake for 13 to 15 minutes, until the tops are browned and the bottoms are fairly dark and crusty. Transfer the biscuits to a cloth-lined basket and serve them hot. ◆

# Blueberry Oatmeal Drop Biscuits

*Makes 12 big biscuits*

Some biscuits are patted out and cut; these are simply dropped onto a baking sheet. Though you can make any biscuit a drop biscuit by adding a little extra liquid to the mix, it makes sense to go this route when you're including fragile berries; the extra handling involved with a shaped biscuit would cause the berries to shatter and turn the biscuits a funny gray shade. This way you can appreciate the whole berries in what looks and tastes like an oversize blueberry oatmeal cookie. You can split and butter these or just eat them out of hand.

1 cup unbleached flour
1/2 cup whole wheat flour
1/2 cup rolled oats (not *instant*)
1/3 cup oat bran
1 teaspoon baking powder
1/2 teaspoon baking soda
3/4 teaspoon salt
1/2 teaspoon ground cinnamon
1/4 cup cold unsalted butter, cut into 1/4-inch
   pieces
1/4 cup white or packed light brown sugar
1 large egg
1/2 cup milk
1/4 cup plain yogurt
1 cup fresh blueberries

Preheat the oven to 400° and lightly oil a large baking sheet. In a large mixing bowl, combine the flours, oats, oat bran, baking powder, baking soda, salt, and cinnamon. Add the butter and cut it in with a pastry blender until it is broken into very small pieces. Stir in the sugar.

Lightly beat the egg, milk, and yogurt in a small bowl. Make a well in the dry ingredients, pour in the liquid ingredients, and stir lightly. When there are only a few traces of dry ingredients visible, *gently* fold in the blueberries. Using about 1/4 cup of batter for each, drop evenly spaced mounds onto the oiled sheet, leaving a little space between them. Bake for 20 minutes, turning the sheet midway through so they brown evenly. Serve at once, from a cloth-lined basket, or transfer them to a rack until serving time. ♦

# Dried Cherry and Rye Scones

*Makes 8 scones*

Dried cherries are one of my big fruit-cake fruits, and because I hoard them around the holidays so I don't come up short when making fruitcakes, I usually end up with leftover cherries until about the following November. That's fine, because I like to bake with them. My dried cherries are usually very dry, so I put them in a small bowl, cover them with boiling water, and let them sit for 15 minutes or so; just drain and proceed. Because of the rye, these are slightly on the dense side. Serve them with soft butter and honey.

1⅓ cups unbleached flour
⅔ cup rye flour
3 tablespoons packed light brown sugar
1 teaspoon baking soda
½ teaspoon salt
¼ teaspoon crushed aniseed (crush it with a
   rolling pin between sheets of wax paper)
finely grated zest of 1 orange
5 tablespoons cold unsalted butter
scant 1 cup plain yogurt
½ cup chopped dried cherries
1 teaspoon milk or cream
sugar for sprinkling on top (optional)

Preheat the oven to 425° and very lightly oil a medium baking sheet. In a large bowl, mix the flours, brown sugar, baking soda, salt, and aniseed. Add the orange zest and butter and cut them in until the mixture has a gravellike texture, with only very small pieces of butter visible.

Make a well in the dry ingredients and add the yogurt, stirring just until it pulls together; fold in the cherries on the last few stirs. Don't worry if the dough is a bit shaggy and damp. If so, work some shakes of flour into the dough, pushing it in with the back of a wooden spoon or a rubber spatula. Heavily flour your hands and work surface, then turn the dough out and knead it for 15 seconds or so. Put the dough on the sheet and pat it into a 9-inch circle about ¾ inch thick.

Using a floured butter knife or dough scraper, score the dough deeply, making 8 wedges as though you were cutting a pie. Brush the top with the milk or cream and sprinkle with sugar if desired. Bake for 20 minutes; it will get quite dark. Slide the scone onto a rack and cool it for several minutes before serving it from a cloth-lined basket; you'll have to recut the score marks to separate the scones. ♦

# *Oat Cream Scones*

*Makes 8 servings*

These are rich enough that you don't really need to put butter on them, just a dab of good preserves or fruit butter. Take a basket of these and a thermos of coffee on a visit to a friend you haven't seen in a while.

1¹/₃ cups unbleached flour
¹/₃ cup whole wheat flour
¹/₃ cup rolled oats (not *instant*)
¹/₄ cup packed light brown sugar
2 teaspoons baking powder
¹/₂ teaspoon salt
¹/₂ teaspoon ground cinnamon
¹/₄ cup cold unsalted butter, cut into ¹/₄-inch pieces
¹/₂ cup chopped pitted dates or dried figs
¹/₂ cup (approximately) heavy cream
1 tablespoon (approximately) oats for sprinkling on top

Preheat the oven to 425° and lightly oil a medium baking sheet. Mix the dry ingredients in a large bowl. Add the butter and cut it in until the pieces of butter are quite small; toss in the dates or figs.

Make a well in the dry mixture and add most of the cream. Stir and see if it will all pull together in a dampish mass; if not, stir in enough of the remaining cream until it does. You may even need a little more than ¹/₂ cup. When the dough pulls together, knead it in the bowl once or twice. Put the dough in the middle of the baking sheet and pat it, with floured hands, into a 9-inch circle. Using a floured butter knife or dough scraper, score the dough deeply into 8 wedges, as you would a pie; leave them in place on the sheet.

Brush the scone sparingly with heavy cream, then sprinkle it with about a tablespoon of raw oats. Brush again with cream, then bake for 20 minutes; it will be a dark golden brown when done. Slide the scone onto a rack and let it sit for several minutes, then cut through the score marks. Tuck the wedges into a cloth-lined basket and serve. ♦

# Honey Walnut Oatmeal Soda Bread

*Makes 2 small free-form loaves*

This soda bread and the following pumpernickel recipe are extensions of my ongoing infatuation with Irish soda bread. This one is lighter than the next, in both color and flavor, the oats being the predominant feature. It makes a fine slicing loaf for breakfast or brunch or a good dinner loaf when you want something fast and filling. Both recipes are also good alternatives when you don't have time to make yeast bread.

1 cup rolled oats (not *instant*)
1²/₃ cups buttermilk
¹/₃ cup honey
2 tablespoons unsalted butter
1¹/₂ cups whole wheat flour
1¹/₂ cups unbleached flour
2 teaspoons baking powder
1¹/₂ teaspoons salt
1 teaspoon baking soda
1 cup (4 to 5 ounces) coarsely chopped
   walnuts

Lightly oil a large, heavy baking sheet, preferably a dark one. Sprinkle it lightly with rolled oats if you want them on the bottoms of your loaves; I recommend it. Preheat the oven to 400°.

Put the oats into a large bowl and pour the buttermilk over them. Gently warm the honey and butter in a small saucepan, just until the butter melts, then stir them into the oats. Reserve.

In a large mixing bowl, combine the remaining ingredients and toss with your hands to mix. Make a well in the center of the dry ingredients, then add the liquid oat mixture. Stir from the center out until you have a soft dough. Turn it out onto a floured surface and divide it in half. With floured hands, knead each half into a ball and place both on the sheet; it's fine if you have a dusting of flour on them.

Bake for 30 minutes, until well browned on all sides. Transfer the loaves to a rack and cool them for at least 10 minutes before slicing. Store thoroughly cooled leftovers in sealed plastic bags.

FREEZING: *If you won't be using one of these loaves within 2 days, wrap the loaf in foil, put it in a plastic bag, and freeze it for up to 1 month.* ♦

# Coarse Pumpernickel Soda Bread

*Makes 2 small free-form loaves*

This bread can bring a table of grainy-bread lovers to moans of pleasure. It is dark, dense, and *very* grainy, in the best peasant tradition. Serve it with a hearty soup or stew, and a big, colorful salad. Slice the pieces thinly and serve with a selection of cheeses. A crock of herb cream cheese is another nice accompaniment.

> 1¹⁄₂ cups whole wheat flour
> 1 cup unbleached flour
> 1 cup rye flour
> ¹⁄₂ cup yellow cornmeal, preferably stone-ground
> 1 tablespoon baking powder
> 1 tablespoon caraway seeds
> 2 teaspoons salt
> 1 teaspoon baking soda
> 2 cups buttermilk
> 3 tablespoons unsulphured molasses

Preheat the oven to 425°. Generously dust a large, heavy baking sheet with cornmeal and set it aside.

Stir the dry ingredients together in a large mixing bowl. Make a well in the dry ingredients and add the buttermilk and molasses. Using a wooden spoon, blend the liquids with little strokes, then widen the strokes to mix the batter together; it will be dense and damp. Sprinkle a little flour over the dough and work it in with the back of your wooden spoon; just get it to the point where it isn't so tacky, then turn it out onto a floured surface. With floured hands, knead the dough gently for about 30 seconds. Divide the dough in half and shape the halves into fat footballs. Place them about 6 inches apart on the sheet. Make a few shallow slashes in each loaf, using a sharp, serrated knife.

Bake the loaves for 35 to 40 minutes, until the tops and bottoms are dark and crusty. The bottoms, when tapped with a finger, should sound hollow; they shouldn't seem rubbery. Transfer the loaves to a rack to cool. Store completely cooled leftovers in sealed plastic bags.

NOTE: *This bread is at its best about an hour out of the oven. Don't slice it much before then.* ♦

## Pumpkin Soda Bread

*Makes 2 free-form loaves*

Sometimes I think I get a little carried away with putting pumpkin and other winter squashes in bread, but it's hard not to bake with pumpkin because the payoff is so pretty, moist, and delicious. Since this is a quick bread, you could make this in the late afternoon and have it in plenty of time for a soup-and-salad dinner. To make things easier, prepare the pumpkin puree ahead or use canned pumpkin.

*3¹/₂ cups cubed peeled pumpkin or 1¹/₂ cups canned*
*¹/₂ cup sour cream, plain yogurt, or buttermilk*
*¹/₂ cup packed light brown sugar*
*1 egg yolk*
*1 tablespoon freshly squeezed lemon juice*
*3¹/₂ cups unbleached flour*
*1¹/₂ cups yellow cornmeal, preferably stone-ground*
*2 teaspoons baking powder*
*1 teaspoon baking soda*
*2 teaspoons salt*
*1 cup dark or golden raisins*

If you're using fresh, put the pumpkin in a large pot with plenty of lightly salted water. Bring to a boil, cover, then reduce the heat and cook at a low boil for 20 to 25 minutes, until the pumpkin is quite tender; drain. Preheat the oven to 400° and dust a large baking sheet liberally with cornmeal.

Cool the pumpkin briefly, then puree it in a food processor, food mill, or blender. Measure out 1¹/₂ cups—saving any remainder for another use—and put it in a bowl. Blend in the sour cream, yogurt, or buttermilk, the brown sugar, egg yolk, and lemon juice. In a separate bowl, mix 3 cups of the unbleached flour with the remaining ingredients. Make a well in the dry mixture, then stir in the liquid with a wooden spoon until the dough pulls together in a slightly damp, shaggy mass.

Using some of the remaining unbleached flour, flour your hands and a kneading surface liberally and turn the dough out. Divide it in half and very gently knead each half into a ball, spending about 20 to 30 seconds on each; during this kneading the dough will soak up more of the remaining flour, but don't feel like you have to incorporate all of it.

Place the balls on the prepared sheet, leaving plenty of room between them. Bake for about 40 minutes, until they are well browned; as with a yeasted bread, the bottom should give a hollow retort when tapped with a finger. Cool the loaves on a rack for at least 30 minutes before slicing. Store leftovers up to 2 days in a sealed plastic bag. To reheat, wrap in foil and place in a hot oven for 5 minutes. ♦

# Lemon Honey Banana Bread

*Makes 1 large loaf*

Here's a good way to rescue those decrepit bananas you've let ripen too long. In fact, this bread is so good it's worth intentionally letting some bananas turn brown. You'll get a good idea, with this loaf, of how honey both sweetens and flavors baked goods when you use a lot of it; it isn't the best choice of sweetener for every recipe, but here the honey is endearing without being cloying or invasive. This is excellent plain, as a snack, for breakfast (toasted in a toaster oven), or after dinner, maybe with a scoop of ice cream.

*1/4 cup unsalted butter, softened*
*3/4 cup honey*
*2 large eggs, at room temperature*
*1 1/2 teaspoons vanilla extract*
*juice and finely grated zest of 1/2 lemon*
*1 1/2 cups unbleached flour*
*3/4 cup whole wheat flour*
*1 tablespoon baking powder*
*3/4 teaspoon salt*
*1/2 teaspoon ground cinnamon*
*1/4 teaspoon freshly grated nutmeg*
*1 cup (about 2 large) mashed very ripe banana*
*1/2 cup (about 2 ounces) coarsely chopped walnuts*

Butter a 4 1/2- by 8 1/2-inch or 5- by 9-inch loaf pan and preheat the oven to 350° (325° if you're using glass).

In a large mixing bowl, cream the butter and honey with an electric mixer. Beat in the eggs, one at a time, followed by the vanilla, lemon juice, and zest. Into a separate bowl, sift the flours, baking powder, salt, and spices; include any pieces of bran that remain in the sifter. Stir half of the dry ingredients into the creamed mixture, then stir in the banana, and finally the remaining dry ingredients; fold in the walnuts on the last few turns. Don't beat the batter.

Turn the batter into the prepared pan and bake for 50 to 55 minutes. When the bread is done, the top will be browned and a tester inserted into the center of the bread will come out clean. Cool the bread in the pan on a rack for 10 minutes, then slip a knife around the edge of the bread and turn it out. Cool thoroughly on a rack before slicing. As soon as it is cool, wrap it in foil or plastic wrap to preserve freshness. ♦

## Whole Wheat Zucchini Bread

*Makes 1 large loaf*

Zucchini season always brings hordes of so-called friends, carrying armloads of zucchini the size of redwoods, to one's door. A *real* friend would make this zucchini bread and drop *it* off. Of course the best thing zucchini does for a tea bread is keep it moist and add some color; I've never been able to discern any real zucchini flavor. But you can appreciate it in this sweet loaf; others will too. Better make a second loaf for a friend.

> 1¹/₃ *cups whole wheat* pastry *flour*
> 1 *cup unbleached flour*
> 2 *teaspoons baking powder*
> ¹/₂ *teaspoon baking soda*
> 1 *teaspoon salt*
> 1 *teaspoon ground cinnamon*
> 2 *large eggs, at room temperature*
> ¹/₃ *cup flavorless vegetable oil*
> 1 *cup packed light brown sugar*
> 1 *tablespoon freshly squeezed lemon juice*
> 2 *teaspoons vanilla extract*
> 1 *cup grated zucchini (leave the skin on, and don't squeeze the pulp dry)*

Butter a 4¹/₂- by 8¹/₂-inch loaf pan, preferably a shiny metal one, and preheat the oven to 350° (325° if you're using glass). Sift the flours, baking powder, baking soda, salt, and cinnamon into a bowl; dump any flakes of bran from the sifter into the bowl.

In a separate bowl, beat the eggs well, then beat in the oil, brown sugar, lemon juice, and vanilla. Stir in the zucchini. Gradually stir the dry ingredients into the liquid, just until combined; there should be no dry streaks visible. Scrape the batter into the prepared pan and bake for 50 minutes, until the top does not give under moderate finger pressure; a tester inserted in the center of the bread should come out clean.

Cool the pan on a rack for 10 minutes, then run a spatula around the sides before turning the bread out. Cool the bread on a rack, then wrap it tightly in plastic wrap and foil. Slice and serve anytime, but keep it wrapped when not in service.

VARIATION: *You can, of course, use grated summer squash instead of zucchini or a combination of both.* ◆

# Whole Wheat Honey Tea Bread

*Makes 1 large or 2 smaller loaves*

This is my basic whole grain quick bread. I'm quick to acknowledge my bias for whole grains, but this bread makes it perfectly clear how whole wheat flour and whole grains in general can add so much character and flavor to baked goods.

Excellent plain, but one of my favorite ways to serve this is with a little vanilla ice cream and orange sherbet on the side.

*1¹/₂ cups whole wheat pastry flour*
*1¹/₂ cups unbleached flour*
*2 teaspoons baking powder*
*¹/₂ teaspoon baking soda*
*1 teaspoon salt*
*1 teaspoon freshly grated nutmeg or other
  favorite spice*
*¹/₂ cup (¹/₄ pound) unsalted butter, softened*
*¹/₂ cup honey*
*¹/₂ cup packed light brown sugar*
*3 large eggs, at room temperature*
*2 teaspoons vanilla extract*
*3 tablespoons sour cream or plain yogurt*
*¹/₂ cup milk, at room temperature*
*coarsely grated orange and lemon zest (a
  generous shaving of each; use the larger
  holes on a box grater)*

Butter a 5- by 9-inch loaf pan, preferably shiny metal, not dark. Preheat the oven to 350° (325° if you're using glass). Sift the flours, baking powder, baking soda, salt, and nutmeg into a bowl; dump in any pieces of bran that won't go through the sifter. In a separate bowl, cream the butter and honey with an electric mixer. When it is well blended, beat in the brown sugar, the eggs, one at a time, and then the vanilla and sour cream.

Stir half of the dry ingredients into the creamed ingredients, just until blended, then stir in the milk, zests, and the rest of the dry ingredients; stir just until no traces of dry ingredients remain. Bake on the center rack for about 55 minutes, until the top does not give easily under gentle finger pressure; a tester inserted in the center of the bread should come out clean.

Let the bread cool in the pan on a rack for 10 to 15 minutes, then carefully run a spatula around the sides before turning the bread out. Cool thoroughly, then immediately wrap the bread in plastic wrap and foil until serving time.

NOTE: *If you don't have a 5- by 9-inch loaf pan, you can use any combination of smaller pans. In general, the bread will look most attractive if the batter fills the pan by about a generous half.* ◆

---

*One tip to pass on about quick breads: I notice that they dry out prematurely if they aren't well wrapped. Our house—because we heat solely with wood—is probably drier than many. But no matter how you heat your home, this is something to remember.*

# Dark and Moist Blueberry Tea Bread

*Makes 1 large loaf*

This is as good a tea bread as you will find, blueberries showcased in a dark background provided by the molasses and a little cocoa. I prefer the small lowbush, wild blueberries that grow near us because they always have the best flavor, but the larger ones are just fine too.

1¹/₃ cups whole wheat pastry flour
1¹/₃ cups unbleached flour
2 teaspoons unsweetened cocoa powder
1 teaspoon baking powder
1 teaspoon baking soda
1 teaspoon salt
¹/₂ teaspoon ground ginger
¹/₂ teaspoon ground allspice
¹/₂ teaspoon ground cinnamon
¹/₂ cup (¹/₄ pound) unsalted butter, softened
¹/₂ cup unsulphured molasses
¹/₂ cup packed light brown sugar
3 large eggs, at room temperature
¹/₄ cup sour cream or plain yogurt
1 teaspoon vanilla extract
coarsely grated zest of 1 orange (use the
    larger holes on a box grater)
¹/₄ cup milk, at room temperature
1 cup fresh blueberries

Butter a 5- by 9-inch loaf pan, preferably a shiny metal one, and preheat the oven to 350° (325° if you're using glass). Sift the flours, cocoa, baking powder, baking soda, salt, and spices into a bowl, including any pieces of bran that remain in the sifter. In a separate, large bowl, cream the butter and molasses with an electric mixer. Beat in the brown sugar, the eggs, one at a time, the sour cream or yogurt, vanilla, and orange zest. Stir half the flour into the liquid, followed by the milk, then the remaining flour; fold in the blueberries while there is still a little dry flour in the batter. Mix just to blend.

Scrape the batter into the prepared pan and bake for 55 minutes, until a tester inserted in the center comes out clean; the top should spring a little under light finger pressure. Transfer the pan to a rack and cool for 15 minutes. Run a spatula around the edges, then turn the bread out and let it cool thoroughly on the rack. Wrap the bread in plastic wrap and foil until serving. ◆

# Whole Wheat Corn Bread

*Makes 8 to 10 servings*

Here's the way we eat corn bread most often—a basic, simple recipe you can commit to memory. I serve this when we have friends over for a special breakfast, for soup-and-salad dinners, and almost always with chili. If there are leftovers, butter and brown them in a skillet, spread on honey or jelly, and have them for breakfast. If you don't have the skillet I specify, you can use another 10-inch round pan, not preheated, and just bake the bread a little longer.

1⅓ cups yellow cornmeal, preferably stone-ground
1 cup whole wheat flour
1 teaspoon baking soda
1 teaspoon baking powder
½ teaspoon salt
1 large egg
2 tablespoons packed light brown sugar
2 cups buttermilk
¼ cup unsalted butter

Before you begin, put a 10-inch cast-iron skillet (not enameled) into the oven and preheat the oven to 400°. In a large mixing bowl, mix together the cornmeal, flour, baking soda, baking powder, and salt. In a separate bowl, beat the egg, brown sugar, and buttermilk. Reserve.

Using a pot holder, take the skillet out of the oven and put the butter in it, shaking the pan to facilitate the melting. After it is all melted, pour the butter into the liquid mixture, leaving a little butter in the pan. Make a well in the dry mixture, then stir in the liquid just until the batter is blended and smooth; do not beat. Scrape the batter into the hot buttered pan, even the top, then bake for 20 minutes. When the bread is done, the sides will have pulled away from the pan and the center should feel springy under gentle finger pressure. Cut and serve right from the pan (but don't use a knife that will scratch the pan). Store leftovers in a sealed plastic bag. ♦

## Oat Bran Raisin Breakfast Bread

*Makes 8 to 10 servings*

Here's a quick, filling breakfast idea when you want something hot and homemade but time is limited. There's nothing to chop or puree or fuss over (the lemon zest is grated, but this is optional), and there's very little to clean up when you're done. A little butter and jelly or honey are nice additions, but this bread has a full flavor that requires no embellishments.

1 1/2 cups oat bran
1/2 cup unbleached flour
1/2 cup whole wheat flour
1 tablespoon baking powder
1/2 teaspoon salt
big pinch of ground cinnamon
1/2 cup honey
2 tablespoons unsalted butter
2 large eggs
2/3 cup milk
1/4 cup flavorless vegetable oil
finely grated zest of 1 lemon (optional)
1/2 cup dark or golden raisins

Butter either a 10-inch pie pan or 9-inch square baking pan, preferably glass or enameled. Preheat the oven to 400° (375° if you're using glass).

In a large mixing bowl, stir together the oat bran, flours, baking powder, salt, and cinnamon. Set aside. In a small saucepan, warm the honey and butter over very low heat, just until the butter melts.

Meanwhile, beat the eggs lightly in a medium mixing bowl. Blend in the milk, oil, honey/butter, and lemon zest, if you are using it. Make a well in the dry ingredients, add the liquid, and stir just until blended. Fold in the raisins. Scrape the batter into the prepared pan and bake for 25 minutes, until the top is fairly firm to the touch. Transfer the baking dish to a cooling rack and cool briefly before serving. Store leftovers in a sealed plastic bag. ◆

# Pecan Streusel Coffee Cake

*Makes 12 servings*

This is one of those recipes that's so delicious that the number of servings listed has absolutely no correlation to reality. Yes, it makes 12 pieces; but given half a chance, three or four hungry souls will polish this off without batting an eye. It is extra-moist, thanks to the molasses and grated apple. With a cup of strong coffee, it teeters near the sublime.

TOPPING

3 tablespoons yellow cornmeal, preferably
    stone-ground
2¹/₂ tablespoons packed light brown sugar
1 tablespoon unbleached flour
pinch of salt
2¹/₂ tablespoons unsalted butter
¹/₃ cup finely chopped pecans

BATTER

1 cup unbleached flour
³/₄ cup yellow cornmeal, preferably stone-
    ground
¹/₂ cup whole wheat flour
2 teaspoons baking powder
1 teaspoon baking soda
1 teaspoon ground cinnamon
¹/₂ teaspoon ground cloves
1 teaspoon salt
¹/₂ cup (¹/₄ pound) unsalted butter, softened
²/₃ cup packed light brown sugar
¹/₃ cup unsulphured molasses
3 large eggs

1 teaspoon vanilla extract
1 large apple, peeled
²/₃ cup buttermilk

Make the topping by combining the cornmeal, brown sugar, flour, salt, and butter in a mixing bowl. Rub them between your fingers until you have a damp, crumbly mixture. Stir in the pecans. Cover and set aside.

Butter a 9-inch square or 7- by 11-inch baking pan; I like glass for this, but metal is fine too. Preheat the oven to 350° (325° if you are using glass).

Make the batter: Into a large mixing bowl, sift the unbleached flour, cornmeal, whole wheat flour, baking powder, baking soda, spices, and salt. Set aside.

In another large bowl, cream the butter and brown sugar with an electric mixer until well blended. Beat in the molasses, the eggs, one at a time, and the vanilla. Set aside. Grate the apple onto a plate, cover, and set aside.

Stir about half the dry mixture into the creamed mixture, just until blended; then add the buttermilk. Blend with a few more strokes, then stir in the remaining dry ingredients; stop mixing when no dry streaks are visible. Fold the apple into the batter with a few deft strokes.

Scrape the batter into the prepared pan and even it out with your rubber spatula. Sprinkle the topping evenly over the cake and bake for about 35 minutes. When done, the coffee cake will be golden brown and the center will be springy to the touch. Transfer the pan to a rack. Serve hot or warm, right from the pan. When cool, cover leftovers with plastic wrap. ◆

# Fresh Blackberry Crumb Cake

*Makes 8 to 10 servings*

If there were ever a cake to be made on a lazy summer day, this is it. It's all the better if you turn it into an event, picking your own berries and inviting the gang over for coffee and a slice. There are three layers here: a buttery cake, a fresh blackberry sauce, and an oat crumb topping. The first time I made this I omitted the topping, but it seemed almost naked without it. Better to go all out.

FRUIT SAUCE
*2 pints fresh blackberries*
*½ cup honey*
*juice of 1 orange*
*1 tablespoon cornstarch*

CRUMB TOPPING
*½ cup unbleached flour*
*¼ cup rolled oats (not instant)*
*⅓ cup packed light brown sugar*
*pinch of ground cinnamon*
*pinch of salt*
*¼ cup unsalted butter, cut into ¼-inch pieces*
*¼ cup unsweetened shredded coconut (available at health food stores) or sweetened flaked coconut*

CAKE
*1 recipe Classic Wheaten Shortcake (page 269)*

To make the fruit sauce, put the blackberries and honey in a medium, nonaluminum pot. Gradually bring to a boil over medium heat, stirring occasionally. When the berries start to boil, mix the orange juice and cornstarch together in a little bowl and add it to the pot. Stir at a low boil for 1 minute; it will thicken just a little. Pour the contents of the pan into a shallow baking dish and cool to room temperature, stirring occasionally, while you prepare the rest of the recipe. (Put it in the refrigerator to hasten the cooling.)

To make the topping, mix the flour, oats, brown sugar, cinnamon, and salt in a bowl. Add the butter and rub or cut it in until the mixture is gravellike in texture. Add the coconut and mix it in by hand. Cover and refrigerate. Lightly butter an 8- by 12-inch shallow baking dish, glass or enameled, and preheat the oven to 375° (350° if you're using glass).

Make the cake and scrape the batter into the prepared pan. Shake a little flour over the batter, flour your hands, and gently pat the batter evenly into the pan. Poke the cake 8 or so times with a fork so the fruit juices can sink in. Carefully pour the fruit sauce over the cake, even it out, then scatter the oat topping over the fruit. Bake the cake on the center rack for 30 minutes, then move the cake up to the top rack and bake for another 15 to 20 minutes. If the top starts to get too dark, cover it loosely with foil. Cool the pan on a rack for about 15 minutes before serving, right from the pan. Store at room temperature, covered, and eat within 24 hours. ◆

# Blueberry Cornmeal Crumb Cake

*Makes 10 servings*

Here's one of the nicest things we make with the harvest from both the highbush and lowbush blueberries—a dense buttery cake with a rich crumb topping. (We would probably eat much *more* of this were it not for our dog, Stina, who, as the self-appointed reincarnation of Euell Gibbons, munches most of the crop off the vine before we get to it.) The cornmeal gives this cake a slightly rough texture, but that's nicely offset by the moisture of the fruit. In fact, if you wrap this well as soon as it's cool, the moisture from the fruit will slowly absorb into the cake, making this even moister on the second day. Try it with blackberries and raspberries too.

BATTER

1/2 cup (1/4 pound) unsalted butter, softened
3/4 cup honey
3 large egg yolks
1 teaspoon vanilla extract
1 teaspoon finely grated lemon zest
1 cup unbleached flour
1 cup yellow cornmeal, preferably stone-ground
3/4 cup (about 4 ounces) very finely chopped pecans
1/2 teaspoon baking soda
1/4 teaspoon salt
pinch of freshly grated nutmeg
1 cup fresh or frozen, unthawed blueberries

CRUMB TOPPING

3/4 cup plus 1 tablespoon unbleached flour
1/3 cup packed light brown sugar
pinch of salt
1/4 cup unsalted butter, melted and cooled

Butter a 9-inch springform or cake pan and set it aside. Preheat the oven to 350° while you make the batter. In a large mixing bowl, cream the butter and honey with an electric mixer. Beat in the egg yolks, vanilla, and lemon zest.

In a separate bowl, combine the flour, cornmeal, pecans, baking soda, salt, and nutmeg. Stir these dry ingredients into the creamed mixture just until blended; do not beat. Spread the batter evenly in the buttered pan and strew the berries evenly over the top.

To make the topping, combine the flour, brown sugar, and salt in a bowl and stir in the melted butter. Rub this mixture lightly through your fingers, creating small, damp pea-size pieces. Spread the crumbs over the blueberries. Bake for 40 to 45 minutes, just until the center of the cake offers moderate resistance when pushed lightly with a fingertip. Transfer the pan to a rack and cool for at least 15 minutes before slicing and serving the cake. Store leftovers at room temperature, covered, for no more than 2 days. ♦

# Oatmeal Sour Cream Coffee Cake

*Makes 9 to 12 servings*

Anyone who thinks whole grain baking has to be dense and heavy should
stop right here; I'd put this up against any
sweet breakfast cake, confident it would
take top honors for lightness, flavor, and
nutrition. Besides all that, it couldn't be simpler to make.

BATTER
2 large eggs
1 cup sour cream or plain yogurt
1/2 cup maple syrup
2 tablespoons flavorless vegetable oil
1 teaspoon vanilla extract
finely grated zest of 1 lemon
1/2 cup whole wheat flour
1/2 cup unbleached flour
1 1/2 teaspoons baking powder
1 teaspoon ground cinnamon
1/2 teaspoon baking soda
1/2 teaspoon salt
1 cup rolled oats (not *instant*)

NUT TOPPING
2 tablespoons unsalted butter
2 tablespoons maple syrup
1/2 cup (2 ounces) finely chopped walnuts
1/3 cup unsweetened shredded coconut
    (available at health food stores) or
    sweetened flaked coconut

Butter an 8 1/2- or 9-inch square baking
pan—I prefer a glass pan here—and sprinkle the inside sparingly with rolled oats. Set
aside. Preheat the oven to 350° (325° if
you're using glass).

In a large mixing bowl, beat the eggs for a
minute and then whisk in the sour cream or
yogurt, maple syrup, the oil, vanilla, and
lemon zest. Set aside.

Sift the flours, baking powder, cinnamon,
baking soda, and salt into another mixing
bowl. Put the oats in a blender or food processor and pulse them on and off until
they're reduced to a coarse meal with some
large flecks remaining. Stir into the dry mixture.

Make the nut topping by melting the butter in a medium skillet over low heat. Immediately stir in the maple syrup, heat briefly,
then stir in the walnuts and coconut. Remove from the heat.

Make a well in the dry ingredients, pour
in the liquid, and stir with a wooden spoon
just to blend; do not beat. Scrape the batter
into the prepared pan, jiggling the pan
gently to distribute the batter. Spoon the
walnut/coconut mixture evenly over the
top. Bake for 30 to 40 minutes—the smaller
pan will take longer—until the top just begins to brown and the center of the cake is
springy to the touch. Cool the cake in the
pan on a rack for 5 to 10 minutes before
serving. Store leftovers at room temperature, covered, for no more than 2 days. ♦

# YEAST
# BREADS

*B*ecause people know I love to bake bread, I have somehow assumed the role of a sympathetic ear that regularly hears tales of baking woe. I don't know how many "My whole wheat bread comes out like bricks" stories I've heard; how many "My kids won't eat it" and "Mine never rises" are out there. But I do know—because all this unwanted baking baggage gets left at my place—that yeast bread baking is an anxiety-provoking subject.

So the first thing I have to say is this: calm down. Take control and realize that it's just your wits—you being a higher form of intelligent life— against the dough's. Even if you've never made yeast bread before, the odds are greatly in your favor that a few hours after you begin you'll have some delicious loaves to eat. (And if you don't, don't take it too hard; chances are you just ran into a particularly intelligent or competitive strain of yeast.) It may not look picture-perfect, and perhaps it'll have a few learner's dings or show some rough edges, but who cares? Nobody should expect perfection on the first try. What counts is that you've got both feet in the ring and you came out swinging.

Bread baking was my first love in the kitchen, something I taught myself nearly 20 years ago. I bought myself a James Beard bread book and started making bread. The one thing that's never changed for me is the excitement I feel over this small miracle of nursing along a batch of dough and seeing it emerge from the oven as the staff of life. I love the flavor, the texture, the wholesomeness and purity of homemade bread. But what keeps me—and I suspect many other bread makers—coming back, is the miracle.

From the very beginning I was never content to be strictly a white flour bread maker. Homemade white bread is good, often excellent, but a bread baker who limits himself to white flour is like the fiddler with only one string: after a while, you get tired of the same few notes.

So the recipes in this yeast bread chapter are, for the most part, grainy. Most use both whole wheat and unbleached flour, in conjunction with another grain or several of them. Grainy breads are no more difficult to make than white breads; they're just a little different, like your kids: you don't expect or even hope they'll all be the same. Like kids, different doughs have their little behavioral quirks; some require a gentler kneading hand; others like a little roughhousing. When I notice these things in a recipe, I point them out to you so you'll know what to expect.

The yeast breads that follow are broken down into three main categories. There are "Daily Breads," the ones I make most often. This category includes a couple of white breads, but the majority are grainy and often feature a single grain, like millet or oats, so you'll have a chance to get acquainted with it. The daily breads are, for the most part, all-purpose, good for a number of things, like French toast, sandwiches, toast, and just to go with dinner.

Next, I have a collection of personal treasures I call "Harvest Breads," loaves based on vegetables and herbs. When I bake, I always have one eye trained on the garden, to see what sort of marriages I can arrange. Winter squash and cornmeal? A fresh herb loaf in the finest Shaker tradition? How about a pesto bread? You'll find recipes here for all of those ideas. I think these breads represent the spirit of country baking, because of their conspicuous association with the soil, because they're synonymous with freshness, and because they carry on in the tradition of country cooks, who've always looked for ways to make thorough use of their resources. Even if you're only an armchair gardener, you'll want to go digging around in this section for something tasty.

Last are the "Sweet and Holiday Breads." These are richer, sweeter special-occasion breads, often more like cake or coffee cake than daily breads. Two things to remember about breads from this category are that the doughs are often a little trickier to handle: the extra fat hinders the elasticity. And they tend to darken from the extra sweetening; most of the daily breads have a minimum of sweetening.

If you have never baked yeast bread before, now is the time to start, with one of the recipes in the "Daily Breads" section, a quick run through the crash course for beginners (page 55), and a little affirmation that you'll give it your best shot. At the risk of sermonizing, I think yeast bread baking takes some level of commitment, because it can be a slow learning process with frustrations along the way. Not so many that you'll bake a lot of inedible bread, because you can be 85 percent competent after your first try; your bread will be wonderful. But the last bit of refinement, that other 15 percent, takes time. Stick with it, though, because there's wisdom in the process. You get attentive, and you get better at reading the messages the bread is sending you. You enjoy it more and place a higher priority on doing it. And your bread gets better.

So, expect a little stumbling. But by all means, make bread. ◆

# Yeast Bread Basics: A Crash Course for Beginners

This quick reference guide to baking with yeast will get you started on the right track.

1. *To dissolve active dry yeast,* sprinkle it over your liquid—usually lukewarm water—and stir with a fork. The liquid should be no hotter than 115°; it should feel warm, but not uncomfortably so, to the touch. If you are uncertain whether or not your yeast is still good, stir it into ¼ cup warm water with a pinch of sweetener; this is called "proofing." If it does not foam within 10 minutes, it's no good. To avoid this uncertainty I buy my yeast in bulk, test it once, then store it in the freezer, tightly sealed, where it will last for at least 6 months.

2. Speaking of warmth, *make sure none of your ingredients—eggs, milk, flour, etc.— are cold.* Cold will inhibit the action of the yeast, and your dough won't rise (or it will rise very slowly). So, let your ingredients warm to room temperature before you begin.

3. *All of these bread recipes use a sponge, or the sponge method.* A sponge is a mixture of liquid, yeast, and enough flour to make a sort of thick batter. A sponge softens coarse particles of grain, so you get a better rise, because the grain is less likely to cut into the gluten, the elastic framework of the bread. Because the particles of flour absorb moisture in the sponge, you'll end up using less flour later, resulting in a moister loaf.

4. *Always add flour gradually to the sponge.* Once your sponge has rested, and you start adding the remainder of the flour, add it no more than a cup at a time. When the dough starts to firm up and becomes hard to stir, shake the flour on by the handful as you need it. This grad-

ual addition of flour will prevent you from accidentally kneading in too much flour, which would give you a dry loaf.

5. *When the dough loses most of its tackiness in the bowl, turn it out onto a floured surface.* Flour your hands and start to knead. Kneading is easier to do than to describe. Basically the idea is to push, fold, turn, push, fold, turn, until the dough forms an elastic, cohesive mass (for remedial instruction, see page 69). *Kneading develops gluten,* which in turn allows your dough to stretch. If you know a good kneader, see if you can go watch. Average kneading time for dough is 10 minutes, a little less for lean doughs, a little more for rich ones.

6. *Putting your dough in an oiled or buttered bowl and covering it with plastic wrap prevents a skin from forming on the dough.* (There are exceptions, where a hard, rustic-looking crust is your aim.) The plastic wrap also traps heat and moisture, both of which are conducive to a good rise. Let your dough rise in a draft-free, comfortably warm, but not hot, spot (for some suggestions, see page 76).

7. Once in the bowl, *the dough will generally take from 1 to 2 hours to double in bulk.* The key factors are temperature and the relative richness of the dough. The more butter and eggs a dough contains, the longer it takes to rise. The standard test for checking a dough to determine whether it is sufficiently doubled is to poke it with a finger; if the impression remains, instead of slowly filling back in, it is supposed to be ready. The one problem I have with this test is that even doughs not fully doubled will hold a finger impression. So let me add this footnote to the finger-poking technique: the dough should feel spongy around your finger when you poke it in. If you use a straight-sided or just gently flared bowl, it will be simple to judge the dough visually, especially if the dough—at the outset—fills the bowl by about half.

8. *To punch the dough down, do just that,* with your fist and with authority, but not so hard that you tear the gluten. Punching down is almost always followed by a brief kneading to reinvigorate the gluten—which at this point is like a relaxed muscle—after its stretch in the bowl.

9. *Shaping* comes next. (For more on shaping pan loaves, see page 73.) Shaping tight balls for free-form loaves is one of the trickiest bread-baking skills to learn. With experience you can teach yourself to knead the dough into a ball, tightening the dough as you push it forward. If you're a beginner, you can hold the dough in two hands and tighten it by stretching the upper surface of the ball with your palms, at the same time tucking the dough up and inside itself with your fingertips. Pinch the dough together where it gathers—the gathered part of the ball sits on the sheet; the smooth side

faces up. In any case, don't be afraid to try shaping free-form loaves; at the very worst, the dough will spread on the sheet, perhaps more than it should, and you'll end up with a wider loaf instead of a taller one. No big deal.

10. *Cover the shaped dough loosely with plastic wrap and set it aside until doubled.* The second rising always takes less time than the first, about two-thirds of the time. At this point you don't want to use the finger-poking method, because you'll leave an impression in the finished loaf. Pan loaves are easy to judge. Free-form loaves are more difficult because some of the *rising* has to be accounted for in *spreading;* in this case, always try to picture whether the *volume,* rather than the height, has doubled.

11. Anticipate the point at which your dough will be ready to bake—it will look quite swollen, nearly doubled, and have a spongy feel (touch it softly)—and *preheat the oven 15 minutes ahead.* If you're using baking tiles or a baking stone, preheat them and the oven for at least 30 minutes. Gather any seeds you may use on top and prepare the egg wash if you're using one.

12. *Bake the loaves with the rack set low enough so the tops don't scorch.* Your loaves are likely to rise at least 1 inch in the oven, perhaps more. If you notice at any point that the tops are getting burned, move the rack down. If you have a small oven, the loaves will brown more evenly if you change their positions halfway through the baking.

13. *To see if a yeast bread is done, tap the bottom* (turn it out of the pan if you've baked it in one) *and listen for a hollow retort.* If you don't hear one, put the loaf back in the oven; you needn't put it back in the pan at this point. Some breads, especially the richer ones, don't sound like that; they don't sound like anything, or they give only a faint echo. Yeast coffee cakes are a good example. When I'm in doubt about a yeast coffee cake, I pull some of the dough apart and check for sticky patches. If you're ever in doubt, better to bake your bread an extra 5 minutes or so than to find out it is undercooked.

14. *Cool your loaves on a rack,* out of the pans. Generally you shouldn't slice a loaf right away, because the structure is too fragile at this point to allow you to do a clean cutting job. Unless otherwise indicated, it's better to wait at least 30 minutes before cutting. Use only a sharp serrated knife to cut yeast bread. Nothing else will do. ◆

# Daily Breads

## Farm-Style Whole Wheat Bread

*Makes 2 large loaves*

This is called "farm-style" because it's the sort of loaf that would have been served, not all that long ago, on working farms all across the country, where there was always a surplus of eggs, butter, and milk. This loaf has similar qualities to, though I think a better flavor than, some commercial whole wheat breads. You might consider that a less than flattering comment to make about a good homemade loaf. But I can't tell you how many times I've heard frustrated young moms say "My kids won't eat my whole wheat bread because it isn't soft like the store-bought kind." They'll eat this one—enthusiastically.

2³/₄ cups lukewarm milk
¹/₄ cup honey or unsulphured molasses
1 ¹/₄-ounce package (about 1 tablespoon) active dry yeast
5¹/₂ cups whole wheat flour
1 tablespoon salt
1 large egg, at room temperature
3 tablespoons unsalted butter, softened
³/₄ to 1 cup unbleached flour for kneading
egg wash: 1 egg beaten with 1 tablespoon milk or cream
1 tablespoon sesame, sunflower, or poppy seeds

Pour the milk into a large mixing bowl and stir in the honey or molasses. Sprinkle the yeast over the milk and set aside for 5 minutes to dissolve. Add 3¹/₂ cups of the whole wheat flour to the milk and beat hard with a wooden spoon for 1 minute. Cover this sponge with plastic wrap and set it aside in a warm, draft-free spot for 30 minutes.

After 30 minutes, beat the salt and egg into the sponge, followed by one more cup of the whole wheat flour. Smear the butter into the dough, intermittently, with the remaining cup of whole wheat flour. Begin working the unbleached flour into the dough. When the dough is firm enough to handle, turn it out onto a floured surface and knead for 10 minutes, using the unbleached flour to keep the dough from sticking. (I find that this dough reaches a point, late in the kneading, where the elasticity kicks in and becomes apparent; once you reach that point, knead a minute or 2 longer.)

Place the dough in a lightly oiled bowl, turning it to cover the entire surface with oil. Cover the bowl with plastic wrap and set it aside until the dough is doubled. While the dough rises, lightly butter 2 4½- by 8½-inch loaf pans.

Once the dough has doubled, punch it down, knead it briefly, and divide it in half. Shape each half into a loaf, then place the loaves in the prepared pans. Cover the pans loosely with plastic wrap and set them aside in a warm, draft-free spot until the dough has doubled again. When the dough appears nearly doubled, preheat the oven to 375°.

Just before baking, lightly brush the tops of the loaves with the egg wash. Sprinkle the loaves with the seeds, then make 3 or 4 diagonal slashes on top of each. Bake for 40 to 45 minutes, until the loaves are nicely browned on all sides and the bottoms give a hollow retort when tapped gently. Remove the loaves from the pans and let them cool on a rack before slicing. Store the loaves in sealed plastic bags. ♦

# *Grainy Bread for the Whole Week*

*Makes 4 loaves*

*L*et's say you have only a little time each week to devote to baking, and you want to make the most of it; this recipe is for you. It will provide a week's supply of bread for a small family, with options. For instance, you can bake three loaves and turn the other quarter of the dough into a pizza dinner. Or, for a little variety, you can top one loaf with sesame seeds, knead raisins into another, put a swirl of brown sugar and cinnamon into the third, and make rolls with the rest. Please note that kneading this much dough is something of an athletic event. Don't let that deter you; the dough may seem to have a mind of its own at first, but it will eventually knead up into a springy ball.

> 1½ *quarts lukewarm water*
> 1½ *cups rolled oats* (not *instant*)
> 2 ¼*-ounce packages* (*about 2 tablespoons*)
>   *active dry yeast*
> ⅓ *cup honey*
> 11 *cups whole wheat flour*
> 3 *tablespoons salt*
> ½ *cup flavorless vegetable oil*
> 1 *cup* (*approximately*) *unbleached flour*

Pour the water into the biggest bowl you have, then add the rolled oats. Stir in the yeast and honey and set aside for 5 minutes. Beat in 7 cups of the whole wheat flour; add

*(continued)*

59

(*continued*)

the first 4 cups all at once, the other 3 one at a time. Using a wooden spoon, beat vigorously for 1 minute, then cover the bowl with plastic wrap and set this sponge aside in a warm, draft-free spot for 30 minutes.

After 30 minutes, beat the salt and oil into the sponge. Beat in the remaining 4 cups of whole wheat flour, 1 cup at a time; by the last cup, you may have to start kneading the flour in by hand. After all the whole wheat flour has been added, cover the dough again with plastic wrap and let it rest for 10 minutes.

Dust your kneading surface with some of the unbleached flour, flour your hands, and turn the dough out of the bowl. Knead for about 15 minutes, flouring your kneading surface when necessary to keep the dough from sticking. (If an experienced kneader is close by, offer him or her half the dough.) After 15 minutes you should have a fairly stiff, elastic, and smooth dough. Place the dough in a lightly oiled bowl, turning it to coat the entire surface of the dough with oil. Cover the bowl with plastic wrap and set it aside in a warm, draft-free spot until doubled in bulk. While the dough is rising, butter 4 loaf pans measuring 4½ by 8½ inches.

When doubled, punch the dough down and turn it out onto a lightly floured surface. Divide the dough into 4 equal pieces. Knead each piece briefly, then shape them into loaves. Place the loaves in the prepared pans, cover loosely with plastic wrap, and let rise in a warm, draft-free spot until doubled. When the loaves appear nearly doubled, preheat the oven to 375°.

Just before you put the loaves in the oven,

make 3 or 4 slashes in the top of each loaf using a sharp serrated knife. Bake the loaves for 40 to 45 minutes, arranging them so none of the pans are too close to the oven walls. Check the loaves about midway through the baking; if they aren't browning evenly, change their positions. (For instance, anything near an oven wall is liable to brown more on the side near the wall; turn the loaf 180°.) The loaves are done when the bottoms give a hollow retort when tapped with a finger.

Transfer the loaves to a rack to cool. Store the cooled loaves in plastic bags.

FREEZING: *Any loaves that you're saving for more than 2 days should be frozen.* ♦

# 60-Minute Bread

*Makes 2 free-form loaves*

Well, maybe 65 or 70 minutes, but I would tell you almost anything to get you to try this. This recipe—a cross between a yeasted and a soda bread—breaks all the rules and wins. It's the best *fast* all-purpose bread I know, the sort of loaf that becomes a staple in a busy household. The kneading time is brief, as is the rising—only 10 minutes. I invented it because I was always coming up short on sandwich bread for the kids' lunches and needed a quick solution.

1/2 cup lukewarm water
1 1/4-ounce package (about 1 tablespoon) active dry yeast
1 cup milk
1 cup plain yogurt
1 tablespoon honey
2 cups whole wheat flour
2 tablespoons flavorless vegetable oil
3 1/4 cups (approximately) unbleached flour
2 teaspoons salt
1 teaspoon baking powder
1 teaspoon baking soda

Pour the water into a small bowl and stir in the yeast. Set aside for 5 minutes to dissolve. Meanwhile, heat the milk and yogurt in a small saucepan, just to about body temperature. Pour the liquid into a mixing bowl, then stir in the dissolved yeast and the honey. Beat in the whole wheat flour until smooth. Cover the bowl with plastic wrap and set the sponge aside in a warm, draft-free spot for 15 minutes. While you're waiting, generously dust a large baking sheet with cornmeal.

After 15 minutes, stir the oil into the sponge. In a separate bowl, mix 2 cups of the unbleached flour with the salt, baking powder, and baking soda. Stir this, about 1 cup at a time, into the sponge, beating well after each cup. Gradually stir in enough of the remaining unbleached flour to make a soft but kneadable dough. Preheat the oven to 425°.

Turn the dough out onto a floured surface and knead for 5 minutes, using the remaining unbleached flour. Don't be too rough with it, because it is a soft dough, but don't baby it either. Keep the surface floured so it doesn't stick. Divide the dough in half, shaping each half into a stumpy football. Place the loaves on the baking sheet, leaving some room for expansion.

Let the loaves sit, uncovered, for 10 minutes in a warm, draft-free spot. Make 3 or 4 slashes on top of each loaf, then bake for 30 minutes; they'll get well browned on all sides, and the bottoms of the loaves should give a hollow retort when tapped, just like yeast bread. Cool the loaves on a rack for at least 30 minutes before slicing; use a sharp serrated knife. ◆

# Honey Whole Grain Swedish Limpa

*Makes 2 free-form loaves*

Swedish limpa was the first bread I really fell in love with—its aroma and flavor, punctuated by aniseed, caraway, dark beer, and orange, brought me to a level of bread pleasure I had never imagined. Given the frequency with which Swedish limpa recipes appear in bread books, I suspect I'm not alone. After years of toying with the standard recipe, this is my current favorite version. It makes wonderful toast, slathered with sweet butter and honey. Great with soup-and-salad meals too.

1 12-ounce bottle dark beer (*Guinness stout is good*)

³/₄ cup water

¹/₃ cup honey

1 tablespoon unsulphured molasses

finely grated zest of 2 oranges

1 teaspoon aniseed

1 teaspoon caraway seeds

1 ¹/₄-ounce package (*about 1 tablespoon*) active dry yeast

2 cups whole wheat flour

1¹/₂ cups rye flour

1 tablespoon salt

3 tablespoons unsalted butter, melted

2¹/₂ cups (approximately) unbleached flour

In a medium saucepan, heat the beer, water, honey, molasses, orange zest, and seeds. When very hot, pour the liquid into a large mixing bowl and cool. When it is lukewarm, sprinkle on the yeast and set aside for 5 minutes.

Using a wooden spoon, stir the whole wheat and rye flours into the liquid. Beat vigorously for 1 minute, cover with plastic wrap, and set this sponge aside in a warm, draft-free spot for 20 minutes.

After 20 minutes, beat the salt and then the butter into the sponge. Stir in the unbleached flour, about ¹/₂ cup at a time, until the dough is too stiff to stir. Turn the dough out onto a floured surface and knead with floured hands for 10 minutes, using as much of the unbleached flour as necessary to keep the dough from sticking. Go easy at first; the dough will be soft and a little sticky. After 10 minutes the dough will be smooth and springy. Put the dough in a lightly oiled bowl, turn to coat the entire surface of the dough with oil, and cover the bowl with plastic wrap. Set it aside in a warm, draft-free spot until the dough is doubled in bulk. While the dough doubles, generously dust a large, heavy baking sheet with cornmeal and set it aside.

When the dough has doubled, punch it down, knead it briefly, then divide it in half. Shape each half into a tight ball and place, diagonally across from one another, on the baking sheet. Cover loosely with plastic wrap and set aside in a warm, draft-free spot until doubled. When the loaves appear nearly doubled, preheat the oven to 375°.

Just before baking, make several long slashes on top of the loaves. Bake for approximately 50 minutes, until the tops and bottoms are well browned. (To equalize the baking, turn the sheet 180° midway through the baking.) When done, the bottoms of the loaves should give a faint, hollow echo when tapped with a finger. Transfer the loaves to a rack to cool. Store completely cooled loaves in sealed plastic bags.

NOTE: *For a glossy appearance you can brush the loaves with an egg white wash (1 egg white beaten with 1 teaspoon water) just before slashing them.* ◆

## Mixing Dough with an Electric Mixer

Though I much prefer mixing and kneading dough by hand, some cooks may want to enlist the aid of their standing electric mixers. The most capable—and probably the most common—of the kneading machines is the large KitchenAid K5A, which comes equipped with a dough hook for kneading.

Obviously the first thing you should do is consult the instruction manual if you are unsure whether your mixer can knead dough. Mixers have particular problems with grainy doughs, which most of these are (If your mixer didn't come with a dough hook, most likely it can't knead). Then you should check for the machine's recommended dough capacity: if a dough is too heavy, the machine may be subject to too much stress, and you could burn out the motor. (To play it safe, you may want to halve the recipe the first time you make it; simply make the recipe as directed, using half the ingredients.)

To make dough in an electric mixer, put the liquid in the machine's mixing bowl. Add the dissolved yeast, as you would normally, then follow the same progression for adding the flour and the other ingredients. For the initial mixing—while the dough is still batterlike—you will probably find that the flat beater does a better job of mixing the dough than the dough hook does. Expect to turn the machine off occasionally, to scrape down the sides of the bowl during the preliminary mixing. Once the dough gets firmer, switch to the hook.

When the dough starts to pull away from the sides of the bowl, you've reached a point roughly equivalent to the point when you turn the dough out—when mixing by hand—and begin kneading on a floured surface. Kneading times with mixers may not be precisely what they are with the hand method, though you will probably find—especially with heavier, grainier doughs—there's not much time saved. The mixer has done its job—stop it periodically to check the progress—when the dough is smooth and elastic; it tends to ball around the hook at this point. Proceed with the recipe as directed.

# Tess's French-Style Whole Wheat Bread

*Makes 2 long loaves*

Tess is one of my daughters, and this is the bread she likes to make most. At the tender age of 6 she could not only recite the ingredients from memory, but she could also make this with no help but an adult kneading contribution; that's how simple this is. What this loaf lacks in French bread authenticity it makes up for by being fast and flavorful. Instead of making 2 long loaves we sometimes make 6 smaller ones so each of us has his or her own loaf. It makes great garlic bread.

> 2 cups lukewarm water
> 2 1/4-ounce packages (about 2 tablespoons) active dry yeast
> 1 tablespoon honey
> 4 cups whole wheat flour
> 1 tablespoon salt
> 1/3 cup (approximately) unbleached flour for kneading

Pour the water into a large mixing bowl and stir in the yeast and honey. Set aside for 5 minutes, then stir in 2 1/2 cups of the whole wheat flour. Beat vigorously with a wooden spoon for 1 minute, then cover this sponge with plastic wrap and set it aside in a warm, draft-free spot for 10 minutes.

After 10 minutes, beat the salt into the sponge. Add the remaining whole wheat flour, about 1/2 cup at a time; the dough may be a little slow to accept the last 1/2 cup, so expect to knead some of it in.

Turn the dough out onto a lightly floured surface and knead for about 8 minutes, using sprinkles of the unbleached flour to keep the dough from sticking. After 8 minutes the dough will be smooth and elastic and somewhat firm. Flour the dough lightly and put it in a bowl. Cover the bowl with plastic wrap and set it aside in a warm, draft-free spot until doubled in bulk; this is a relatively quick riser due to the amount of yeast and absence of fat. While the dough is rising, generously sprinkle a large baking sheet with cornmeal and set it aside.

Once the dough has doubled, punch it down and knead briefly on a lightly floured surface. Divide the dough in half, shape the halves into rounds, and let rest for 5 minutes. Working with one piece of dough at a time, roll each half into an oval about 13 inches long on a lightly floured surface. Roll the oval up lengthwise, like you would a carpet, keeping a fair amount of tension on the dough; pinch the seam to seal, then lay the loaf on the prepared sheet. Repeat for the other piece of dough, leaving plenty of room between them on the sheet. Cover the dough loosely with a foil tent; the foil shouldn't touch the dough or it will stick. Set the loaves aside in a warm, draft-free spot until doubled in bulk; the loaves will spread as well as rise. When the loaves appear nearly doubled, preheat the oven to 425°.

Just before baking, make several diagonal slashes in the top of each loaf. Bake for 30 to 35 minutes, until the tops are nicely browned and the bottoms give a hollow thud when tapped with a finger. Serve hot or cool on a rack. Any bread that won't be eaten right away should be frozen, wrapped in foil. ♦

## *About Yeast*

Yeast is a single-celled plant in the fungus family. Though there are many different types of yeast, the kind we use to leaven bread—bakers' yeast—is composed of yeast strains that excel at producing carbon dioxide. This gas raises bread dough as it becomes trapped in the gluten, the elastic framework of the dough.

Bakers' yeast is commonly sold in two forms: in granular form, called *active dry yeast,* and in *compressed cakes.* The active dry yeast is usually sold in 1/4-ounce foil packages, though 4-ounce vacuum-packed jars are also available in many supermarkets. Compressed yeast is most commonly available in cakes measuring 3/5-ounce. (To substitute cake yeast for active dry, replace one 3/5-ounce cake for one 1/4-ounce package. Crumble it into the liquid—where you normally sprinkle on the dry yeast—and stir to dissolve.)

Throughout this section on yeast breads I specify active dry yeast, because this is what I have always used, not because I feel it has superior qualities to cake yeast. In fact, there are bakers who swear by compressed cake yeast. Nonetheless, I prefer active dry yeast since it has a much longer shelf life than cake yeast, generally a year after the date of manufacture, provided it has been properly stored in a cool, dry, airtight environment. Compressed cake yeast, on the other hand, only has a refrigerated shelf life of 4 to 6 weeks after manufacture. Once purchased, it should be used within 2 weeks, though it will keep up to 2 months in the freezer. In every case, check the expiration date on the package, to be sure you aren't buying yeast that's outdated.

In the past several years, manufacturers have introduced new "fast" yeasts, stronger strains of yeast that can reduce the rising time by as much as half. The mixing method for this type of yeast is different from the conventional way: rather than dissolving the yeast in water, it is mixed in with the flour, and hotter liquids are called for.

I have only limited experience with these fast yeasts. Because I learned to bake with regular active dry yeast, I have long since become accustomed to its pace, which suits me fine, and never really seemed particularly "slow." I suppose it might if one sat around waiting for the dough to rise. But you don't. You go rake leaves, or run to the store, or cook dinner. Two common complaints I have heard about fast yeast are that bread made from it dries out quickly (since the starches in the dough don't absorb as much moisture during the shortened rising) and that the flavor, especially in "plainer" breads—like French bread—suffers due to the abbreviated fermentation of the dough.

# Wheaten French Bread

*Makes 3 loaves*

I firmly believe that instructions for homemade French bread should be kept as simple as possible. I admire and sometimes even envy bakers who explore and report on French bread in all its minutiae, citing narrow and precise temperatures for rising, espousing the virtues of this or that starter formula, and the like. But more often than not, I'm afraid, the findings are dauntingly counterproductive: home bakers get scared off, and nobody makes *any* French bread.

Here, then, is a pared-down recipe for French bread, or at least for the long narrow loaves (baguettes) we commonly refer to as French bread. The flavor is fantastic, with pleasant wheaty overtones; the crust is very chewy and shatters with appropriate crackerlike brilliance when you break the loaf in half.

This recipe is written around loaves baked on oven tiles; that's key, in my opinion. (See page 130 for information on buying and using tiles.) Only on tiles can you get well-rounded loaves with a superior crust. Special French bread pans that look like shallow metal troughs are available, but I think they're overrated and entirely unnecessary; I had such a sticking problem with mine I just gave up and went back to this simple system, which uses things you already have on hand. The bread needs intermittent attention for the better part of a day, so best to make this on a weekend.

2¹/₄ *cups lukewarm water*

2 *teaspoons (a little less than 1 ¹/₄-ounce*
  *package) active dry yeast*

5 *cups unbleached flour*

1 *cup whole wheat flour*

3 *tablespoons yellow cornmeal, preferably*
  *stone-ground*

2 *teaspoons salt*

Pour the water into a large mixing bowl and stir in the yeast. Set it aside to dissolve for 5 minutes, then beat in 2¹/₂ cups of the unbleached flour, ¹/₂ cup of the whole wheat flour, and the cornmeal. Beat vigorously with a wooden spoon for 1 minute, cover with plastic wrap, and set this sponge aside in a draft-free environment—at average room temperature, not a warm spot—for 2 to 4 hours.

After the allotted time, beat the salt and remaining whole wheat flour into the dough. Stir in enough of the remaining unbleached flour to make a kneadable dough, then turn the dough out onto a lightly floured surface. Knead for 10 minutes, using sprinkles of flour to keep it from sticking. After 10 minutes the dough will be smooth and elastic, though it may still have a tendency to stick if it isn't floured. That's all right. Flour the dough, then put it in a ceramic bowl and cover the bowl with plastic wrap. Let the dough rise at room temperature until at least doubled but no more than tripled in bulk.

While the dough is rising, prepare the cloth pleats in which the loaves will rise. Take a dish towel—a smooth-surfaced one, not terry—and sprinkle one side of it heavily with flour; brush your hand over it so it gets into the weave. Have it standing by in your kneading area.

Once the dough has risen, punch it down and turn it out onto a lightly floured surface. Knead vigorously for 30 seconds, then divide the dough into equal thirds. Working with one piece at a time, knead the dough into a ball, flatten it slightly, then give it a karate chop in the center. Fold the dough over, using the impression as your hinge; push down with your palm to flatten. Make another karate chop down the length of the dough and fold in half again, pressing down with your palm to seal the edge; notice the loaf growing longer. If the dough isn't cooperating, let it rest a minute to loosen the gluten. Do another chop and fold, then roll the dough under your palms to round and stretch it into a 10- or 11-inch strand.

Center the length of dough between the 2 long sides of the towel, laying it down about 6 inches in from the end. Pinch opposite sides of the towel and pull up, making a half pleat to the outside of the loaf; it should come not quite an inch above the loaf. Support the pleat with something long and heavy, like a bread pan with a can in it. Pull up another half pleat on the other side of the dough, creating a cloth trough. Lay the next loaf in the next partial trough, pull up a pleat, put in the next loaf, and pull up one last pleat and support it. Leave about ¹/₂ inch of space between loaves; you don't want to crowd them at the outset, even though they'll eventually be pushing against one another for support. Dust the loaves generously with flour and let rise, uncovered. Once the loaves have clearly begun to

*(continued)*

*(continued)*

swell—after about 30 minutes—line your oven with tiles (see page 130) and preheat the oven to 450°.

Find a piece of sturdy cardboard, or cut one from a box, measuring about 13 inches long and 8 inches wide. Flour one side of it. When the loaves have doubled, remove the support and pull down one of the end pleats. Lay the long side of the cardboard right next to the loaf. Now, grasping the sides of the towel about halfway up the other supporting pleat, roll the dough onto the cardboard; what was the bottom is now the top of the loaf. Using a sharp serrated knife, carefully make 3 or 4 shallow diagonal slashes on top of the loaf, then slide it onto the tiles. Repeat for the remaining loaves.

As soon as the loaves are all in place, put 2 ice cubes in a pie pan, put the pan somewhere in the oven, and shut the door; this will create the steam you need for a crusty loaf. Bake the loaves for 30 minutes. The loaves will be quite crusty when you first take them out, but as the initial steam is released from within, the crust will start to go slightly soft; at any point the loaves can be put back in a hot oven for about 10 minutes to bring back the crust. Cool the loaves on a rack, then immediately freeze any you don't eat right away.

NOTES:

♦ The good flavor of this loaf comes, in large part, from not forcing the rising in a warm environment. This loaf doesn't like to be rushed; thus the lengthy rest for the sponge.

♦ Though I prefer baking this bread on tiles, you can simply shape the dough into loaves and transfer them to a cornmeal-dusted baking sheet. Let them rise under a foil tent—don't let it touch the dough—then bake in a preheated 450° oven for about 35 minutes. With this method you do, however, lose the superior bottom crust and roundness of shape the tiles contribute to.

♦ Instead of using cardboard to get the loaves in the oven, you can buy a wooden paddle, called a *peel,* at a kitchen store. The problem with many of these, I find, is that the shape and size are limiting; a peel for this type of bread, for instance, probably wouldn't work for pizza.

♦ If you own a plant mister, you can skip the ice; spray the loaves lightly with water just after they go in, then again about 10 minutes later.

♦ I'm always proud of this loaf and like to bring it to the table and break it in half (with pot holders)—the sound of the shattering crust and whoosh of escaping steam never fail to unleash the requisite chorus of oohs and aahs.

♦ If you knead in the bowl for the first minute or 2, while the dough is still very tacky, you'll keep your kneading surface from getting all gummed up.

♦ Knead gently at first, with well-floured hands, so you don't tear the dough's fragile elastic structure. As you feel the dough cohere and become more elastic, use a little more muscle.

♦ Don't use whole wheat flour for kneading. It does a poor job of preventing the dough from sticking. Use unbleached flour.

♦ As you knead, don't use any more flour than necessary to prevent the dough from sticking. Otherwise, you may knead in too much and end up with a dry loaf. ♦

## *Kneading 101*

One of the frustrations most common to beginning bread bakers revolves around this manipulation of the dough we call kneading. Getting the knack of it is the problem, and this is not surprising, given the limitations of words: it just isn't that easy to tell someone how to knead. The standard line is to "push, fold, turn" the dough—and that will get you started. But if you've ever watched an experienced baker knead dough, you know that "push, fold, turn" no more describes the beauty of kneading than "tap, tap, tap" describes the way Fred Astaire moved on the dance floor.

The challenge, then, is to translate that "push, fold, turn" into something fluid, something that feels like more of a dance. That takes some experimenting with your hands and the way you manipulate the dough. Don't be timid. Using little half-turns, push the dough

this way and that until you find the rhythm that feels right. Start with your basic "push, fold, turn" idea and then branch out from there.

A good way to find your kneading rhythm is to play music while you knead. I used to think that kneading had to be some sort of meditative exercise, done in absolute silence in a contemplative state of mind; heaven knows where I got that idea. Anyway, that never worked for me; 10 minutes of contemplative kneading can seem like an eternity. Eventually I discovered I was more of a rock-and-roll kneader. Give me some loud Talking Heads or George Harrison and I'll knead all day. Maybe you're a classical kneader or a country-western kneader or a rap kneader. Whatever works.

# Buttermilk Honey Bran Bread

*Makes 2 loaves*

Over the years I've put bran into numerous yeast breads, only to find that I like it best in an otherwise white loaf such as this one. In grainy breads the bran is either lost or obscured by the flour itself; here, the off-white background of the unbleached flour provides a sharp contrast for the dark bran. This is a soft, somewhat tacky dough. Even after 10 minutes of kneading, don't be surprised if it still feels a little sticky. Don't keep kneading flour in, however, or the loaf will be dry. An excellent all-purpose loaf, with a slightly sour bite.

1¹/₃ cups buttermilk
1 cup milk
¹/₃ cup honey
1¹/₂ cups wheat bran
1 ¹/₄-ounce package (about 1 tablespoon) active dry yeast
¹/₄ cup lukewarm water
7¹/₂ cups (approximately) unbleached flour
1 tablespoon salt
¹/₄ cup unsalted butter, melted and cooled
2 large eggs, at room temperature
egg wash: 1 egg beaten with 1 tablespoon milk

In a large nonaluminum saucepan, heat the buttermilk, milk, and honey until hot to the touch; don't worry if it looks curdled. Put the bran into a large mixing bowl and stir the heated liquid into it. While this cools, sprinkle the yeast over the warm water in a separate bowl and set it aside for 5 minutes to dissolve.

When the bran mixture has cooled to lukewarm, stir in the dissolved yeast. With a wooden spoon, stir in 2¹/₂ cups of the unbleached flour and beat vigorously for 1 minute. Cover the bowl with plastic wrap and set this sponge aside in a warm, draft-free spot for 30 minutes.

After 30 minutes, beat in the salt, melted butter, and eggs. Beat in the remaining flour, 1 cup at a time, until the dough is too stiff to stir. Turn the dough out onto a lightly floured surface and knead for 10 minutes with floured hands, adding flour as needed to prevent sticking. Place the dough in a lightly oiled bowl, turning to coat the entire surface of the dough with oil. Cover the bowl with plastic wrap and set it aside in a warm, draft-free spot until doubled. As the dough rises, butter 2 4¹/₂- by 8¹/₂-inch loaf pans.

Punch the dough down, knead it briefly on a lightly floured surface, then divide it in half. Shape the halves into loaves and place them in the buttered pans. Cover loosely with plastic wrap and set aside in a warm, draft-free spot until almost doubled. When the dough appears nearly doubled, preheat the oven to 375° and brush the loaves lightly with the egg wash. When fully doubled, bake the loaves for about 45 minutes. The top crusts will be deep brown, and the bottoms, should give a hollow retort when tapped lightly with a finger.

Remove the loaves from their pans and cool on a rack. Store in sealed plastic bags when completely cooled. ◆

# Toasted Sunflower Seed Bread

*Makes 2 large loaves*

Here's a whole wheat bread that incorporates toasted sunflower seeds.

3 cups lukewarm water or potato water

1 ¼-ounce package (about 1 tablespoon) active dry yeast

1 tablespoon packed light brown sugar or unsulphured molasses

4 cups whole wheat flour

1½ cups raw hulled sunflower seeds

1 tablespoon soy sauce or tamari

1 tablespoon salt (less if you've used salted potato water)

¼ cup flavorless vegetable oil

2 to 2½ cups unbleached flour

egg wash: 1 egg beaten with 1 tablespoon milk

Pour the water into a large mixing bowl and stir in the yeast and brown sugar or molasses. Set aside for 5 minutes to dissolve the yeast. Using a wooden spoon, stir in the whole wheat flour and beat vigorously for 1 minute. Cover this sponge with plastic wrap and set it aside in a warm, draft-free spot for 30 minutes.

While the sponge activates, prepare the sunflower seeds. In a cast-iron skillet, toast 1 cup of the sunflower seeds over medium heat, stirring often. After 5 minutes or so, when they are nicely golden, stir in the tamari or soy sauce. Turn off the heat but keep stirring to coat the seeds well. Scrape the seeds out of the skillet onto a baking sheet and let them cool in a single layer. Once they've cooled, put them into a blender or food processor and grind to a coarse meal; some remaining chunks of whole seeds are desirable.

Stir the salt into the sponge, followed by the oil and sunflower meal. Mix in the unbleached flour, about ½ cup at a time, until you have a stiff, kneadable dough. Turn the dough out onto a lightly floured surface and knead for 10 minutes, until smooth and elastic. Place the dough in a lightly oiled bowl, turning it to coat the entire surface of the dough with oil. Cover the bowl with plastic wrap and set aside in a warm, draft-free spot, until doubled in bulk. While the dough rises, butter 2 4½- by 8½-inch loaf pans and sprinkle the insides with half the remaining seeds; pat some up against the sides, but don't be surprised if they tend to fall off. Set aside.

When the dough has doubled, punch it down, knead briefly, then divide it in half. Shape the halves into loaves and place them in the prepared pans. Cover loosely with plastic wrap and set aside in a warm, draft-free spot to rise again. When the loaves appear nearly doubled, preheat the oven to 375°.

Brush the loaves lightly with the egg wash and sprinkle them with the rest of the seeds. Pat *lightly* with your hands to embed the seeds a little. When fully doubled, bake the loaves for approximately 45 minutes, until the bottom crusts give a hollow retort when tapped with a finger. Cool the loaves on a rack before slicing. Store the cooled loaves in sealed plastic bags. ♦

## Nubby Brown Rice Bread

*Makes 2 free-form loaves*

There's a whole generation of young people for whom brown rice has become the staple grain, virtually replacing white rice. That amounts to a lot of leftover brown rice, and here's one wholesome way to press it into service. Thanks to the rice, the golden surface of this bread is broken with crisp kernels and the interior is extra-chewy. All the flour is whole wheat, except for what you knead in—a very nutritious bread. One variation is to knead raisins into half the dough after you punch it down— kids love this bread.

2¾ *cups lukewarm water*

1 ¼-*ounce package (about 1 tablespoon) active dry yeast*

¼ *cup honey*

5 *cups whole wheat flour*

1 *tablespoon salt*

¼ *cup flavorless vegetable oil*

1½ *cups leftover (cooked) brown rice, at room temperature (see note below)*

¾ *cup (approximately) unbleached flour for kneading*

Pour the water into a large mixing bowl and stir the yeast into it. Set it aside for 5 minutes to dissolve. Using a wooden spoon, stir in the honey and 3 cups of the whole wheat flour; beat vigorously for 1 minute. Cover this sponge with plastic wrap and set it aside in a warm, draft-free spot for 30 minutes.

After 30 minutes, stir the salt and oil into the sponge. Add the brown rice. Beat in the remaining 2 cups of whole wheat flour, ½ cup at a time, after which the dough should feel very stiff.

Turn the dough out onto a floured surface and knead it with floured hands (using the unbleached flour) for about 7 minutes. It will be a bit sticky and will absorb a lot of flour in the kneading; to minimize sticking, don't press too hard on the dough as you knead. After 7 minutes the dough won't be as elastic as other yeast doughs, but it will be cohesive and soft. Place the dough in a lightly oiled bowl, turning to coat the entire surface of the dough with oil. Cover the bowl with plastic wrap and set it aside in a warm, draft-free spot until the dough is doubled. In the meantime, generously dust a large, heavy baking sheet with cornmeal and set it aside.

When the dough has doubled, punch it down and knead briefly on a floured surface. Divide in half, then shape the halves into balls. Place them in diagonally opposite corners of the sheet and cover loosely with plastic wrap. Set aside in a warm, draft-free spot to rise again. When the loaves appear nearly doubled, preheat the oven to 375°.

When the loaves have doubled, slash a long X into each surface with a sharp serrated knife, cutting about ½ inch into the surface. Bake for about 45 minutes, until the bottoms give a hollow retort when tapped with a finger. To help the loaves bake evenly, turn the sheet 180° about halfway into the baking. Transfer the loaves to a rack to cool. Store in sealed plastic bags when totally cooled.

NOTE: *If you want to make this bread and have no brown rice on hand, bring 1½ cups of water to boil in a small saucepan. Stir in ¾ cup raw brown rice and ¼ teaspoon salt and cover. Cook over very low heat for about 40 minutes, undisturbed, until all the water is absorbed. Cool and proceed.* ◆

## How to Shape a Well-Rounded Loaf

Are you one of those bakers who gaze with envy at the next guy's loaf, standing there all proud and tall, while your own loaves always seem to fall over the edge of the pan? If so, here are some points to consider.

◆ First, you may not be kneading enough. Insufficient kneading will leave the dough slack, without the elasticity it needs to hold a nicely rounded top. The other possibility is that you're letting the dough rise too long in the pans, in which case the dough overextends itself and collapses in the heat of the oven.

◆ More often than not, however, the secret to a well-rounded loaf lies in the shaping, and the trick is putting enough tension into the dough so it springs up and not out. Here's the method I think works best: your basic jelly-roll roll.

Once you've punched the dough down and kneaded it briefly, give it a 5-minute rest to relax the gluten. Then, using a heavy rolling pin, roll the dough into a tapered oblong about 12 inches long and about as wide as the pan you're using; it should look something like a narrow guitar pick, pointing at you. Don't flour your surface heavily at all, or the flour inside the roll will prevent a good seal.

Now, starting at the narrow end, roll the dough up like a jelly roll; keep tension on it, but not so much that you rip the surface of the dough. When you get to the end, pinch the seams together and tuck the ends under slightly. Then lay the loaves in the pans seam side down, pressing them down with the palm of your hand. Or, just lay the loaves directly on a cornmeal-dusted baking sheet.

# Seven-Grain Bread

*Makes 2 loaves*

Words can barely describe how much I like this bread. I used to stay away from these many-grain bread recipes because I thought the result would be a confused mishmash. But somehow all the little parts add up to a wonderfully rich whole. One of the key elements here is the millet, which adds that nice crunch.

- ½ cup uncooked millet
- 1 cup boiling water
- 2 cups lukewarm water
- 2 tablespoons packed light brown sugar or honey
- 1 ¼-ounce package (about 1 tablespoon) active dry yeast
- ½ cup yellow cornmeal, preferably stone-ground
- ½ cup barley flour
- ½ cup rolled oats (not *instant*)
- ½ cup rye flour
- ¼ cup buckwheat flour
- 4½ cups whole wheat flour
- 1 tablespoon salt
- ⅓ cup flavorless vegetable oil or good-quality corn oil
- ⅓ to ½ cup unbleached flour for kneading

Put the millet in a medium mixing bowl and pour the boiling water over it. Cover and set aside for 30 minutes. When the 30 minutes are almost up, put the lukewarm water into a large mixing bowl and stir in the brown sugar or honey and yeast. Set aside for 5 minutes to dissolve. Pour the millet and its soaking water into the yeast water, then add the cornmeal, barley flour, oats, rye flour, buckwheat flour, and 2 cups of the whole wheat flour. Beat vigorously with a wooden spoon for 1 minute, cover the bowl with plastic wrap, and set aside in a warm, draft-free spot for 30 minutes.

After 30 minutes, stir the salt and oil into the sponge. Beat in the remaining whole wheat flour; it may get too stiff to stir, at which point you can knead it right in the bowl until it absorbs the rest of the whole wheat.

Now turn the dough out and knead for 10 minutes, using as much of the unbleached flour as necessary to keep the dough from sticking. The dough may stick a little at first, but it will eventually lose most of the tackiness as it becomes more elastic. Place the dough in a lightly oiled bowl, turning to coat the entire surface of the dough with the oil. Cover the bowl with plastic wrap and set it aside in a warm, draft-free spot until the dough is doubled in bulk. As the dough rises, butter 2 4½- by 8½-inch loaf pans.

Once the dough has doubled, punch it down, knead briefly, and divide the dough in half. Shape into loaves and place them in the buttered pans. Cover loosely with plastic wrap and set aside in a warm, draft-free spot until doubled in bulk. When the dough appears nearly doubled, preheat the oven to 375°.

Bake the loaves for 45 to 50 minutes, until all sides are nicely browned and the bottoms, when tapped with a finger, give a hollow retort. Remove the loaves from the pans and cool on a rack before slicing. Store in sealed plastic bags. ◆

## Four-Grain Pumpernickel Prune Bread

*Makes 2 free-form loaves*

This dough, frankly, isn't my favorite to work with, but the end result for one's patience is a dark, grainy loaf of exceptional merit. Whereas many doughs are responsive to kneading, this one stays rather sticky and dense, building up very little springiness, due to the high proportion of grains other than wheat. Unlike most other fruit breads, it makes a really fine loaf for savory sandwiches. The prunes are not at all obtrusive with meats; actually they combine quite nicely (think of the classic French dish, pork with prunes).

*1 cup chopped pitted prunes*
*¹/₂ cup rolled oats (not instant)*
*2¹/₄ cups boiling water*
*1 ¹/₄-ounce package (about 1 tablespoon) active dry yeast*
*¹/₄ cup unsulphured molasses*
*1 cup rye flour*
*¹/₂ cup buckwheat flour*
*3 cups whole wheat flour*
*1 tablespoon salt*
*¹/₄ cup flavorless vegetable oil*
*¹/₂ cup (approximately) unbleached flour for kneading*
*egg wash: 1 egg white beaten with 1 tablespoon water*
*about 2 tablespoons poppy seeds to sprinkle on top*

Put the prunes and oats into a large mixing bowl and pour the boiling water over them. When cooled to lukewarm, sprinkle the yeast over the liquid and set aside for 5 minutes to dissolve. Stir in the molasses, then beat in the rye and buckwheat flours and 1 cup of the whole wheat flour. Beat vigorously for 1 minute, then cover the bowl with plastic wrap and set aside in a warm, draft-free spot for 30 minutes.

After 30 minutes, beat the salt and oil into the sponge. Add the remaining whole wheat flour, ¹/₂ cup at a time, beating well after each addition; the dough will be dense and almost unstirrable.

Start kneading the dough (in the bowl if there's room) with floured hands. Each time it starts to stick, add sprinkles of unbleached flour; if you knead gently at first, you'll minimize sticking. Knead for 10 minutes, after which the dough will feel moderately soft and spongy but still quite dense. Put it in a lightly oiled bowl, turning to coat the entire surface of the dough with oil. Cover the bowl with plastic wrap and put the dough in a warm, draft-free spot to rise until doubled in bulk. As the dough rises, generously dust a large, heavy baking sheet with cornmeal and set it aside.

Once the dough has doubled, punch it down and turn it out onto a floured surface. Divide it in half, knead each half briefly, then shape the halves into loaves that look something like blunt-ended footballs. Place them on the sheet, well spaced, then cover loosely with plastic wrap. Set aside in a

*(continued)*

(*continued*)

warm, draft-free spot until doubled. When the loaves appear nearly doubled, preheat the oven to 375°.

When the loaves are doubled, brush them sparingly with the egg wash and sprinkle each with about 1 tablespoon of poppy seeds. Make several slashes across the top of each loaf with a sharp serrated knife. Bake for about 45 minutes, until well browned on the bottoms and slightly less so on the tops; the bottoms, when tapped with a finger, should give a hollow retort. Transfer the loaves to a rack and cool for at least 30 minutes before slicing. Store in sealed plastic bags. ♦

## Microclimates and Misadventures in Baking

Every home—but especially old country ones like the converted camp we live in—has its warm and cool spots, areas that for one reason or another defy your home's median temperature. We call these areas *microclimates,* and, as any cook who has ever put a pie on the windowsill to cool knows, these microclimates can be a valuable resource to the home baker.

For example: nearly every yeasted bread recipe you'll ever read says to let the dough rise in a warm spot. How many warm spots can you think of in your home? How about near the clothes dryer or radiator? On a high shelf above the kitchen stove? In your gas oven, where the heat from the pilot light alone provides a cozy environment? All of these would be good places for rising dough.

The warm spots I use most often are near our two woodstoves, our only source of heat. After years of softening butter, setting out sponges and doughs to rise, and warming honey to a loose, pourable consistency, I've developed an intimate and useful relationship with the layers of microclimates in our stoves' environs. But, like all intimate relationships, things can sometimes go awry.

There was the night when I awoke to

76

what sounded like someone throwing mud against the back door. Now, with four youngsters, you can understand that mud hitting the back door wouldn't usually strike me as anything too out of the ordinary. But this was January, and the kids were snoring, so visions of being attacked by some crazed, mud-slinging cult danced in my head. Anyway, after several unsuccessful attempts to convince Karen she should investigate, I took bat in hand and headed down the stairs. I rounded the corner just in time to see a blob of bread dough blurp from the bowl where I had stuck it earlier in the day—and proceeded to forget about it—on top of the exposed floor joist near the woodstove; on the floor beneath the bowl was a random pile of dusty bread dough under close examination by our dog.

Then there was the time, as I lay in bed reading late one evening, when I swore I smelled cookies baking in the oven. So I went to investigate, only to find a stream of melted butter cascading onto the woodstove from above, where my wife had put a stick of it earlier in the day—again on the joist—when she planned to make cookies. I guess if there's a lesson in any of this, it's that a microclimate is only as smart as the baker who's using it.

So keep microclimates in mind when you bake. They'll be most useful to you if you plan in advance. Read your recipe through several hours ahead. Need soft butter? Put it, still in the wrapper, on a sunny windowsill. (Use your timer to remind you it's there.) Should you take the chill off the eggs? Sit them near the gas stove or, for quick results, in a bowl of warm water. Want to make the honey blessedly easy to pour and measure? Loosen the lid and put it in a pan of warm water or on a trivet above a turned-off gas burner. Need to slow down a rising bread dough because you've been called away unexpectedly? Punch the dough down and put it in the mudroom, basement, root cellar, apartment balcony—in cool weather—or refrigerator, where it's cool.*

* *Almost any dough can be made ahead and immediately stored in the fridge—tightly covered—for later shaping and baking. Someone, for instance, who has a few extra minutes before work can prepare a dough early in the day and store it in the fridge. When you come home, the dough—which will be fully risen by now—can be punched down, kneaded, and shaped (a little extra kneading is good, because the heat from your hands will help warm the dough). The second rising will be a little slow, due to the chill in the dough, but not so slow that you'll have to burn the midnight oil.*

# Light Yogurt Rye Bread

*Makes 2 free-form loaves*

Here's an easy rye bread, not as difficult to handle as some. Thanks to the yogurt, this loaf has a nice, sharp tang and a soft, light texture. And there's a good-looking contrast between the crust, which gets quite dark because of the honey, and the creamy-colored interior. Good with soups and for grilled cheese sandwiches.

*1/4 cup lukewarm water*

*1 1/4-ounce package (about 1 tablespoon) active dry yeast*

*2 cups plain yogurt*

*1/3 cup honey*

*2 cups rye flour*

*2 tablespoons caraway seeds*

*2 teaspoons salt*

*2 tablespoons flavorless vegetable oil*

*3 1/2 cups (approximately) unbleached flour*

*egg wash: 1 egg beaten with 1 tablespoon milk or cream*

Put the lukewarm water in a small bowl, stir in the yeast, and set aside for 5 minutes to dissolve. Meanwhile, put the yogurt and honey in a small nonaluminum saucepan and heat gently, to just slightly warmer than body temperature. Scrape this mixture into a large mixing bowl and stir in the dissolved yeast, the rye flour, and the caraway seeds. Cover the bowl with plastic wrap and set aside in a warm, draft-free spot for 30 minutes.

After 30 minutes, beat the salt and oil into the sponge. Using a heavy wooden spoon, beat in the unbleached flour, a cup at a time, until you have a soft, kneadable dough. Turn the dough out onto a floured surface and knead—never too roughly, because this is a soft dough—for 10 minutes, using as much of the remaining flour as necessary to keep the dough from sticking. After 10 minutes the dough will be soft and elastic, but not as elastic as a white dough would be. Place the dough in a lightly oiled bowl, turning to coat the entire surface of the dough with oil. Cover the bowl with plastic wrap and set aside in a warm, draft-free spot until doubled in bulk. As the dough rises, generously dust a large, heavy baking sheet with cornmeal and set it aside.

Once the dough has doubled, punch it down, knead briefly, and divide it in half. Shape each half into a tight football and place the loaves on the prepared sheet, leaving plenty of room between them. Cover loosely with plastic wrap and set aside in a warm, draft-free spot until doubled. When the loaves appear nearly doubled, preheat the oven to 375°.

Once the loaves have doubled, brush them sparingly with the egg wash. Make 3 or 4 slashes across the top of each loaf with a sharp serrated knife and then bake for 45 minutes, turning the sheet around about halfway through the baking. The loaves are done when the bottoms, tapped with a finger, give a hollow retort. Transfer the loaves to a rack and cool before slicing. Store the cooled loaves in plastic bags.

VARIATION: *Replace 1 teaspoon of the caraway seeds with fennel seeds.* ◆

# Soft Oatmeal Sandwich Bread

*Makes 2 loaves*

This is about the most ideal sandwich bread I know: wholesome yet soft enough—due to the oats and the yogurt—to wrap around any sandwich without falling apart. Incidentally, the oats will make the dough, even when fully kneaded, a little slack.

*1 cup rolled oats* (not *instant*)
*2 cups hot milk*
*¹/₃ cup honey or unsulphured molasses*
*¹/₄ cup lukewarm water*
*1 ¹/₄-ounce package (about 1 tablespoon)*
 *active dry yeast*
*¹/₃ cup plain yogurt or buttermilk*
*2¹/₂ cups whole wheat flour*
*1 large egg, at room temperature*
*1 tablespoon salt*
*¹/₄ cup unsalted butter, softened*
*3 to 3¹/₂ cups unbleached flour*
*about 2 extra tablespoons of oats, to sprinkle*
 *in the pans*

Put the oats in a large mixing bowl and pour the hot milk over them. Stir in the honey or molasses and let cool to body temperature. Meanwhile, put the water in a small bowl and stir in the yeast. Set aside for 5 minutes to dissolve. Once the oats have cooled, stir in the dissolved yeast, the yogurt or buttermilk, and the whole wheat flour and beat vigorously for 1 minute with a wooden spoon. Cover this sponge with plastic wrap and set aside for 30 minutes in a warm, draft-free spot.

Using a wooden spoon, beat in the egg, salt, and butter until well blended. Add the unbleached flour, ¹/₂ cup at a time, beating well after each addition. When the dough is too dense to stir, turn it out onto a lightly floured surface and knead for 10 minutes, periodically dusting your kneading surface with flour; knead gently at first to prevent the dough from sticking. Place the dough in a lightly oiled bowl, turning it to coat the entire surface of the dough with oil. Cover the bowl with plastic wrap and set aside, in a warm, draft-free spot, until the dough is doubled in bulk. Butter 2 4¹/₂- by 8¹/₂-inch loaf pans and sprinkle the inside of each with about 1 tablespoon of oats.

When the dough has doubled, punch it down, knead briefly, and divide in half. Shape the halves into loaves and place them in the prepared pans. Cover loosely and let rise in a warm, draft-free spot until doubled in bulk, preheating the oven to 375° when the loaves appear nearly doubled.

Bake the loaves for approximately 40 minutes, until nicely browned. When done, the bottom crusts should give a hollow retort when tapped with a finger. Cool the loaves on a rack before slicing. Store in sealed plastic bags. ♦

## Double Oat Bread

*Makes 2 loaves*

Basically a white bread, fortified with rolled oats and oat bran, this is a good practice loaf for yeast bread beginners. Even though the dough is denser than some, it is responsive to kneading and soon takes on that nice, tight elasticity common to white breads. (Whole grain doughs also become elastic, but seldom as much.) The actual oat flavor here is rather subtle and most apparent when the bread is barely warm or toasted. An excellent sandwich loaf.

*1 cup oat bran*
*½ cup rolled oats* (not *instant*)
*2 cups hot milk*
*¼ cup honey or unsulphured molasses*
*¼ cup lukewarm water*
*1 ¼-ounce package (about 1 tablespoon) active dry yeast*
*5½ cups (approximately) unbleached flour*
*1 tablespoon salt*
*¼ cup unsalted butter, melted, or flavorless vegetable oil*
*1 large egg, at room temperature*
*egg wash: 1 egg beaten with 1 tablespoon milk*
*2 extra tablespoons rolled oats, to sprinkle on top of the loaves*

Put the oat bran and rolled oats into a large mixing bowl and pour the milk over them. Stir in the honey or molasses and let cool to lukewarm. As that cools, pour the water into a small bowl and stir in the yeast. Set aside for 5 minutes to dissolve.

When the oats have cooled to about body temperature, stir in the dissolved yeast. Add 2½ cups of the unbleached flour and beat vigorously with a wooden spoon for 1 minute. Cover this sponge with plastic wrap and set aside in a warm, draft-free spot for 30 minutes.

After 30 minutes, beat the salt, melted butter or oil, and egg into the sponge. Beat in the remaining flour, ½ cup at a time, until you have a stiff, kneadable dough. Turn the dough out onto a floured surface and knead for 10 minutes, using sprinkles of flour to prevent the dough from sticking. After 10 minutes the dough will be soft and elastic, though somewhat nubby because of the oat bran and oats. Put the dough in a lightly oiled bowl, turning to coat the entire surface of the dough with oil. Cover the bowl with plastic wrap and set the dough aside in a warm, draft-free spot until doubled in bulk. Butter 2 4½- by 8½-inch loaf pans, sprinkling the insides with a few oats if you like.

When the dough has doubled, punch it down and turn it out onto a lightly floured surface. Divide it in half, knead each half briefly, then shape the halves into loaves. Put the loaves in the prepared pans, cover loosely with plastic wrap, and set aside in a warm, draft-free spot until doubled in bulk. When the loaves appear nearly doubled, preheat the oven to 375°.

Just before baking, brush the tops of the loaves sparingly with the egg wash. Sprinkle the top of each loaf with about 1 tablespoon of the extra oats if you like (if you do, brush them a second time with the egg wash; they'll stick better), then make one lengthwise slash down the center of each loaf with a sharp serrated knife. Bake the loaves for 40 to 45 minutes, until the tops and bottoms are well browned and the bottoms give a hollow retort when tapped with a finger.

Transfer the loaves to a rack, to cool. Don't try to slice this bread for at least an hour, because it is very soft. Store the completely cooled loaves in plastic bags.

VARIATION: *You can make a fine raisin bread with this recipe by kneading up to 1 cup of raisins into the dough when you punch it down. Or you can knead ¹/₂ cup or less into half the dough.* ♦

### Tools of the Trade: Some Personal Observations

Aside from baking sheets and pans—the front line of one's basic baking battery—there's an odd assortment of secondary tools that are all but essential to the home baker. Here are a few random observations about some.

*Wooden Spoons:* By no stretch of the imagination are all wooden spoons created equal. At one end of the spectrum are the serious, heavily constructed spoons, and at the other end you have the flimsy ones you get in dime stores. Stay away from this latter type. They're utterly useless for stirring heavy yeast bread doughs, and I have a trash can full of broken ones to prove it. You're apt to find the best spoons in stores that specialize in wooden ware, where the selection is wide. Test some. Look for sturdy handles, just long enough to grip comfortably. For a longer life, don't let your wooden spoons sit in dishwater.

*Rubber Spatulas:* It's virtually impossible to do a good job of bowl scraping without a rubber spatula. Since you'll often need more than one to finish a recipe, you'll save time by keeping two or three at hand; you won't have to rinse one in mid-recipe. Cheap rubber spatulas come with the rubber part just shoved over the handle, and they generally go their separate ways after the third or fourth washing. Rubbermaid makes an

*(continued)*

(*continued*)

excellent one—the handle flares into the scraper, to which it is permanently glued.

*Dough Scraper:* A dough scraper looks like a small square of sheet metal with a handle on one edge. It's almost a third hand if you make a lot of yeast breads, because it can be employed to divide dough (safer than keeping a knife on the counter, especially with kids around), lift sticky doughs off your work surface, and scrape your bread board clean after you've kneaded. (In a pinch it even makes a respectable putty knife.) I've had a professional-quality one (called a Dexter) for about 10 years. The handle, I think, is rosewood, and the blade is riveted to it. Recently someone gave me one with a slightly sharper blade, which makes for easy scraping, but it has a cheap pine handle that's already starting to crack.

*Pastry Blender:* This is used for cutting fat into flour and is nothing more than some stiff, curved wires attached to a short handle. Don't buy one with rigid blades (as opposed to wire strands), because you can cut yourself cleaning the fat off the blades. One of the home baker's handiest tools.

*Flour Shaker:* This looks like a tin measuring cup with a lid. I got along without one for years and just grabbed flour from a cup. But this puts down a nicer, more even dusting of flour than you can with your hand; that's especially good for rolling pie pastry and for kneading dough. Keep this right in front of you at your baking area, on the counter or a shelf.

*Pastry Brushes:* Don't bother with heavy, clunky brushes; they can do damage to the surface of a raised yeast bread if you poke it too hard; I've done that often. My favorite is a feather brush. I also have a soft bristle type. Look for handles without a painted or lacquered finish, because this stuff inevitably cracks and peels off and lands on your baked things. Don't leave brushes sitting in hot pans; wash them out right away in warm, soapy water. All the better if they are designed to be hung on a cup hook.

*Measuring Cups:* At least two glass measuring cups are essential for measuring liquids, the 2- and 4-cup size. As for dry measures, a nesting set—in graduated sizes—is very handy.

*Measuring Spoons:* Ideally you should own several sets so you don't need to wash them in mid-recipe. The sets should be attached by a common ring. Long-handled spoons are a blessing, because they enable you to reach way down into baking soda boxes and spice jars.

# Millet and Corn Bread

*Makes 2 loaves*

illet is an important food for at least half a billion people worldwide, according to the food writer Waverley Root. I wouldn't call it a staple in our family, but we do like the crunch and delicate flavor that millet gives yeast bread. Here the entire crust is shot through with pretty yellow millet pellets. A sturdy bread, this makes great toast and open-face sandwiches.

*1¹/₂ cups uncooked millet*

*2³/₄ cups boiling water*

*1 ¹/₄-ounce package (about 1 tablespoon) active dry yeast*

*2 tablespoons packed light brown sugar*

*4 cups whole wheat flour*

*³/₄ cup yellow cornmeal, preferably stone-ground*

*1 tablespoon salt*

*¹/₃ cup flavorless vegetable oil*

*1¹/₂ cups (approximately) unbleached flour*

Put the millet into a large mixing bowl and pour the boiling water over it. Cover and let sit for 1 hour. After an hour, stir in the yeast and set aside for 5 minutes to dissolve.

Using a heavy wooden spoon, stir in the brown sugar, 2 cups of the whole wheat flour, and the cornmeal, beating vigorously for 1 minute. Cover the bowl with plastic wrap and set aside in a warm, draft-free spot for 30 minutes.

After 30 minutes, stir in the salt and oil, then the remaining whole wheat flour. Add enough of the unbleached flour to make a kneadable dough, then turn it out onto a floured surface and knead for 12 minutes, using the unbleached flour to keep it from sticking. (As you knead, bits of millet will fly all over the place; nothing you can do about it, really). After 12 minutes the dough will be somewhat elastic and perhaps a little tacky; that's okay. Place the dough in a lightly oiled bowl, turning it to coat the entire surface of the dough with oil. Cover the bowl with plastic wrap and place it in a warm, draft-free spot until the dough is doubled in bulk. As the dough rises, butter 2 4¹/₂- by 8¹/₂-inch loaf pans.

Once the dough has doubled, punch it down, knead briefly, and divide the dough in half. Shape the halves into loaves and place them in the buttered pans. Cover loosely with plastic wrap and set aside in a warm, draft-free spot until doubled in bulk. When the loaves appear nearly doubled, preheat the oven to 375°.

When the loaves have doubled, make several diagonal slashes across the top of each, using a sharp serrated knife. Bake for 45 minutes, until the tops are nicely browned and the bottoms, when tapped with a finger, give a hollow retort. Transfer the loaves to a rack and cool before slicing. Store in sealed plastic bags.

VARIATION: *This bread is wonderful with a cupful of toasted walnuts kneaded into the dough (when you punch it down).* ♦

## Whole Wheat Buttermilk Burger Buns

*Makes 8 large buns*

Consider your standard, packaged burger bun: so pale, so limp, so blah, that there's practically no *there* there. A shame, because to know the Total Burger Experience the bun must be an equal, not a passive partner. Like this one, it should be soft but sturdy, flavorful, and of sufficiently generous proportions to cradle your quarter pound of beef or compressed tofu without spilling over the sides. Do try these at your next barbecue. They also make great sloppy Joes and all-purpose sandwich rolls too.

½ cup lukewarm water
1 tablespoon (or 1 ¼-ounce package) active
  dry yeast
1 cup buttermilk
1 tablespoon honey
2½ cups whole wheat flour
2 teaspoons salt
1 large egg, at room temperature
1 tablespoon unsalted butter, softened
1 cup (approximately) unbleached flour
egg wash: 1 egg beaten with 1 tablespoon
  milk
toasted sesame seeds, for sprinkling on top

Pour the lukewarm water into a small bowl and stir in the yeast. While the yeast dissolves, put the buttermilk in a small saucepan and heat to about body temperature. Pour the buttermilk into a large mixing bowl, then stir in the honey and dissolved yeast. Stir in 1½ cups of the whole wheat flour, beating vigorously with a wooden spoon for 1 minute. Cover and set this sponge aside for 30 minutes.

After 30 minutes beat the salt, egg, and remaining whole wheat flour into the sponge. Stir in the butter, then work in enough of the unbleached flour to make a soft, kneadable dough. Turn the dough out onto a floured surface and knead, gently at first, for 10 minutes. Keep the surface well floured with unbleached flour, because this is an absorbent dough. After 10 minutes of kneading the dough will be smooth, soft, and moderately elastic. It may even be slightly sticky; that's okay. Place the dough in a lightly oiled bowl, turning to coat the entire surface. Cover with plastic wrap and set aside in a warm, draft-free spot until doubled. While the dough rises, lightly oil a large, heavy baking sheet and set it aside.

When fully doubled, punch the dough down, knead briefly, then divide the dough into quarters. Cut each quarter in half, leaving you with 8 pieces. Shape the pieces into balls, then flatten them—with your fingers—into 3-inch circles. Transfer them to the prepared sheet, not quite touching, keeping the shaped pieces loosely covered with plastic wrap. After all the pieces are on the sheet, go back and slightly flatten each one again, increasing the circle to about 3½ inches. Cover the buns loosely with plastic wrap and set aside in a warm, draft-free spot, until doubled in bulk. Preheat the oven to 400° about 15 minutes before the rising is complete.

Just before baking, brush the rolls gently and sparingly with the egg wash. Sprinkle the buns generously with the sesame seeds, then bake for 20 minutes. When done, the tops will be richly browned and the bottoms slightly more so; don't let the bottoms get too dark. Transfer the buns to a rack to cool. Store completely cooled leftovers in a sealed plastic bag. ♦

## Barley Corn Bread

*Makes 2 loaves*

Barley doesn't have a forward flavor, but using whole barley, along with some barley flour, helps to accentuate it. I like to use hulled organic barley here, purchased at a health food store, but I see no reason you couldn't use pearled barley from the grocery store. If you need an extra nudge to try this, it makes an excellent crust for the Mushroom Barley-Crusted Pizza (page 140). These are big, brawny, pretty loaves.

3/4 *cup uncooked hulled barley (see note below)*

2 *cups water*

1/2 *teaspoon salt*

2 1/2 *cups lukewarm water*

2 *tablespoons honey*

1 1/4-*ounce package (about 1 tablespoon) active dry yeast*

2 *cups barley flour (available at health food stores)*

1 *cup whole wheat flour*

1/2 *cup yellow cornmeal, preferably stone-ground*

5 1/2 *to 6 cups unbleached flour*

1 *tablespoon salt*

1/4 *cup flavorless vegetable oil*

*egg wash: 1 egg beaten with 1 tablespoon milk or cream*

Several hours before you start the bread, bring the barley, 2 cups water, and salt to a boil in a medium nonaluminum pot. Reduce the heat to very low, cover, and cook undisturbed for 60 to 70 minutes, until the water is absorbed by the grain. Scrape the barley into a bowl and cool to body temperature.

When the barley has cooled, pour the lukewarm water and honey into a large mixing bowl. Stir in the yeast and set aside for 5 minutes to dissolve. Using a heavy wooden spoon, beat in the barley flour, whole wheat flour, cornmeal, and 2 cups of the unbleached flour. Stir in the barley, then cover with plastic wrap and set aside for 30 minutes.

After 30 minutes, beat in the salt, oil, and enough of the remaining unbleached flour, 1 cup at a time, to make a soft, kneadable dough. Turn the dough out onto a floured surface and knead for 12 minutes, using unbleached flour as necessary to keep the dough from sticking. Even after 12 minutes the dough may still be slightly tacky; that's okay. Put the dough in a lightly oiled bowl, turning to coat the entire surface of the dough with oil. Cover the bowl with plastic wrap and place in a warm spot until the dough is doubled. While the dough rises, generously dust a large, heavy baking sheet with cornmeal and set it aside.

*(continued)*

(*continued*)

When the dough is fully risen, punch it down, knead briefly, and divide in half. Working with one half at a time, roll each half into a long oval, then roll up, as you would a carpet. Pinch the seam to seal, then lay the loaf on the prepared sheet, seam side down, leaving plenty of room between the loaves for expansion. Cover loosely with plastic wrap, place the loaves in a warm, draft-free spot, and let rise until doubled in bulk. When the loaves appear nearly doubled, preheat the oven to 375°.

Once the loaves have fully doubled, brush them sparingly with the egg wash. With a sharp serrated knife, make several long slashes down the length of the bread on each surface. Bake for 50 to 55 minutes, until the loaves are golden and crusty all over and the bottoms, when tapped with a finger, give a hollow retort. Transfer the loaves to a rack and cool before slicing. Store the cooled loaves in sealed plastic bags.

NOTE: *If you are using packaged pearled barley, cook until just tender according to the package directions.* ◆

# The Sandwich Board

Good homemade bread is the foundation for one of life's simple pleasures: the homemade sandwich. Pity, then, that we should let sandwich making fall into an architectural and gastronomic rut: a slab of this or that deli meat with mayo or mustard. Let's expand our sandwich consciousness, loudly intoning sandwich mantras like *big, bold, beautiful, fresh,* and *colorful.* To that end, here are some sandwich suggestions to get the creative juices flowing.

*Steak and Slaw:* Warm leftover steak slices, coleslaw, and crumbled blue cheese on Whole Wheat Buttermilk Burger Buns (page 84).

*Radish and Watercress:* Herb cream cheese on Four-Grain Pumpernickel Prune Bread (page 75), topped with sliced radishes and watercress sprigs.

*Fresh Mexican:* Herb cream cheese on toasted Seven-Grain Bread (page 74) with sliced cherry tomatoes, avocado chunks, salsa, and fresh spinach.

*Smoked Cheddar and Chicken Club:* Sliced cooked chicken, smoked Cheddar, bacon, lettuce, tomato, and mayo—club style—on toasted Double Oat Bread (page 80).

*Herb Cream Cheese and Salmon:* Herb cream cheese on Wheaten French Bread (page 66), topped with thin slices of smoked salmon and watercress sprigs.

*Cold Meat Loaf:* Cold sliced meat loaf on Honey Whole Grain Swedish Limpa (page 62), topped with Dijon mustard, chopped sweet onion, and sliced gherkins.

*Oriental Stir-Fry:* Leftover cooked chicken, steak, or shrimp pieces quickly sautéed in oil and garlic with tender vegetables, seasoned with soy sauce and served on Whole Wheat Buttermilk Burger Buns (page 84).

*Sautéed Mushrooms and Swiss:* Sliced butter-sautéed mushrooms, tomato slices, and Swiss cheese on Light Yogurt Rye Bread (page 78), run under the broiler (open-face).

*Pesto and Provolone Melt:* Slices of Sage-Scented Parmesan Cheese Bread (page 105), spread lightly with pesto, topped with sliced tomatoes and provolone, and run under the broiler (open-face).

*Cheddar and Apple Melt:* Herb cream cheese on toasted Seven-Grain Bread (page 74), covered with butter-sautéed apple and onion slices, sauerkraut, and Cheddar, run under the broiler (open-face).

And finally, *to make herb cream cheese,* mix ½ pound soft cream cheese with 2 tablespoons sour cream or mayo, a squirt of freshly squeezed lemon juice, 1 minced garlic clove, a pinch of cayenne pepper, and about ½ cup loosely packed fresh herbs, such as parsley, basil, dill, and oregano. Add salt and pepper to taste.

# Snappy Sharp Cheddar Muffin Rolls

*Makes about 18 rolls*

New Englanders have a word to describe our good, very sharp Cheddar: snappy. These rolls are based on that Cheddar, with a few other snappy touches, like mustard and cayenne. If you think you want extra snap, those last are the two ingredients you could increase. This is an easy way to make rolls, with a good-looking result. If you don't want to bake all of the dough in muffin cups, you can make 12 muffins and then bake the remaining dough in a small loaf pan or free-form on a pie tin. Or, you can freeze the unused dough—punch it down and slip it into a plastic bag—for later use.

*¼ cup lukewarm water*

*1 ¼-ounce package (about 1 tablespoon) active dry yeast*

*1 12-ounce bottle of beer*

*2 tablespoons Dijon mustard*

*1 tablespoon unsulphured molasses*

*½ teaspoon cayenne pepper*

*1 cup whole wheat flour*

*½ cup yellow cornmeal, preferably stone-ground*

*4 cups (approximately) unbleached flour*

*1 tablespoon salt*

*1 large egg, at room temperature*

*3 tablespoons unsalted butter, melted*

*a little extra cornmeal, for sprinkling in the muffin cups*

*1½ cups (about ¼ pound) grated extra-sharp Cheddar cheese*

*egg wash: 1 egg beaten with 1 tablespoon milk*

Pour the water into a small bowl, stir in the yeast, and set aside for 5 minutes to dissolve. Meanwhile, heat the beer to lukewarm, then pour it into a large mixing bowl. Stir in the dissolved yeast, mustard, molasses, and cayenne. Using a wooden spoon, beat in the whole wheat flour, cornmeal, and 1 cup of the unbleached flour. Beat vigorously for 1 minute, cover the bowl with plastic wrap, and set aside in a warm, draft-free spot for 30 minutes.

After 30 minutes, beat in the salt, egg, and melted butter. Stir in enough of the remaining flour, ½ cup at a time, to make a stiff, kneadable dough. Turn the dough out onto a floured surface and knead for 10 minutes, flouring the surface as needed to prevent sticking. After 10 minutes of kneading, the dough will be smooth, soft, and elastic. Place the dough in a lightly oiled bowl, turning to coat the entire surface of the dough with oil. Cover the bowl with plastic wrap and set aside in a warm, draft-free spot until doubled. While the dough rises, butter 18 muffin cups and dust them lightly with cornmeal.

Sprinkle half the cheese over the risen dough, punch it down, then gradually knead in the remaining cheese. Turn the dough out onto a lightly floured surface and knead it for 1 minute. Cut off pieces of dough large enough to form 2-inch-diameter balls; the balls should fill the bottom half of the cups, with the tops reaching almost to the top of the pan. Before you place the balls of dough in the cups, make 3 shallow slashes across the top of each with a serrated knife. (You're doing this now because it's difficult to slash them in the cups once they've risen.) If you have any empty muffin cups, fill each one with 1/2 inch of water before you put the pans in the oven. Cover the pans loosely with plastic wrap and set them aside in a warm, draft-free spot until doubled and swollen above the tops of the cups. Preheat the oven to 375° as they are nearing the end of the second rise.

Just before baking, brush the rolls very gently and sparingly with the egg wash. Bake for 25 to 30 minutes, until the tops are golden brown. Remove the rolls from the cups and put them in a cloth-lined basket, if you're serving them hot. Otherwise, transfer them to a rack to cool. As soon as they are cool, seal them in plastic bags to prevent them from drying out.

NOTE: *If you like, you can sprinkle each of these with a large pinch of poppy or sesame seeds after you brush on the egg wash. Also, instead of putting these rolls in muffin cups, you can shape and slash them as above and put them directly on a baking sheet dusted with cornmeal.* ◆

## Three-Grain Potato-Onion Pinwheels

*Makes 18 rolls*

These fragrant rolls are something like a savory version of sticky buns, with sautéed onions in place of the sweet stuff. They're one of the most popular rolls I make, with just enough cornmeal and rye flour to make a grainy statement but not enough to overwhelm the onions. The potatoes, which act as a sort of natural preservative here, help to keep these fresh for days, so they stand up well when reheated in foil. These are a lot of fun to make; it helps to read the recipe through first to get the hang of the technique.

1 large potato, peeled and cut into 1-inch dice
1 1/4-ounce package (about 1 tablespoon) active dry yeast
1/2 cup cold milk
3/4 cup rye flour
1/2 cup yellow cornmeal, preferably stone-ground
1/3 cup flavorless vegetable oil
1 tablespoon salt
4 cups (approximately) unbleached flour
1/4 cup unsalted butter
1 1/2 cups (about 2 to 3 medium-size) minced onions
egg wash: 1 egg beaten with 1 tablespoon milk

In a medium saucepan, cover the potato with about a quart of water. Bring to a boil, reduce the heat a little, and cook at a gentle boil until tender, 10 to 15 minutes. Drain the potatoes, reserving 3/4 cup of the potato water. Pour 1/4 cup of the reserved potato water into a small bowl. Cool to lukewarm, then sprinkle on the yeast and set aside for 5 minutes to dissolve.

Combine the cold milk and the remaining 1/2 cup potato water. Pour about 1/4 cup of this liquid into a mixing bowl, add the cooked potatoes, and beat with an electric mixer until smooth. Beat in the remaining 3/4 cup liquid. Let cool to lukewarm, then stir in the dissolved yeast, rye flour, and cornmeal. Beat vigorously with a wooden spoon for 1 minute. Cover the bowl with plastic wrap and set aside in a warm, draft-free spot for 30 minutes.

After 30 minutes, beat in the oil and salt. Using a wooden spoon, beat in enough of the unbleached flour, 1 cup at a time, to make a stiff dough. When too stiff to stir, turn out onto a floured surface and knead with floured hands for 10 minutes, using only as much additional unbleached flour as necessary to prevent the dough from sticking. After 10 minutes it should be moderately elastic and quite smooth, but perhaps still a little tacky; that's okay. Put the dough into a large, lightly oiled bowl and turn to coat the entire surface of the dough with oil. Cover the bowl with plastic wrap and let the dough rise in a warm, draft-free spot until doubled in bulk.

While the dough rises, melt the butter in a large skillet. Add the onions and cook over moderate heat, stirring occasionally, until softened and lightly browned, about 10 minutes. Scrape the onions onto a plate. Butter 2 10-inch pie pans or 2 8-inch square baking pans; I like glass here.

Punch the dough down, knead briefly, then let the dough sit for several minutes. On a lightly floured surface, roll the dough into an 18- by 12-inch rectangle; it won't be a perfect rectangle, so don't worry about it. Cover the entire surface evenly with the cooked onions. Cut the dough in half to form 2 9- by 12-inch rectangles.

Starting at a short edge, roll up one of the rectangles. Pinch the dough at the seam to seal. Slice the log into 1-inch-thick rounds and arrange the slices, spiral side up, in one of the prepared pans. Repeat with the remaining rectangle of dough. Cover the pans loosely with plastic wrap and set aside in a warm, draft-free spot until the rolls are touching and have doubled in bulk. When they appear nearly doubled, preheat the oven to 375° (350° if you're using glass).

When the rolls are doubled, brush them lightly with the egg wash. Bake for 25 to 30 minutes, until lightly browned. Remove the rolls from the pans, transfer to a cloth-lined basket, and serve hot. If you're not serving them right away, transfer the rolls to a rack to cool. Seal and store completely cooled leftovers in a plastic bag. ◆

## Pesto and Walnut Bread

*Makes 2 medium loaves*

This recipe is adapted, with much gratitude for the idea, from a recipe in Carol Field's wonderful book, *The Italian Baker* (Harper & Row). It's one of the classier yeast breads I know, one that will turn heads and make mouths water at a summer gathering, as well as seal your reputation as a cutting-edge baker—all for putting a slug of pesto into a batch of dough. You can do all sorts of things with this: halve it and make summer garden subs, or cover half with cheese and tomatoes and broil it, or just serve it plain with any Italian entrée.

1 cup lukewarm water
1 1/4-ounce package (about 1 tablespoon)
    active dry yeast
1 teaspoon sugar
1/2 cup whole wheat flour
3 1/4 cups (approximately) unbleached flour
1 1/4 teaspoons salt
1/2 cup pesto (page 145)
1/2 cup (about 2 ounces) finely chopped
    walnuts

Pour the water into a large mixing bowl and stir in the yeast and sugar. Set aside for 5 minutes to dissolve, then stir in the whole wheat flour and 1 cup of the unbleached flour, beating vigorously with a wooden spoon for 1 minute. Cover the bowl with plastic wrap and set aside in a warm, draft-free spot for 15 minutes.

After 15 minutes, beat the salt and pesto into the sponge. Stir in enough of the remaining unbleached flour, about 1/2 cup at a time, to make a soft, kneadable dough. Turn the dough out onto a floured surface and knead for 10 minutes, using as much of the remaining unbleached flour as necessary to keep the dough from sticking. After 10 minutes the dough should be fairly elastic, though the pesto may keep it a trifle sticky. Put the dough in a lightly oiled bowl, turning it to coat the entire surface with oil. Cover the bowl with plastic wrap and set aside in a warm, draft-free spot until the dough is doubled in bulk. While the dough is rising, generously dust a large, heavy baking sheet with cornmeal and set aside.

Once the dough has doubled, punch it down and divide it in half. Let the dough rest, covered, for 5 minutes. Working with half the dough at a time, roll the dough into a 12- to 14-inch oval. Sprinkle the dough with half the walnuts, then roll it up along the long edge like you would a carpet, pinching at the seam to seal. Place the dough on the sheet, seam down; repeat for the other half, leaving room between the loaves for expansion. Cover the loaves loosely with plastic wrap and place in a warm, draft-free spot until doubled in bulk. When they appear nearly doubled, preheat the oven to 425°.

Just before baking, make several diagonal slashes on the top of each loaf with a sharp serrated knife. Bake for 30 to 35 minutes, until the bottoms give a hollow retort when tapped with a finger. Transfer the loaves to a rack and cool before slicing. ◆

# *Italian Herb Bread*

*Makes 2 long loaves*

This crusty bread has a lot in common with French bread, but it's grainier, faster to make, and generally less fussy. You can bake the loaves on a baking sheet, but I'm actually more inclined to slide the loaves onto hot oven tiles; you just can't beat a tile-baked crust. Half of this recipe makes a wonderful pizza dough for the Herb Cream Cheese and Tomato Pizza (page 142).

*2 cups lukewarm water*

*1 1/4-ounce package (about 1 tablespoon) active dry yeast*

*3 cups (approximately) unbleached flour*

*1 cup yellow cornmeal, preferably stone-ground*

*1/2 cup rye flour*

*1/4 cup chopped fresh herbs (any combination of oregano, basil, and sage) or 1 to 2 tablespoons dried*

*2 tablespoons good-quality olive oil*

*2 teaspoons salt*

*1 cup whole wheat flour*

Pour the water into a large mixing bowl and sprinkle on the yeast. Set aside for 5 minutes to dissolve. Stir in 1½ cups of the un-bleached flour, the cornmeal, and the rye flour; beat vigorously with a wooden spoon for 1 minute, adding the herbs at the end. Cover the bowl with plastic wrap and set aside in a warm, draft-free spot for 30 minutes.

After 30 minutes, beat the oil, salt, and whole wheat flour into the sponge; it will become quite dense. Add enough of the remaining unbleached flour to make a kneadable dough, then turn it out onto a flour-dusted surface. Knead for 10 minutes, using the unbleached flour to keep the dough from sticking. After 10 minutes the dough will be somewhat elastic, though it may retain some of its stickiness. Place the dough in a lightly oiled bowl, turning to coat the entire surface of the dough with oil. Cover the bowl with plastic wrap and set aside in a warm, draft-free spot until dou-bled in bulk. As the dough rises, generously dust a large, heavy baking sheet with corn-meal and set it aside.

Punch the dough down, knead it briefly, and divide in half. Shape each half into a tight torpedo about 10 inches long—you can roll the dough out and then roll it up—and place the loaves on the prepared sheet, leaving plenty of room between them for expansion. Dust the tops very lightly with cornmeal and cover loosely with plastic wrap. Set the loaves aside in a warm, draft-free spot to double in bulk. When the loaves appear nearly doubled, preheat the oven to 400°.

When the loaves are fully doubled, make 3 diagonal slashes on top of each with a sharp serrated knife. Spray or brush with water and bake for 30 to 35 minutes, until hard and quite crusty on all sides. Remove the loaves to a cooling rack. Eat hot, with dinner, or cool thoroughly. You can freeze one loaf, but I normally keep leftovers at room temperature, unwrapped, to retain the crisp crust. ◆

## Making Garlic Bread

Several of the "plain" breads in this section—namely the Italian Herb Bread (page 93), Wheaten French Bread (page 66) and Tess's French-Style Whole Wheat Bread (page 64)—make particularly good garlic bread, which we like to serve with hearty soups, stews, Italian food, or with whole meal-type salads. Nothing could be simpler.

To one stick (¼ pound) of soft, unsalted butter add as much finely minced garlic as you like; we like it very garlicky, so 5 cloves is not out of the question. Blend the garlic and butter, adding a teaspoon or two of dried basil if you like (more, if you're using fresh basil). Another really special addition is a tablespoon or two of fresh, finely grated Parmesan cheese.

Cut your loaves—which should be at room temperature—in about ¾-inch-wide slices, on the diagonal if you like. If you can manage, don't slice all the way through—leave the pieces barely connected by the bottom crust. Spread the pieces apart and butter one side of each slice generously with the garlic butter. You should have plenty of garlic butter for at least two 12-inch-long loaves. Any extra can be refrigerated for another time, tightly covered.

To heat, just wrap the loaf in foil and place in a 400° oven for about 15–20 minutes.

# Bulgur and Dried Mushroom Bread

*Makes 2 large free-form loaves*

Dried mushrooms are now available in many supermarkets; here's a good way to become acquainted with them. I've used both oyster and shitake mushrooms here, but any kind will do. First you make up a sort of bulgur pilaf, then you add that to a sponge along with the dried mushrooms. As the dough rises, the mushrooms slowly rehydrate from the moisture in the dough, but they never get too soft. So they hold their shape and maintain their identity in the finished loaf. This is fine sandwich bread, and I've even used it for pizza, for company I knew would appreciate a grainy crust.

2 tablespoons flavorless vegetable oil
1 medium-size onion, chopped
½ cup uncooked bulgur
1 garlic clove, minced
¾ cup water
2¾ cups lukewarm water
1 ¼-ounce package (about 1 tablespoon)
    active dry yeast
2 tablespoons honey
5½ cups whole wheat flour
1 tablespoon salt
¼ cup flavorless vegetable oil
½ cup (about ½ ounce) finely chopped dried
    mushrooms
½ to 1 cup unbleached flour for kneading

Heat the 2 tablespoons oil in a small, heavy saucepan. Stir in the onion and sauté over medium heat for 5 minutes, stirring occasionally. Stir in the bulgur and garlic, cook for another minute, then add the ¾ cup water. Bring to a boil, reduce the heat to very low, and cover. Cook for 15 minutes, until the water is absorbed. (Check after 10 minutes to make sure the bulgur isn't sticking.) Scrape the grain onto a plate to cool.

While that cools, pour the lukewarm water into a small bowl and stir in the yeast and honey. Set aside for 5 minutes to dissolve. Using a wooden spoon, stir in 3½ cups of the whole wheat flour and beat vigorously for 1 minute. Cover this sponge with plastic wrap and set aside in a warm, draft-free spot for 30 minutes.

After 30 minutes, stir the salt, oil, dried mushrooms, and cooked bulgur into the sponge. Beat in the remaining whole wheat flour, and let the dough sit for 10 minutes.

With floured hands, knead the dough— right in the bowl if there is room—for a minute. Turn the dough onto a floured surface and knead for 10 minutes, using sprinkles of unbleached flour to prevent the dough from sticking. After 10 minutes of kneading, the dough will be somewhat elastic. If it is still a little tacky, don't try to work any more flour into it, or the loaves may come out dry. Place the dough in an oiled bowl, turning to coat the entire surface of the dough with oil. Cover the bowl with plastic wrap and set aside in a warm, draft-free spot until doubled in bulk. While the dough is rising, generously dust a large, heavy baking sheet with cornmeal and set it aside.

When doubled, punch the dough down and turn it out onto a lightly floured surface. Divide the dough in half, knead each half briefly, then shape the halves into tight balls. Place them on the prepared sheet, diagonally across from one another, and cover loosely with plastic wrap. Put the sheet in a warm, draft-free spot and let the loaves expand until doubled in bulk. When the loaves appear nearly doubled, preheat the oven to 375°.

When doubled, spray or lightly brush the loaves with water. Using a sharp serrated knife, slash the top of each loaf 4 or 5 times. Bake the loaves for 45 minutes, brushing or spraying with water once or twice more in the first 10 minutes. About midway into the baking, turn the sheet 180° for even baking and browning. When done, the finished loaves should look lightly browned and the bottoms should give a hollow retort when tapped with a finger. Transfer the loaves to a rack to cool. Store the loaves in sealed plastic bags. ♦

# Italian Pepper, Onion, and Olive Rolls

*Makes 2 loaves*

I think this is one of the most attractive breads in this collection—a big blossom of pepper-studded rolls that really brings the house down. All you do is make up the simple Italian Herb Bread and roll sautéed peppers, onions, and olives up in it. Then you slice off pieces and overlap them on a baking sheet (I describe an alternate shape below). Serve this with spaghetti and red sauce or any pasta dish. Good party fare.

1 recipe Italian Herb Bread (*page 93*)

FILLING
1/4 cup good-quality olive oil
2 medium-size green bell peppers, seeded and chopped
2 medium-size red bell peppers, seeded and chopped
1 large onion, chopped
2 garlic cloves, thinly sliced
salt and freshly ground pepper to taste
1/2 cup coarsely chopped pitted black olives, preferably a good imported variety, like Kalamata
egg wash: 1 egg beaten with 1 tablespoon milk
a little celery seed to sprinkle on top (optional)

Prepare the Italian Herb Bread as directed and set aside to rise in a warm spot. As that rises, prepare the filling. Heat the olive oil in a large skillet. Stir in the peppers and onion and cook over fairly high heat, stirring occasionally, for about 10 minutes. Stir in the garlic, cook for another minute, then remove from the heat and scrape the contents of the pan onto a plate to cool; season to taste with salt and pepper. Lightly oil 2 medium or large baking sheets and set them aside.

Once the dough has doubled, you can assemble the bread. Punch the dough down, knead it briefly, and divide in half. Put one half aside, covered. On a lightly floured surface, roll the other half into a 12-inch square. Spread half the cooled, sautéed vegetables over the dough right up to the sides, but leave about a 1-inch margin on each end. Sprinkle half the olives over the dough and moisten the far end with a wet finger. Starting at the near end, roll the dough up snugly, like a carpet. Pinch at the seam to seal, then plump the dough with your hands so you have a neat, 12-inch-long log.

Score the log on top with a serrated knife, in 1-inch sections. Cut the sections with a sharp serrated knife, using a sawing motion. As you make each cut, lay the pieces on the sheet; put the first one in the middle, then lean 4 up against it, evenly spaced. The 4 will probably just touch one another. With the remaining slices, make another ring of leaners outside the previous row, overlapping the last row by a little. Repeat this procedure for the other half of the dough or try the lattice log shape as described below. Cover loosely with plastic wrap and set aside in a warm, draft-free spot, until very swollen and obviously much increased in size, maybe 1 hour. About 15 minutes before that point, preheat the oven to 375°.

Just before baking, brush the breads sparingly with the egg wash. Sprinkle each bread lightly with celery seeds, if desired, and bake for 40 minutes; the tops should be deep golden. Transfer the breads to a rack if you're not serving them right away. If you have a large, flattish basket, line it with a cloth and serve the breads in it.

VARIATIONS: *Here's another way to shape this into what I call a lattice log. Proceed as directed, rolling the dough up into a 12-inch log. Transfer the log to the baking sheet. Now, instead of slicing the log all the way, stop about 1/2 inch from the bottom, leaving you with 12 connected sections; don't cut straight down, but slice at about a 45° angle. Carefully pull the sections to either side, alternating as you go—one to the right, the next to the left, and so on. Each slice should overlap the previous one by about half. Let rise and finish as above.*

*Also, I have used diced mozzarella cheese in the filling of this bread, as a little dividend. Some of the pieces fall out and burn on the sheet, but the ones that stay put taste great.* ♦

# Golden Squash and Sesame Loaf

*Makes 2 loaves*

This is one of the prettiest harvest breads I make, tinted light orange like the harvest moon. As with potato breads, the squash helps to preserve the bread, so this is a good keeper. We especially like it for French toast. Because the dough is just a tad slack, you'll get a higher, more rounded loaf if you follow the shaping instructions outlined on page 73.

2 cups cubed peeled butternut or other winter squash (a 1¹/₂-pound squash should be plenty)
1¹/₂ cups lukewarm milk
¹/₃ cup sugar
1 ¹/₄-ounce package (about 1 tablespoon) active dry yeast
¹/₄ cup lukewarm water
1 teaspoon finely grated lemon zest
1 cup yellow cornmeal, preferably stone-ground
2 cups whole wheat flour
1 egg, lightly beaten
¹/₄ cup unsalted butter, softened
1 tablespoon salt
3¹/₂ to 4 cups unbleached flour
¹/₄ cup toasted sesame seeds
1 cup dark or golden raisins
egg wash: 1 egg beaten with 1 tablespoon milk

In a medium saucepan, cover the squash with about a quart of water. Bring to a boil, cover, and reduce to an active simmer. Cook the squash until very tender, about 15 minutes; drain. In a blender or food processor, puree the squash until smooth. Scrape the puree into a large mixing bowl and beat in the milk and sugar.

In a small bowl, stir the yeast into the lukewarm water. Set aside for 5 minutes to dissolve, then stir into the squash mixture along with the lemon zest. Add the cornmeal and whole wheat flour and beat vigorously with a wooden spoon for 1 minute. Cover this sponge with plastic wrap and set aside in a warm, draft-free spot for about 30 minutes.

After 30 minutes, beat the egg, butter, and salt into the sponge with a wooden spoon. Beat in about 3 cups of the unbleached flour, 1 cup at a time, until the dough becomes too stiff to work. Turn the dough out onto a floured surface and knead with floured hands for 12 minutes, incorporating enough of the remaining flour to keep the dough from sticking. The dough should be smooth and able to hold its shape fairly well, though it won't be extremely elastic. Place the dough in a lightly oiled bowl, turn to coat the entire surface of the dough with oil, and cover the bowl with plastic wrap. Let rise in a warm, draft-free spot until doubled in bulk. While the dough rises, butter 2 4¹/₂- by 8¹/₂-inch loaf pans. Sprinkle the sides and bottom of each pan with 1 tablespoon of the toasted seeds.

Spread half the raisins over the top of the dough and punch down. Add the remaining raisins, punching and kneading them into the dough. Divide the dough in half, knead each half briefly, then shape the halves into loaves. Place the loaves in the pans, cover loosely with plastic wrap, then set aside in a warm, draft-free spot until doubled in bulk.

When the loaves appear nearly doubled, preheat the oven to 375° and brush the loaves with a little of the egg wash. Using a sharp serrated knife, make 3 or 4 diagonal slashes on the top of each loaf. Sprinkle the top of each loaf with 1 tablespoon of the sesame seeds. When fully doubled, brush the loaves again with the egg wash and bake in the lower third of the oven for 45 to 50 minutes. When done, the loaves will be well browned and the bottoms will give a soft, hollow retort when tapped with a finger. Remove the loaves from the pans and cool them on a rack for at least 30 minutes before slicing. Cool thoroughly before storing in plastic bags. ◆

# Wheat Flake Potato Bread

*Makes 2 free-form loaves*

Wheat flakes are to wheat what rolled oats are to oatmeal. In this loaf, compact and potato-rich, they add just a slight chewiness and variation in texture. This is a very responsive dough, quite easy and gratifying to knead if you are a beginner looking for a surefire loaf. One of my favorite sandwich breads.

1 cup diced peeled potatoes
1 quart water
1 cup wheat flakes
1 1/4-ounce package (about 1 tablespoon)
    active dry yeast
4 1/2 cups whole wheat flour
1 tablespoon salt
1/3 cup flavorless vegetable oil
1/3 cup (approximately) unbleached flour for
    kneading

Put the potatoes and water into a large saucepan and bring to a boil over high heat. Boil, uncovered, for 10 minutes, until the potatoes are quite tender. Drain, reserving 2 1/2 cups of the potato water; if you're just a little low, add tap water.

Put the wheat flakes in a large mixing bowl and pour the potato water over them. When cooled to lukewarm, sprinkle on the yeast and set aside for 5 minutes to dissolve. Meanwhile, mash the potatoes with a hand masher; they don't have to be perfectly smooth. When the potatoes are lukewarm, stir them into the wheat flake water along with 2 cups of the whole wheat flour. Beat hard with a wooden spoon for 2 minutes, cover the bowl with plastic wrap, and set aside in a warm, draft-free spot for 30 minutes.

After 30 minutes, beat the salt and oil into the sponge. Gradually stir in the remaining whole wheat flour, kneading right in the bowl if the dough gets too dense. Turn the dough out onto a lightly floured surface and knead for 8 to 10 minutes, using the unbleached flour as necessary to prevent the dough from sticking. When fully kneaded, the dough will be soft and responsive, though perhaps very slightly tacky; that's okay. Place the dough in a lightly oiled bowl, turning to coat the entire surface of the dough with oil. Cover the bowl with plastic wrap and set aside in a warm, draft-free spot until the dough is doubled in bulk. While the dough rises, lightly oil a large, heavy baking sheet and dust it generously with wheat flakes or cornmeal.

Punch the dough down, knead briefly, and divide in half. Knead each half into a tight ball and place the balls on the sheet, leaving plenty of room for expansion. Cover with plastic wrap and let rise and widen on the sheet in a warm, draft-free spot until doubled, about 30 to 45 minutes. When the loaves appear nearly doubled, preheat the oven to 375°.

Just before baking, make several slashes in the top of each loaf with a sharp serrated knife. Bake for 40 to 45 minutes, until the bottoms give a clear, hollow echo when tapped with a finger. Transfer the loaves to a rack and cool before slicing. Store loaves in sealed plastic bags. ♦

# Garlic Lovers' Bread

*Makes 1 loaf*

Here's a fine conversation piece—a bread that not only tastes of garlic but also looks like a big garlic bulb. You can make this as one big loaf, for slicing, or you can make 2 smaller loaves and break off individual "cloves" at the table. Read the recipe through before you start to shape it, to familiarize yourself with the process. Serve this bread with Italian food, soups, and stews. Makes excellent toast.

*1 tablespoon unsalted butter*

*10 garlic cloves, minced*

*1 1/2 cups milk*

*1/4 cup lukewarm water*

*1 1/4-ounce package (about 1 tablespoon) active dry yeast*

*1 cup whole wheat flour*

*3 3/4 cups (approximately) unbleached flour*

*2 teaspoons salt*

*1 large egg, at room temperature*

*2 tablespoons good-quality olive oil or unsalted butter, melted*

*egg wash: 1 egg beaten with 1 tablespoon milk*

Melt the 1 tablespoon butter over medium heat in a small saucepan. Stir in the garlic and cook for 15 seconds. Pour in the milk and remove the pan from the heat. Let the milk sit in the pan for 5 minutes to take the chill off, then pour it into a large mixing bowl. Pour the water into a small bowl and stir in the yeast. Set aside for 5 minutes to dissolve.

Once the yeast has dissolved, blend it with the milk, then stir in the whole wheat flour and 1 cup of the unbleached flour. Beat vigorously with a wooden spoon for 1 minute, then cover this sponge with plastic wrap and set aside in a warm, draft-free spot for 30 minutes.

After 30 minutes, beat the salt, egg, and oil or melted butter into the sponge. Stir in enough of the remaining unbleached flour, about 1/2 cup at a time, to make a kneadable dough. Turn the dough out onto a floured surface and knead for 8 minutes, using more flour as necessary to keep the dough from sticking. After 8 minutes the dough will be smooth and elastic. Place it in a lightly oiled bowl, turning to coat the entire surface of the dough with oil. Cover the bowl with plastic wrap and set aside in a warm, draft-free spot until the dough is doubled in bulk. In the meantime, generously dust a large heavy baking sheet with cornmeal.

Once the dough has doubled, punch it down and knead it into a tight ball on a lightly floured surface; put the ball in the center of the sheet. Now, imagine there's a shaft, about the size of a nickel, extending straight down from the top center of the dough. You'll be making cuts right up to that imaginary shaft, but you want to keep it intact as much as possible.

Lightly oil a sharp knife or dough scraper and, from the shaft out, cut all the way down through the ball. Make the first cuts at 12:00 and 6:00, then two on each side, at 2:00 and 4:00 and 8:00 and 10:00. At this

*(continued)*

*(continued)*

point you will have tapered sections of dough, attached at the middle. Take each section, one at a time, and gently push it over so it leans a little; lean each one the same way, then plump the bottom of what should now look like a bulb of garlic with your cupped hands. Cover the loaf loosely with plastic wrap and set aside in a warm, draft-free spot until doubled. When the loaf appears nearly doubled, preheat the oven to 400°.

Once the loaf has doubled, brush it with the egg wash and bake for approximately 30 minutes, until well browned on all sides. The bottom, when tapped with a finger, should give a hollow retort. Cool on a rack for at least 10 minutes before serving.

NOTE: *If you plan to eat most of this at one meal, and you would like a crustier loaf, more akin to French bread, leave out the egg and the extra 2 tablespoons of oil or butter; use 1³/₄ cups lukewarm water for the liquid and omit the milk. Don't use the egg wash, but instead spray or brush the loaves with water before baking.* ◆

## Shaker Fresh Herb Bread

*Makes 2 large free-form loaves*

*I*f there was ever a group of people in America whose cooking exemplified the highest values of country cooking, it is the Shakers. Among their many contributions to American cookery was their extensive and creative use of herbs; at one time the sale of herbs—both culinary and medicinal—was a major cottage industry for the Shakers. This bread is not unlike a loaf that would have been found on their supper tables. It makes superb sandwich bread for almost any savory filling, from chicken salad to fresh vegetable concoctions. Dried herbs—in roughly half the listed quantities—can be substituted.

> ¹/₄ cup lukewarm water
> 1 ¹/₄-ounce package (*about 1 tablespoon*) active dry yeast
> ¹/₂ cup rolled oats (not *instant*)
> ¹/₂ cup buttermilk
> 1¹/₂ cups hot milk
> 1 tablespoon sugar
> 3 tablespoons minced fresh dill
> 2 teaspoons minced fresh thyme
> 2 teaspoons minced fresh sage
> 1 teaspoon caraway seeds
> 1 cup whole wheat flour
> 4 cups (*approximately*) unbleached flour
> 1 large egg, lightly beaten
> 3 tablespoons unsalted butter, melted
> 2 teaspoons salt
> egg wash: 1 egg beaten with 1 tablespoon milk

Pour the water into a small bowl and stir in the yeast. Set aside for 5 minutes to dissolve. Put the oats in a small mixing bowl. Warm the buttermilk to about body temperature and pour it over the oats. Stir and set aside for 10 minutes.

Pour the hot milk into a large mixing bowl and stir in the sugar, dill, thyme, sage, and caraway seeds. Cool to lukewarm, then blend in the buttermilk/oat mixture and the dissolved yeast. Add the whole wheat flour and 1 cup of the unbleached flour and beat vigorously with a wooden spoon for 1 minute. Cover this sponge with plastic wrap and set aside in a warm, draft-free spot for 30 minutes.

After 30 minutes, beat the egg, melted butter, and salt into the sponge with a wooden spoon. Beat in the remaining unbleached flour, 1 cup at a time, until the dough is too stiff to stir, then turn the dough out onto a floured surface. With floured hands, knead the dough for 10 minutes, using just enough additional flour to prevent sticking. After 10 minutes it will be smooth, soft, and moderately elastic. Place the dough in a lightly oiled bowl, turning to coat the entire surface of the dough with oil.

Cover the bowl with plastic wrap and set aside in a warm, draft-free spot until doubled in bulk. While the dough rises, generously dust a large, heavy baking sheet with cornmeal and set it aside.

When the dough has doubled, punch it down and turn it out onto a floured surface. Divide the dough in half, knead each half briefly, and form the halves into tight balls. Place the balls on the prepared baking sheet, leaving plenty of room between them for expansion. Cover loosely with plastic wrap and set aside in a warm, draft-free spot until doubled in bulk. When the loaves appear nearly doubled, preheat the oven to 375°.

Brush each loaf sparingly with the egg wash; try to keep it from running onto the sheet. Using a sharp serrated knife, make several slashes on the surface of each loaf. When fully doubled, bake for 45 minutes, until the crust is nicely browned and the bottom sounds hollow when tapped with a finger. For uniform baking, turn the baking sheet 180° about midway through the baking. Transfer the loaves to a rack to cool. Cool thoroughly before sealing in plastic bags. ◆

# Tarragon and Sun-Dried Tomato Bread

*Makes 1 large free-form loaf*

A harvest tomato bread sounded good to me, but I was afraid fresh tomatoes wouldn't stand out enough and using tomato juice for the liquid was just a little too gimmicky. Then it dawned on me that sun-dried tomatoes would be the perfect, stylish angle, since they wouldn't get all mushy or turn the bread some weird shade of pink. The tarragon entered the picture when this bread was in the experimental phase, and the two became fast friends. I wanted to give this earthy bread a rough look, so I let it rise in the bowl and then just turned it out onto a baking sheet (or oven tiles) and baked it. This is great for savory sandwiches; I like it for a grilled cheese sandwich made with Fontina.

1 cup sun-dried tomatoes (not *oil-packed*)
1 cup boiling water
1 1/4-ounce package (*about 1 tablespoon*)
    active dry yeast
1 tablespoon sugar
1/4 cup chopped fresh tarragon
2 cups whole wheat flour
2 teaspoons salt
2 tablespoons good-quality olive oil
2 cups (approximately) unbleached flour

Put the tomatoes in a medium mixing bowl and pour the boiling water over them. Let stand for 10 minutes, then drain the tomatoes, pouring the water into a 2- or 4-cup measure. Squeeze the tomatoes, letting their water drip into the measuring cup, then add enough additional cool water to make 1 1/2 cups. Blot the tomatoes dry on a paper towel; chop coarsely and reserve.

When the water is just warm to the touch, pour it into a large mixing bowl and stir in the yeast and sugar. Set aside for 5 minutes to dissolve the yeast, then stir in the tarragon and whole wheat flour. Beat vigorously with a wooden spoon for 1 minute, then cover the bowl with plastic wrap and set aside in a warm, draft-free spot for 30 minutes.

After 30 minutes, stir the salt, oil, and reserved tomatoes into the sponge. Add enough of the unbleached flour, about 1/2 cup at a time, to make a soft but kneadable dough. Turn the dough out onto a floured surface and knead for 8 minutes, until smooth and fairly elastic. Oil a bowl lightly, then place the dough in it, turning to coat the entire surface of the dough with oil. Cover and let rise in a warm spot until doubled.

Punch the dough down and turn it out onto a lightly floured surface. Find a bowl that is likely to just hold the bulk of the dough once it has doubled, line it with a tea towel—*not* a terry one—and dust the towel generously with flour. Knead the dough into a ball, dust it with flour too, then place it in the towel-draped bowl smooth side up; you want the area where the dough gathers at the bottom, so the loaf blossoms open somewhat after it is inverted and baked. Dust the top of the dough with a little more flour and let rise in a warm, draft-free spot, uncovered, until doubled in bulk. Preheat the oven to 400° when the dough appears nearly doubled.

Once the dough has doubled, put a baking sheet on top of the bowl and invert it, letting the dough slip out onto the sheet. Remove the bowl and towel. Bake the bread for 40 minutes, until well browned. The bottom, when tapped with a finger, should give a hollow echo. Cool on a rack, then store the bread in a sealed plastic bag.

NOTE: *To bake on tiles, just before you turn it out of the bowl, give the top of the dough another dusting of flour. Invert it onto the bottom of a small baking sheet or a piece of cardboard. Slide it onto the tiles and bake for about 35 minutes.* ♦

# Sage-Scented Parmesan Cheese Bread

*Makes 1 tube loaf or 2 smaller loaves*

Years ago I self-published a small bread book, and though it brought me neither fame nor fortune, it brought many compliments for this particular bread. Out of the blue I'd meet somebody who would say, "Hey, you're the guy who wrote that little bread book; love that Parmesan bread!" It got to the point where it happened so much I was beginning to have doubts about all the *other* breads ("Gee, thanks, but have you tried anything else in the book?"). My new (optional) touch here is the sage, which can be quite dominating against more subtle flavors, and that's why I line the pan with the leaves, so it only perfumes the bread. I love the way this looks baked in the kugelhopf pan, though lacking that you can use loaf pans, randomly lining them with the sage leaves. Serve this with Italian foods, soups, or as an after-dinner savory with a glass of port. It's best eaten warm.

1/4 cup lukewarm water
1 1/4-ounce package (about 1 tablespoon) active dry yeast
1 tablespoon sugar
3/4 cup sour cream
1/4 cup milk
1/2 cup yellow cornmeal, preferably stone-ground
1/2 cup whole wheat flour
1 cup (1/4 pound) freshly grated Parmesan cheese
1 1/2 teaspoons salt
2 large eggs, at room temperature
1 large egg yolk, at room temperature
2 tablespoons unsalted butter, melted and partially cooled
3 cups (approximately) unbleached flour
20 fresh sage leaves

Pour the water into a small bowl and stir in the yeast and sugar. Set aside for 5 minutes to dissolve. Meanwhile, gently heat the sour cream and milk in a small saucepan, just until slightly warmer than body temperature. Pour into a large mixing bowl and

*(continued)*

*(continued)*

stir in the dissolved yeast, the cornmeal, and the whole wheat flour. Beat vigorously with a wooden spoon for 1 minute, then cover this sponge with plastic wrap and set aside in a warm, draft-free spot for 30 minutes.

After 30 minutes, beat the Parmesan cheese, salt, eggs, egg yolk, and butter into the sponge. Stir in the unbleached flour, 1/2 cup at a time, until you have a soft but kneadable dough. Turn the dough out and knead for 8 minutes, using the unbleached flour as necessary to keep the dough from sticking. Place the dough in a lightly oiled bowl and turn to coat the entire surface of the dough with oil. Cover the bowl with plastic wrap and set aside in a warm, draft-free spot, until the dough is doubled in bulk. While the dough is rising, generously butter a 9-inch kugelhopf pan (or 2 4½- by 8½-inch loaf pans) and press a whole sage leaf into each flute; the butter should hold it in place.

When the dough has doubled, punch it down and knead briefly on a floured surface, shaping the dough into a ball. Using a floured thumb, press down through the center of the dough, making a hole clear through. Pick the dough up and rotate it in your hands to enlarge the center hole. When the hole is about the size of the tube, slip the dough over it and lightly press it down. Cover the top of the mold with plastic wrap and set aside in a warm, draft-free spot until the dough has doubled. When the dough appears nearly doubled, preheat the oven to 375°.

When the dough has fully doubled, bake it on the lower rack (because the bread may rise well out of the pan) for 45 minutes. Remove the bread from the oven and invert it onto a baking sheet, removing the mold. Bake for 10 more minutes. Transfer the loaf to a rack and cool for 5 minutes before slicing. Store leftovers in a sealed plastic bag. To reheat, cut individual slices, wrap them flat in foil, and place in a hot oven for 5 minutes. ◆

# Sweet and Holiday Breads

## Oatmeal Maple Pecan Twists

*Makes 2 twisted free-form loaves*

One thing I've always loved about bread baking is how something as basic as dough can take on so many graceful forms. I have a soft spot for braids, crescents, and other breads with a twist—like this one. I call this a lazy braid: you just lay two strands next to one another and twist the ends in opposite directions. The visual effect is much the same as a three-strand braid and just as attractive, but simpler. The maple aroma of these loaves, when you take them from the oven, will send you. Perfect toasted, with nothing more than soft sweet butter to spread on it. Also a much appreciated gift bread for the holidays.

1 cup rolled oats (not *instant*)
2 tablespoons sugar
1½ cups hot milk
¼ cup lukewarm water
1 ¼-ounce package (about 1 tablespoon) active dry yeast
1¼ cups whole wheat flour

1 tablespoon salt
1 large egg, at room temperature
¼ cup unsalted butter
½ cup pure maple syrup
3½ cups (approximately) unbleached flour
1 cup (4 to 5 ounces) chopped pecans
egg wash: 1 egg white beaten with 1 teaspoon water
2 extra tablespoons of oats, to sprinkle on the loaves before baking

Put the rolled oats and sugar in a large mixing bowl. Stir in the hot milk. As the mixture cools, pour the water into a small bowl and stir in the yeast. Set aside for 5 minutes to dissolve.

When the milk/oat mixture has cooled to lukewarm, stir in the dissolved yeast and the whole wheat flour and beat vigorously with a wooden spoon for 1 minute. Cover this sponge with plastic wrap and set aside in a warm, draft-free spot for 30 minutes.

After 30 minutes, stir the salt and then the egg into the sponge. Gently melt the butter in a small pan, turn off the heat, and add the maple syrup. Swirl the pan, then pour this into the sponge and beat well. Add the unbleached flour, 1 cup at a time, beating well after each addition. When the dough is too

*(continued)*

107

(*continued*)

stiff to stir, turn it out onto a floured surface and knead the dough for 10 minutes, until smooth and somewhat elastic (oat doughs are never terribly elastic). Add unbleached flour as needed to prevent the dough from sticking. Put the dough in a lightly oiled bowl, turning to coat the entire surface of the dough with oil. Cover the bowl with plastic wrap and place the dough in a warm, draft-free spot until doubled in bulk. In the meantime, lightly oil a large baking sheet and sprinkle it with rolled oats.

When doubled, sprinkle half the pecans over the dough and punch it down. Knead in the rest of the pecans, then turn the dough out onto a lightly floured surface and knead the dough for 1 minute. Divide the dough into 4 equal pieces and shape each piece into a strand 12 inches long. Put 2 strands side by side, touching, and pinch the ends together. Now grasp both ends and twist the ends in opposite directions, about a half-turn. Put the first one down, start the second loaf, then go back and twist the first one as before. Put the first twist on the sheet, finish twisting the second one, and put that on the sheet, leaving room between them for expansion. Cover the twists loosely with plastic wrap and set aside in a warm, draft-free spot until doubled. When they appear nearly doubled, preheat the oven to 375°.

When the loaves have fully doubled, brush them lightly with the egg wash. Sprinkle about a tablespoon of oats over each loaf and brush again with the egg wash. Bake the loaves for 20 minutes, turn the heat down to 350°, and bake for about another 30 minutes. When done, the tops will be glazed to a dark brown and the bottoms will be dark and crusty; they should give a faint, hollow echo when tapped with a finger. Transfer the loaves to a rack to cool. Store cooled leftovers in sealed plastic bags. ♦

## Banana Oat Bread

*Makes 2 large loaves*

Banana is often seen in quick breads, much less often in yeast bread. This bread may have limited use as a sandwich bread, but there may not be a better loaf for French toast. If you don't often make French toast, make 3 or 4 smaller loaves and freeze some of them. The pecan swirl variation is excellent.

*¼ cup lukewarm water*
*1 ¼-ounce package (about 1 tablespoon)*
   *active dry yeast*
*1½ cups milk*
*⅓ cup honey*
*1 cup (about 2 large) mashed ripe bananas*
*1 cup rolled oats (not* instant*)*
*1 cup whole wheat flour*
*7 cups (approximately) unbleached flour*
*1 tablespoon salt*
*2 large eggs, at room temperature*
*¼ cup very soft unsalted butter*
*egg wash: 1 egg beaten with 1 tablespoon*
   *milk*

Pour the water into a small bowl and stir in the yeast; set aside for 5 minutes to dissolve. In the meantime, heat the milk to slightly warmer than body temperature and blend it, in a large mixing bowl, with the honey and mashed bananas. Stir in the dissolved yeast. Using a wooden spoon, stir in the oats, whole wheat flour, and 2 cups of the unbleached flour, beating vigorously for 1 minute. Cover this sponge with plastic wrap and set aside in a warm, draft-free spot for 30 minutes.

After 30 minutes, stir in the salt, eggs, and butter. Add enough of the remaining unbleached flour—a cup at a time at first, more gradually as the dough stiffens—to make a soft, kneadable dough. Turn it out onto a lightly floured surface and knead for 10 to 12 minutes, until smooth and fairly elastic; use as much of the remaining flour as needed to keep the dough from sticking. Transfer the dough to a lightly oiled bowl, turning to coat the entire surface of the dough with oil. Cover the bowl with plastic wrap and set aside in a warm, draft-free spot until the dough is doubled in bulk. While the dough rises, butter 2 5- by 9-inch loaf pans.

Once the dough has doubled, punch it down and turn it out onto a lightly floured surface. Divide the dough in half and knead each half briefly. Shape into loaves—and I recommend the procedure for shaping outlined on page 73—and place them in the buttered pans. Cover loosely with plastic wrap and set them aside in a warm, draft-free spot until doubled in bulk. When the loaves appear nearly doubled, preheat the oven to 350°.

When the loaves have fully doubled, brush them sparingly with the egg wash and bake for 50 to 55 minutes; when done, the loaves will be well browned and the bottoms should give a hollow retort when tapped with a finger. Cool the loaves on a rack for at least 30 minutes before slicing.

VARIATION: *To make a Pecan Swirl Banana Oat Bread, roll the dough into a tapered oblong, as described on page 73, working with half the dough at a time. Brush each loaf with 1 tablespoon melted butter, then sprinkle with 2 tablespoons sugar and 1 teaspoon ground cinnamon. Scatter 1 cup chopped pecans (4-5 ounces) evenly over the dough, then roll up and place in the pan. Let rise and bake as directed.* ♦

## Scotch Oatmeal Christmas Bread

*Makes 3 loaves*

Observant cooks will quickly recognize the similarities between this and the traditional stollen it is modeled after. There are, however, some major breaks from tradition. First, I use Scotch or steel-cut oats, which give the bread a nubby texture. Second, I've used dried—rather than candied—fruit because I think their color and flavor are more natural than candied fruits. Use the dried fruits and nuts you like best. This bread makes a great Christmas present.

*1 cup Scotch oats (steel-cut oats; available at health food stores)*
*1 cup boiling water*
*¼ cup lukewarm water*
*1 ¼-ounce package (about 1 tablespoon) active dry yeast*
*1¼ cups hot milk*
*½ cup packed light brown sugar*
*coarsely grated zest of 2 oranges (use the larger holes on a box grater)*
*2½ cups whole wheat flour*
*1 tablespoon salt*
*1 tablespoon vanilla extract or brandy*
*2 large eggs, at room temperature*
*4 cups (approximately) unbleached flour*
*6 tablespoons unsalted butter, softened*
*rolled oats for sprinkling on the baking sheet*
*1½ cups coarsely chopped dried fruit (see note below)*
*½ cup (2 ounces) coarsely chopped nuts*
*2 tablespoons unsalted butter, melted*
*confectioners' sugar to sprinkle on the loaves*

At least 2 hours before you start this bread (or the night before), put the Scotch oats in a mixing bowl and pour the boiling water over them. Cover with foil and leave at room temperature.

When you're ready to start the bread, pour the lukewarm water into a small bowl and stir in the yeast; set aside for 5 minutes to dissolve. Pour the hot milk into a large mixing bowl and stir in the brown sugar and orange zest. Let the milk cool to lukewarm, then stir in the dissolved yeast.

Pour the soaked oats into the milk along with the whole wheat flour and beat vigorously with a wooden spoon for 1 minute. Cover this sponge with plastic wrap and set it aside in a warm, draft-free spot for 30 minutes.

After 30 minutes, using a wooden spoon, beat the salt, vanilla or brandy, and eggs into the sponge. Beat in 1 cup of the unbleached flour, then 2 tablespoons of the soft butter; continue like this until all the butter and 3 cups of flour have been incorporated. By this point you should have a nearly kneadable dough.

Sprinkle the dough with flour and start to knead in the bowl, very gently. When the dough loses much of its original tackiness, turn it out onto a well-floured surface and knead for 10 minutes, adding unbleached flour as needed to keep the dough from sticking; it will be a little sticky for much of the kneading, but try not to go overboard adding flour. Put the dough into a lightly oiled bowl and turn to coat the entire surface of the dough with oil. Cover the bowl with plastic wrap and set aside in a warm, draft-free spot until the dough is doubled. As the dough rises, lightly oil 1 very large or 1 medium and 1 small baking sheet and sprinkle them lightly with rolled oats.

Sprinkle half the fruit and nuts over the risen dough, then punch it down. Turn the dough out onto a floured surface and knead in the remaining fruit and nuts. (If the dough sticks to your surface, a scraper or spatula will help.) Divide the dough into 3 equal pieces, shaping them into balls. Cover loosely with plastic wrap and let them sit for 5 minutes.

Working with one piece at a time, roll each piece into an oval about 10 inches long and 6 inches wide. Brush the surface well with some of the melted butter, then fold the dough over lengthwise, leaving about 1 inch of the bottom half exposed; it will look like a pair of lips. Transfer each to the baking sheet, leaving at least 4 inches between them. Cover loosely with plastic wrap and set aside in a warm, draft-free spot until doubled. When the loaves appear nearly doubled, preheat the oven to 350°.

Bake the loaves for 45 minutes. When done, the bottoms will be golden brown, though because of the oats and richness of the dough they may not give the usual hollow sound when tapped. As soon as the loaves come out of the oven, transfer them to a rack and brush well with the remaining melted butter. When fully cooled, dust them generously with the confectioners' sugar. As good as this bread tastes fresh, it gets even better if wrapped in foil, sealed in a plastic bag, and refrigerated for several days. It will keep for at least a week so wrapped.

NOTE: *If your dried fruits are very dry, you may want to soak them first; otherwise they'll pull moisture out of the bread. Simply put the fruits in a small bowl and pour on enough boiling water to cover. Let them sit for at least 10 minutes, then drain and squeeze gently before adding to the dough.* ♦

## Cranberry Maple-Pecan Sticky Buns

*Makes 12 large buns*

*E*very home baker needs one item, the appearance or mention of which represents the ultimate bargaining tool with one's mate; this is mine. It incorporates everything Karen, my wife, finds irresistible. With a trayful of these I could dissolve any differences, arrange for a full body massage, or trade away a counterful of dirty dishes. Because they take a little time, start them early on a weekend morning and plan to serve them for a late breakfast or a mid-morning snack.

*1 recipe Farm-Style Whole Wheat Bread (page 58)*

FILLING
*3 cups (almost 1 full 12-ounce bag) fresh cranberries*
*2/3 cup water*
*3/4 cup packed light brown sugar*
*3/4 cup dark or golden raisins*
*1 teaspoon ground cinnamon*

GLAZE
*6 tablespoons unsalted butter*
*1/2 cup maple syrup*
*1/3 cup packed light brown sugar*
*1 cup (4 to 5 ounces) finely chopped pecans*

Prepare the dough as directed and set it aside to rise in a warm spot. As the dough rises, prepare the filling. Put the cranberries and water into a large nonaluminum pot, preferably a heavy one. Bring to a boil, cover, and boil gently for 5 minutes, letting the skins pop and the mixture thicken. Stir in the brown sugar and raisins, reduce the heat, and simmer, covered, for 5 more minutes, stirring occasionally. Stir in the cinnamon, then remove the pot from the heat and scrape the filling onto a plate to cool. Butter the sides only of a 9- by 13-inch baking pan, glass or enameled.

Make the glaze. Melt the butter over gentle heat in a medium saucepan. Pour off approximately 1 tablespoon of the butter into another small pan and reserve for later. Add the maple syrup and brown sugar, increase the heat, and bring to a boil. Boil for 1 minute, then pour the glaze into the buttered pan. Tilt the pan to distribute the glaze, then scatter the nuts evenly in the pan.

To assemble the buns, punch the dough down once it has doubled, knead briefly, and divide in half. (Set one half aside to bake as a loaf.) Roll the other half out into a 12- by 15-inch rectangle on a lightly floured surface, with the long side facing you; if at first it is hard to roll, let it rest for 5 minutes. Spread the cooled filling evenly over the dough, pushing it right up to the short edges but leaving a 3/4-inch margin on both of the long sides. Starting at the long edge closest to you, roll the dough up snugly, as you would a carpet. Pinch the seam to seal.

Using a sharp serrated knife, score the roll at the middle point and then at the middle of each half; those are your reference marks. Cut each quarter section into 3 equal pieces, laying them in the pan as you go, on the flat;

you should end up with 3 rows of 4. Cover the pan with plastic wrap and set aside in a warm spot until doubled in bulk. When the buns appear nearly doubled, preheat the oven to 350° (325° if you're using glass).

Bake the buns for 35 minutes; you can probe the dough with a fork to see if it is cooked through. When they come out of the oven, reheat the remaining tablespoon of butter, then brush it over the buns with a pastry brush. Lay a large baking sheet over the buns and, using pot holders, quickly invert the pan of buns onto the sheet; they should drop right out. Lift one end of the pan up slowly to make sure they've dropped, then take the pan off. Serve the buns hot. Store leftovers loosely covered with foil. ♦

# Whole Wheat Kugelhopf

*Makes 1 large kugelhopf*

A kugelhopf is an enriched yeast bread, baked in a special kugelhopf mold shaped like the turban it is said to be designed after. Traditionally a kugelhopf is made with white flour, but we like it better with whole wheat—all whole wheat, except for a little unbleached flour for kneading. Kugelhopf connoisseurs claim that the slightly dry interior of a 1- or 2-day-old kugelhopf actually improves the flavor, but I'm not convinced; still warm and fresh, this is grand. Here's a gift idea for your baker friends: buy the kugelhopf mold as a present (most kitchen shops carry them), bake this, and when it is completely cool, put it back in the mold. Wrap it up and you have a nice combination gift.

*1/4 cup lukewarm water*
*1 1/4-ounce package (about 1 tablespoon) active dry yeast*
*1 cup milk*
*1/2 cup packed light brown sugar*
*1 teaspoon finely grated orange zest*
*3 1/2 cups whole wheat flour*
*2 1/2 teaspoons salt*
*2 large eggs, at room temperature*
*3 tablespoons unsalted butter, softened*
*1/3 cup (approximately) unbleached flour for kneading*
*about 18 whole almonds to lay in the flutes (optional)*
*1/2 cup dark or golden raisins*
*1/2 cup (about 2 ounces) chopped almonds*
*Confectioners' sugar to sprinkle on top (optional)*

Pour the water into a small bowl and stir in the yeast. Set aside for 5 minutes to dissolve. In a small saucepan, gently heat the milk and brown sugar just until the sugar dissolves. Pour this into a large mixing bowl and, when it is slightly warm to the touch, stir in the dissolved yeast. Stir in the orange zest. Using a wooden spoon, stir in 1 1/2 cups of the whole wheat flour, beating vigorously for 1 minute. Cover this sponge with plastic wrap and set aside in a warm, draft-free spot for 30 minutes.

After 30 minutes, beat the salt into the

*(continued)*

*(continued)*

sponge, followed by the eggs, one at a time. Stir in about another cup of the whole wheat flour, then break the butter into pieces and smear it on the dough; work it in as well as you can with your spoon. Stir in the rest of the whole wheat flour.

Lightly flour your work area with the unbleached flour. Turn the dough out and knead for 5 or 6 minutes, using sprinkles of flour to keep the dough from sticking; because of the richness of this dough, it won't become terribly elastic. Put the dough in a lightly buttered bowl, turning to coat the entire surface with butter. Cover the bowl with plastic wrap and set aside in a warm, draft-free spot until the dough is doubled in bulk (this *isn't* a quick riser).

While the dough is rising, butter an 8½- or 9-inch kugelhopf pan and—if you want a decorative touch—lay one whole almond in each bottom flute, points facing center. Put the raisins in a small bowl and pour on enough hot water to just cover. Set aside for 15 minutes, then drain and pat dry between paper towels. Reserve.

Once the dough has risen, punch it down. Turn it out onto a lightly floured surface and knead in the raisins and chopped almonds. Knead the dough into a ball and flatten it slightly. Using a floured thumb, press down all the way through the dough. Enlarge the hole by twirling the dough around on your hand until the hole is about the same size as the center tube of the pan. Put the dough in the pan, feeding the tube through the hole in the dough. Press down on the dough to level it. Cover with plastic wrap and set the pan aside in a

warm, draft-free spot until the dough has doubled, or not quite risen up to the rim of the pan. When the dough appears nearly doubled, preheat the oven to 375°.

When the dough has fully doubled, bake for 45 minutes on one of the lower oven racks. Check the top of the bread about two-thirds of the way through, and if it is getting too dark, cover loosely with foil. After 45 minutes, invert the bread onto a baking sheet, remove the pan, and bake for 10 more minutes. Cool on a rack, then sprinkle generously with confectioners' sugar. To serve, slice into wedges. ♦

## Basic Yeasted Sweet Dough

*Makes enough dough for 1 large or 2 smaller coffee cakes*

With this wonderful dough, enriched with rolled oats and whole wheat, you can create some of the most delectable home-baked items imaginable, chosen from the collection of yeasted coffee cakes that follow. Yeasted coffee cakes take more time and more dexterity than the quick bread type, but that just makes them all the more appreciated. Early risers can make a yeasted coffee cake for a late family breakfast; or you could make one on Saturday for Sunday breakfast or to carry to church coffee hour. About the dough: as rich as it is, it feels a bit less responsive than some, because the fat inhibits gluten formation. And it tends to be a little sticky. Don't worry. Just knead easily and keep your surface dusted lightly with flour. I use some white sugar with the brown here, but you can substitute ⅓ cup honey for one or the other. Just be aware that with the honey the surface of the coffee cake will have a darker, less golden, tone to it.

*¼ cup lukewarm water*

*2 ¼-ounce packages (about 1½ tablespoons) active dry yeast*

*1¼ cups lukewarm milk*

*⅓ cup sugar*

*⅓ cup packed light brown sugar*

*½ cup rolled oats (not instant)*

*1½ cups whole wheat flour*

*4 cups (approximately) unbleached flour*

*2 large eggs (at room temperature), lightly beaten*

*½ cup (¼ pound) unsalted butter, melted and slightly cooled*

*2 teaspoons salt*

Pour the water into a small bowl and stir in the yeast. Set aside for 5 minutes to dissolve. In the meantime, pour the milk into a large mixing bowl and stir in the sugars, oats, whole wheat flour, and ½ cup of the unbleached flour. Add the dissolved yeast. Beat vigorously with a wooden spoon for 1

minute, then cover this sponge with plastic wrap and set it aside in a warm, draft-free spot for 30 minutes.

After 30 minutes, stir the eggs, butter, and salt into the sponge. Start adding the remaining unbleached flour, about ½ cup at a time, stirring well after each addition. When the dough is too stiff to stir, cover the bowl with plastic wrap and let rest for 5 to 10 minutes.

After the short rest, shake some flour on the dough and start to knead it, right in the bowl if there is room. When it loses its original tackiness, turn the dough out onto a floured surface and knead for 10 minutes, using as much of the remaining flour as necessary to keep the dough from sticking. Place the dough in a lightly buttered bowl, turning to coat the entire surface of the dough with butter. Cover the bowl with plastic wrap and set aside, in a warm, draft-free spot, until the dough is doubled in bulk. Once the dough has doubled, it is ready to use in the following recipes.

NOTE: *If you are using only half of this dough, you can shape the other half into a loaf and bake it in a 4- by 8-inch loaf pan for 35 to 40 minutes, in a preheated 350° oven. This unadorned loaf makes excellent toast or French toast. Or, once the dough has risen, punch it down, place in a plastic bag, and freeze for future use. Thaw and proceed.* ♦

# Holiday Mixed-Grain, Fruit, and Nut Bread

*Makes 3 loaves*

A spin-off of the Basic Yeasted Sweet Dough (page 114), this includes some rye flour, grated orange zest, an assortment of fruits—including rum-soaked raisins—and pecans. I bake this in 3 shapes: like a doughnut, a stollen, and a quasi star shape that looks like a holiday bread but is actually a variation on the way I shape the Garlic Lovers' Bread (page 101). You can choose one of these, do all 3, or make up your own. And if you want small instead of medium-size loaves, you can divide the dough into quarters instead of thirds. Feel free to go heavier with the amounts of nuts and fruits; you'll never get complaints about too much.

*1/2 cup dark or golden raisins*
*1/4 cup dark rum*
*1 modified recipe Basic Yeasted Sweet Dough (page 114), as outlined below*
*finely grated zest of 1 or 2 oranges*
*1/2 teaspoon ground cardamom*
*1/2 teaspoon ground coriander*
*1/2 teaspoon ground cinnamon*
*1/2 cup finely chopped dried figs*
*1/2 cup finely chopped pitted prunes*
*1/2 cup chopped fresh cranberries*
*1/2 to 1 cup chopped pecans or pecans and walnuts (2 to 4 ounces)*
*egg wash: 1 egg beaten with 1 tablespoon milk or cream*

*Confectioners' sugar to sprinkle on top (optional)*

At least an hour before you start the bread, put the raisins and rum in a small bowl to soak.

To make the dough, prepare the Basic Yeasted Sweet Dough up to the point of making the sponge. Once the sponge has rested for 30 minutes, proceed as directed, making the following changes and additions: stir into the sponge the raisins and rum, orange zest, and spices and replace 1 cup unbleached flour with 1 cup rye flour. Add the eggs, butter, and salt, as usual, and proceed with the recipe, adding the unbleached flour and kneading as directed.

Once the dough has doubled, mix all the remaining fruits and nuts together and spread about one-third of it over the dough. Punch the dough down, fold it over, and sprinkle on another third. Fold again and work in the rest of it. Turn the dough out and knead it for a minute to distribute the fruits and nuts. Lightly butter 2 large baking sheets.

Divide the dough into thirds and shape each as follows.

TO MAKE A RING OR DOUGHNUT: Knead the dough into a ball, then push your floured thumb down through the center. Pick up the ring of dough and move it in a circular direction with your hands to enlarge the hole. Once the hole is about 4 inches wide, put the ring on the baking sheet.

TO MAKE A STOLLEN: Roll the dough into an oval about 10 inches long and 7 inches wide. Lightly brush the surface with melted butter and fold half of the dough over the other, lengthwise, to form what looks like a big pair of lips. The top lip should not line up perfectly with the bottom but rather be set about ¾ inch back from the edge. Place it on the sheet.

*TO MAKE A STAR:* Knead the dough into a ball and place it on the baking sheet. Imagine a continuous shaft of dough, as big around as a quarter, running down the center of the dough. Using a sharp knife or dough scraper, cut down through the dough—at 12:00, 2:00, 4:00, 6:00, 8:00, and 10:00—but keep the shaft intact so it holds the pieces together; in other words, don't bring the cuts together at the center of the dough.

Take the resulting pieces and turn each one 90°, in the same direction, so they're lying on edge. Plump the edge with cupped hands to even.

At this point you should have 2 breads on one sheet, well spaced, and 1 on another. Cover the dough loosely with plastic wrap and set aside in a warm, draft-free spot until doubled in bulk. Preheat the oven to 350° when it appears nearly doubled.

Just before baking, brush the loaves sparingly with the egg wash. Bake for 35 to 40 minutes, until well browned. Transfer the breads to a cooling rack and cool before slicing. When the breads have cooled thoroughly, dust with confectioners' sugar if you wish. These will last many days, well wrapped in foil and sealed in plastic bags. ◆

# Panettone

*Makes 2 cylindrical loaves*

I like the legend behind this bread, as told in *The Cooking of Italy* (Time-Life Books). Originally it was called Tony's bread (*pan de Tonio*), after a fifteenth-century baker in Milan. Tony had a daughter, Adalgisa, much desired by a poor, young commoner who wanted her hand in marriage. So to get on the good side of Pop, the young man sold off his prize possessions—his hunting falcons—and used the money to buy the baker the best flour, sultana raisins, and lemons he could afford. Tony, naturally, parlayed those ingredients into a bread that would make him a rich and famous man, and of course the young man won the daughter and everybody lived happily ever after. Take care, when you make this, that there's no chill in any of the ingredients; as rich and sluggish as this dough is, a chill in the dough will slow the rising considerably. This is the perfect holiday gift bread—plump, pretty, and richly colored.

*1 modified recipe Basic Yeasted Sweet Dough
  (page 114), as outlined below
4 egg yolks, at room temperature
finely grated zest of 2 lemons
1¹/₂ cups golden raisins
2 tablespoons unsalted butter, melted*

Prepare the dough, making the following changes: Reduce the amount of milk to 1 cup. After the sponge has rested for 30 minutes, stir in—in addition to the regular ingredients—the 4 large egg yolks and the lemon zest. Also, after the dough has risen once, knead in the raisins when you punch it down.

To make the loaves—this is the fun part—evenly cut off the top 7 inches of 2 medium or large grocery sacks. Cut them so you have two long 7-inch-wide strips and heavily butter one side of each. Roll each one up so you have 2 7-inch cylinders, buttered part on the inside. Secure each cylinder with a staple or pin at the top and bottom. Put the cylinders on a large, lightly buttered baking sheet.

After the dough has doubled and you've worked in the raisins, divide the dough in half and knead each half into a ball. Put one ball of dough in the center of each cylinder; they'll spread to the edge and then start to rise. Put a not-too-heavy book on top of each cylinder to discourage the dough from creeping under the cylinder. Set the cylinders in a warm, draft-free spot to rise until doubled. When they appear nearly doubled, preheat the oven to 375°.

When the dough looks doubled, take the books off and bake for 40 minutes; when done, the loaves will be on the dark side. Transfer the loaves to a rack, then carefully remove the collars by snipping them with scissors or taking out the pins. Generously brush the surfaces of both loaves with the melted butter. Cool thoroughly, then wrap well in foil and plastic bags.

NOTE: *You can, if you like, add about ¹/₄ cup chopped candied citron to the dough; that's a traditional touch.* ◆

# Honey Wheat Crumb Cake

*Makes 12 servings*

As much as I love rich, sweet coffee cakes, here's one that's much less so, and I still can't get enough of it. This is a yeasted coffee cake, so it's a good weekend choice; figure about 2½ hours from the time you start this until the time it comes out of the oven. I like to start this, have coffee and do some chores, then plan for a late breakfast, so this is done right about the time we're all good and hungry.

CAKE BATTER
³/₄ *cup hot milk*
¹/₃ *cup honey*
¹/₄ *cup lukewarm water*
*1 ¹/₄-ounce package (about 1 tablespoon) active dry yeast*
*1¹/₂ cups whole wheat flour*
*2 large eggs, at room temperature*
*1¹/₂ teaspoons salt*
*5 tablespoons unsalted butter, softened*
*1¹/₂ cups unbleached flour*

CRUMB TOPPING
³/₄ *cup plus 1 tablespoon unbleached flour*
¹/₃ *cup packed light brown sugar*
*pinch of salt*
¹/₄ *cup unsalted butter, melted and cooled*

To make the batter, pour the hot milk into a large mixing bowl and stir in the honey. While that's cooling, put the warm water in a small bowl and stir in the yeast. After the milk has cooled to about body temperature, stir in the dissolved yeast. Using a wooden spoon, beat in the whole wheat flour, stirring vigorously for 2 minutes. Cover this sponge and set it aside in a warm spot for 30 minutes. Butter a 9-inch square or 7- by 11-inch baking pan; I like glass for this.

After 30 minutes, beat the eggs and salt into the sponge. Beat in the butter and the unbleached flour, ½ cup at a time, beating for 1 full minute after each addition and 2 full minutes after the final ½ cup. The dough will become quite hard to stir; take a break if your arm gets tired. Scrape the dough into the prepared pan, then lightly butter your fingertips and pat the dough out evenly. Lightly butter a piece of plastic wrap and loosely cover the pan with it. Set the pan in a warm, draft-free spot to let the dough rise. Preheat the oven to 375° (350° if you're using glass) 20 minutes into the rising.

As the dough rises, make the topping. Combine the flour, brown sugar, and salt in a mixing bowl. Stir in the melted butter and rub with your fingers to form damp pea-size crumbs. Set aside.

When the dough has doubled, no higher—in about 35 to 45 minutes—sprinkle the crumbs evenly over the top. Bake for approximately 35 minutes, until the top is golden brown. Transfer the pan to a rack to cool. Cut and serve warm from the pan. Keep leftovers covered with plastic wrap. ♦

# Toasted Hazelnut Coffee Cake

*Makes 1 large round coffee cake*
*(about 10 servings)*

You could use pecans or walnuts here, but hazelnuts are sort of a classy change of pace, and this blend of cocoa, spice and powdered coffee brings out their best. The instant coffee in the filling gives it a slightly bitter but still sweet flavor. Karen, my wife, doesn't care for that slight bitterness; instead, she likes to mix a little powdered coffee into the glaze. You could do both, too.

1 recipe Basic Yeast Sweet Dough (page 114)

FILLING
1½ cups (about 6 ounces) hazelnuts
½ cup packed light brown sugar
2 teaspoons unsweetened cocoa powder
1 teaspoon instant coffee or espresso powder
½ teaspoon ground cinnamon
¼ cup unsalted butter, cut into ¼-inch pieces
½ cup unsweetened shredded coconut (available at health food stores) or sweetened flaked coconut
egg wash: 1 egg beaten with 1 tablespoon milk

GLAZE
½ cup confectioners' sugar
1 to 1½ tablespoons milk

Prepare the dough as directed, letting it rise in a warm spot. While you're waiting for it to double, make the filling.

Preheat the oven to 350°. Spread the hazelnuts on a baking sheet and roast them for 8 minutes. Transfer the nuts to a tea towel, fold it over, and rub the skins off as well as you can. Chop the nuts finely and reserve.

Using your hands, rub together the brown sugar, cocoa, instant coffee, and cinnamon. Add the butter and rub it in to spread it around, then add the coconut and reserved hazelnuts. Continue to rub with your hands to blend the ingredients evenly. Set aside. Lightly butter a large baking sheet, preferably not a dark one.

Once the dough has doubled, punch it down and knead briefly on a lightly floured surface; cut off half for this recipe (see note on page 115). Let half the dough rest, covered, for 5 minutes, then roll it into a 10- by 15-inch rectangle. Spread the filling evenly over the dough, right up to the short sides but leaving a ¾-inch margin on the long sides. Starting at one of the long sides, roll the dough up like you would a carpet. Keep a little tension on the dough to get a nice, uniform roll. Before you finish rolling, lightly moisten the other long margin of dough with water, then pinch there to seal when you have a finished log.

Lift the log and place it, seam down, on the baking sheet. Pull the ends around to meet, shaping the dough into a nice, even doughnut. Using a sharp serrated knife, cut down into the dough—but not quite through it—at about 1-inch intervals; you'll be left with a number of rings. Pull each ring out just a little to widen the circle, at the same time leaning it over just slightly; each ring should lean against the next. Cover the coffee cake loosely with plastic wrap and set aside in a warm, draft-free spot to rise. It won't actually double in bulk, but in about 30 minutes it should look swollen, and feel somewhat spongy when poked with a finger. At that point, preheat the oven to 350°.

While the oven heats, brush the ring sparingly with the egg wash. As soon as the oven is preheated, bake for 30 minutes, until the surface is a deep golden brown. Slide the ring onto a rack and cool for 30 minutes before drizzling on the glaze with a fork or small whisk.

To make the glaze, stir together the confectioners' sugar and enough of the milk (start with a tablespoon) to make an emulsion that falls from a fork in a thick thread. ♦

# Yeasted Galette Dough

*Makes 1 large or 2 smaller galettes*

This is nothing more than a slightly sweet, enriched yeast dough—though just barely kneaded—used for any number of galettes, which are something like sweet pizzas, attractive and delicious way out of proportion to your investment of time. Because it is kneaded for less than a minute, the dough has very little structure, which is fine because it doesn't need much and the structure would detract from the dough's tenderness. Here I give the basic dough, followed by a handful of sweet possibilities; but you'll be able to take this idea and run with all sorts of personal interpretations, as I have. I find that the choice of pan here is important: a shinier, reflective one seems to work better than a dark one, which makes the crust darken too quickly. But if your only pan is dark, simply lower the temperature by 25°.

1/2 cup lukewarm water
1 1/4-ounce package (about 1 tablespoon) active dry yeast
1 2/3 cups unbleached flour
1/2 cup whole wheat flour
2 tablespoons sugar
1/2 teaspoon salt
finely grated zest of 1 lemon
1/4 cup cold unsalted butter, cut into small pieces
1 large egg, lightly beaten

Pour the water into a small bowl and stir in the yeast. Set aside for 5 minutes to dissolve. Mix the flours, sugar, salt, and lemon zest in a large bowl. Add the butter and cut it in with a pastry blender until the mixture resembles coarse meal; the pieces of butter will be almost invisible.

Make a well in the center of this mixture and pour in the dissolved yeast and egg. Stir until the dough pulls together in a dampish mass; cover with plastic wrap and let it sit for a few minutes. Flour your hands and a kneading surface and turn the dough out. Knead gently for 15 seconds, using more sprinkles of flour to keep the dough from sticking; then flour the dough lightly and put it in a medium bowl. Cover the bowl with plastic wrap and set aside in a warm, draft-free spot until doubled in bulk. Once the dough has doubled, you can proceed with one of the following variations.

## General Information and Galette Variations

Each of the variations here makes 2 10-inch round galettes. I like this size best because it is easier to work with a smaller piece of dough *and* you can make 2 variations with the same batch of dough. For these smaller ones you can use small pizza pans, 10-inch tin pie pans, the removable bottoms from springform pans, or small baking sheets. Rather than make and bake both at once, roll and assemble the first one, get it in the oven on the lower shelf, then start on the second one; it can be put in the oven when the first has been moved up to the higher oven shelf or after it comes out.

To make 1 large galette, roll the dough approximately the same size as a large baking sheet—12 by 18 inches is a good size—then transfer the dough to the pan, pushing the dough slightly up the sides. For the topping, double the quantities listed for each 10-inch galette.

To shape 10-inch galettes, gently punch down the doubled dough. Divide it in half and shape each half into a disk. On a lightly floured surface, roll each half into an 11-inch circle. Lightly flour the surface of the dough, fold it in half, and lift it onto a lightly oiled baking sheet or one of the pans suggested above. Unfold the dough and play around with it to shape it into a respectable circle. Fold back 1/2 to 3/4 inch of the dough's edge so you have a raised perimeter. Pinch the edge between the thumbs and second fingers of both hands; do this at closely spaced intervals all around, creating a wavy edge.

Now you are ready to proceed with one or two of the following variations. The quantities listed are for 1 10-inch galette; double if making 2 of the same.

*GALETTE PÉROUGIENNE:* This, I understand, is the way they do it in the small town of Perouges, near Lyons in France; sounds like my kind of place. Dot the surface of the dough, but not the edge, with 3 tablespoons cold unsalted butter. Sprinkle with 2 tablespoons sugar. Bake on the lower shelf of a preheated 450° oven for 6 minutes, transfer it to the upper shelf, and bake for another 6 minutes, until the surface is lightly browned.

*MAPLE ALMOND GALETTE:* Dot the surface of the dough, but not the edge, with 3 tablespoons cold unsalted butter. Sprinkle with 1 tablespoon sugar and drizzle with 2 tablespoons maple syrup. Bake on the lower shelf of a preheated 450° oven for 6 minutes. Remove from the oven and sprinkle with 1/4 cup thinly sliced almonds. Move it to the upper shelf and bake for 6 more minutes.

*FRESH FRUIT GALETTE:* This works beautifully with fresh seasonal fruit. Dot the surface of the dough, but not the edge, with 3 tablespoons cold unsalted butter. Slice either 1 large peach, 1 large peeled apple, or several ripe plums and arrange the slices randomly over the dough. Sprinkle with 2 tablespoons white or light brown sugar. Bake on the lower shelf of a preheated 450° oven for 6 minutes. Then transfer it to the upper shelf and bake 6 more minutes. Any juices the fruit has released can be brushed over the fruit just before serving.

*CUSTARD GALETTE:* This idea is from an old James Beard newspaper column. When you shape the galette, instead of making a wavy edge, pinch it to form a rim at least 1/4 inch high. Sprinkle the surface of the dough with 2 tablespoons sugar. Lightly beat 1 egg with 1/2 cup heavy cream. Get everything near the oven—you don't want to walk across the room with this—and slowly pour the custard into the galette shell. Bake on the lower rack of a preheated 425° oven for 5 minutes. Lower the heat to 325° and transfer the galette to the center rack. Bake about 10 more minutes, just until the custard is set.

FRUIT AND CUSTARD GALETTE: Proceed as for the custard galette, adding slices of fresh fruit, as in the fruit galette. (Put the fruit on first, then pour on the custard.)

*In every case,* cool the galette directly on a rack if you're not slicing and serving it right away. Slice it into big wedges. ◆

# SAVORY
# BAKING

The premise of this chapter on savory baking—a rather large net that we cast over such favorites as pizza, calzone, quiches, dinner pies, and the like—is that there's almost no savory dish you can't improve by putting a pastry or bread crust over, under, or somehow around it. As eaters, we know this instinctively. Have you ever eaten—or served—soup without crackers or bread? Gravy without rolls or biscuits to sop it up? A thick stew or an Italian meal without crusty bread on the side? Even if we can accept such oversights intellectually, body and soul perceive them as letdowns of the highest order. The fact is, we crave something bready, crisp, or crusty with every meal.

This craving, of course, explains our collective excitement over savory baking, the fine art of marrying a pastry or bread wrapping with a savory filling. From chicken pot pies to quiche to calzone and the contemporary pizza revival, our recent culinary history celebrates these earthy, primal dishes as sustenance for a nation grown weary of too much food introspection, too many new and restrictive diets, and too many fast-food meals.

Like all worthwhile pursuits, the execution of a savory baked entrée takes a little time and planning. You don't rush home from the workplace at 5:30 and hope to pull one of these babies out of the oven by 6:00. In fact, you don't even think about rushing one of these meals, because that goes against the grain of their casual, down-home, I-got-all-the-time-in-the-world personality. Take it slow. Find something that sounds good; buy the ingredients, if you don't have them on hand; prep the filling as far as you can (cut the vegetables for a pot pie, grate cheeses, and so on); and make the crust. That sequence can take place over a day, a weekend, or a week, depending on your skills, your inclinations, and the exact workings of the recipe.

One skill a savory baker should hone is pastry making, because it is the basis for so many crusted entrées. Further, one should develop the habit of keeping partially baked tart shells in the freezer, a practice that puts a quiche in the running for a mid-week meal, since all that's left to do is make the filling, which can usually be done in 10 or 20 minutes. Don't feel intimidated by the prospect of making pastry. If you're in the habit of buying frozen pie shells, just try—for a change one weekend—to make a pastry shell from scratch; do it when nobody is around and there are no distractions. Get yourself a tart pan from the local hardware store or cookware shop and stick with it until you have pastry shell making down pat. And don't be discouraged by less-than-perfect results. Anybody who aspires to be a proficient home cook has to realize that the road to proficiency is littered with imperfect—though generally still edible—experiments. It's an unfair expectation of yourself to think you'll master pastry making—or bread or pie making, for that matter—overnight. It won't happen. Learn to be happy with incremental improvements—and even occasional setbacks—in your baking skills, secure in the knowledge that home baking is a craft that's learned over an entire lifetime, not a few weeks or months. In these days of instant gratification that isn't always easy.

When you plan one of these savory baked entrées, give the rest of the meal some thought too. Most of these main dishes are substantial enough that little else is needed. A thoughtful, varied salad is always a good partner, and that includes a good homemade dressing. Depending on how filling the dish is and how many people you are serving, you may not need dessert at all, just a bowl of fresh fruit.

Sit down, count your blessings, and dig in. ◆

## Kale and Three-Cheese Calzones

*Makes 4 individual calzones*

I have eaten these calzones for days on end without tiring of them. There is something so gratifying about cracking one open, releasing a hot cloud of kale, Kasseri, mozzarella, and Parmesan vapors. The hard part is restraining yourself from biting into it too quickly, but do; otherwise you'll bite into a pocket of steam that could burn your mouth terribly. I've done it. Kids are especially vulnerable, so warn them or cut theirs in half about 5 minutes before you're ready to eat. I like to serve calzones with a salad, tomato sauce on the side, and red wine.

*1 recipe Light Wheat Pizza or Calzone*
 *Dough (page 129)*

FILLING
*½ pound kale*
*1 cup (¼ pound) freshly grated Parmesan*
 *cheese*
*1 cup (3 ounces) diced mozzarella cheese*
*1 cup (3 ounces) crumbled Kasseri cheese*
*2 tablespoons minced onion*
*2 teaspoons dried basil* or *2 tablespoons*
 *chopped fresh*
*freshly ground pepper*

Prepare the dough as directed and, while it is rising, prepare the filling as follows. Strip the kale leaves from their stems, placing them in a very large bowl as you work; discard the stems. Fill the bowl with lukewarm water and agitate the leaves with your hands to free any sand and dirt. Put about ½ inch of water into a large non-aluminum pot and lift the wet leaves right into it. Bring to a boil over high heat, reduce to medium-low, then cover. Steam for 15 minutes, tightly covered, then drain in a colander, saving the steaming water for soup if you like. Cool.

In a medium mixing bowl, combine the remaining ingredients except the pepper. When the kale is cool enough to handle, squeeze out almost all of the liquid. Chop well and mix with the cheeses. Season to taste with pepper. Generously dust a large, heavy baking sheet with cornmeal and set it aside.

Once the dough has doubled, punch it down and turn it out onto a floured surface. Knead briefly, then divide it into 4 equal parts. Shape each quarter into a ball, then lay them on a lightly floured surface, loosely covered with plastic wrap. Let rest for 5 minutes; they'll roll easier with this short rest. Preheat the oven to 450°.

Working with one piece at a time, roll each into an oblong about 9 inches long and 5 or 6 inches wide. Now, draw an imaginary line across the width of the oblong at the very center. Spoon one-quarter of the filling, compacted, onto one-half of the dough, keeping it about ½ inch shy of the center line. Try to leave a ¾-inch margin of dough around the outside of the filling. Very lightly moisten with water a thin band of the perimeter, all around, then fold the other half of the dough over and pinch to seal. After you pinch the edge, curl it up and pinch it some more to secure. Transfer it to the baking sheet, then repeat for the remaining pieces of dough.

After the last calzone has been placed on the sheet (leave some room between them), wait 5 minutes, then bake them in the oven for 25 minutes, until well browned. Transfer the calzones to a rack and cool for 5 minutes before serving.

VARIATIONS: *Other additions to this filling might include up to ¹/₃ cup finely chopped prosciutto, a few sautéed sliced mushrooms, or a little sautéed chopped green bell pepper. To accommodate any additions, cut back on one of the other ingredients by an equal amount.* ♦

## Light Wheat Pizza or Calzone Dough

*Makes enough dough for 1 large or 3 small pizzas or 4 individual calzones*

From this one easy dough you can make all sorts of wonderful dishes. You can make calzones, one big pizza or several smaller ones, or two skillet breads, recipes for all of which can be found in "Savory Baking." This is a lovely dough to knead; because it has very little fat it responds quickly to kneading, becoming smooth and elastic within several minutes. There's just a shade of whole wheat and cornmeal here, which I think lends this a rugged, distinctive characteristic not usually found in pizzeria dough. Try it this way first, then make it more or less grainy if you like. This dough rises quickly, which is a good thing, because impatience reigns around here when pizza is on the menu.

> 1¹/₂ cups lukewarm water
> 1 ¹/₄-ounce package (about 1 tablespoon) active dry yeast
> 3¹/₄ cups (approximately) unbleached flour
> ¹/₂ cup whole wheat flour
> ¹/₃ cup yellow cornmeal, preferably stone-ground
> 1¹/₂ teaspoons salt
> 2 tablespoons good-quality olive oil

Pour the water into a large mixing bowl, stir in the yeast, and set aside for 5 minutes to dissolve. When the yeast has dissolved, beat in 1¹/₂ cups of the unbleached flour, the whole wheat flour, and the cornmeal. Beat vigorously with a wooden spoon for 1 minute, cover the bowl with plastic wrap, and set aside in a warm, draft-free spot for 10 minutes.

After 10 minutes, stir in the salt and olive oil. Add the remaining unbleached flour, about ¹/₂ cup at a time, until you have a soft, kneadable dough. Turn the dough out onto a floured surface and knead vigorously for about 8 minutes, using sprinkles of flour to prevent sticking; you should have a soft, smooth, and elastic dough. Place the dough in a lightly oiled bowl and turn to coat the entire surface of the dough with oil. Cover the bowl with plastic wrap and set the dough aside in a warm, draft-free spot until doubled, about 1 hour.

Once the dough has doubled, it is recipe ready. Proceed according to recipe instructions. ♦

## Baking Tiles

In a far corner of my oven there's a stack of blackened tiles. These are my baking tiles, every home baker's inexpensive ticket to the best crust in town. When only pizza with an authentic crust will do, I resurrect my tiles from their chaotic encampment and arrange them on my lower baking rack. I don't use them every time I bake pizza, but when I don't bother, I could kick myself. (For advice on tile-baking pizza, see page 138.)

There's baking magic in those tiles: not only do you get a little extra lift when your dough hits the preheated tiles, but their porousness steals moisture from the bottom crust, leaving you with a wonderfully chewy, crisp-dry crust.

Baking tiles—actually unglazed quarry tiles—are available from most home improvement centers/lumberyards, though there's a fair chance you will have to order them specially. I have two kinds, ordered from different stores: one size measures about 4 by 8 inches and the other 6 by 6 inches; I have about eight of each. There's only one thing that bothers me about the square ones, and that's two small protrusions on all four sides; you can't get them to butt up against one another, which leaves a crease on the bottom crust of whatever you are baking. It can also impede you from sliding breads around on the tiles; just something to watch for if you order tiles.

Tiles are usually placed on the bottom rack of the oven, near where the hottest heat is; that leaves you plenty of headroom for getting things in and out of the oven, since baking on tiles inevitably involves reaching your hands and arms—to some extent—into the oven. So order only as many tiles as you need to cover the rack—leaving 2 inches of space around the edges, for circulation—plus a couple to cover against breakage. They *will* break, which is the reason I use tiles instead of the larger *baking stones* I see in kitchen shops for $25 or $30, which work the same way.

Baking tiles need to be preheated no less than 30 minutes ahead of baking. Get them in place before you turn on the oven. If you forget, and turn the oven on first, no big deal; you just have to cope with a faceful of heat and potential finger burns.

Most free-form breads that are low in fat and sugar can be baked directly on tiles. There are a couple of useful tricks to baking bread on tiles. The first is to let your rounded loaves rise in a bowl that's been draped with a tea towel (*not* a terry one). Ideally, the volume of the bowl should be roughly half the size of the unrisen dough, so the dough more or less fills the bowl once it has risen. Dust the towel generously with flour, place the dough in it and dust the top with a little more flour. You needn't cover it with plastic wrap as it rises. When the dough is fully risen, dust the top (which is about to become the *bottom*) again with flour, cornmeal, or semolina, and quickly but carefully invert the risen dough onto another rigid surface, like a small baking sheet. Pull the towel off carefully, then slash the top surface of the dough several times, if you like, with a sharp serrated knife and slide it onto the hot tiles with a little flick of the wrist, just as you do with pizza. This technique is explained in a little more detail on page 138.

# *Big Broccoli Calzone*

### *Makes 1 big calzone (about 8 servings)*

*H*ere's a calzone for a crowd. You could easily feed 8 people with just one, as long as you have a few other nice things on the side, like a green salad, marinated vegetables, and a big jug of red wine. Please don't skip the step of draining the ricotta cheese; it seems like such a minor thing, but it really isn't. The small amount of liquid you'll get out of the ricotta is enough to blow a major hole in the side of your calzone, which will sputter and smoke like a submarine that's just taken a torpedo to starboard. Plan to let the calzone cool for about 10 minutes so the filling has time to firm up a bit.

*1 pound ricotta cheese*
*1 recipe Light Wheat Pizza or Calzone Dough (page 129)*

FILLING

*1 medium-size head of broccoli, cut into small flowerets (about 4 cups)*
*salt to taste*
*3 tablespoons good-quality olive oil*
*1 large onion, chopped*
*2 garlic cloves, minced*
*1 1/2 cups (about 1/4 pound) grated provolone cheese*
*1 cup (1/4 pound) finely grated Parmesan cheese, preferably a good, imported variety*
*1/4 cup chopped pitted black or green olives*
*1 tablespoon dried basil or up to 1/4 cup chopped fresh*
*freshly ground pepper to taste*

In the early morning of the day you plan to serve this, put the ricotta cheese in a fine-mesh strainer and let it drain at room temperature for at least 5 hours, stirring occasionally without pushing it through the strainer. Later in the day, prepare the dough as directed and set it aside in a warm spot. As the dough rises, make the filling.

Steam the broccoli in a covered pot for about 5 minutes, until not quite tender. Remove the steamer from the pot, sprinkle the broccoli with a pinch or 2 of salt, and set aside.

Heat the olive oil in a large skillet and add the onion. Sauté over medium heat for 5 minutes, stir in the garlic, and cook another minute or 2. Remove from the heat.

In a large bowl, combine the drained ricotta cheese, the onions, provolone and Parmesan cheeses, olives, and basil. Season to taste with a little salt and pepper. When the dough appears nearly doubled, preheat the oven to 450°. Generously dust a large, heavy baking sheet—12 by 18 inches is a good size—with cornmeal and set it aside.

When the dough has doubled, punch it down, knead briefly, and then let it rest for 5 minutes. On a floured surface, roll the dough into an oval roughly 19 inches long and 15 inches wide. Draw an imaginary line down the center of the dough, lengthwise, and spoon the cheese filling just to one side of it, spreading it out but leaving at least a 1-inch margin at the edge. Arrange the broccoli on top of the cheese. Run a fingertip moistened with water around the outer edge, then fold the other half of the dough over *without stretching it*. Pinch the seam to-

*(continued)*

(continued)

gether and curl it up to seal it. Find a helper, if you can, then carefully lift the dough onto the prepared sheet, laying it on diagonally. (If you have to curl the calzone into a crescent to fit it on, that's fine. And if you can't find a helper, slowly slide a skinny baking sheet under it to move it.)

Bake the calzone on the lower rack of the oven for 25 minutes, until nicely browned. Slide it onto a big rack and cool for 10 minutes before slicing. You can wrap cooled leftovers in foil and reheat them right in the foil. ◆

## Broccoli and Sausage Torta

*Makes 10 servings*

This "cake"—like a calzone—is yet another way to bake a savory filling in bread, in this case the Parmesan cheese bread on page 105. There's nothing rigid about the filling; I just included some of my favorite things, and you should do the same. Leftover cooked chicken would be great in addition to the sausage, as would cooked shrimp if you're splurging. Try not to overcook the broccoli at the outset, remembering that it will cook further in the oven. And though you can vary the cheese in the filling, do use Parmesan as the base, because it will help soak up excess liquid that might otherwise dampen the bottom crust. Because this is so substantial, all you really need with it is wine and a salad.

1 recipe Sage-Scented Parmesan Cheese Bread (*page 105*), omitting the sage

FILLING

1 pound hot Italian sausage
1 large head of broccoli (about 1½ pounds)
1 large onion, chopped
1 large green bell pepper, seeded and chopped
3 garlic cloves, minced
¼ cup canned crushed tomatoes in puree or chopped fresh
2 teaspoons dried basil or 2 tablespoons chopped fresh
salt and freshly ground pepper to taste
½ cup (2 ounces) freshly grated Parmesan cheese
1½ cups (¼ pound) grated provolone or mozzarella cheese
egg wash: 1 egg beaten with 1 tablespoon milk

Prepare the dough as directed and set it aside to rise. As the bread rises, prepare the filling.

Bring several quarts of water to a boil in a medium saucepan. Prick the sausage a number of times with a fork, then drop it in the water. Bring the water back to a boil and boil for 5 minutes to render some of the fat. Transfer the sausage to a plate and cool.

Cut the broccoli—including the peeled stalk—into bite-size pieces; don't cut through the flowerets—keep them whole. Put an inch of water and a steamer basket in a medium-large pot and add the broccoli. Steam for a few minutes, then remove from the heat while the broccoli still offers resistance to a knife point. Transfer the broccoli to a plate and cool.

When the sausage is cool enough to handle, cut it into 1-inch pieces. Heat a large skillet and brown the sausage in it over medium-high heat for 5 minutes. Remove the sausage pieces with a slotted spoon, then add the onion and pepper to the skillet. Sauté over medium-high heat for 5 to 8 minutes, stirring often; then stir in the garlic and cook for another few seconds. Stir in the crushed or chopped tomatoes and the basil. Cook briefly, then scrape the contents of the skillet into a large bowl. Season to taste with salt and pepper. Cool, then fold in the broccoli and sausage. Generously sprinkle a large baking sheet with cornmeal or semolina.

To assemble the torta, punch the fully doubled dough down and knead briefly on a floured surface. Cover and let rest for 5 minutes, then roll the dough into an approximate 16-inch-diameter circle; it doesn't have to be a perfect circle. Transfer the circle of dough to the baking sheet and center it.

Imagine a 9-inch circle in the center of the dough and sprinkle the Parmesan cheese over it. Arrange the broccoli/sausage mixture over it, then the provolone or mozzarella on top. Starting anywhere along the edge, grab the edge and pull it toward the center of the filling, coming to rest at a point on the filling just short of center. Now go back to the edge and pull it up again at the point where the dough overlaps. (This is a little tricky to explain. Just try to visualize the finished bread: a circle with about 6 or 7 pleats, with a small hole in the center where the tops of the pleats don't quite meet; it will look something like a pleated volcano.) As you pull each pleat up, moisten the edge of it with a pastry brush dipped in water so the next pleat will adhere. Cover loosely with plastic wrap and set aside for 15 minutes; preheat the oven to 400°.

After 15 minutes, brush the surface sparingly with the egg wash. Bake for 40 minutes, then transfer to a rack and cool for several minutes before slicing into wedges. ◆

# Eggplant Strudel

*Makes 8 servings*

In this loose adaptation of a strudel, a moussaka-type filling is layered in the center of a dough rectangle; the sides of the dough are cut into strips, then folded over to create a sort of mock braid. It looks very spiffy and tastes festive, so it's perfect for an intimate gathering of friends. This strudel, a bottle of Greek wine, and perhaps the High-Fiber Peach and Raspberry Crunch (page 280) would be a splendid way to pass a cool summer evening.

1 recipe Light Wheat Pizza or Calzone
   Dough (page 129)

FILLING
10 to 12 sun-dried tomatoes (not oil-packed)
1 large eggplant
1/3 cup (approximately) good-quality olive oil
a little unbleached flour (for dredging the
   eggplant)
salt
1 large onion, chopped
3 garlic cloves, minced
2 cups (about 8 ounces) crumbled feta cheese
1/2 cup ricotta cheese
1 egg
1/3 cup chopped fresh parsley
1/3 cup chopped fresh basil
pinch of ground cinnamon
1/2 cup (2 ounces) lightly toasted chopped
   walnuts
freshly ground pepper to taste
egg wash: 1 egg beaten with 1 tablespoon
   milk

Prepare the dough as directed and set aside to rise. As it rises, prepare the filling. Pour enough boiling water over the tomatoes to cover. Let sit for 10 minutes, then drain and chop. Set aside.

From the thickest part of the eggplant, cut 8 1/2-inch-thick slices; save the rest of the eggplant for another use. Heat a little less than half the olive oil in a large, heavy skillet. When it is hot, dredge half the eggplant slices in the flour and put them in the skillet. Over medium-high heat, fry the slices for several minutes on each side, until they brown. If they seem to soak up all of the oil, just press down on the slices with a fork; that should put some oil back in the pan. Transfer the pieces to a large plate.

Add all but about 2 tablespoons of the remaining oil to the pan and fry the second batch of eggplant. Remove those to the plate also and sprinkle all the slices very lightly with salt. Reserve.

Wipe the skillet dry with paper towels, then heat the rest of the olive oil. Add the onion and sauté over medium-high heat for about 5 minutes, stirring occasionally; stir in the garlic, cook for another few seconds, then remove from the heat.

In a mixing bowl, combine the cheeses, egg, parsley, basil, cinnamon, walnuts, and sun-dried tomatoes; stir in a few generous grinds of pepper.

When the dough has doubled, assemble the strudel as follows. Punch the dough down and knead briefly on a floured surface. Pinch off a small piece of dough, not quite the size of a tennis ball, and reserve. Let the bulk of the dough rest, covered with plastic wrap, for 5 minutes. Lightly flour your work area and roll the dough into a 12-by 18-inch rectangle. Mentally divide the dough into thirds, lengthwise, then lay the eggplant slices down the center third, overlapping slightly. Pile the cheese mixture on top of that, flatten a little, then spread the onions over that.

Cut the flanking thirds of dough into 1½-inch strips at right angles to the filling. Starting at one end, fold the strips of dough over the filling, alternating from side to side; don't fold them straight over, but at about a 45° angle. When you get to the end, tuck the end strips under the strudel.

Find a second pair of hands to help move the strudel to a large cornmeal-dusted baking sheet. Using a pastry brush, lightly moisten with water a narrow band of dough around the bottom of the strudel. Roll the reserved piece of dough into a rope, 36 inches long, and trim the moistened bottom of the strudel with it. Cover with a foil tent and let rest for 25 minutes while you preheat the oven to 400°.

Just before baking, brush the surface of the strudel sparingly with the egg wash. Bake for 10 minutes, then reduce the heat to 375° and bake for another 45 minutes. Transfer the strudel to a large rack and cool for 10 minutes before slicing and serving.

VARIATION: *You could easily add a layer of browned, seasoned ground lamb to the filling; cook it with the onion.* ♦

# Basic Pizza

*Makes 1 12- by 18-inch
pizza (6 to 8 servings)*

Homemade pizza is so easy to make, and so superior to all others, that there's really no reason to settle for anything else. I think if there's one secret to really good homemade pizza, it's the crust. Unfortunately, that's usually the first thing to go if there's a time crunch. But you just can't buy a frozen crust—and seldom run across a pizza parlor crust—that can compare to homemade. The other thing that sets your own apart from the others is the care that's taken with the toppings; I've discussed some possibilities below.

*1 recipe Light Wheat Pizza or Calzone
Dough (page 129)*

TOPPING

*¼ cup good-quality olive oil*

*2 large onions, halved lengthwise and thinly
sliced*

*2 medium-size green bell peppers, seeded
and chopped or thinly sliced*

*salt and freshly ground pepper*

*2 garlic cloves, minced*

*2 to 3 cups tomato sauce, preferably
homemade*

*3 cups (½ pound) grated cheese, any one or
a combination of mozzarella, provolone,
Havarti, etc.*

Prepare the pizza dough as directed and set it aside to rise, covered, in a warm, draft-free spot. As the dough rises, prepare the topping. Heat the olive oil in a very large, heavy skillet. Add the onions and peppers and cook them over high heat, stirring often. Season to taste with salt and pepper. When the onions are just beginning to turn golden—about 10 minutes—stir in the garlic and remove the pan from the heat. When the dough is nearly doubled, dust a very large, heavy cookie or baking sheet—12 by 18 inches is perfect—with cornmeal and set it aside.

Once the dough has doubled, punch it down, knead briefly, then let the dough rest for 5 minutes. Roll the dough into a rectangle the same size as the pan, then lift it into the pan; what I find works well is to *lightly* flour the dough, fold it in half, and then very quickly lift it into the pan and unfold it before the dough has a chance to stick to itself. Push the dough up against the sides of the pan so the edge runs a little up the sides.

Pour the tomato sauce over the dough and spread it around evenly with a spoon, to within ½ inch of the outer edge. Spread the onions and peppers evenly over the sauce, then bake on the center rack for 15 minutes. Slide the pizza out of the oven, then sprinkle the cheese evenly over the top. Bake for another 7 minutes, until the cheese is just starting to brown. Lift one end of the pizza out of the pan with a spatula and slide it onto a cutting surface. Cut and serve right away.

NOTES AND VARIATIONS: *There must be a zillion ways to vary this, and I go half crazy trying to accommodate my own clan with one big pizza.*

On any given day we might add some steamed broccoli or cooked, drained kale; chopped olives; cooked sausage; fried eggplant slices; steamed or fried summer squash or zucchini slices; marinated artichoke hearts. And in the summer, we might use half the amount of tomato sauce and substitute sliced tomatoes for the rest. And if you'd rather, you can make 2 or 3 smaller pizzas and bake them on tiles, as described on page 130.

Just in case you don't have a favorite tomato sauce recipe in your memory file, we usually just sauté one small onion and one minced garlic clove in 2 or 3 tablespoons of olive oil, add one 28-ounce can of crushed tomatoes (in puree) and maybe 1¹/₂ teaspoons each of dried basil and oregano. (When available, we'd use fresh tomatoes and herbs of course, to taste.) Simmer over low heat, covered, for about 10 minutes and season to taste with salt and pepper. ♦

Homemade pizza, baked in a pan, is a fine meal indeed. But connoisseurs will tell you, rightly, that there's nothing quite like the cracker-crisp crust you get with tile-baked pizza. (See page 130 for information on buying and using tiles.) Like anything else, it takes practice to get the hang of it, so here are a few secrets worth sharing.

*Start small.* I find that individual-size pizzas are simpler to slide onto tiles than one humongous one, though—with a little practice—you may find it easy to maneuver a large pizza into the oven. I have four sheets of heavy-duty cardboard I build my pizzas on, each of which is just large enough to hold an 8- to 10-inch pizza. You don't have to use cardboard; it could be thin plywood or the bottom of a removable tart pan. Kitchen shops sell wooden paddles, called *peels,* that are also good for this, but be sure to buy one that's small enough to move around easily in your oven. No matter what you use:

*Dust it heavily with cornmeal.* Failure to do this is likely to cause the rolled dough to stick, resulting in that syndrome feared by all home bakers known as The Slide, Dangle, and Splat (you try to slide it, but the pizza just dangles off the edge, and the topping goes splat on the tiles). After you roll your dough, put it on the cornmeal-dusted cardboard, peel, or whatever, pressing down lightly with your fingertips all around to make little depressions that will help contain the sauce; keep the very edge on the thick side. Sauce it, top it, and get it in the oven as quickly as you can. The longer you wait, the more likely the dough will start to stick. Agitate your board a tad, just before you slide the pizza in the oven, to make sure it isn't stuck to the sheet. If it is, gently pull up the part that's stuck and dust underneath with cornmeal.

*Slide the back pizzas in first and then the front ones.* Just get the board down near the tiles, about where you want the pizza to land, say a little prayer, and pull back quickly. The pizza should drop right off. Once you get the knack, you'll find yourself doing a little forward flick of the wrist before you pull back.

*Be careful, when you're doing all this, not to get burned.* Reaching unprotected arms around in your oven can be hazardous to your health. Wear long sleeves. Oven mitts are a good idea too, but they are liable to make sliding the pizzas onto the tiles a bit more cumbersome. If you aren't comfortable reaching into your oven, I suggest you buy a peel, which will keep your arms away from the hot interior surface of the oven.

*You can finish a big pan pizza on the tiles for the last 5 or 7 minutes to crisp the crust.* Just slip a spatula under one end, lift the crust out of the pan, and slide the pizza onto the hot tiles.

# Creamy Onion Pizza with Fontina and Cheddar

*Makes 1 12- by 18-inch pizza*
*(6 to 8 servings)*

*T*his is for people who like a rich, cheesy pizza with no red sauce. Because it is creamy, it should be served with something lean and sharp: a salad plate of marinated artichoke hearts and mushrooms, perhaps with a selection of sliced raw vegetables—what you might call a vegetarian antipasto. A cooked green such as kale or spinach, drizzled with red wine vinegar, would be excellent. I prefer big, sweet Vidalia onions for this, but the regular yellow onions will do just as well.

*1 recipe Light Wheat Pizza or Calzone*
  *Dough (page 129)*

TOPPING
*2 tablespoons unsalted butter*
*2 tablespoons good-quality olive oil*
*6 cups (2 to 3 large) halved (lengthwise) and*
  *thinly sliced large onions*
*1/4 teaspoon salt*
*3 garlic cloves, minced*
*freshly ground pepper*
*1/3 cup heavy cream*
*10 to 15 black olives, preferably a good*
  *imported variety like Kalamata, pitted and*
  *sliced*
*2 cups (5 to 6 ounces) grated sharp Cheddar*
  *cheese*
*2 cups (5 to 6 ounces) grated Fontina cheese*

Prepare the dough as directed and set it aside in a warm, draft-free spot to rise. To make the filling, heat the butter and oil in a very large skillet. Add the onions and salt and sauté over medium heat for about 20 minutes, stirring often; you want them to turn a nice golden shade. If they start to get crispy brown, turn the heat down. Stir in the garlic near the very end, cook for another minute, then remove from the heat. Preheat the oven to 450° and generously dust a 12- by 18-inch baking sheet with cornmeal.

Once the dough has doubled, punch it down and knead briefly. Let the dough rest for 5 minutes, then roll it out on a lightly floured surface until it is the same size as the pan. Transfer the dough to the pan, pushing it up against the sides.

Spread the onions evenly over the surface of the dough, then sprinkle them with plenty of pepper. Spoon the cream over the onions, covering as much territory as possible, then scatter the olives over the onions. Bake the pizza on the center rack for 15 minutes, then pull the pan out. Mix the cheeses and sprinkle evenly over the surface of the pizza. Bake for about another 7 minutes, just until the cheese melts and starts to bubble. Slice and serve right away. ♦

# Mushroom Barley-Crusted Pizza

*Makes 1 12- by 18-inch pizza*
*(6 to 8 servings)*

Mushrooms and barley, no strangers to one another, are joined here to make one of the earthiest, most mouthwatering pizzas to come down the pike in a while. You'll need to make the Barley Corn Bread; bake one half of the dough as a loaf and use one half for this. Be sure to buy fresh, firm mushrooms, because a bad batch can ruin this. Other melting cheese—like Fontina or Jarlsberg—can be substituted for the mozzarella.

*1 recipe Barley Corn Bread (page 85)*

TOPPING
*3 tablespoons unsalted butter*
*2 large onions, halved lengthwise and thinly sliced*
*1¹/₂ pounds fresh mushrooms, stems removed, cleaned and sliced*
*2 garlic cloves, minced*
*salt*
*3 tablespoons good-quality olive oil*
*freshly ground pepper*
*3 cups (¹/₂ pound) grated mozzarella cheese*
*¹/₄ cup green or black olives, preferably a good imported variety like Kalamata, pitted and sliced*
*¹/₄ cup minced fresh parsley*

Prepare the dough as directed and set it aside in a warm, draft-free spot to rise. As that rises, generously dust a very large, heavy baking sheet with cornmeal and set it aside. (If you don't have one that's 12 by 18 inches, it would be better to bake this on 2 medium sheets.) Preheat the oven to 450° when the dough has almost doubled. After the dough has risen, punch it down, knead briefly, and divide in half. (Set aside half to bake as a loaf.) Let the other half rest, covered, as you prepare the topping.

In a very large enameled or stainless-steel skillet (best not to use bare cast iron because it will darken the mushrooms too much), melt the butter over medium-high heat. Add the onions and sauté, stirring occasionally, for about 7 minutes, until translucent. Stir in the mushrooms and garlic, add a big pinch of salt, and stir to coat. Cover for 2 to 4 minutes, then uncover, turn the heat up, and cook off almost all of the excess moisture. Scrape onto a plate to cool.

Roll the dough out into a rectangle the same size as the pan. Carefully lift it into the pan, pushing the dough a little up the sides. Spread evenly with the mushroom mixture and drizzle the olive oil over the top. Give the pizza a healthy dusting of pepper, then bake on the center rack for 15 minutes. Remove the pizza from the oven, sprinkle on the cheese and olives, and bake for 5 more minutes, just until the cheese melts. Lift one end of the pizza out of the pan with a spatula and slide it onto a cutting surface. Spread the parsley over the top, slice, and serve hot.

NOTE: *This will make as many as 4 individual pizzas, baked on tiles. See page 130 for pointers.* ◆

# *Potato and Jarlsberg Pizza*

*Makes 1 12- by 18-inch pizza (6 to 8 servings)*

This pizza uses pesto, though you could easily skip that layer and you'd still have something great to eat. If you do leave out the pesto, however, at least jazz up the potatoes in the skillet by adding some chopped fresh or dried herbs of your choice. Basil, chives, or parsley would be good.

*1 recipe Light Wheat Pizza or Calzone Dough (page 129)*

TOPPING

*¼ cup good-quality olive oil*
*4 cups (about 1½ pounds) scrubbed, very thinly sliced red-skinned potatoes, with skins on*
*1 large onion, chopped*
*salt and freshly ground pepper*
*2 garlic cloves, minced (omit if you're using pesto)*
*¾ cup pesto (page 145)*
*3 cups (½ pound) grated Jarlsberg cheese*

Prepare the pizza dough as directed and set it aside to rise in a warm, draft-free spot. As that rises, make the topping. Heat the olive oil in a very large skillet. Add the potatoes and cook over high heat, stirring almost constantly—otherwise they'll stick. As you stir, try to separate the slices from one another so everything cooks evenly.

After 5 minutes, add the onion and continue to cook, stirring, for 2 to 3 more min-

utes. Lower the heat a little, season the potatoes with salt and pepper, and scatter the garlic on top if you're using it. Cover and let cook for about 5 minutes, until the potatoes are just tender. Scrape the potatoes from the pan onto a large plate, then correct the seasoning with salt and pepper. Preheat the oven to 450°. Generously dust a large, heavy baking sheet—12 by 18 inches is a good size—with cornmeal and set it aside.

When the dough has doubled, punch it down and knead briefly. Cover and let rest for 5 minutes, then roll it into a rectangle the same size as the pan. Lift the dough into the pan and push it up the sides slightly. (It helps, when you're lifting it into the pan, to flour the dough lightly, quickly fold it in half, lift into the pan, and unfold.)

Spread the pesto evenly over the dough, then spread the potatoes evenly over that. Bake on the center rack for 15 minutes, pull the pizza out, and sprinkle the cheese over the top. Bake for 5 to 7 minutes more, just until the cheese is bubbly. Lift one end of the pizza out of the pan with a spatula and slide it onto a cutting surface. Slice and serve right away.

NOTE: *You can, if you wish, bake 3 individual pizzas on oven tiles using this recipe, dividing the ingredients evenly among them. See page 138 for pointers.* ♦

## Herb Cream Cheese and Tomato Pizza

*Makes 1 12- by 18-inch pizza
(6 to 8 servings)*

*I*n August, a slice of this pizza, with an ear of fresh corn and a frosty brew on the side, and a fellow couldn't ask for anything more out of life. But even in winter, with not-very-good tomatoes and dried herbs, you'll love this pizza.

*1 recipe Light Wheat Pizza or Calzone
Dough (page 129) or ¹/₂ recipe Italian
Herb Bread (page 93)*

TOPPING
*¹/₂ pound cream cheese, softened*
*3 cups (¹/₂ pound) grated Monterey Jack
cheese*
*3 tablespoons milk or light cream*
*¹/₃ cup chopped fresh herbs (any combination
of basil, oregano, parsley, etc.) or 2
tablespoons dried*
*¹/₂ teaspoon Dijon mustard*
*large pinch of cayenne pepper*
*2 large fresh tomatoes, thinly sliced*

Prepare the dough as directed and let it rise in a warm, draft-free spot. As the dough rises, prepare the topping. Using a wooden spoon, cream the cream cheese, half the Monterey Jack, the milk or cream, herbs, mustard, and cayenne. Set aside.

When the dough has nearly doubled, preheat the oven to 425°. Generously dust a large, heavy baking sheet—12 by 18 inches is the best size—with cornmeal and set it aside. Once the dough has doubled, punch it down, knead briefly, and let rest for 5 minutes on a lightly floured surface. Roll the dough out about the same size as the baking sheet, then carefully maneuver it onto the sheet. It sometimes helps to lightly flour the surface of the dough, fold it in half, quickly lift it into the pan, then unfold it before it has a chance to stick to itself.

Dot the surface of the dough with the herb cream cheese and spread it around with a fork; it doesn't have to be perfectly even or cover every speck of the dough—it will spread out. Bake for 10 minutes on the bottom rack of the oven.

Remove the pizza from the oven and arrange the tomato slices evenly over the cream cheese. Bake for 10 minutes more, this time on the center rack. Slide the pizza out again and sprinkle with the remaining Monterey Jack cheese. Bake for 5 minutes more, just until the cheese melts and bubbles. Slip a spatula under one end of the pizza and then slide it out onto a cutting board. Slice and serve right away. ◆

# Onion Skillet Bread

*Makes 2 10-inch breads*

This recipe and the following one are what I call skillet breads, or skillet pizzas, though the finished product is much thicker than most pizzas. One other difference is that the emphasis here is on the bread, and the goal to just give it an interesting flavor, whereas with pizza the crust generally plays second fiddle to the toppings. These two breads will serve 6 as a main course (2 big pieces each) or 8 to 10 if you include a number of other dishes—maybe a big salad or antipasto, a hearty soup, slices of fresh tomato, and a dessert.

*1 recipe Light Wheat Pizza or Calzone*
  *Dough (page 129)*

TOPPING
*7 tablespoons plus 1 teaspoon good-quality*
  *olive oil*
*2 medium onions, halved lengthwise and*
  *thinly sliced*
*2 garlic cloves, thinly sliced*
*2 teaspoons dried rosemary or 1 tablespoon*
  *chopped fresh*
*salt and freshly ground pepper*

Prepare the dough as directed and set it aside. While the dough rises, heat 3 tablespoons of the olive oil in a 10-inch cast-iron skillet. Add the sliced onions and sauté them over medium-high heat, stirring occasionally, for 5 minutes. Stir in the garlic and rosemary, cook for another minute, then remove from the heat. Scrape the onions onto a plate, keeping the skillet nearby. Preheat the oven to 425°.

You will need a second 10-inch cast-iron skillet or a 10-inch glass or tin pie pan. Oil this second pan with the teaspoon of olive oil, then rub the same paper towel around in the original skillet to distribute the oil.

Once the dough has doubled, punch it down, turn it out onto a lightly floured surface, and divide it in half. Knead each half briefly, cover with plastic wrap, and let them rest for 5 minutes. Then roll each one into a 10-inch circle on a lightly floured surface. Lift a circle into each pan and flatten with your fingers, just so the dough pushes up snugly against the sides.

Let the dough sit in the pans, covered with plastic wrap, for 5 minutes. Slash the surface of each about 1/8 inch deep using a sharp paring knife; make 5 or 6 slashes, in a random pattern. Drizzle 2 tablespoons of olive oil over each bread, followed by a pinch of salt and a dusting of black pepper. Divide the onions between the 2 breads, scattering them around the top, then bake them for 30 to 35 minutes, until the bottoms are golden brown. They can be baked side by side, if you have the room, or one above the other, in which case you should keep them staggered and switch their positions about midway into the baking. If the onions are getting too dark, cover with foil. Lift the breads out of the pans and onto a cutting board. Slice into wedges and serve hot.

NOTE: *One of these can be cooled and frozen for a later meal. Wrap in foil and warm the frozen bread in a hot 400° oven for about 20 minutes before cutting.* ◆

## Pesto and Walnut Skillet Bread

*Makes 2 10-inch breads*

This pan-style pizza—like a number of other creations in this book—is flavored with pesto, that basil-based sauce of summer people tend to deify once they've tasted it. I came up with this recipe one day when I was scraping the bottom of a jar of pesto a friend had given me—the same day I happened to have some pizza dough on the rise. In the flash of a light bulb I brushed pesto on the dough, added some walnuts and onions, and stuck it in the oven. Life hasn't been quite the same since. I have given a basic pesto recipe below, which yields more than you'll actually need. But there's no use making just a small amount, because you'll quickly use the rest as a pasta sauce. These 2 breads will serve as many as 10 people, as part of a nice big summer meal including corn on the cob, sliced fresh tomatoes, green beans vinaigrette, and a fruit pie.

*1 recipe Light Wheat Pizza or Calzone Dough (page 129)*

TOPPING

*3 tablespoons plus 1 teaspoon good-quality olive oil*

*2 medium-size onions, halved lengthwise and thinly sliced*

*1/2 cup pesto (recipe follows)*

*1/2 cup (about 2 ounces) chopped walnuts*

Prepare the dough as directed and set it aside. Make the topping: While the dough rises, heat the 3 tablespoons of olive oil in a 10-inch cast-iron skillet. Add the sliced onions and sauté them over medium-high heat, stirring occasionally, for 5 minutes. Remove from the heat, then scrape the onions onto a plate, keeping the skillet nearby. Preheat the oven to 425°.

You will need a second 10-inch cast-iron skillet or a 10-inch glass or tin pie pan. Using a paper towel, oil this second pan with the teaspoon of olive oil, then rub the same paper towel around in the original skillet to distribute the oil.

Once it has doubled, punch the dough down, turn it out onto a lightly floured surface, and divide it in half. Knead each half briefly, cover with plastic wrap, and let them rest for 5 minutes. Then roll each one into a 10-inch circle on a lightly floured surface. Lift a circle of dough into each pan and flatten with your fingers, just so the dough pushes up snugly against the sides.

Let the dough sit in the pans, covered with plastic wrap, for 5 minutes. Slash the surface of each about 1/8 inch deep (*not through the dough*) using a sharp paring knife; make about 5 or 6 slashes, at random, so the oil in the topping saturates the dough. Spoon 1/4 cup of pesto onto each, spreading it evenly with the back of the spoon. Sprinkle 1/4 cup of walnuts over each, then divide the onions between them, scattering them around the top. Bake for 30 to 35 minutes, until the bottoms are golden brown. They can be baked side by side, if you have the room, or one above the other, in which case you should keep them staggered and switch their positions about midway through the baking. If the tops of the breads start to get too dark near the end of the baking, cover loosely with foil. Lift the breads out of the pans and onto a cutting board. Slice into wedges and serve hot.

VARIATION: *I sometimes melt a little cheese on these during the last few minutes. Provolone is especially good.*

FREEZING: *If you like, the bread (without any cheese) can be cooled and frozen for a later meal. Just wrap well in foil and warm the frozen bread in a hot 400° oven for 20 minutes before cutting.* ♦

## *Basic Pesto*

*Makes about 1 cup*

2¹/₂ *cups lightly packed fresh basil leaves*
2 *to 3 garlic cloves, peeled*
²/₃ *cup good-quality olive oil*
¹/₄ *cup (about 1 ounce) walnuts or pine nuts*
¹/₈ *teaspoon salt*
³/₄ *cup freshly grated Parmesan cheese*

In a blender or food processor, process the basil, garlic, olive oil, nuts, and salt until smooth, stopping occasionally to scrape the sides down. Scrape the mixture into a small bowl and stir in the Parmesan cheese. Refrigerate until needed, tightly covered. If you won't use it within a few days, freeze it. ♦

## *Rye-Crusted Potato and Cumin Seed Galette*

*Makes 1 large galette (8 servings)*

This is a big, very attractive free-form tart of overlapping potatoes baked with a little cream and cheese in a rye crust. And it is *really* sensational. I would serve this hot, with tomato soup, to a crowd of hungry skiers or at room temperature as part of a summer buffet. Because the filling is dry, it can be partially assembled in advance, covered, and refrigerated for several hours before baking, without fear of the crust becoming soggy. I love the seasoning here, toasted cumin with a shake of chili powder.

*1 recipe Sour Rye Pastry (page 189)*

FILLING
*6 (about 2 pounds) medium-large red-skinned potatoes, peeled and sliced ¹/₈ inch thick*
*1¹/₂ cups (¹/₄ pound) grated Monterey Jack cheese*
*¹/₃ cup heavy cream*
*salt and freshly ground pepper*
*1 teaspoon toasted cumin seed (see note below)*
*¹/₄ teaspoon mild chili powder*
*2 garlic cloves, minced*
*2 tablespoons chopped fresh parsley*

Prepare the pastry as directed, using cumin seed. Chill the dough whole instead of di-

*(continued)*

(continued)

viding it in half. As the dough chills, prepare the filling.

Put the potatoes in a medium pot with about 2 quarts of salted water. Bring to a boil and cook the potatoes for about 6 or 7 minutes, until not quite tender; this is important, because you don't want to assemble this with fragile potatoes. Slowly pour the potatoes into a colander and rinse under cold running water for 30 seconds. Drain for several minutes, then lay the potatoes on sheets of paper towels to dry.

After the dough has chilled, get out your largest *cookie* sheet; you need something without sides, so you can roll the dough right on it. Place the dough in the center of the sheet and roll it into a large oval or circle, roughly 1/8 inch thick; on my biggest, squarish sheet I can get about a 13-inch circle. Sprinkle half the grated cheese over the dough.

Starting in the center, arrange the potatoes in overlapping concentric circles; sprinkle just a little of the remaining cheese over each circle before you put down the next one. Continue making circles of potatoes up to the edge, leaving a 1-inch margin of dough all around. Fold the margin of pastry up and over the last row of potatoes; it may help to slip a spatula under the edge to lift it. Cover the galette with plastic wrap and refrigerate for at least 15 minutes and up to several hours; preheat the oven to 400° toward the end of the chilling time.

Just before baking, brush half the cream over the potatoes. Sprinkle the galette with a big pinch of salt and lots of pepper, then bake on the center rack for 20 minutes. Take

the galette out and slowly pour the remaining cream over the top. Sprinkle on the cumin seed, dust with several big pinches of chili powder, and scatter the garlic over the top. Bake on the top rack for 20 minutes more, until lightly browned and a little bubbly. Slide the galette onto a large cooling rack and leave it there until you slice it into wedges; sprinkle with the parsley just before slicing.

NOTE: *To toast the cumin seed, put it in a small, heavy skillet and toast over medium heat for several minutes, shaking the pan often. The seeds are done when they've turned a shade or two darker and their fragrance is released; they burn easily, so watch them carefully. Pour the seeds onto a plate to cool.* ◆

## Spiced Chicken, Spinach, and Cheese Hand Pies

*Makes 4 to 6 servings*

A hand pie is the same thing as a half-moon pie, basically just a savory turnover, an informal little pie. This variation uses leftover chicken, quickly cooked in spices and tomatoes, then layered in the pastry with spinach, goat cheese, and Monterey Jack. To hasten the process you can use defrosted frozen spinach, adding it where I add the fresh and cooking it basically the same way; the important thing is to cook off the moisture so the pie doesn't leak. My first choice for the pastry here is the Three-Grain Butter Pastry (page 193); the egg in it makes it just that much easier to handle. The All-American Pie Pastry (page 184) is also excellent. I would make a meal of these pies, guacamole with chips, and beer.

*1 recipe Three-Grain Butter Pastry (page 193)*

FILLING

*2 tablespoons flavorless vegetable oil*

*2 tablespoons unsalted butter*

*1 medium-size onion, chopped*

*2 garlic cloves, minced*

*2 teaspoons ground cumin*

*2 teaspoons dried oregano*

*1 teaspoon mild chili powder*

*1 teaspoon ground coriander*

*1¹/₂ cups leftover cooked (skinless) chicken, cut into bite-size strips*

*¹/₂ cup canned crushed tomatoes in puree*

*salt and freshly ground pepper*

*10 ounces fresh spinach, stems removed, washed, and chopped, or 1 10-ounce box defrosted frozen chopped spinach*

*1 cup (3 ounces) Monterey Jack cheese in ¹/₂-inch cubes*

*3 ounces chèvre or other goat cheese, crumbled*

Prepare and chill the pastry as directed. Meanwhile, make the filling. Heat the oil and butter in a heavy Dutch oven or pot. Add the onion and sauté over medium heat for 5 minutes, stirring occasionally. Stir in the garlic, spices, herbs, and chicken. Cook, stirring, for 1 minute; then add the tomatoes. Heat the ingredients through, then re-move from the heat and season to taste with salt and pepper. Scrape the contents of the pan onto a plate to cool, then put the pot back on the stove.

If you're using fresh spinach, add just enough water to the pot to cover the bottom of it, then add the spinach and a pinch of salt. Bring to a boil, cover, then reduce the heat and cook at a low boil for 3 minutes. Uncover and cook off the excess moisture, then transfer the spinach to a plate to cool. If you're using frozen spinach, squeeze as much liquid out of it as possible. Preheat the oven to 400°.

When the ingredients have cooled, roll half the pastry into a 12-inch circle on a piece of wax paper. Draw an imaginary line down the center of it, then—leaving a ³/₄- to 1-inch margin of dough around the edge—layer half the ingredients just to one side of that line: half the Jack cheese first, then the chicken mixture, spinach, and finally the goat cheese. Lightly moisten the edge with water, then fold the uncovered edge over, line up the edges, and press to seal. Curl the edge up and pinch down again for a better seal.

Transfer the pie to a large, ungreased baking sheet and poke several steam vents in the top. Repeat this procedure for the other pie, then bake for 40 minutes. Cool the pies on a rack for several minutes, then slice and serve.

NOTE: *Any of these hand-held pies or turnovers can be brushed with a little milk or cream just before baking if you want a glossy finish.* ◆

# North Country Turnovers

*Makes 6 large turnovers*

Perhaps you've heard of the *pasty* (page 151), that half-moon of pastry filled with meat and potatoes that Cornish miners brought with them to Michigan's Upper Peninsula. Well, this is its slightly refined New England cousin. Instead of the lard crust you'd get with a pasty, I use a cream cheese pastry, and instead of meat and potatoes there's sauerkraut, ham, and apples. At dinner I'd serve them with stewed kale or a steamed green vegetable, preceded by a thick seafood soup.

1 recipe Cream Cheese Pastry (*page 197*)

FILLING

1 cup sauerkraut

1 teaspoon mustard, preferably a good German-style brand

1/2 cup finely chopped Canadian bacon or ham

1/2 cup (about 2 ounces) finely diced sharp Cheddar cheese

1/2 cup finely chopped peeled Granny Smith apple

egg wash: 1 egg beaten with 1 tablespoon milk

Prepare the pastry as directed. After it has chilled, lightly flour a work surface and roll the dough into an approximate 16-inch circle, about 1/8 inch thick; dust the surface of the dough lightly with flour if it sticks to the pin.

Using a 6-inch-diameter cereal bowl or other round object as a guide, cut 4 circles of dough with a sharp paring knife. Stack the circles between sheets of wax paper on a plate. Cover and refrigerate. Dust the excess flour from the dough scraps and pack them into a ball. Divide the ball in half, then flatten each half into a thin disk. Roll each disk into a circle slightly larger than 6 inches. Trim the circles with the bowl and knife, then stack with the other disks between sheets of wax paper. Cover with plastic wrap and refrigerate for 30 minutes.

Meanwhile, make the filling: Put the sauerkraut and any of its lingering juices into a small, nonaluminum saucepan and stir in the mustard. Cook over medium-high heat, stirring occasionally, until almost all of the excess liquid evaporates, about 5 minutes. Remove the pan from the heat before the sauerkraut begins to stick, then spread it on a plate to cool. Arrange the sauerkraut in 6 roughly equal piles. Preheat the oven to 400°.

Clear a large work area, then arrange all your ingredients in front of you. Have the bacon or ham, Cheddar cheese, and apple in separate bowls. Put a small bowl of water nearby.

Take one circle of dough from the refrigerator and place it in front of you. Draw an imaginary line across the center of the dough, from side to side, then spread a pile of sauerkraut just forward of the line, keeping it a good 1/2 inch back from the edge. On top of the sauerkraut, spread a slightly rounded tablespoon each of the ham or Canadian bacon, Cheddar cheese, and apple, keeping the filling back from the edge. Dip a finger into the bowl of water and lightly moisten about ¼ inch of the outer edge. Fold the back half of the circle over the front, lining up the edges. Press gently to seal, then transfer the turnover to a large, heavy baking sheet; better not to use a very dark one here. Crimp the edge with the tines of a fork to make a decorative, tightly sealed edge. Repeat for the remaining circles of dough.

Using a pastry brush, brush each of the turnovers with a little of the egg wash. Poke the surface of each turnover 2 or 3 times with the tines of a fork.

Bake the turnovers on the center rack for 10 minutes, then reduce the heat to 375°. Move the turnovers to the top rack and bake for another 15 to 20 minutes, until the bottoms are a dark golden and the tops a light golden. Transfer the turnovers to a rack and cool for 5 to 10 minutes before serving; use caution, because even after 10 minutes the filling can be very hot. ♦

# Broccoli Half-Moon Pie

*Makes 2 servings*

I often have an extra half recipe of pie pastry stored in the fridge. If there's no pie in my immediate future, I like to use the pastry to make this big turnover, or some variation on it, for a quick lunch or dinner. Start by collecting leftovers; then let your imagination tell you what might taste good together. In this case I had a little broccoli, which I steamed quickly, then I filled the rest of the pie out with basic stock items. Don't add anything that's too juicy.

*½ recipe any leftover pie pastry (pages 184–201)*

FILLING
*2 cups cut broccoli, mainly flowerets*
*2 tablespoons good-quality olive oil*
*1 small onion, halved lengthwise and sliced*
*1 garlic clove, minced*
*½ cup (2 ounces) freshly grated Parmesan cheese*
*6 to 8 green or black olives, preferably a good imported variety, pitted and chopped*
*about 5 cherry tomatoes*
*small handful of cheese cubes (Cheddar, Fontina, or other melting cheese)*
*salt and freshly ground pepper*

Preheat the oven to 400°. In a medium saucepan, steam the broccoli in a basket steamer until barely tender. Remove the basket and spread the broccoli on a plate to cool.

Meanwhile, heat the olive oil in a small skillet. Add the onion and sauté over medium heat for about 5 minutes, stirring occasionally. Stir in the garlic, cook for 5 more seconds, then remove from the heat.

To assemble the pie, roll the pastry into a 12-inch circle on a sheet of wax paper. Draw an imaginary line down the center of the circle and sprinkle the Parmesan cheese on one half, leaving a 1-inch margin of dough at the edge. On top of the Parmesan arrange the broccoli, onion and garlic, olives, cherry tomatoes, and cheese cubes. Season with a little salt and pepper.

Moisten the edge of the dough with water, then fold the uncovered half of pastry over the filled half, lining up the edges. Pinch the edges to seal the package, then curl the edge up a little for a better seal. Transfer the pie to an ungreased baking sheet and poke several steam vents in the top. Bake for 40 minutes. Cool briefly, then slice and serve. ♦

# Traditional Cornish Pasties

*Makes 4 large turnovers (4 ample servings)*

Here is the traditional hand-held meat-and-potatoes pie that put Michigan's Upper Peninsula—where Cornish miners first settled—on the culinary map. I use the All-American Pie Pastry for these, and I sometimes substitute lard for part of the vegetable shortening. Many of the apparently authentic recipes I've seen for pasty dough use suet, which I've never tried though other good cooks I know swear by it. And there is considerable debate, as there often is over traditional recipes, as to the precise ingredients: one source says no carrots allowed, another recipe uses them, and so forth. The cabbage isn't heretical, and I like the way it adds moisture to the filling.

*1 recipe All-American Pie Pastry (page 184)*

FILLING
*2 tablespoons unsalted butter*
*1 medium-size onion, halved lengthwise and sliced*
*2 cups thinly sliced green cabbage*
*1/2 pound boneless pork loin, cut into 1/4- to 1/2-inch cubes*
*1 1/2 cups diced peeled potatoes*
*salt and freshly ground pepper*

Prepare the pastry as directed, dividing it into 4 equal disks instead of 2; chill. Meanwhile, make the filling.

Heat the butter in a large skillet. Add the onion and cabbage and sauté over medium heat for 10 minutes, stirring occasionally. Scrape the contents of the pan into a bowl, stir in the pork and potatoes, and season to taste with salt and pepper. Preheat the oven to 425°.

Working with one disk of pastry at a time, roll it into an 8- to 9-inch circle on a sheet of lightly floured wax paper. Pile one-quarter of the filling onto half the pastry, leaving a 1-inch border of dough. Moisten the entire edge of the circle with water and fold the unfilled half of pastry over the filled half. Line up the edges and press to seal. Curl the edge up and pinch it again for a better seal. Transfer the pasty to a large, ungreased baking sheet, then repeat for the remaining ones. Poke several steam vents in the top of each with a fork.

Bake for 15 minutes, then reduce the heat to 350° and bake for another 45 minutes. Let the pasties cool for 5 minutes before serving. Be careful; all turnovers hold quite a bit of heat for some time. ♦

## Hot Ham and Cheese Turnovers

*Makes about 14 small turnovers*

H ere's an impressive appetizer or party nibble with a little zing to it. What you do is make a cream cheese and Cheddar spread, season with hot peppers and other tidbits, then fill little rounds of cream cheese pastry with it and bake to a turn. Do follow the instructions carefully, avoiding the temptation to put too much filling in each turnover; if they're over-stuffed, they almost always blow open, leaving you with a sheet of beautiful but empty turnovers, each attached to a little pile of burned cheese.

*1 recipe Cream Cheese Pastry (page 197)*

FILLING
*1/4 pound cream cheese, softened*
*1 1/2 cups (1/4 pound) grated sharp Cheddar cheese*
*1/4 cup minced ham*
*2 tablespoons minced fresh parsley*
*2 tablespoons green or black olives, preferably a good imported variety, pitted and minced*
*2 tablespoons minced jalapeño peppers*
*2 tablespoons minced onion*
*1 garlic clove, minced*
*1 teaspoon dried oregano*
*1/4 to 1/2 teaspoon cayenne pepper*
*egg wash: 1 egg beaten with 1 tablespoon milk*

Prepare the pastry as directed. After it has chilled, roll it out 1/8 inch thick on a lightly floured surface or sheet of wax paper. Keeping the cuts close together, cut as many 4-inch circles as you can (see note below) and transfer them to a wax paper–lined platter; if you need to make a second layer, cover the first with another sheet of wax paper and arrange the extras on it. Dust the flour off the scraps and keep rolling and cutting until all the dough is used up. Cover with plastic wrap and refrigerate while you make the filling.

To make the filling, combine all of the ingredients (except for the egg wash) in a bowl and mix well with a wooden spoon. Put a piece of wax paper nearby. Measure out a level tablespoon of the filling. Push it off the spoon and form it into a little foot-ball shape. Put it on the wax paper. Now, using your hands, form as many footballs of the same size as you have circles of dough, putting them on the wax paper. You'll prob-ably have leftover filling—good; save it for an omelet or spread it on crackers. Preheat the oven to 400°.

Take your dough circles out of the fridge. Put a small bowl of water in front of you and get out a fork. Working with one circle at a time, take a rolling pin and roll the circle just slightly to make a 5-inch-long oblong. Draw an imaginary line, from side to side, across the center of the oblong and put one ball of filling just forward of that line, leav-ing a good 3/4-inch margin of dough. Stick a finger in the water and lightly moisten the outer edge of the dough. Fold the back edge of the dough over the front, line up the edges, and press down to seal. Transfer the turnover to a large baking sheet, preferably not a very dark one, and crimp the edge with the tines of the fork. Repeat for the remaining circles of dough, leaving just a little space between them on the sheet.

When all of the turnovers are on the sheet, brush them sparingly with the egg wash and poke the top once with the fork so steam can escape. Bake in the center of the oven for 10 minutes, then reduce the heat to 375°. Move them to the top rack of the oven and bake for another 15 minutes, until the tops are a rich golden color. Transfer the turnovers to a cooling rack if you're not serving them right away.

NOTE: *I use an empty, washed tomato can—the 28-ounce size—for my 4-inch cutter. I've also used a doughnut cutter with the center hole cutter removed.* ◆

## Three-Cheese Apple Turnovers

*Makes 4 large turnovers (4 full or 8 half servings)*

I like cheese and fruit, but I like it even better in a crust. This is a classy, adult dessert—my kids aren't crazy about these—and one that can be made in a flash once the pastry is done. I like either of the pastries listed below. You wouldn't think so, but these turnovers are even better at room temperature than they are warm from the oven. So if you can, give them at least 15 minutes to cool. You can also make these with pears or pears and apples.

1 recipe Cream Cheese Pastry (*page 197*) or
 Three-Grain Butter Pastry (*page 193*)

FILLING
²/₃ cup ricotta cheese
²/₃ cup crumbled blue cheese (2 to 3 ounces)
1 tablespoon milk or cream
pinch of cayenne pepper
1 large Granny Smith apple, peeled, cored,
 and quartered
¹/₂ lemon
¹/₂ cup Gouda cheese, cut into small cubes

Prepare the pastry as directed, dividing the dough into 4 equal pieces. Flatten each one into a ¹/₄-inch-thick disk, then wrap each disk in plastic wrap and chill. Meanwhile, make the filling and preheat the oven to 375°.

Combine the ricotta, blue cheese, milk or cream, and cayenne in a small bowl. Work the mixture with a fork to blend. Set aside.

Working with one piece of pastry at a time, assemble the turnovers by rolling the dough into an 8-inch circle on a sheet of lightly floured wax paper. Cut one-quarter of the apple into 5 or 6 pieces and arrange them on one half of the turnover, the smaller slices on the ends and longer ones in the center. Squeeze a few drops of lemon juice over the apples, then spread one-quarter of the cheese filling on top, followed by one-quarter of the Gouda cubes.

Lightly moisten the edge of the circle with water, then fold the dough over to close, lining up the edges. Pinch and curl the edge to seal, crimping with a fork if you like to make an attractive edge. Transfer the turnover to a large, ungreased baking sheet, poke a few steam vents in the top, then repeat for the remaining turnovers.

Bake for 35 to 40 minutes, until golden brown. Transfer the turnovers to a rack and cool for at least 15 minutes before serving. ◆

# Curried Tofu and Broccoli Pot Pie

*Makes 6 servings*

Our kids like this a lot, which says something for how open little kids are to interesting, good flavors. You have to go very easy on the cayenne, however, for kids; I don't use any, or just a pinch, when I make this for the family. You can substitute about 2 tablespoons prepared curry powder for the individual spices called for. Commercial curry powders are, however, by no means the same in heat or flavor, so I can't take full responsibility for the possible outcome—you may end up breathing fire. Serve this with plain yogurt and chopped apples and pears, mixed and tossed with lemon juice. The 100 Percent Whole Wheat Pie Pastry (page 188) is excellent here.

1/2 recipe pie pastry (*see note above*)

FILLING
1/4 cup flavorless vegetable oil
1 medium-size onion, chopped
3 garlic cloves, minced
1 bay leaf
2 teaspoons turmeric
2 teaspoons paprika
2 teaspoons ground coriander
1 teaspoon mild chili powder
1 teaspoon ground ginger
1/4 teaspoon ground cardamom
1/4 teaspoon cayenne pepper
1 cup sliced fresh mushrooms
1 1/4 cups water

1/2 cup carrots in small dice
1 cup broccoli flowerets
1 teaspoon salt
1/2 cup canned crushed tomatoes in puree or tomato puree
1 pound firm tofu
1/4 cup sour cream
2 tablespoons chopped fresh parsley

Prepare and chill the pie pastry as directed. Heat the oil in a large, heavy pot or Dutch oven and add the onion. Sauté over medium heat for 5 minutes, stirring often, then add the garlic, bay leaf, and all the spices. Cook, stirring, for 1 minute, then stir in the mushrooms, water, carrots, broccoli, and salt and bring to a boil. Lower the heat, cover, and simmer for about 5 minutes, then stir in the tomatoes and cook for another 5 minutes.

While you're waiting, cut the tofu into 3/4-inch slabs, laying them between paper towels. Press down on them firmly to blot up excess moisture, then cut the slabs into cubes. Carefully stir them into the sauce. Remove from the heat and stir in the sour cream and parsley. Turn the filling into a 10-inch deep-dish pie pan, preferably ceramic or glass, and cool for 15 minutes. Meanwhile, preheat the oven to 400°.

On a sheet of wax paper, roll the pastry into a 12-inch circle. Invert it onto the filling, tucking the edge down along the inside edge of the pan. Poke a few steam vents in the top and bake for 40 minutes. Cool on a rack for 5 to 10 minutes before serving. ◆

# Seafood and Broccoli Pot Pie Parmesan

*Makes 6 to 8 servings*

Pot pies you can make at home are so superior to what you find in the frozen food case. Here's a creamy seafood version that makes a good winter dish. I've tried various vegetables with the seafood, and broccoli works well because the flowerets sop up the flavorful juices better than any other. The types of seafood you use depend on personal taste; scallops and mussels give the pie definition. The fillet gets all broken up, which some cooks might object to, but I like little seafood chunks spread throughout. Plus, I can usually find fish fillets that are a lot less expensive than scallops. Choose any pastry you like for the top crust; the Three-Grain Butter Pastry is always an excellent choice.

*½ recipe (or more) Three-Grain Butter Pastry (page 193) or other pie pastry*

FILLING
*1½ cups dry white wine*
*1 bay leaf*
*1 small onion, halved and peeled*
*1 pound bay or sea scallops (see note)*
*½ pound cod, haddock, or other inexpensive fillet*
*1 pound mussels*
*1½ to 2 cups broccoli flowerets*
*¼ cup unsalted butter*
*2 shallots, minced*

*1 celery stalk, finely chopped*
*¼ cup unbleached flour*
*1 cup light cream or ½ cup each heavy and light cream*
*½ teaspoon dried thyme*
*salt and freshly ground pepper*
*½ cup (2 ounces) freshly grated Parmesan cheese*
*¼ cup chopped fresh parsley*

Prepare and chill the pastry as directed. If you want a slightly thicker crust, the top pastry can use up to two-thirds of the dough instead of half the recipe. Save the remainder of the dough for another use.

To make the filling, bring the wine, bay leaf, and onion to a boil in a large, non-aluminum pot. Add the scallops and simmer for 2 to 3 minutes, just until they turn white; remove them to a bowl with a slotted spoon. With the heat still on, put the fillet into the pot and simmer, covered, for 2 minutes. Using a spatula, remove it—and any pieces that flake off—to a plate. Turn the heat off while you prepare the mussels.

Clean the mussels by scrubbing them with a brush under cold running water; pull off any beards. If some are partially open, stick a thin-bladed knife through the crack and tickle the meat. If they still don't close, discard them. Put them into the pot you've been using and bring to a boil. Boil gently, covered, for 5 minutes. Remove from the heat, uncover, and—when the steam subsides—remove the mussels with tongs or a slotted spoon and put them on a plate. Discard any that haven't opened. When cool enough to handle, remove the meat and discard the shells. Strain the fish water in the pot through cheesecloth or paper towels.

In a medium saucepan, steam the broccoli in a steamer basket until not quite tender, about 4 minutes. Remove the steamer from the pot and let the broccoli cool.

Melt the butter in a large, nonaluminum pot. Add the shallots and celery and sauté over medium heat for 2 minutes, stirring often. Stir in the flour and cook, stirring, for 2 minutes, taking care not to let it color more than slightly. Measure out 1 cup of the fish broth and stir it into the celery mixture. When it starts to thicken, stir in the cream and cook, stirring, for 5 minutes. Add the thyme and salt and pepper to taste. Stir in the Parmesan cheese and parsley, then fold

in the scallops, broccoli, and mussels. Flake the fillet and fold it in, then turn the mixture into a 10-inch deep-dish pie pan, glass or ceramic, or some other deep casserole. Cool for 15 minutes as you preheat the oven to 400°.

Just before baking, roll the pastry into a 12-inch circle on a sheet of wax paper. Invert it over the filling, tucking it down along the inside edge. Poke several steam vents on top, then bake for 40 minutes. If it starts to bubble over, put a baking sheet under it. Cool on a rack for 5 to 10 minutes, then serve.

NOTE: *If you use the larger sea scallops, cut them in half or quarters before folding them into the filling.* ◆

## Deep-Dish Sausage and Shrimp Pie

*Makes 8 servings*

I've seen this combination of sausage and shrimp in a number of cookbooks on Louisiana cooking, always in a rich, spicy hot, and flavorful broth. Since one of my basic cooking philosophies is that there's almost no dish you can't improve by putting it in a crust or baking it in dough, I did my best little Paul Prudhomme imitation and came up with this Louisiana-style dinner pie. Paul's reputation, I suppose, will remain intact, but I do think y'all gonna like this.

*½ recipe (or more) Three-Grain Butter Pastry (page 193)*

FILLING

*1 pound hot Italian sausage*
*¼ cup flavorless vegetable oil*
*1 large onion, chopped*
*2 celery stalks, chopped*
*1 large green bell pepper, seeded and chopped*
*1 small eggplant, peeled and cubed*
*¾ teaspoon salt*
*1 teaspoon paprika*
*1 teaspoon dried thyme*
*1 teaspoon dried oregano*
*¼ teaspoon mild chili powder*
*⅛ teaspoon cayenne pepper*
*2 garlic cloves, minced*
*1 tablespoon unbleached flour*
*⅔ cup water*
*½ cup canned crushed tomatoes in puree*

*1½ tablespoons Worcestershire sauce*
*½ pound medium-size shrimp, shelled and deveined*
*¼ cup chopped fresh parsley*
*freshly ground pepper*

Prepare and chill the pastry as directed; you will need at least half of this recipe, but use slightly more if you want a thicker crust.

Bring several quarts of water to a boil in a small pot. Pierce the sausage several times with a fork and drop it into the boiling water. Cook for 5 minutes, then drain. When cool enough to handle, slice into ½-inch pieces.

Heat the oil in a large, heavy pot or Dutch oven. Add the onion, celery, and green pepper and sauté over fairly high heat for 5 minutes, stirring occasionally. Stir in the eggplant and salt and reduce the heat to medium. Cover and cook for 5 minutes more, stirring several times.

Stir in the paprika, thyme, oregano, chili powder, cayenne, garlic, and sliced sausage. Cook for 1 minute, add the flour, and cook for another minute, stirring often. Stir in the water, tomatoes, and Worcestershire sauce and simmer for 5 minutes. Stir in the shrimp, parsley, and a few good grinds of pepper and remove from the heat. Turn the filling into a 10-inch deep-dish ceramic or glass pie pan or other casserole and cool for 15 minutes. Preheat the oven to 400°.

On a sheet of wax paper, roll the pastry into a 12-inch circle. Lay it over the filling, tucking the edge down inside the pan. Poke several steam vents in the top crust, then bake for 40 minutes, until nicely browned. Cool on a rack for 5 minutes, then serve. ◆

# Summer Seafood Pie with Cornmeal Crust

*Makes 6 servings*

This is a light seafood pie, ideal for summer entertaining, when some of the key ingredients are at their peak. I wouldn't call this a snap, but if you start early and do just a little prep here and there—make the pastry, steam the mussels, poach the scallops—this will be a summer breeze to make. Wine, cheese, and a light fruit dessert will turn this into a real feast.

²/₃ *recipe Cornmeal Cheddar Pastry (page 194)*

FILLING

*3 pounds mussels*

*1 cup dry white wine*

*1 bay leaf*

*¹/₂ pound bay or sea scallops*

*3 tablespoons good-quality olive oil*

*1 large onion, chopped*

*¹/₂ pound fresh mushrooms, stems removed,
caps cleaned and quartered*

*2 garlic cloves, minced*

*2 cups chopped fresh tomatoes (halve them
first and squeeze out the seeds and juice)*

*1 cup (no more than 3 ears) fresh corn kernels*

*¹/₃ cup chopped fresh basil*

*¹/₂ teaspoon salt*

*freshly ground pepper*

Prepare the cornmeal pastry as directed and chill. Meanwhile, make the filling: Clean the mussels by scrubbing them with a stiff brush under cold running water; pull off any beards. If some are partially open, stick a knife through the crack and tickle the meat; discard any that still don't close. Put the scrubbed mussels, wine, and bay leaf in a large, nonaluminum pot with a lid. Bring to a boil over high heat, cover, and steam the mussels for 5 minutes. Remove from the heat, uncover, and remove the mussels from the pot with tongs or a slotted spoon and put them in a large bowl. Discard any that have not opened. Save the broth.

While the mussels cool, bring the mussel broth to a simmer and add the scallops. Poach for 2 to 3 minutes—less time for the smaller scallops—then remove them to a plate with a slotted spoon. (If you are using sea scallops, cut them into halves or quarters at this point.)

When the mussels are cool enough to handle, remove the meat and discard the shells. Reserve.

Heat the olive oil in a large enameled or stainless-steel skillet. Add the onion and cook over medium-high heat for 5 minutes, stirring occasionally. Add the mushrooms and garlic, cover, and let the mushrooms cook for 2 to 3 minutes. Add the tomatoes, cover again, and cook over medium heat for 5 minutes. Remove from the heat and pour the contents of the pan into a large bowl. Stir in the corn, basil, salt, a generous amount of pepper, and the reserved scallops and mussels. Cool for 15 minutes and preheat the oven to 400°.

On a sheet of wax paper, roll the pastry into an 11-inch circle; keep it nearby. Turn the partially cooled filling into a 10-inch

*(continued)*

(continued)

deep-dish pie pan, glass or ceramic, and in-vert the pastry over the filling. Tuck the edge down between the filling and the pan. Poke a few steam vents in the top of the pie with a paring knife—twist the knife to open the vent. Bake for 40 minutes, until the filling is quite bubbly and the crust is slightly browned. Cool on a rack for 5 to 10 minutes before spooning it out. ♦

## Spinach and Spud Dinner Pie

*Makes 8 servings*

An easy pie, made from basic ingre-dients, this is a fine family dish any time of year.

1 9-inch pie shell, partially baked (see page 200 for baking instructions)

FILLING

2 cups ⅛-inch-thick sliced peeled new potatoes

10 ounces fresh spinach, stems removed, washed and coarsely chopped

1 cup (3 ounces) grated Gouda, Fontina, or Cheddar cheese

¾ cup milk or cream

½ cup ricotta cheese

2 large eggs

½ teaspoon salt

1 teaspoon dried basil

freshly ground pepper

2 scallions, thinly sliced

Cool the partially baked pie shell on a rack. Meanwhile, make the filling.

Put the potatoes into a large saucepan with about a quart of lightly salted water. Bring to a boil, lower the heat, and simmer for about 5 minutes or less; take them off when they're not quite tender. Drain, run cold water over them to stop the cooking, and then lay them on paper toweling to dry. Preheat the oven to 375°.

Put the spinach into a large pot with barely enough water to cover the bottom of the pot. Bring to a boil, add a pinch of salt, and cover. Steam over high heat for about 4 minutes, then drain. When cool enough to handle, squeeze out most—but not all—of the liquid.

To assemble the pie, sprinkle half the melting cheese over the bottom of the crust, followed by about one-third of the po-tatoes. Spread the spinach evenly over the potatoes, followed by the rest of the po-tatoes and the rest of the cheese.

Puree the milk or cream and the ricotta cheese in a blender and whisk together with the eggs, salt, basil, and pepper to taste. *Slowly* pour the custard over the pie and sprinkle the scallions over the top. Bake for 40 minutes, until the custard is set and the pie is golden brown. Cool briefly, then slice and serve. ♦

# Onion, Havarti, and Dill Dinner Pie

*Makes 8 servings*

This is thick with sweet, browned Vidalia onions, couched in a sour-creamy and Havarti custard. My preference is the Sour Rye Pastry (page 189), but if you have the makings of another shell on hand, then by all means use it. I might serve this with corn on the cob and hot buttered beets in the summer; with a light, brothy soup in the colder months. The consistency of this filling is just a little loose, but you can tighten it up some by including another egg or an egg yolk if need be.

1 9-inch pie shell (see note above), partially baked (see page 200 for baking instructions)

FILLING
1/4 cup unsalted butter
2 large onions, halved lengthwise and sliced (about 4 cups)
salt
1 or 2 garlic cloves, minced
2 large eggs
3/4 cup light cream or milk
1/2 cup sour cream
1/2 teaspoon salt
freshly ground pepper
1 teaspoon dried dill or 2 to 3 teaspoons fresh
3/4 cup (2 ounces) grated Havarti cheese

Cool the partially baked pie shell on a rack while you prepare the filling.

Melt the butter in a large, heavy skillet. Add the onions and a pinch of salt and cook, stirring often, over medium heat for 12 to 15 minutes, until nicely browned, lowering the heat a little toward the end. Stir the garlic in for the last minute, then scrape the onions onto a plate to cool. Preheat the oven to 350°.

As the onions cool, beat the eggs with the cream or milk, sour cream, 1/2 teaspoon salt, a good grind of pepper, and the dill. To assemble the pie, spread about one-third of the grated Havarti over the cooled shell, followed by the onions. *Slowly* pour on the custard, then spread the remaining cheese evenly over the top. Bake for 35 to 40 minutes, just until lightly browned. Cool the pan on a rack for at least 10 minutes before slicing and serving. ♦

# Three-Grain-Crusted Chicken Pot Pie

*Makes 6 to 8 servings*

I don't think I'm alone in having a real soft spot for old-fashioned dishes like this, the ones whose remarkable quality is a direct result not of fancy or expensive ingredients but rather of the care and time invested in them. Which is not to say this takes forever to make; it doesn't, especially if you play your cards right. Think of this as a Sunday night dinner. Poach the chicken on Saturday, make the pastry when convenient, then assemble the dish Sunday afternoon. Not feeling rushed, you'll be able to sit down and really enjoy the meal. Yeast rolls are nice with this, or serve just a salad.

1 recipe Three-Grain Butter Pastry (*page 193*)

FILLING
1 quart water
1 bay leaf
1 teaspoon salt
1 4-pound (approximately) chicken
2 celery stalks, finely chopped
1 cup thinly sliced carrots
2 medium-size potatoes, peeled and cut into
  ¹/₂-inch dice
6 tablespoons unsalted butter
2 cups chopped onions
3 tablespoons unbleached flour
1¹/₃ cups heavy cream
¹/₂ teaspoon dried thyme

salt and freshly ground pepper
¹/₄ cup chopped fresh parsley

Prepare the pastry as directed, but instead of shaping it into 2 disks, shape it into a rectangle about ¹/₂ inch thick. Wrap in plastic wrap and chill.

Meanwhile, make the filling. Put the water, bay leaf, and salt in a large pot. Add the chicken and bring to a boil over high heat. Reduce to a simmer, cover, and poach the chicken for 30 minutes. Turn off the heat and let the chicken cool right in the pot. Remove the chicken to a platter and, when convenient, skin it, pick the meat off the bones, and cut into bite-size pieces. Strain and reserve the chicken broth, refrigerated if overnight. (If you do refrigerate the broth, you can skim off the fat the next day.)

Put the broth back in the pot and add the celery, carrots, and potatoes. Bring to a boil, reduce the heat, and simmer for several minutes, until the potatoes are not quite tender. Drain the vegetables, reserving the broth.

Using the same large pot, melt 3 tablespoons of the butter over medium heat and add the onions. Sauté, stirring occasionally, for 10 minutes, until golden. Add the remaining butter, letting it melt, then sprinkle in the flour and cook, stirring constantly, for 2 minutes.

Stir 1¹/₂ cups of the reserved chicken broth into the onions. Cook over medium heat for about 2 minutes, stirring, until it starts to thicken, then stir in the cream and thyme. Cook for 5 minutes, stirring occasionally, then season the sauce to taste with salt and pepper. Add the parsley, the reserved chicken and vegetables, and salt and pepper if needed. Turn the filling into a buttered 8- by 12-inch baking dish and let cool for 15 to 30 minutes. Preheat the oven to 400° 15 minutes before you assemble the dish.

To assemble, tear off a sheet of wax paper a little longer than your baking dish. Roll the pastry on the wax paper into a rectangle roughly 9 by 13 inches. Invert the pastry over the filling, tucking the edges down along the inside edges. Poke several steam vents in the surface with a paring knife or a fork. Put the dish on a foil-lined baking sheet and bake for about 40 to 45 minutes, until the top is nicely browned. Cool on a rack for 10 minutes before serving.

VARIATIONS: *There are many possibilities. You could use a different pastry, such as the 100 Percent Whole Wheat Pie Pastry (page 188) or the All-American Pie Pastry (page 184). And poke around the fridge for little leftover containers of vegetables, like corn or peas or green beans. Make the dish work for you; there's not one magic formula.* ◆

# Kale Dinner Pie with Ricotta Spoon Bread Topping

*Makes 8 servings*

There are enough kale recipes in this book to leave the impression that kale is the New Hampshire state vegetable. Because kale is so well suited to hardy climates, I can always find a local source, which is probably why it tastes so good to me. Actually, you could use other greens here—spinach, Swiss chard, or beet greens—or even broccoli or cauliflower, for that matter; just steam with a little water in a covered pot until tender and add it where the kale goes in the skillet. The special touch here is the corn topping, a spoon-bread-like custard, some of which seeps down through the kale but most of which stays on top and forms an upper crust; sounds involved, but it's really very simple. My first choice for the shell is the 100 Percent Whole Wheat Pie Pastry (page 188).

1 9-inch pie shell (see note above), partially baked (see page 200 for baking instructions)

FILLING
1 pound kale
3 tablespoons good-quality olive oil
1 medium-size onion, chopped
1 small carrot, grated
2 garlic cloves, minced
1/2 teaspoon mild chili powder

salt and freshly ground pepper
1 cup ricotta cheese
3 large eggs
1/2 cup (almost 2 ounces) finely grated Parmesan cheese
2 tablespoons yellow cornmeal, preferably stone-ground
3/4 cup fresh or thawed frozen corn kernels
1/2 teaspoon salt

Let the partially baked pie shell cool completely while you make the filling.

Strip the kale leaves from their stems, placing them in a large bowl as you work; discard the stems. Fill the bowl with lukewarm water and agitate the leaves with your hands to free any sand and dirt. Put about 1/4 inch of water into a large pot and lift the wet leaves right into it. Bring to a boil over high heat, reduce to medium-low, then cover. Steam for 15 minutes, tightly covered, then drain in a colander. Cool. Preheat the oven to 400°.

While the kale is cooling, heat the oil in a large skillet. Add the onion and carrot and sauté over medium heat for 5 minutes, stirring occasionally. Stir in the garlic and chili powder, cook for another minute, then remove from the heat. Squeeze some, but not all, of the water out of the kale and chop it coarsely. Stir it into the sauté, season to taste with salt and pepper, then scrape the sauté onto a plate to cool.

Puree the ricotta cheese and eggs in a blender. Scrape into a bowl and whisk in the Parmesan cheese, cornmeal, corn, 1/2 teaspoon salt, and a few good grinds of pepper.

To assemble the pie, spread the sautéed mixture in the pie shell; pat it down lightly to even the top. Pour the topping over the kale and even it out with a spoon. Bake for 15 minutes, reduce the heat to 350°, and bake 15 minutes more. Slice and serve hot, warm, or at room temperature.

VARIATION: *A little tomato gives this an added flavor dimension, so if you like, spoon some salsa over the kale before you pour on the topping.* ♦

# Cheddar and Winter Vegetable Dinner Pie

*Makes 8 servings*

Winters in New Hampshire tend to be long and physically demanding; dishes like this one are the perfect antidote. It's economical, filling, very tasty, and so easy to throw together—one of the easiest dinner pies I make, in fact. If you make the pie shell in the morning or the night before, you can have this in the oven in less than 30 minutes. Note that this is a vegetarian pie, but it is also excellent if you substitute a little chopped, cooked sausage or diced ham for some of the cabbage.

*1 recipe Cornmeal Cheddar Pastry (page 194)*

FILLING
*2 cups (about 4 medium) peeled potatoes in ³/₄-inch dice*
*2 tablespoons flavorless vegetable oil*
*1 tablespoon unsalted butter*
*2 medium-size onions, chopped*
*4 cups very thinly sliced green cabbage*
*1 garlic clove, minced*
*¹/₂ teaspoon salt*
*²/₃ cup sour cream*
*2 teaspoons Dijon or German-style mustard*
*salt and freshly ground pepper*
*several thin slices of Cheddar cheese for lining the pastry*

*(continued)*

*(continued)*

Chill the pastry. When it is cold, roll half of the pastry into a 12-inch circle on a sheet of lightly floured wax paper and line a 9-inch pie pan with it; let the edge hang over. Cover loosely with plastic wrap and refrigerate.

Put the potatoes into a medium saucepan, cover with about a quart of lightly salted water, and bring to a boil. Boil the potatoes until they are barely tender, then drain, saving ⅓ cup of the water. (You could save all of it and use it in a yeasted bread.)

In a very large skillet, warm the oil and butter over medium heat. Add the onions and sauté, stirring occasionally, for 5 minutes. Stir in the cabbage and garlic, cook for another minute, then stir in the ½ teaspoon salt and reserved potato water. Raise the heat a little, then cover and cook for 5 minutes, stirring once or twice; then uncover and cook for another 5 minutes. You want to cook off all the excess liquid in these last 5 minutes, but it's fine to add a tablespoon or so more water if the skillet is getting too dry. Remove the pan from the heat when the cabbage is somewhat tender and limp. Preheat the oven to 425°.

Blend the sour cream and mustard in a large mixing bowl. Stir in the cooked vegetables from the skillet and the potatoes; season to taste with salt and pepper. Set aside.

On a sheet of wax paper, roll the other half of the pastry into a 12-inch circle and keep it close by. Line the refrigerated pie shell with the Cheddar cheese; it's fine if the slices overlap a little. Scrape the filling into the shell and even it out. Moisten the very outer rim of the pie shell with water, then invert the top crust over the filling. Press down around the edge to seal, then trim the pastry flush with the pan with the back of a knife. Crimp the edge with the tines of a fork, then use the fork to poke several steam vents in the top of the pie.

Bake the pie for 20 minutes, turn the heat down to 375°, then bake for another 40 minutes. Cool the pie on a rack for 10 minutes before slicing. ♦

## Asparagus and Havarti Quiche

*Makes 8 servings*

We're fortunate to have lots of friends who are avid gardeners, some of whom grow only one or two crops in a big way. Come May—when the sight of asparagus is like the first glimpse of land after a winter of hard sailing—we're always swapping baked things for big bunches of the freshest asparagus you ever laid eyes on. The season is so short that we never get past our favorite ways with asparagus—this recipe is one of the top three. A touch of sour cream in the custard here gives the quiche a light but very tasty tang, well suited to the dill and mustard.

1 9-inch Tart Pastry shell (*page 201*),
  *partially baked (see page 230 for baking instructions*)

FILLING
1 pound fresh asparagus with finger-size
  stalks
2 large eggs
³/₄ cup light cream
2 tablespoons sour cream
¹/₂ teaspoon dried dill
¹/₂ teaspoon Dijon mustard
¹/₂ teaspoon salt
freshly ground pepper
3 scallions, thinly sliced
1¹/₂ cups (¹/₄ pound) grated Havarti cheese

Let the partially baked tart shell cool completely on a rack. Preheat the oven to 375° as you prepare the filling.

Prepare the asparagus by cutting off all the tips, leaving them approximately 4 inches long. Slice the rest of the stalks into ¹/₂-inch pieces, using only the green part of each stalk. (If the bottoms of the stalks are tough, you should peel them first, using a sharp paring knife.) Put all the asparagus into a steamer basket and steam it for about 4-5 minutes in a saucepan. Using pot holders, take the steamer basket out of the saucepan while the asparagus is still a little crunchy; it will finish cooking as it cools and when it bakes. Set the steamed tips aside on a separate plate.

As the asparagus cools, beat the eggs lightly in a mixing bowl, then whisk in the cream, sour cream, dill, mustard, salt, and a few good grinds of pepper. Set aside.

To assemble the quiche, sprinkle the small pieces of asparagus—not the tips—over the bottom of the tart shell. Spread the scallions on next, followed by the Havarti. *Slowly* pour on the custard. Arrange the asparagus tips on top like the spokes of a wheel, with the tips pointing outward. Bake for about 40 minutes, until the quiche is lightly browned and puffy. Cool for 5 to 10 minutes on a rack before slicing and serving. ◆

# Green Pepper and Corn Pudding Tart

*Makes 8 servings*

I'm crazy about anything with corn pudding in, on, under, or anywhere near it—this tart especially; in this case the corn pudding, made with cottage cheese, goes over sautéed green peppers, though you could use a combination of colorful peppers or even a combination of other summer vegetables. Whether you use a blender or food processor to mix the pudding, keep the texture on the rough side so you have nubby little corn flecks in the custard. For a casual summer meal you might include hot buttered beets and either a cold soup—gazpacho would be perfect—or a simple fruit and cheese dessert.

1 9-inch Tart Pastry shell (*page 201*),
   partially baked (*see page 230 for baking
   instructions*)

FILLING
2 tablespoons unsalted butter
2 medium-large green bell peppers, seeded
   and chopped
1¹/₂ cups fresh or thawed frozen corn kernels,
   patted dry between paper towels
²/₃ cup cottage cheese
¹/₃ cup milk
2 large eggs
¹/₂ teaspoon salt
¹/₄ teaspoon freshly ground pepper

1 cup (about 3 ounces) grated sharp Cheddar
   cheese
1 tablespoon chopped fresh parsley

Let the partially baked tart shell cool on a rack. Meanwhile, preheat the oven to 375° and make the filling.

Heat the butter in a medium skillet and add the peppers. Sauté over medium heat for about 8 minutes, stirring often; scrape onto a plate to cool.

Put the corn kernels, cottage cheese, and milk in a blender or food processor and pulse on and off, keeping it on the textured side. Crack the eggs into a bowl, beat them until frothy, then whisk in the corn puree, salt, and pepper.

To assemble the tart, arrange the peppers in an even layer in the bottom of the tart shell, sprinkle on half the Cheddar, then *slowly* pour the corn pudding over the top. Sprinkle with the remaining cheese and bake for 35 to 40 minutes, until the top is set and just starting to brown. Cool for at least several minutes on a rack, top with the fresh parsley, then slice and serve. ♦

# Scallop and Smoked Cheddar Quiche

*Makes 8 servings*

*Y*ou'll love the way the smoky Cheddar pairs up with the brininess of the scallops in this recipe adapted from one by Richard Sax in *Cooking Great Meals Every Day* (Random House, 1982). Try this for a New Year's Eve party contribution, a Super Bowl party dish, or a hearty winter brunch.

1 9-inch Tart Pastry shell (*page 201*), *partially baked (see page 230 for baking instructions)*

FILLING
2 tablespoons unsalted butter
1 large onion, quartered and sliced
¹/₂ pound bay or sea scallops (cut sea scallops into halves or quarters)
1 garlic clove, minced
salt
2 large eggs
³/₄ cup light cream
¹/₂ teaspoon Dijon mustard
¹/₄ teaspoon salt
¹/₈ teaspoon cayenne pepper
2 tablespoons minced fresh parsley
1¹/₂ cups (¹/₄ pound) grated smoked Cheddar cheese

Cool the partially baked tart shell on a rack. Meanwhile, preheat the oven to 375° and make the filling.

In a large, nonaluminum skillet, melt the butter over medium heat. Add the onion and sauté, stirring occasionally, for 5 minutes. Add the scallops, garlic, and a pinch of salt and cook, stirring often, for about 4 minutes. (If there is a large buildup of moisture in the pan, move the solids to the perimeter of the pan and cook it off.) Scrape the contents of the pan onto a plate and let cool.

In a large mixing bowl, beat the eggs lightly, then whisk in the cream, mustard, ¹/₄ teaspoon salt, cayenne, and parsley.

To assemble the quiche, sprinkle half the smoked Cheddar over the shell, then scrape the scallop sauté over that, spreading it evenly. *Slowly* pour on the custard, then top with the remaining cheese. Bake for 35 minutes, until the quiche is lightly browned and slightly puffy. Cool for 5 to 10 minutes before serving.

VARIATION: *Instead of scallops, you could use leftover cooked (flaked) fish; add it when the onions come off the heat (paragraph 2).* ◆

# Cauliflower Parmesan Quiche

*Makes 8 servings*

One bite of this rich quiche and you'll get as worked up over cauliflower as you might over, say, fresh asparagus or the season's first sweet corn. The Parmesan cheese and the cream, with the onion base, give the understated cauliflower just the pizzazz it needs. This bakes to a pretty shade of gold that looks perfectly seductive with a sprinkling of chopped fresh chives or parsley on top.

1 9-inch Tart Pastry shell (page 201), partially baked (see page 230 for baking instructions)

FILLING
2 quarts water
1¼ teaspoons salt
4 cups (1 small head) cauliflower flowerets
2 tablespoons unsalted butter
2 cups chopped onions
2 garlic cloves, minced
1 large egg
1 large egg yolk
¾ cup heavy cream
¾ cup (almost 2 ounces) finely grated
    Parmesan cheese
a little chopped fresh parsley or chives

Cool the partially baked tart shell thoroughly on a rack. Meanwhile, make the filling.

Bring the water to boil in a large pot. Add 1 teaspoon of the salt and the cauliflower, return to a boil, and boil for about 4 minutes, until the cauliflower is not quite tender. Drain in a colander and let cool. Preheat the oven to 375°.

While the cauliflower is cooking, melt the butter in a medium skillet over moderate heat. Add the onions and sauté, stirring occasionally, for 5 minutes. Stir in the garlic, cook briefly, then scrape the onions onto a plate and let cool.

In a medium bowl, lightly beat the egg, egg yolk, cream, and remaining ¼ teaspoon of salt. Stir in all but 2 tablespoons of the Parmesan cheese.

To assemble the quiche, sprinkle the remaining 2 tablespoons of Parmesan cheese over the crust. Spread the onions over the cheese, then arrange the cauliflower in the shell, stems pointing down. You'll have a lot of leaners; don't worry. *Slowly* pour the custard over the top, then bake on the center rack for 45 to 50 minutes, until the custard is set and the top is golden and slightly puffy. Remove the pan to a cooling rack and cool for 5 to 10 minutes. Sprinkle with the fresh herbs, slice, and serve. ♦

## Vegetarian Kale, Tomato, and Provolone Quiche

*Makes 8 to 10 servings*

Here's a great party-size quiche you might make to impress the vegetarians in your life. Provolone is just one of the cheeses I might use here, depending on what's on hand. Mozzarella is also excellent, though milder. Half Kasseri is wonderful, for a stronger flavor. As for any quiche, don't barge into this recipe at the last minute. It's a lot less stressful to make and partially bake the pastry at your leisure, then prep the remaining ingredients without feeling rushed. Once you have all the components ready, assembly takes only minutes. To round out your vegetarian feast you could serve this with soup and/or a salad, or a raw vegetable and dip platter, and a light dessert.

1 10-inch Tart Pastry shell (page 201),
   partially baked (see page 230 for baking
   instructions)

FILLING
1 pound kale
¼ cup unsalted butter
2 medium-size onions, halved lengthwise and
   thinly sliced
1 garlic clove, minced
salt and freshly ground pepper
1 large tomato, halved and seeded
3 large eggs
1 egg yolk
1½ cups light cream

¾ teaspoon salt
¼ teaspoon freshly ground black pepper
1½ teaspoons dried basil or 3 tablespoons
   minced fresh
2 cups (5 to 6 ounces) grated provolone or
   other cheese

While the partially baked tart shell cools on a rack, make the filling.

Strip the kale leaves from their stems, placing them in a large bowl as you work; discard the stems. Fill the bowl with lukewarm water and agitate the leaves with your hands to free any sand and dirt. Put about ¼ inch of water into a large pot and lift the wet leaves right into it. Bring to a boil over high heat, reduce heat to medium-low, cover tightly, and steam for 15 minutes; then drain in a colander. (You might want to save the steaming water for a soup.) Cool.

While the kale is cooling, heat 3 tablespoons of the butter in a medium skillet and sauté the onions over medium heat. Sauté for 10 minutes, stirring occasionally, until the onions start to brown. Stir in the minced garlic, cook for another minute, then remove the pan from the heat.

When the kale is cool enough to handle, pick it up with your hands and squeeze out *almost* all of the liquid; if you squeeze all of it out, the kale will seem dry. Finely chop the kale and stir it into the onions. Lightly underseason this vegetable mixture with salt and pepper to taste. Preheat the oven to 375°.

Slice the tomato thinly, placing the slices on a paper towel–lined plate. Salt them

(continued)

*(continued)*

lightly and set aside. In a medium mixing bowl, lightly beat the eggs, egg yolk, cream, salt, pepper, and basil.

To assemble the quiche, sprinkle one-third of the grated cheese over the tart shell. Layer the kale/onion mixture over that, followed by all but a small handful of the remaining cheese. Blot the tomato slices with a paper towel and arrange them in a single layer on top of the cheese. Sprinkle on the rest of the cheese. *Slowly* pour the egg mixture into the shell, then cut the remaining tablespoon of butter into pieces and sprinkle them over the top. Bake for approximately 40 minutes, until puffed and nicely browned on top. Cool on a rack for 5 to 10 minutes, then slice and serve. ♦

## Eggplant, Feta, and Tomato Quiche

*Makes 8 to 10 servings*

Here's another big, excellent vegetarian quiche, especially good in the summer, when tomatoes and eggplant are at their best. This takes a little bit of work, but just imagine how rewarding it will be to have your friends fighting over seconds of your contribution at your next summer potluck while the five variations of potato and green bean salad languish in the sun. If you have a tart pan with high sides, all the better, because this is a very full pie. If your tart pan has low sides, try to keep the dough a little above the rim when you put the pastry in the pan, and don't trim it flush. Everyone loves the look of this tart, with its overlapping row of eggplant and the tomatoes in the center. To make this more of a manageable production, prepare this in stages, perhaps preparing the tart shell and prepping some of the vegetables the day before.

1 10-inch Tart Pastry shell (*page 201*),
   partially baked (*see page 230 for baking
   instructions*)

FILLING
1 medium (about ¹/₂-pound) eggplant
up to ¹/₃ cup olive oil for frying the eggplant
¹/₂ cup unbleached flour
salt
2 large tomatoes, halved and seeded
3 tablespoons good-quality olive oil

2 medium-size onions, halved lengthwise and
 thinly sliced
2 garlic cloves, minced
3 large eggs
1 cup light cream
2 tablespoons minced fresh parsley
3/4 teaspoon salt
1/8 teaspoon freshly ground pepper
1/8 teaspoon ground cinnamon
1/8 teaspoon freshly grated nutmeg
1 cup (almost 1/4 pound) crumbled feta cheese
1 cup (almost 3 ounces) grated mozzarella or
 provolone cheese

As the partially baked tart shell cools on a rack, prepare the filling.

Slice the eggplant into 1/2-inch-thick rounds. Heat a very thin layer of olive oil in a heavy skillet, preferably cast iron. Dredge the eggplant slices in the flour, dusting them lightly. When the oil is hot, fry the pieces over medium-high heat, browning both sides but not letting the eggplant get too soft; you'll probably have to do this in 2 or 3 batches, adding extra oil to the pan as it is absorbed by the eggplant. Remove the pieces to a paper towel-lined platter. Sprinkle them very lightly with salt. Set aside.

Cut the tomatoes into 1/4-inch-thick slices and lay them on a paper towel-lined baking sheet. Sprinkle them very lightly with salt and set aside.

Heat the 3 tablespoons of olive oil in a medium skillet and add the onions. Sauté over medium heat for 10 minutes, stirring occasionally. Stir in the garlic, cook for another minute, then scrape the onions onto a plate to cool.

In a medium mixing bowl, beat together the eggs, cream, parsley, 3/4 teaspoon salt, pepper, cinnamon, and nutmeg. Preheat the oven to 375°.

To assemble the tart, blot the tomatoes dry with a paper towel and arrange all but 5 slices in the bottom of the tart shell. Spread the onions over the tomatoes, followed by the feta cheese and all but a small handful of the mozzarella or provolone. Arrange the eggplant slices in an overlapping row around the perimeter of the tart. *Slowly* pour the custard into the center of the tart, then arrange the remaining tomato slices in a small, overlapping circle in the center. Sprinkle the remaining cheese over the top.

Bake the tart for 45 minutes, until puffed and well browned. Remove the tart pan to a rack and cool for at least 10 minutes before slicing and serving.

NOTE: *One nice addition to this tart is a few good-quality green or black olives, preferably imported (pitted and chopped) with the cheese layers. Also, if you're making this with customarily tasteless winter tomatoes, you'll find that they benefit from a very quick flash in the pan with a splash of oil. Just cook them on one side, for 15 seconds or so, to soften slightly.* ◆

# Fresh Corn Quiche

*Makes 8 to 10 servings*

A dish like this is a great focal point for a summer feast with good friends. To round the meal out I might include a garden coleslaw, a platter of fresh tomatoes (drizzled with olive oil and topped with mozzarella cubes and fresh basil), and maybe fresh strawberries and cream or strawberry shortcake for dessert.

1 10-inch Tart Pastry shell (*page 201*),
   partially baked (*see page 230 for baking instructions*)

FILLING
3 large eggs
1 large egg yolk
1¹/₂ cups light cream
¹/₂ teaspoon salt
pinch of freshly grated nutmeg
1¹/₂ cups (¹/₄ pound) grated Cheddar or other
   melting cheese
1¹/₂ cups (3 medium-large ears) fresh or
   thawed frozen corn kernels (see note below)
2 tablespoons minced fresh parsley
1 tablespoon minced onion

Let the partially baked tart shell cool on a rack. Preheat the oven to 375° while you make the filling.

In a large mixing bowl, lightly beat the eggs and egg yolk. Whisk in the cream, salt, and nutmeg just until blended. Set aside.

To assemble the quiche, sprinkle about ¹/₂ cup of the cheese over the shell and spread the corn, parsley, and onion over it. *Slowly* pour the custard into the shell, then sprinkle the remaining cheese on top. Bake for approximately 40 minutes, until slightly puffed and golden brown. Transfer the tart pan to a rack and cool for 5 to 10 minutes. Slice and serve. This is good served fairly hot, warm, or at room temperature.

NOTE: *If you use frozen corn, pat the kernels dry before using.* ♦

# Blue Cheese and Toasted Walnut Tart

*Makes 8 servings*

Here's an easy tart—there are no vegetables to prep, just walnuts to toast—for blue cheese lovers. Blue cheese seems to be an adult taste, so one of the other quiches in this section might be more appropriate if you're cooking for a mixed crowd. For best flavor and texture, be sure to serve this hot or warm, not cold.

*1 9-inch Tart Pastry shell (page 201), partially baked (see page 230 for baking instructions)*

FILLING
*³/₄ cup walnuts (3 ounces)*
*2 large eggs*
*¹/₂ cup heavy cream*
*¹/₂ cup light cream*
*¹/₈ teaspoon salt*
*1¹/₂ teaspoons Dijon mustard*
*¹/₈ teaspoon cayenne pepper*
*1¹/₄ cups (about ¹/₄ pound) crumbled blue cheese*

Set the partially baked tart shell aside on a rack to cool. Preheat the oven to 350° and prepare the filling.

Spread the walnuts on a small baking sheet and toast them in the oven for about 8 minutes, just until they are fragrant and take on a rich but not-too-dark tone. Cool slightly, then chop coarsely.

In a medium mixing bowl, lightly beat the eggs with the creams, salt, mustard, and cayenne. To assemble the tart, scatter the nuts and blue cheese evenly in the shell. *Slowly* pour or ladle in the custard, then bake the tart for 30 to 35 minutes. When done, the top will be a very light brown and the custard will be set; do not overbake. Transfer the tart pan to a rack and cool for several minutes before slicing and serving.

NOTE: *This quiche could serve up to 12 people as an after-dinner savory, thinly sliced, with a pear slice or 2, tossed in lemon juice, on the side.* ♦

# Savory Oatmeal Skillet Bread

*Makes 8 servings*

This could just as easily be called a flat vegetable loaf as a savory bread. We often depend on this bread to serve as the homemade focal point of an easy meal—for instance, to go with applesauce and a green salad or a soup. This is adapted from a recipe by Jacques Pépin.

*1 medium-size potato, peeled and cut into ¹/₂-*
*inch dice*
*milk (no more than 1 cup)*
*1 cup rolled oats (not instant)*
*1 small onion, minced*
*1 small green bell pepper, seeded and minced*
*1 medium-size carrot, grated*
*1 large egg, lightly beaten*
*1 teaspoon dried basil*
*1 teaspoon dried oregano*
*¹/₂ teaspoon dried thyme*
*³/₄ teaspoon salt*
*¹/₄ teaspoon freshly ground pepper*
*¹/₂ cup fine unseasoned bread crumbs (see*
*page 286 for suggestions on how to make*
*your own bread crumbs)*
*2 teaspoons baking powder*
*¹/₄ cup good-quality olive oil*
*1 garlic clove, minced*

Preheat the oven to 400°. Put the potato into a small saucepan with enough lightly salted water to barely cover. Bring to a boil and cook at a low boil for about 8 minutes, until barely tender. Drain the water off into a measuring cup, leaving the potatoes in the saucepan.

Add enough milk to the potato water to equal 1 cup. Put the oats into a large mixing bowl, then pour in the potato water and milk. Mash the potatoes a little with a fork, then add them to the mixing bowl. Stir in the vegetables, egg, herbs, salt, and pepper. Mix ¹/₄ cup of the bread crumbs with the baking powder and reserve.

Heat 2 tablespoons of the oil in a 10-inch cast-iron skillet. Turn off the heat and add the garlic, but keep it all in one spot in the pan. Wait 10 seconds, then scrape out the garlic with a rubber spatula and add it to the batter. Add the reserved bread crumb/baking powder mixture to the batter, then stir until everything is blended. Tilt the skillet to spread the oil around, then scrape the batter into the pan. Spread it evenly with a fork, then sprinkle on the remaining ¹/₄ cup bread crumbs. Drizzle the rest of the olive oil over the crumbs, then bake the bread for 30 minutes. Cool in the pan for 5 minutes. Slice and serve directly from the pan. ◆

# Savory Vidalia Onion Corn Cake

*Makes 6 to 8 servings*

To me, this is down-home cooking at its best: sweet, golden-sautéed Vidalia onions in, and spread over, a sort of potato-cornmeal biscuit. You cook it right in the onion sauté pan, and 25 minutes later you have something really delicious and substantial. This cake would be great with a stew, with soup and salad, or with breakfast alongside your scrambled eggs or omelet; you can forget the toast and hash browns. If you can't find Vidalia onions, yellow ones will do.

1 cup (1 medium-large) *diced peeled potato*
6 tablespoons *unsalted butter*
1 large Vidalia or yellow onion, *quartered and thinly sliced (about 2 to 2¹/₂ cups)*
1¹/₄ cups *unbleached flour*
¹/₂ cup yellow cornmeal, *preferably stone-ground*
2 teaspoons *baking powder*
¹/₂ cup *milk*
1 large egg, *lightly beaten*
1 teaspoon *salt*
¹/₂ teaspoon *dried dill*
¹/₄ teaspoon *caraway seeds*

Put the potatoes in a medium saucepan and cover with plenty of water. Add a pinch of salt and bring to a boil. Boil for 10 minutes or so, until the potatoes are very tender. Drain, saving the water for soup or yeast bread if you like.

While the potatoes boil, melt 3 tablespoons of the butter in a 9- or 10-inch cast-iron skillet over medium heat. Add the onions and sauté, stirring occasionally, for about 15 minutes; let them turn a golden hue but not get crispy brown. Scrape the onions onto a plate to cool. Keep the skillet handy, unwashed. Preheat the oven to 400°.

As the onions cook, mix the flour, cornmeal, and baking powder in a small bowl and set aside.

Using an electric mixer, beat the potatoes with 2 tablespoons of the remaining butter (put the last tablespoon of butter on the stove to melt). Blend in the milk, egg, salt, dill, and caraway seeds. Stir in half the onions. Add the dry ingredients to the liquid and stir, just until it gathers into a soft, shaggy mass. Scrape it into the skillet, smoothing it out with a fork. Spread the remaining onions on top, then drizzle the tablespoon of melted butter all over the top. Bake for 25 minutes. Slice and serve hot from the pan. This is also good at room temperature. ♦

# Corn Bread Chili Cobbler

*Makes 8 large servings*

This is the sort of informal, meatless main dish that was made for a cold night, good friends, and plenty of frosty brew. It isn't all that involved either, just a well-seasoned chili with a simple muffin recipe spooned over the top. You can, if you like, bypass the dried beans and use 2 19-ounce cans, rinsed, but I've never much cared for either the tinny flavor or the texture of canned beans. If you opt for dried, allow time for soaking. Along with this I'd serve a creamy coleslaw or a big green salad and maybe Brown Sugar Yogurt Pie (page 227) for dessert.

*½ pound (about 1½ cups) dried kidney beans (see note below), or canned beans (see note above)*

*1 modified recipe Double-Corn and Cheese Muffins (page 27), as outlined below*

*¼ cup plus 1 tablespoon flavorless vegetable oil or good-quality olive oil*

*3 medium-size onions, chopped*

*1 large green bell pepper, seeded and chopped*

*1 celery stalk, minced*

*3 to 4 garlic cloves, minced*

*1½ tablespoons mild chili powder*

*1 tablespoon dried oregano*

*2 teaspoons ground cumin*

*1 teaspoon unsweetened cocoa powder*

*¼ to ½ teaspoon cayenne pepper*

*2¼ cups water*

*1 cup canned crushed tomatoes in puree*

*¼ cup chopped fresh green chilies or 1 4-ounce can (if fresh, choose a mild variety such as Anaheim)*

*1 teaspoon salt*

Put the beans in a colander and pick them over for small stones and sticks. Rinse well, put them in a large bowl, and cover with plenty of water. The next day (or at least 6 hours later), drain the beans and put them in a pot. Cover with water by about 3 inches, bring to a boil, reduce to an active simmer, and cover partially. Cook until tender, 60 to 90 minutes, while you prepare the rest of the recipe.

Prepare but do not mix the corn bread ingredients, reducing the sugar to 1 tablespoon and the baking powder to 2 teaspoons. Reserve the dry and liquid ingredients separately.

Warm the ¼ cup oil in a large, heavy nonaluminum pot. Add the onions and sauté over medium heat, stirring occasionally, for 10 minutes. Stir in the green pepper and celery and cook for 5 minutes more, stirring occasionally. Add the garlic, chili powder, oregano, cumin, cocoa, cayenne, and remaining tablespoon of oil, stirring constantly over medium-low heat for 2 minutes; it will seem dry, but just keep stirring to minimize the sticking to the pot. Stir in the water, bring to a boil over high heat, then add the tomatoes, chilies, and salt. Reduce the heat and let simmer, covered, over very low heat.

When the beans are tender, add them to the sauce and simmer for 15 minutes. While the chili simmers, preheat the oven to 425°. Pour the chili into a 9- by 13-inch glass or enamel casserole. Cover with foil and place in the oven for about 15 minutes, until the chili is good and bubbly. Mix up the corn bread, take the casserole out of the oven, and spoon the corn bread over the chili in 3 long, equal rows. Bake for 15 minutes more, uncovered, until the top of the cobbler is lightly browned and the corn bread is cooked through; probe it with a fork to find out. Serve hot, offering a dollop of sour cream on the side.

NOTE: *Given the amount of time it takes to soak and cook dry beans, it makes sense to prepare more than you need—in this case, a whole pound—and freeze them for later use in soups or marinated bean salads. If you haven't remembered to soak them overnight, use the quick-soak method. Bring them to a boil with plenty of water, boil for 5 minutes, cover, and turn off the heat. Let them soak for 1 to 2 hours, drain, and cook.* ♦

# PIES
# AND
# TARTS

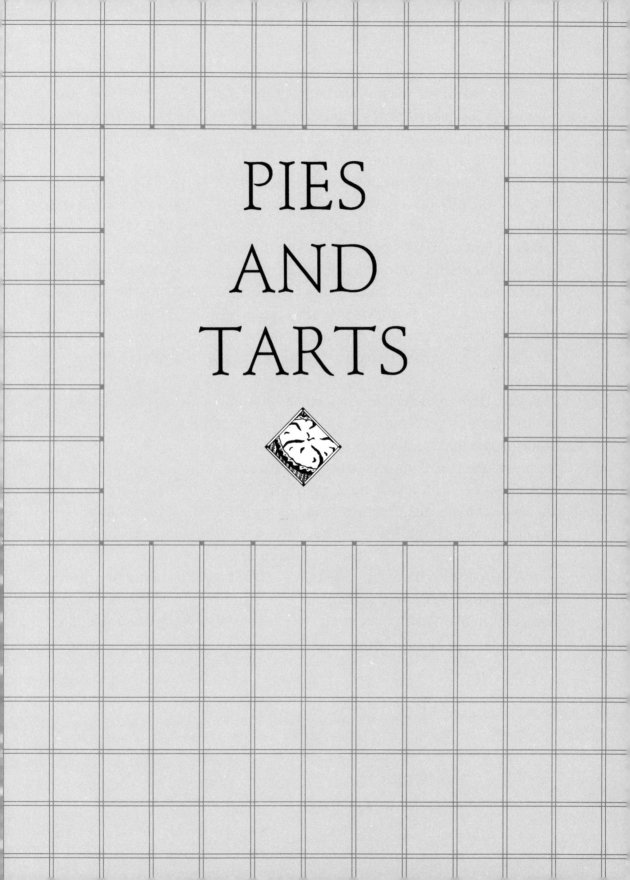

*I* think one of the most noble aspirations a person can have in life is to make good pies. It tastes good, smells good, and makes people happy. I can't think of too many other things in life for which you can make the same claims and get so much in return for your time.

So ultimately pie making is about pleasure, both giving and receiving. The pleasure of working with the raw ingredients, like plump, sun-drenched fruits. The shared pleasure of gathering those fruits, for both you and your family, if you have the opportunity. And the unabashed pleasure of digging in, watching others swoon, and waving off the rounds of compliments—"Oh, it was nothing." But don't you believe it, because a homemade pie is never nothing. It's a very personal affair, an investment of goodwill toward your fellow man. It sends a message of caring to everyone who eats it. Pies are always a cause for celebration, some of the sweetest of life's edible pleasures.

You can only fantasize so much about homemade pies before you actually have to get down, roll up your sleeves, and make them. And for some people that means overcoming a fear that has haunted them for years—namely, making a piecrust. Beneath every limp excuse I hear for not making pies—"I broke my rolling pin" or "They're too fattening"—I hear the voice of a piecrust phobic calling out for help. If this sounds at all familiar, I think the best way to deal with piecrust phobia is to confront it, get to know it, talk about it. So let's talk. And then let's practice.

A pie pastry is basically just flour and fat and a little water to help hold things together. Because solid fat, like butter and vegetable shortening, gets soft at room temperature, pie pastry needs to be chilled before you roll it out. You *can* roll a pie pastry that hasn't been chilled, but it is never as easy, and the result is never as tender. After you chill it, you roll out the pastry with gentle authority; just don't whale on it like you're beating a rug. With any luck at all, the now-firm fat will hold the pastry together, and even if you get a crack here and there, don't worry, because you can patch it up. *And* while you're doing all this you must visualize success and forget about any bumbling "I Love Lucy" images of yourself as a piecrust maker.

And those are really the most important things to know about making pie pastry. The rest is mainly practice.

On the following pages you'll find lots of practice: a variety of crusts, many with grainy overtones, and 30 or so pies and tarts (which are really just open-face pies) you can make with them. My family and I call these our best pies, the ones we keep coming back to season after season, year after year, to deliver pleasure in a big way.

Much as we would love a fresh blackberry pie in February, we wait and let the expectation whet our appetites. That's the country attitude, having the patience to wait things out until nature runs its course. This waiting is nature's gift to pie makers, because it keeps us from thinking we've ever "arrived" as pie makers. We never have, because with each changing season comes new promise and a fresh perspective, the chance to rekindle good pie times from the past.

So take a casual stroll through these pages and look for something that sounds good; you shouldn't have to go far. Then take out your rolling pin, roll up your sleeves, and start making the good pie times happen right now, for you and yours. ♦

# All-American Pie Pastry

*Makes enough pastry for 1 9-inch
double-crust pie or 2 9-inch pie shells*

I call this pastry All-American because it is made with all white flour, in the American tradition, and a fair amount of vegetable shortening, the standard pie pastry fat. The greater amount of fat, however, is butter, because any less and I think you get a bland crust, without much character. This pastry sports the good flavor and the flakiness butter provides, plus the tenderness imparted by vegetable shortening—in other words, the best of both worlds. It is excellent for almost any pie.

> 2¹/₄ cups unbleached flour
> 1 tablespoon sugar (omit if you're making a savory pie)
> ¹/₂ teaspoon salt
> ¹/₂ cup (¹/₄ pound) cold unsalted butter, cut into ¹/₄-inch pieces
> ¹/₃ cup cold vegetable shortening
> 4 to 6 tablespoons ice-cold water

Mix the flour, sugar, and salt in a large mixing bowl. Add the butter and cut it in until the pieces are somewhat broken down. Add the vegetable shortening, breaking it up with your hands, and continue to cut until the mixture has a coarse, gravellike consistency.

Sprinkle on the water, a tablespoon at a time, tossing and compacting the mixture with a fork as you go. After the fourth table-spoon, add the water in little sprinkles until the dough can be packed together. Knead the dough once, right in the bowl, to distribute the fat.

Divide the dough in half, then flatten each half into a disk about ¹/₂ inch thick; flatten it with your palm, right onto sheets of plastic wrap. Wrap the halves in the plastic wrap and refrigerate for at least 45 minutes before rolling.

For complete rolling and baking instructions, see page 200.

FREEZING: *This pastry can be frozen, overwrapped in foil, for up to 1 month. Thaw it in the fridge, then let it sit briefly at room temperature before rolling it.* ◆

# Half-and-Half Pastry

*Makes enough pastry for 1 9-inch
double-crust pie or 2 9-inch pie shells*

This pastry isn't exactly half and half, since there's a little more unbleached flour here than whole wheat. You can, naturally, tilt the balance the other way, in favor of the whole wheat. Keep in mind, however, that the more you increase the whole wheat flour, the less flaky your crust is likely to be. It will also be slightly more difficult to get into the pan, because whole wheat flour tends to make pastry brittle. This recipe is ideal for someone who likes the idea of a whole wheat crust but has little experience working with it. If and when you want to graduate to something grainier, there's always the 100 Percent Whole Wheat Pie Pastry (page 188). This is a fine pastry for any double-crusted fruit pie.

1¼ cups unbleached flour
1 cup whole wheat flour
1 tablespoon sugar (omit if you're making a
    savory pie)
½ teaspoon salt
9 tablespoons cold unsalted butter, cut into
    ¼-inch pieces
¼ cup cold vegetable shortening
4 to 5½ tablespoons ice-cold water

Mix the flours, sugar, and salt in a large mixing bowl. Add the butter and cut it in until the pieces are somewhat broken down. Add the vegetable shortening, breaking it up somewhat with your hands, and continue to cut until the mixture has a gravellike consistency.

Sprinkle on the water, a tablespoon at a time, tossing and compacting the mixture with a fork as you go. After the 4th tablespoon, add the water in little sprinkles until the dough can be packed together. (Unlike some pastry, it is beneficial if this dough feels *slightly* damp to the touch. Because the whole wheat flour is coarse, it will soak up the moisture gradually. It should not, however, feel *wet*.) Knead the dough once, in the bowl, to distribute the fat.

Divide the dough in half, then flatten each half into a disk about ½ inch thick; flatten it with your palm, right onto sheets of plastic wrap. Wrap the halves in the plastic wrap and refrigerate for at least 45 minutes before rolling.

For complete rolling and baking instructions, see page 200.

FREEZING: *This pastry can be frozen, overwrapped in foil, for up to 1 month. Thaw it in the fridge, then let it sit briefly at room temperature before rolling it.* ◆

## Rolling Pins

Every home baker needs one, maybe two good rolling pins; I have seven. Rolling pins, I've found, are like pairs of pants: however many you own, you settle on a couple of comfortable ones and the rest collect dust.

♦ The key word on pins is *durability,* with a capital D. I have literally broken the handles off the ends of lesser pins, leaning into cold pie pastry. That's when I learned that handles shouldn't just be stuck in the ends. Better pins have a continuous steel rod running through the rolling cylinder and into the handles. The cylinder itself should ride on sealed ball bearings to prevent rusting and ensure a smooth roll.

♦ The surface of a good pin should be made of a polished hardwood such as maple. A polished finish helps to keep your pastry from sticking and prevents odors from seeping into the grain of the wood.

♦ Check the handles. How do they fit in your hands? I like a hefty grip, because I have big hands. And do the handles taper in near the cylinder, so your hands won't want to slide off?

♦ Cylinder size, both diameter and length, is another consideration. With my big hands, I've noticed that unless the cylinder is 3 inches in diameter, my hands tend to scrape the surface I'm rolling on. As for length, a 12-inch cylinder is probably as big as you'll ever need. I have one with a 15-inch cylinder, a regular behemoth—25 inches when you count the handles. But there never seems to be enough room for it on my baking table, nor do I find myself making many recipes where I need the extra length.

In addition to the American-style pins I've been discussing there are French-style rolling pins. Unlike American pins, the French ones are made of one continuous cylinder of wood, in some cases tapered at the ends and in others not. The method of rolling is different: you roll the pin forward under your palms, instead of pushing down on the handles while you roll. This technique gives you more direct contact with your pastry or dough and, in certain cases, an advantage in "reading" the dough. I have two pins like this, and the thinner one, a 1¼-inch cylinder, gives me a better feel for my pie pastry than my 2-inch pin, which feels too fat—even in my big hands—for good control.

Experience will teach you when to use which pin. I often use both types of pins on the same baking project. Cold pie pastry, for instance, responds better under the direct pressure of a thin French pin. Once it loosens up, however, I like to switch to my bigger American pin. For making semolina crackers (page 323) a thin pin is much easier. A big pin is by far preferable for rolling out a batch of yeast dough for, say, coffee cake.

A French-style pin is pretty inexpensive, so it's worth getting one to try out. A good American pin is liable to cost $20. A Connecticut company named Thorpe makes the best ones I know of. Several companies, such as Rowoco, sell Thorpe pins under their own name.

Stay away from pins you fill with ice water (they seep), pins made of marble (they're expensive and unnecessary), and people who try to tell you an empty wine bottle makes a great rolling pin (they're nuts).

## 100 Percent Whole Wheat Pie Pastry

*Makes enough pastry for 1 9-inch
double-crust pie or 2 9-inch pie shells*

*I* have been making whole wheat pie-crusts for years, so I know it is entirely possible to make a good one. All it takes is butter—I like all butter here because it sets the nuttiness of the wheat off nicely— patience, moderate dexterity, and a little practice. There are some things you should know about an all–whole wheat crust. For one, it will never have the flakiness of a white flour crust; the nature of the flour, coarse and grainy, just won't allow it. These crusts tend to have a more crumbly texture. Also, the coarse flour can make them slightly brittle, so I include an egg yolk for added strength and don't roll the dough when it is too cold, because it will crack. Other than that, most of the rules that pertain to standard pie pastry apply here. This versatile crust can be used anywhere you would use a typical white flour pastry.

> 2¹/₂ cups whole wheat flour
> 1 tablespoon sugar (omit if you're making a savory pie)
> ¹/₂ teaspoon salt
> 14 tablespoons cold unsalted butter, cut into ¹/₄-inch pieces
> 1 egg yolk
> 5 tablespoons (approximately) ice-cold water

Mix the whole wheat flour, sugar, and salt in a large mixing bowl. Add the butter and, using a pastry blender, cut it in until the mixture resembles coarse crumbs; the butter pieces will be very small, with a few slightly larger ones.

Whisk the egg yolk with 3 tablespoons of the cold water and sprinkle this liquid over the flour. Toss and compact the mixture with a fork, and don't be afraid to really push on it so it starts to cohere. Sprinkle on another tablespoon and toss and compact some more. At this point, take note of the pastry's consistency—it should be starting to pull together, with some dry gaps. Use as much of the last tablespoon of water as necessary to get a dough that coheres, with neither a too-dry nor a too-moist feel; a little damp is fine, however. (You might even need a little more than 5 tablespoons of water.)

Knead the dough once in the bowl, pushing down on it with your palm. Divide the dough in half, then flatten each half into a disk about ¹/₂ inch thick; do this right on a sheet of plastic wrap. Wherever the disk has cracks along the edge, smooth them out by pushing against the dough. Wrap the halves in the plastic wrap and refrigerate for 30 to 45 minutes before rolling. Be sure not to roll the dough while it is too cold, or you may have a cracking problem. If you do get cracks while you're rolling, immediately push/pinch the dough back together.

For complete rolling and baking instructions, see page 200.

FREEZING: *This pastry can be frozen, over-wrapped in foil, for up to 1 month. Thaw it in the fridge, then let it sit briefly at room temperature before rolling it.* ♦

# Sour Rye Pastry

*Makes enough pastry for 1 9-inch
double-crust pie or 2 9-inch pie shells*

*H*ere's an excellent and unusual
pastry for savory pies and galettes
(don't miss the Rye-Crusted Potato and Cumin Seed Galette, page 145). Part of the
liquid is yogurt, and part is water, so the
texture of the pastry is somewhat softer
than you might be used to. It has a little bit
of a sour bite.

1½ cups unbleached flour

1 cup rye flour (better if it isn't too coarse)

1 teaspoon caraway seeds or toasted cumin
   seeds (see note below)

¾ teaspoon salt

½ cup (¼ pound) cold unsalted butter, cut
   into ¼-inch pieces

2 tablespoons cold vegetable shortening

2 tablespoons plain yogurt

2 tablespoons (approximately) ice-cold water

Mix the flours, seeds, and salt in a large
mixing bowl. Add the butter and cut it in
until the pieces are somewhat broken
down. Add the vegetable shortening, breaking it up with your hands, and continue to
cut until the mixture has a coarse, gravellike
consistency.

Using a fork, stir in the yogurt, tossing
and compacting the mixture. Add the water,
sprinkling it on a tablespoon at a time; after
the second tablespoon, try packing the
pastry like a snowball. It should cohere. If it
doesn't, or it has obvious dry spots, use a

little more water. When it can be packed,
knead it in the bowl once or twice to distribute the fat. Divide the pastry in half, then
flatten each into a ½-inch-thick disk on a
piece of plastic wrap. Wrap the pastry
halves in the plastic wrap and refrigerate for
at least 45 minutes before rolling.

For complete rolling and prebaking instructions, see page 200.

FREEZING: *This pastry can be frozen, overwrapped in foil, for up to 1 month. Thaw it in the
fridge, then let it sit briefly at room temperature
before rolling it.*

NOTE: *To toast the cumin seeds, put them in a
small, heavy skillet over medium-high heat—
shaking the skillet often, so they don't burn—for
several minutes; they'll probably start to make a
popping sound. Immediately pour the seeds onto a
small plate to cool.* ♦

## Cutting In the Fat

Of all the arcane and sometimes perplexing language of baking, one of the choicest little tidbits is "cutting in the fat," an expression found in virtually every piecrust recipe ever written. What sounds suspiciously like a segment from a Jane Fonda workout video is, in fact, a term that's used to describe the process of incorporating the fat in question into the dry ingredients. The objective of fat cutting is to create hundreds or thousands (no one has ever counted, to my knowledge) of tiny flour-coated fat particles. Upon baking, the moisture in these particles creates steam and expands, leaving one with that flaky texture cherished by pie lovers around the globe.

The mystery of fat cutting is further compounded by the fact that recipe writers use no standard reference to tell you just how much to cut the fat. The standard used to be "cut until the size of small peas."

Today, however, recipe writers will tell you to cut the fat until it is the size of steel-cut oats, capers, brown rice, sprouted mung beans, and a thousand other pet expressions. (I'm into gravel myself.) But basically you just want to get the particles pretty small. Generally speaking, the smaller you make them, the more crumbly the crust will be; leave bigger pieces, and you'll get more flake.

The best thing to do is play around with fat cutting until you are satisfied with your own results. Here is a rundown of the preferred methods.

*Using Your Hands:* With this method the fat and flour are actually rubbed together between the thumb and other fingers. I use this method for breaking up big clods of butter when I first add them to the flour. But when the butter is cold—as it should be—I find this method too strenuous for the amount of time it takes to get the fat broken down. And the warmth of your hands is likely to melt the butter—resulting in a less flaky crust—when you really want it to stay cool.

*Using Two Knives*: You see this method mentioned often in old cookbooks. What happens here is the blades of two knives are drawn across one another, slicing the fat into bits. Or, maybe you're supposed to hold the blades at right angles to one another. Frankly I'm not sure, and it doesn't really matter because I abandoned this technique long ago; it felt so klutzy.

*Using a Pastry Blender*: This is my gadget of choice, nothing more than a handle attached to a series of curved, rigid wires. It's pushed repeatedly down through the fat and flour with one hand, while the other clears the occasional buildup between the strands. Makes short work of the whole business.

*Using a Food Processor*: I don't own one, but I have used a food processor for making pie pastry. It is a little faster than using a pastry blender. Food-processed doughs have a reputation for being less flaky and more crumbly than others, due to the very fast, efficient cutting action of the blade. And they tend to require less water.

To make any pie pastry in a food processor, add the flour(s), sugar (if using), and salt to the bowl of the processor. Combine with several quick on/off pulses. Add the fat (butter, shortening, etc.) in large pieces and cut it in with a few more quick on/off pulses, until you have a coarse, gravellike meal. At this point, I recommend transferring the mixture to a bowl and working in the water by hand; it's the most accurate way to judge the proper consistency of the dough. You can, however, add the lesser amount of liquid to the processor and combine it with the other ingredients using quick on/off pulses. Once you have added the water, try pressing the pastry together with your fingers. If it coheres, pack it together, form into a disk, and refrigerate. Or, add more water—a teaspoon at a time—until you can pack it.

Pie lovers, in our ongoing quest for the perfect crust, have expended a fair amount of hot air over the longstanding issue of which fat makes for the best pie-crust. There are those who swear by lard for the flakiness it imparts. Butter lovers throw a considerable amount of weight behind their candidate. And solid vegetable shortening is always a favorite. The truth is, any of these solid fats—alone, or in combination—can yield a flaky crust, with certain nuances in texture from one fat to the next. Basically it boils down to a matter of individual taste, and the best way to learn about each of your choices is to experiment freely, using fats interchangeably, to find out what you like. Here is a breakdown of the main choices.

*Lard:* Poor lard: once the standard fat for country pie makers, it has fallen out of favor in today's atmosphere of healthier eating, the victim of poor public relations. That's really a shame, because it makes an unbeatably tender and flaky crust; nobody who has ever had a good lard crust will deny that. Lard, of course, is fat rendered from pork. Leaf lard, though you seldom see it in supermarkets, is considered the best. It's the fat that surrounds beef kidneys, not—as a customer once asked a friend who works at the local health food store—lard that is sold in leaf form (like sage).

Ask your butcher about the availability of lard. Rendered lard you buy at the butcher's tends to be far superior and fresher than commercial supermarket lard. And lard has less saturated fat than butter.

*Butter:* I'm a big butter crust fan—more so than lard—because I love the delicate, caramellike flavor of a butter crust and the rich golden color butter imparts. An all-butter crust tends to be more crumbly than does a lard or solid vegetable shortening crust.

*Solid Vegetable Shortening:* This has replaced lard as the standard American pie pastry fat. Frankly, as much as people use it, I think solid vegetable shortening isn't the greatest for pies: it adds nothing in the way of flavor and it leaves a greasy film in your mouth, which deadens the taste buds. I use it in small proportions, however, in combination with butter, because then you get the butter flavor along with the flaky attributes of shortening.

*Oil:* I've never had an oil crust I liked, and therefore I don't use or recommend it. Oil is absorbed by the flour, rather than remaining separate, and therefore you end up with a heavy, mealy, dense crust.

# Three-Grain Butter Pastry

*Makes enough pastry for 1 9-inch
double-crust pie or 2 9-inch pie shells*

I often mix grains in a piecrust, sometimes to achieve a particular blend,
other times just to finish off odd bags of
flour. This happened to be one of those
whimsical combinations I liked enough to
repeat until the proportions were just right.
To keep this pastry pliable, I've included an
egg yolk; it helps in the rolling. If you like,
you can replace some of the unbleached
flour with whole wheat, though the end
result won't have quite the same flaky texture. This is an excellent pastry for just
about any pie—especially when you want
something with a yellow-gold cast to contrast with a dark filling.

*½ cup yellow cornmeal, preferably stone-
   ground*
*½ cup rolled oats* (not *instant*) *or oat flour*
*1½ cups unbleached flour*
*1 tablespoon sugar* (omit if you're making a
   savory pie)
*½ teaspoon salt*
*14 tablespoons cold unsalted butter, cut into
   ¼-inch pieces*
*1 egg yolk*
*3½ to 4½ tablespoons ice-cold water*

Put the cornmeal and rolled oats into a
blender and pulse the machine on and off
until the oat flakes are reduced to small
flecks; a few remaining larger pieces are fine
(if you're using oat flour, skip this first step).

Transfer to a large mixing bowl and stir in
the flour, sugar, and salt. Add the butter and
cut it into the dry ingredients until the mixture resembles a coarse, damp meal, with
the largest pieces about the size of split
peas.

Beat the egg yolk with 3 tablespoons of
the cold water. Sprinkle this liquid over the
dry mixture, working the mixture with a
fork; push on it with the tines to help pack
it. If the mixture is still dry, add another
tablespoon of water, this time packing the
dough with your hands. Pack it with some
authority—you'll be surprised how it coheres when you do. If the dough still seems
dry, add more cold water in dribbles. Stop
adding cold water when the dough pulls
together in a dampish but not tacky-wet
ball.

Divide the dough in half, then flatten
each half into a disk about ½ inch thick;
flatten it with your palm, right onto a piece
of plastic wrap. Wrap the dough in the plastic wrap and refrigerate for at least 30 minutes before rolling.

For complete rolling and baking instructions, see page 200.

FREEZING: *This pastry can be frozen, overwrapped in foil, for up to 1 month. Thaw it in the
fridge and let it sit briefly at room temperature
before rolling it.* ◆

# Cornmeal Cheddar Pastry

*Makes enough pastry for 1 9-inch
double-crust pie or 2 9-inch pie shells*

One of the things I love most about this pastry is the aroma. Within minutes of putting a pie in the oven you get this heavenly cloud of Cheddar fragrance hanging at head level. This is, of course, a natural for apple pies, and pear pies too. One of my personal favorites using this pastry is the Cheddar-Crusted Tart Apple Pie (page 203).

1²/₃ *cups unbleached flour*
¹/₃ *cup yellow cornmeai, preferably stone-
    ground*
¹/₂ *teaspoon salt*
¹/₂ *cup (¹/₄ pound) cold unsalted butter, cut
    into ¹/₄-inch pieces*
2 *tablespoons cold vegetable shortening*
1 *cup (almost 3 ounces) grated extra-sharp
    Cheddar cheese*
¹/₄ *cup (approximately) ice-cold water*

Mix the flour, cornmeal, and salt in a large mixing bowl. Add the butter and shortening and cut it into the dry ingredients until the mixture has a gravellike consistency, with the largest pieces about the size of split peas. Mix in the grated Cheddar cheese.

Sprinkle on 3 tablespoons of the water, tossing and packing the mixture with a fork as you go. Add enough of the remaining water to make a dough that will pack together without dry pockets. (If the dough feels dampish at this point—it might— sprinkle it and your hands lightly with flour before you handle it.) Divide the dough in half, then flatten each half into a disk about ¹/₂ inch thick; flatten it with your palm, right onto a piece of plastic wrap. Wrap the dough in the plastic wrap and refrigerate for at least 45 minutes before rolling.

For complete rolling and baking instructions, see page 200.

FREEZING: *This pastry can be frozen, over-wrapped in foil, for up to 1 month. Thaw it in the fridge, then let it sit briefly at room temperature before rolling it.* ◆

## The Wisdom of Wax Paper

I'd like to say a few words on behalf of wax paper—not normally a hot topic of conversation, but a little item home bakers would do well to keep on hand.

First, the stuff is without equal when it comes to rolling out pie pastry, for the simple reason that nothing will stick to it—it's incredibly forgiving that way. Compare that to the problems most of us have had rolling pastry on a bare counter: you'll be rolling along beautifully for 5 minutes, only to find your pastry has long since become one with the Formica.

Wax paper won't let you do that. You can pretty much roll to your heart's content, and it will release your pastry on command. Just lift the wax paper right over the pan, center it, then peel it off. Never fails.

Wax paper also lets you break some of the traditional rolling rules. One of the things you can do on it that I wouldn't try on a bare surface is running your pin around the perimeter of the dough, in short strokes, to close up cracks that often start to develop there. Try it sometime.

And take advantage of the fact that with wax paper you have a built-in ruler. In order to roll the right-size bottom pastry for a standard 9-inch pie you need a circle of dough 12 inches in diameter. Since wax paper comes 12 inches wide, just start with a piece 12 inches long, then roll your circle of dough until it touches the center on all four sides of the square. Pretty neat, huh?

One trick I never have quite gotten the knack of is rolling pastry between 2 sheets of wax paper: it always buckles and crimps in the oddest fashion. It has always worked better for me to lightly flour the top of the pastry if my pin starts to stick.

## What I Really Do with Pastry Scraps

Pie makers inevitably must face the decision of what to do with pastry scraps, those trimmings from around the edge of a double-crust pie. Industrious bakers like to roll them out, dust with sugar and cinnamon, then roll them up and bake them off. Or they cut decorations from them to grace the top of a pie. Some just throw them out, which is convenient, though when I've done that I've suffered terrible spasms of guilt, the same way I do when I throw broccoli stalks away, instead of "saving them for another use"—cookbook double-talk for "Now they're your problem, pal."

Nowadays I do only one or two things with pastry scraps. The first is to just give them to the kids. This is almost as big a cop-out as throwing them away, though I can justify it to the extent that pastry scraps, like clay, are an educational tool, a way for children to express their inner selves; in other words, it keeps them out of my hair while I'm trying to finish my own pie.

But more often than not, I turn my pastry scraps into small pies because it involves so little work and the kids like them. I have several 4-inch pie tins just for this purpose; you can pick them up at most kitchen shops. The kids like to make these too, and this too will often keep them busy long enough for me to finish the pie I'm working on. Just gather your scraps, flatten them out, and chill briefly. Then let the kids roll them without butting in too much. As for the filling, just add an extra half apple or peach or whatever to your own pie in progress and save some out. Or, let the kids dig around the fridge for odd bits of fruit that need to be used up. Little pies like this need to be baked only about half as long as big ones.

## Cream Cheese Pastry

*Makes enough pastry for 6 large
or 12 small turnovers*

Here's the dough I use for a number of turnovers, both sweet and savory. It's quite rich and soft and bakes up flaky and tender, with an ever-so-slight tart bite.

*1¼ cups unbleached flour*
*¼ cup whole wheat flour*
*1 tablespoon sugar (omit if you're making a savory pie)*
*¼ teaspoon salt*
*10 tablespoons cold unsalted butter, cut into ¼-inch pieces*
*¼ pound cold cream cheese, cut into small pieces*
*2 to 3 tablespoons ice-cold water*

Mix the flours, sugar, and salt in a large bowl. Add the butter and cream cheese and cut them into the dry ingredients until the mixture has the consistency of small, split pea–size crumbs. Just when the mixture starts to clump together, sprinkle on the water, a tablespoon at a time, tossing and compacting with a fork. The dough should not have any dry pockets; if it does, add a few more drops of cold water to the dry area.

Knead the dough once in the bowl, then put it on a piece of plastic wrap. Flatten it into a disk about ½ inch thick, wrap it in the plastic wrap, and refrigerate for 1 hour. (It may be refrigerated for up to 24 hours but will need to sit at room temperature for several minutes before rolling if it is very cold.)

FREEZING: *This dough can be frozen, over-wrapped in plastic, for up to 1 month. Thaw it in the refrigerator, then let it sit briefly at room temperature before rolling it.* ♦

# Graham Cracker Crust

*Makes 1 9-inch pie shell*

This is a pretty standard graham cracker crust recipe—just cracker crumbs, butter, and sugar. One little thing I find with this crust is that when you're pressing the crumbs into place, try to keep the upper edge squared off rather than tapering it to a point, because a thin pointed edge tends to burn. Also, spread the loose crumbs around as evenly as you can before you start pressing. If, like me, you don't have a food processor, you can put the full crackers into a double plastic bag and pulverize them with a rolling pin.

1¹/₃ cups (about 11 whole crackers) graham
 cracker crumbs
1¹/₂ tablespoons sugar
5 tablespoons unsalted butter, at room
 temperature, cut into ¹/₄-inch pieces

Mix the crumbs and sugar in a large mixing bowl. Add the butter and rub it in until all of the crumbs are dampened by the fat. Distribute the crumbs evenly in a 9-inch pie pan, pushing them up the side even with the top of the rim. Press the crumbs into the pan with your fingertips. If the shell is going to be filled and baked, simply cover and chill for 15 minutes beforehand. If the pie isn't going to be baked, bake the crust (it isn't necessary to chill it first) for 10 minutes in a preheated 350° oven. Cool thoroughly on a rack before filling.

VARIATION: *For Chocolate Graham Cracker Crust, mix 1¹/₂ tablespoons unsweetened cocoa powder into the crumbs and sugar before proceeding.* ◆

## Country Bakers and Pastry Art: Perception vs. Reality

Since "country" has become a marketable concept, even pie baking hasn't escaped the sort of image posturing we normally associate with political campaigns. You can check this. Just spend a minute leafing through your local magazine rack or the country cookbook section of the local bookstore. Country pie makers, you'll see, *never* just make pies. We make *lattice-top pies,* decorate our edges with *braided pastry borders,* and think nothing of constructing a top crust of *interlocking leaves or grapevines.* These—as far as I can tell—are the kinds of country images that hit a soft spot with our counterpart city pie makers, who apparently have no interest in decorating pies with scenes from their own lives, such as interlocking subway cars or surly cabdrivers.

Although I can appreciate pie pastry art, I am not one of its vocal proponents, and I doubt if I'll ever be. Naturally, each of us must define what constitutes the limits of acceptable fancification; for some reason, I'll take yeast bread art a little further than I will pie decoration. But given the choice, I will almost always choose to bake more often than more elaborately; we're busy, with four youngsters, and the subtlety of pastry-as-art escapes the average toddler. Kids are more into the concept of pastry-as-part-of-a-pie-I-wanna-eat-right-now.

I think a pie should have an attractive edge, and there are a number of ways to make one. On a single-crust pie, start by trimming the edge and then turning the overhang back and down, as you sculpt it into an upstanding, even ridge. With that ridge you can do several things.

I generally just do the basic flute or scallop, where you push the ridge with thumb and forefinger from the outside, at the same time pushing the dough between those fingers with the forefinger from the other hand. It's easier than it sounds.

Beyond that you can flatten the ridge, instead of having it come to a peak, then score it diagonally with the back of a butter knife. Or you can do the old standby, the fork crimp, where you mash the edge down with the tines of a fork and then trim it flush with the edge of the pan.

The same techniques apply to double-crust pies. As for the top crust itself, a few well-placed slashes—cut into the rolled-out dough before it goes over the filling—can give a pie a graceful flourish. Leaving a quarter-size round of dough intact in the center of the crust, cut evenly spaced slashes out from it, either straight or arced; not too many, just a few.

And if you do make a lattice, here's a hint: weave it on a sheet of wax paper, then slide it right onto the pie. It's a lot easier than doing it on the pie.

## Piecrust Particulars

*To roll a piecrust with relative ease,* chill it first, but not so long that it becomes hard and stiff. When pastry is hard, it requires more handling, in the form of rolling pin strokes, which causes it to become tougher as it is worked. It will also crack if it is too cold. Better only to chill it long enough to firm up the fat, no more than 1 hour. If you chill pastry longer than that, let it sit at room temperature for about 10 minutes before rolling.

*To avoid sticking,* roll pastry on a lightly floured sheet of wax paper, keeping the top of the pastry dusted with flour also.

*To transfer pie pastry into the pan,* invert the wax paper and pastry over the pan, center it, then peel off the wax paper. Tuck the dough into the pan *without stretching it.* It won't stretch if you relieve the overhanging slack with one hand as you press it into the bottom crease with the other.

*To finish an edge,* trim your overhang so it is a fairly even ½ inch all around. Turn the overhang back and under, more or less pinching it to itself to beef up the edge; a beefy edge is less likely to burn than a thin one. As you do this, if the edge is thin in spots you can always pinch/press trimmings along the edge to even it out. You can leave the edge as is or flute it (see page 199).

*To prebake a pie shell,* preheat the oven to 400°. Freeze the unbaked pie shell for at least 15 minutes to firm up the pastry, then line it with foil, tucking it in as you did the pastry. Weight the foil down with enough dried beans, rice, or pie weights to nearly fill the pan, pushing them up the side toward the top rim. (I use dried beans, the same ones over and over, and I store them in a jar in my baking cabinet; don't use them for cooking once you've used them for weights. Pie weights—sold in kitchen shops—are fine too, but more costly than either rice or beans.) Bake for 20 minutes, then remove the pan from the oven. Carefully remove the foil (with the beans still in it) from the pan. Pierce the bottom of the shell several times with the tines of a fork and put the shell back in the oven. Bake for 7 more minutes for a *partially baked* crust or about 12 minutes for a *fully baked* crust. A fully baked crust will turn a golden brown; a partially baked one won't.

## Tart Pastry

*Makes enough pastry for 1 9-inch
or 10-inch tart shell*

Here's a tart shell for both savory and sweet tarts. It uses all butter, but some cooks like to replace a tablespoon or 2 of the butter with cold vegetable shortening to give the crust a more crumbly, less flaky texture; try it if you like. Because of the large amount of butter in this, the dough gets very hard if it stays in the fridge much longer than 45 minutes; it's easier to roll if you catch it before it gets too hard. Since this is not really a flaky dough, but a short one, starting with really cold butter isn't necessary. Somewhere between cool and room temperature is ideal.

FOR A 10-INCH CRUST
*1 1/2 cups unbleached flour*
*1 tablespoon sugar (omit if you're making a
  savory tart or quiche)*
*1/2 teaspoon salt*
*10 tablespoons unsalted butter, cut into 1/4-
  inch pieces*
*2 tablespoons (approximately) cold water*

FOR A 9-INCH CRUST
*1 cup plus 2 tablespoons unbleached flour*
*1 tablespoon sugar (omit if you're making a
  savory tart or quiche)*
*1/4 teaspoon salt*
*1/2 cup (1/4 pound) unsalted butter, cut into
  pieces*
*1 tablespoon cold water*

In a large bowl, mix the flour, sugar, and salt. Add the butter and cut it in until the mixture resembles very small crumbs, with all the flour having been dampened by the fat; it should actually be starting to clump together without the water. At that point add the cold water, a teaspoon at a time, tossing and compacting the mixture with a fork until the dough coheres.

When the dough coheres, knead it once in the bowl to distribute the butter, then flatten it on a sheet of plastic wrap into a disk about 1/2 inch thick. Wrap and refrigerate for about 30 minutes before rolling. It can be refrigerated for up to 2 days, but take it out of the refrigerator about 10 minutes before you plan to roll it.

To roll the dough: Put the dough on a sheet of lightly floured wax paper. Lightly flour the top of the dough, then roll it into a circle 13 to 13 1/2 inches in diameter for a 10-inch pan or almost 12 inches in diameter for a 9-inch pan. Carefully invert the dough over the pan and tuck the dough down into the pan without stretching it. Trim the dough off flush with the top of the pan. Cover and refrigerate or freeze until baking.

For baking instructions, and more information about rolling tart pastry, see page 230.

FREEZING: *This dough can be frozen, overwrapped in foil, for up to 1 month. Thaw it in the refrigerator and let it sit briefly at room temperature before rolling it.* ◆

# Whole Wheat Press-In Nut Crust

*Makes 1 9-inch pie or tart shell*

I've used many combinations of nuts here and have yet to find one that doesn't work; my favorites for this crust are walnuts, almonds, and pecans. You don't have to roll out this crust; just mix and press the mixture into the pan. It pays to take your time and press it in evenly, especially around the edges. Keep it thick near the top edge, because if the crust tapers off it over-browns and often shatters when you cut your pie.

1 1/4 cups (about 5 ounces) nuts, one type or a
  combination
3/4 cup whole wheat flour
1/4 teaspoon salt
1/4 cup unsalted butter, softened
1/3 cup packed light brown sugar
1 egg yolk

If you have a food processor, simply process the nuts in the workbowl, using the steel blade, until you have a very fine—though not powdery—consistency. If you're using a blender, put the nuts in it with half of the whole wheat flour. Turn the blender on and off quickly and repeatedly to grind the nuts; each time the machine is off, stick the handle of a wooden spoon all the way down and stir so the nuts don't compact at the bottom. Or, chop the nuts very finely by hand. Pour the nuts into a bowl and mix with all (or the rest) of the whole wheat flour and the salt.

In a separate bowl, cream the butter and sugar. Beat in the egg yolk, then add the ground nut mixture, in 3 stages, blending with a wooden spoon. By the last stage it will be easiest to work the mixture with your hands, until you have what feels like uniform, damp crumbs. When ready to use, spread the crumbs evenly in the pie or tart pan and press the mixture evenly into place. Cover and refrigerate until you're going to use it.

To partially bake the nut crust, place it in a preheated 350° oven for 15 minutes, 20 minutes for a fully baked crust.

NOTE: *If I'm in the mood, I sometimes toast the nuts in a 350° oven (usually for about 6 minutes, a little less than usual) before I grind them. It enhances the flavor.* ♦

# Cheddar-Crusted Tart Apple Pie

*Makes 8 servings*

I love this rustic pie, though I'm still not sure whether to call it a sweet pie or a savory pie; it walks a fine line in between. One moment your mouth is getting sweet apple-and-brown-sugar messages, and the next it's dancing to the sharp tunes of Cheddar and mustard. Sounds like there's a lot going on here, and there is, but somehow it all manages to pull together in one beautiful symphony. I'd serve this with a ham dinner or after a simple light meal.

1 recipe Cornmeal Cheddar Pastry (*page 194*), *chilled*

FILLING
1/2 cup packed light brown sugar
2 tablespoons apple cider vinegar
1 teaspoon Dijon mustard
1/4 teaspoon ground cloves
5 to 6 (about 2 pounds) large firm baking apples, such as Granny Smith, McIntosh, or Gravenstein, peeled, cored, and sliced
1 1/2 tablespoons unbleached flour

Preheat the oven to 425°. On a sheet of lightly floured wax paper, roll half the chilled pastry into a 12-inch circle and line a 9-inch pie pan with it. Leave the edges hanging over. Cover loosely with plastic wrap and refrigerate while you make the filling.

In a large bowl, whisk together the brown sugar, vinegar, mustard, and cloves. Stir in the apples to coat thoroughly, then sprinkle on the flour and stir again. Set aside. On a piece of wax paper, roll the top pastry into an 11-inch circle and keep it close by.

Scrape the filling into the refrigerated shell and then moisten the very outer rim with water. Invert the top pastry over the filling. Gently press down where you've moistened to seal. Trim the overhang to about 1/2 inch, then turn the edge under, sculpting it into an upstanding ridge. Form a decorative edge if you like. With a sharp paring knife or a fork, poke several steam vents in the top pastry; put one of the vents in the valley below the edge so you can check the juices there later.

Bake the pie for 15 minutes, then reduce the heat to 375° and bake for another 45 minutes, until the juices bubble thickly. The crust will be a lovely, dark mottled shade of gold. Transfer the pie to a rack to cool. Serve warm with a wedge of Cheddar on each plate. ◆

# Dried Apple and Walnut Pie

*Makes 8 servings*

Reading through one of the old Time-Life cookbooks in the Foods of the World series, I came across a reference to—but no recipe for—a dried apple pie. Seems as though a pie of this sort was common back in the old days, before fresh and canned apples started coming to market year-round. Farm families, the author said, dried their own apples, often organizing "apple-paring bees" to make the job more of a pleasure. Intrigued by the idea of a dried apple pie, I started playing around, and this is what I came up with, something both similar to (in flavor) and different from (mainly in texture) a fresh apple pie. I hope you try it. I recommend either the Half-and-Half Pastry (page 185) or All-American Pie Pastry (page 184) for this.

*1 recipe 9-inch double-crust pie pastry, chilled*

FILLING
*3¹/₂ cups fresh apple cider without*
  *preservatives*
*1 3 to 4 inch cinnamon stick (see note below)*
*4 cups (about ¹/₂ pound) dried apples*
*1 cup (4 to 5 ounces) chopped walnuts*
*¹/₄ cup honey*
*3 tablespoons unsalted butter, cut into ¹/₄-inch*
  *pieces*
*1 teaspoon light cream*
*sugar to sprinkle on the pie*

Roll half the chilled pastry into a 12-inch circle on a sheet of lightly floured wax paper and line a 9-inch pie pan with it, letting the edge hang over. Cover the dough with plastic wrap and refrigerate.

Put 2 cups of the apple cider into a medium nonaluminum pot. Add the cinnamon stick and the dried apples and bring to a boil over high heat. Reduce the heat to very low, cover, and simmer the apples for 10 minutes. Pour the contents of the pot into a large bowl and let cool. Remove the cinnamon stick and stir in the walnuts. Keep the pot handy, unwashed.

Pour the remaining cider into the original pot and bring it to a frothing boil. Reduce the cider by half; it may take only 5 minutes or less. (You might have to remove the pot from the heat to let the bubbling subside enough to check the level.) When reduced by about half, whisk in the honey and butter. Bring back to a boil, letting the butter melt, then remove from the heat and stir into the apples.

When the apples have cooled to about body temperature, preheat the oven to 425°. Roll the other half of the pastry into an 11-inch circle on a sheet of wax paper. With a sharp paring knife, cut a 6-inch-long X in the middle of the circle, all the way through the pastry. (This X gives the apples some swelling room—and they do swell—as they bake. Otherwise the top crust is likely to crack rather unceremoniously.)

Turn the apples into the unbaked shell, then lightly moisten the outer edge of the shell with water. Leaving the pastry right on the wax paper, invert the top crust over the filling, peel off the paper, and press down around the edge to seal, then trim the overhang to about ½ inch. Turn the overhang down and under, sculpting it into an upstanding ridge. Form a decorative edge if desired. Brush the pie lightly with the cream, then sprinkle it with several generous pinches of sugar.

Bake the pie for 20 minutes, reduce the heat to 350°, and bake for another 40 minutes, until the top is golden brown. Transfer the pie to a rack and cool for no less than 30 minutes before slicing. I like this pie served warm, with sweetened whipped cream.

NOTE: *Instead of using a cinnamon stick, you can add ¼ teaspoon cinnamon to the filling.* ♦

205

## Rum Raisin Apple Pie

*Makes 8 servings*

Observant eaters will no doubt detect the thinly disguised mentality of a rum raisin ice cream lover here; I plead guilty. Indeed I often find that the degree to which I enjoy summer is directly proportional to the number of pints of rum raisin ice cream I can pack away. Here's a pie that lends an added dimension to my fixation. The smell alone—of maple syrup (or honey) mingling with the rum, brown sugar, cinnamon, and raisins—is intoxicating. I like the Half-and-Half Pastry (page 185) with this, but almost any double-crust recipe will do.

1 recipe 9-inch double-crust pie pastry (see note above), chilled

FILLING
1/2 cup maple syrup or honey
1/3 cup dark rum
1 cup dark raisins
5 large firm baking apples, such as Golden Delicious, Granny Smith, or McIntosh, peeled, cored, and sliced
1/4 cup packed light brown sugar
1/4 cup unbleached flour
1/2 teaspoon ground cinnamon
2 tablespoons cold unsalted butter
1 teaspoon light or heavy cream (optional)

On a sheet of lightly floured wax paper, roll half the chilled pastry into a 12-inch circle and line a 9-inch pie pan with it, letting the edge hang over. Cover with plastic wrap and refrigerate while you make the filling.

In a small saucepan, warm the maple syrup or honey and rum, just until hot. Add the raisins, cover, and remove from the heat. Set aside for 15 minutes.

Preheat the oven to 425°. In a large mixing bowl, mix the apples with the brown sugar, flour, and cinnamon. Stir in the raisins and their soaking liquid. On a sheet of wax paper, roll the other half of the pastry into an 11-inch circle; keep it nearby. Turn the filling into the refrigerated shell, dot with the cold butter, then moisten the outer rim of the shell with water. Invert the top pastry over the filling and press around the edge to seal. Trim the overhang to about 1/2 inch, folding it down and under as you shape it into an upstanding ridge. Form a decorative edge if desired.

Using a paring knife or fork, poke several steam vents in the top crust. Put one in the valley below the outer ridge so you can check the juices there later. Lightly brush the pie with the cream, if desired, then bake for 20 minutes. Reduce the heat to 375° and bake for about another 40 minutes. When done, the top will be golden brown and any visible juices should run thickly. Cool the pie on a rack for at least 30 minutes before slicing. ♦

# Cranberry Apple Pie

*Makes 8 servings*

Every fall I buy a case of cranberries while they're in season, and stash them in my freezer, and this terrific pie is not the least of the reasons why. The sweet/tart red jewels, slightly mellowed by the apples, nestle in a flaky double crust. I'm surprised cranberry pie recipes aren't all that common, because cranberries are one of the simplest fruits to handle: they're already clean and picked over when you buy them, so there's little fuss involved, no peeling to do or anything like that. Being a little on the tart side, this pie likes a little vanilla ice cream on the side; so do oblige. I like the All-American Pie Pastry here, because the bright red filling looks nice with the lighter-colored crust.

1 recipe All-American Pie Pastry (*page 184*), chilled

FILLING
1 12-ounce package (*about 3¹/₂ cups*) fresh cranberries
2 large Granny Smith apples, peeled, cored, and coarsely chopped
1¹/₄ cups packed light brown sugar
1¹/₂ tablespoons quick-cooking tapioca
finely grated zest of 1 lemon
juice of ¹/₂ lemon
¹/₄ teaspoon ground cloves
1 teaspoon light or heavy cream

Preheat the oven to 425°. On a sheet of lightly floured wax paper, roll half the chilled pastry into a 12-inch circle and line a 9-inch pie pan with it, letting the edge hang over. Cover with plastic wrap and refrigerate. Make the filling.

In a large bowl, mix the remaining ingredients except the cream. On a sheet of wax paper, roll the other half of the dough into an 11-inch circle; keep it nearby. Turn the filling into the refrigerated pie shell, then lightly moisten the outer rim of the shell with water. Invert the top crust over the filling and press around the edge to seal. Trim the overhang to about ¹/₂ inch, then turn the edge of the pastry down and under, sculpting it into an upstanding ridge. Form a decorative edge if desired.

Brush the top of the pie sparingly with the cream, then poke a few steam vents in the pie with a fork or paring knife; put one in the valley below the edge so you can check the juices later. Bake for 20 minutes, reduce the heat to 375°, then bake for another 40 minutes. When done, the top of the pie will be a rich gold and the juices should bubble thickly. Transfer the pie to a rack and cool for at least 30 minutes before slicing. ♦

# Andy's Cranberry Maple Nut Pie

*Makes 8 servings*

Not only do we buy a lot of cranberries every fall, but our good friend Andy Johnson brings us bags full of wild bog berries he harvests himself on his occasional road trips through our area in his decrepit car. This pie—chock full of his favorite things to eat—is dedicated to Andy.

*1 recipe Half-and-Half Pastry (page 185) or another 9-inch double-crust pastry, chilled*

FILLING
*1 12-ounce bag (about 3¹/₂ cups) cranberries*
*³/₄ cup (about ¹/₄ pound) chopped walnuts*
*³/₄ cup dark or golden raisins (a combination is nice too)*
*1 large ripe but firm pear, peeled, cored, and chopped*
*²/₃ cup maple syrup or honey*
*¹/₂ cup packed light brown sugar*
*3 tablespoons quick-cooking tapioca*
*¹/₂ teaspoon ground cloves*
*¹/₂ teaspoon ground cinnamon*
*1 tablespoon milk or cream*
*sugar to sprinkle on top*

Preheat the oven to 425°. On a sheet of lightly floured wax paper, roll half the chilled pastry into a 12-inch circle and line a 9-inch pie pan with it, letting the edge hang over. Cover with plastic wrap and refrigerate while you make the filling.

In a large mixing bowl, combine the cranberries, nuts, raisins, pear, maple syrup or honey, brown sugar, tapioca, and spices. Mix thoroughly. On a sheet of wax paper, roll the other half of the dough into an 11-inch circle. Scrape the filling into the chilled shell, then lightly moisten the outer rim of the shell with water. Invert the top pastry over the filling, pressing around the edge to seal. Trim the overhang to about ¹/₂ inch, then turn the edge of the pastry down and under, sculpting it into an upstanding ridge. Form a decorative edge if desired.

Lightly brush the top of the pie with the milk, then poke a few steam vents in the top with a fork or paring knife; put one in the valley below the outer edge so you can check the juices later. Sprinkle the pie lightly with sugar if you like. Bake for 20 minutes, then reduce the heat to 350° and bake for about another 45 minutes. When done, the pie will be a deep golden brown and the juices should bubble thickly. Transfer the pie to a rack and cool for at least an hour before slicing. ♦

# All-Pear Molasses Spice Pie

*Makes 8 servings*

I've noticed that pear pie recipes aren't all that common. When you do see one, it's usually pears playing a bit role alongside some produce sensation like apples or cranberries. Here, for a pleasant change, is an all-pear pie, boldly spiced with molasses, ginger, cinnamon, and cloves, which underscore the pear's particular personality. The ginger flavor is fairly pronounced, especially if you'll be eating the pie warm; if you like, it can be reduced to ¹/₂ teaspoon. But if you plan to have the pie at room temperature, best to leave the amount of ginger as is. Excellent served with coffee ice cream.

*1 recipe Half-and-Half Pastry (page 185) or another double-crust pastry, chilled*

FILLING

*5 cups (about 6 large) peeled, cored, and sliced ripe but firm pears such as Anjou or Bartlett*

*¹/₄ cup packed light brown sugar*

*¹/₄ cup unsulphured molasses*

*2 tablespoons quick-cooking tapioca*

*1 tablespoon freshly squeezed lemon juice*

*1 teaspoon ground ginger*

*¹/₂ teaspoon ground cloves*

*¹/₂ teaspoon ground cinnamon*

*1 teaspoon heavy or light cream (optional)*

Preheat the oven to 425°. On a sheet of lightly floured wax paper, roll half the chilled pastry into a 12-inch circle and line a 9-inch pie pan with it, letting the edge hang over. Cover with plastic wrap and refrigerate. Make the filling.

In a large mixing bowl, stir the pears with the remaining ingredients except the cream. Roll the other half of the pastry into an 11-inch circle on a sheet of wax paper. Turn the filling into the pie shell, then moisten the outer rim of the shell with water. Invert the top pastry over the filling, pressing around the edge to seal. Trim the overhang to about ¹/₂ inch, then turn it down and under, sculpting it into an upstanding ridge. Form a decorative edge if you like. Poke a few steam vents in the top crust, using a paring knife or fork; put one down in the valley below the ridge so you can check the juices later. Brush the top of the pie sparingly with the cream if you like.

Bake the pie for 20 minutes, then reduce the heat to 375° and bake for another 40 minutes; the juices should bubble thickly. Transfer the pie to a rack and let cool for at least 30 minutes before slicing. ♦

# Plum Port Pie with Coconut-Almond Topping

*Makes 8 servings*

Plums are an underused pie fruit—why I'm not sure—but this blend of plums and port should put an end to our plum pie innocence. I've put this in a double crust, with few complaints, but the coconut-almond topping plays a sweeter harmony with the fruit. Just about any piecrust would work here.

*1 9-inch unbaked pie shell, chilled*

FILLING
*5 cups (12 to 14) sliced ripe plums, not the small prune plums*
*1/3 cup sugar*
*1/4 cup port*
*finely grated zest of 1 lemon*
*juice of 1/2 lemon*
*1/3 cup unbleached flour*

TOPPING
*1/2 cup unbleached flour*
*1/2 cup sugar*
*3 tablespoons cold unsalted butter*
*1/4 cup unsweetened shredded coconut (available at health food stores) or sweetened flaked coconut*
*1/4 cup slivered almonds*

Preheat the oven to 425°. To make the filling, blend all of the filling ingredients in a large mixing bowl and let the mixture stand for 10 minutes. Turn the filling into the chilled pie shell and bake for 20 minutes. As soon as it starts to bake, make the topping.

Mix the flour and sugar in a bowl and add the butter. Rub it into the dry ingredients until you have uniform, gravellike crumbs. Rub in the coconut and almonds. Cover and chill.

After the pie has baked for 20 minutes, pull the shelf out and spread the topping evenly over the pie. Reduce the heat to 350° and bake for another 45 minutes, until the juices around the edge bubble thickly. Cool the pie on a rack for at least 30 minutes—but preferably longer—before slicing and serving. ◆

# Triple Strawberry Cream Pie

*Makes 8 servings*

Here's a pie that's so good it threatens to dethrone strawberry shortcake as the reigning king of strawberry desserts: strawberry-streaked whipped cream, on top of fresh berries and a berry puree, all within a chocolate graham cracker crust. In fact this is so good I often succumb to those dubious preseason berries to make this; poor as they are, even *they* taste good in this pie. For best results, assemble the pie not more than half an hour before you plan to eat it.

1 recipe Chocolate Graham Cracker Crust
  (page 198), prebaked

FILLING
1 quart fresh strawberries, rinsed clean,
  blotted dry, and hulled
1 tablespoon plus 1/4 cup sugar
finely grated zest of 1 lemon
1 tablespoon cornstarch
1 1/2 cups heavy or whipping cream
1/4 cup confectioners' sugar

Cool the baked crust on a rack, cover it with plastic wrap, and refrigerate it until needed.

Halve half the berries and put them in a bowl. Stir in 1 tablespoon of the sugar and the lemon zest and set aside for 10 minutes. Then crush the berries with a fork until you have a chunky puree.

Put the puree into a small nonaluminum saucepan. Mix the remaining sugar with the cornstarch and stir it into the puree. Bring the mixture to a boil over medium heat, stirring often. Boil gently for about 1 minute, stirring, until the mixture thickens and turns from opaque to translucent. Scrape into a bowl and cool completely. Cover with plastic wrap and refrigerate until cold.

About 30 minutes before serving, chill beaters and a bowl to whip the cream in. Whip the cream in the chilled bowl until it begins to thicken. Add the confectioners' sugar and continue to beat until fairly stiff but not grainy. Fold in 1/3 cup of the reserved berry puree. Cover and refrigerate.

To assemble the pie, spread the remaining strawberry puree in the chilled crust. Halve the rest of the berries and arrange them, flat side down, on top of the puree. If you run out of room, chop the extra berries and spread them over the halves. Mound the strawberry whipped cream over the berries. Cut and serve or cover loosely with foil and chill briefly. ◆

# Meader All-Raspberry Pie

*Makes 8 servings*

Given the cost of raspberries, this might seem a bit extravagant. Indeed, if it weren't for our raspberry-growing friends (we go out of our way to make friends with folks who grow expensive crops we'd rather not buy), this probably would have been a raspberry-peach, raspberry-plum, or raspberry-apple pie, all of which are wonderful, but not all-raspberry wonderful like this is. We like just a couple of little touches to lift the flavor of the raspberries: orange and a bit of mint. We sweeten with both sugar and honey and use a pecan crumb topping. A top crust, we think, holds in too much moisture and doesn't settle down nicely on the berries after they've cooked. I like the 100 Percent Whole Wheat Pie Pastry (page 188) here.

Incidentally, the Meader I refer to in the title is Dr. Elwyn Meader, the plant breeder who developed this berry. (See note below.)

1 9-inch unbaked pie shell *(see note above),*
  *chilled*

FILLING
*5 cups raspberries*
*²/₃ cup sugar*
*2 tablespoons freshly squeezed orange juice*
*10 (approximately) fresh mint leaves*
  *(optional)*
*¹/₃ cup warm honey*
*¹/₄ cup quick-cooking tapioca*

PECAN CRUMB TOPPING
*¹/₂ cup unbleached flour*
*¹/₂ cup sugar*
*¹/₄ cup cold unsalted butter, cut into ¹/₄-inch*
  *pieces*
*¹/₄ cup (about 1 ounce) finely chopped pecans*

Preheat the oven to 425° while you make the filling.

To make the filling, puree ¹/₂ cup of the raspberries in a blender with the sugar, orange juice, and mint leaves. Put the remaining berries in a large bowl and pour the puree, honey, and tapioca over them; stir very gently so you don't smash the berries. When the oven is preheated, turn the filling into the chilled shell and bake for 20 minutes; start making the topping right away.

To make the topping, put the flour, sugar, and butter in a large bowl and rub them together until you have uniform, gravellike crumbs. Mix in the pecans and refrigerate.

After 20 minutes, slide the pie out and spread the crumbs evenly over the fruit, leaving a little margin around the edge. Lower the heat to 350° and bake for another 45 minutes, by which time the juices around the edge should be bubbling thickly. Cool the pie on a rack for several hours before slicing; if you cut this while it is still warm, it will be too runny.

NOTE: *A brief footnote here regarding Dr. Elwyn Meader, whose efforts have made it possible for North Country gardeners to grow not just raspberries (including the ones I use in this pie) but an entire roster of popular produce. As one person put it, this plant breeder based in Rochester, New*

Hampshire, is responsible for more of the food we northern gardeners grow than any other single human being. He has developed the Reliance peach, which in my opinion would make any Georgian turn green with envy, the Royalty green bean, the New Hampshire Midget watermelon, three kinds of raspberries, two apricots, an apple, a blueberry, and a persimmon, to name just a handful. This dedicated man clearly has revolutionized gardening in our region.

If you would like to know more about Dr. Meader's work, a good primer can be found in the July 1989 issue of Yankee magazine ("He's Still Designing the Perfect Plant"). ◆

## Peach and Fresh Currant Pie

*Makes 8 servings*

For a very short time each summer we are lucky enough to have a modest supply of red currants for the picking. Fresh red currants aren't all that common in the marketplace. They're small and delicate, not easy to harvest, and highly perishable; grocers don't like to handle them. Nonetheless, if you keep your eyes open, especially during the months of July and August, you may find a supplier. Snatch some up if you do, because this recipe is too good to pass up; I have seen otherwise sedate and well-mannered friends make utter pigs of themselves with this pie. For the crust, choose the All-American Pie Pastry (page 188) or the Three-Grain Butter Pastry (page 193).

1 recipe 9-inch double-crust pie pastry (see note above), chilled

FILLING
4 cups (about 5 or 6 large) sliced peeled ripe peaches
2 cups fresh red currants
1 cup sugar
1/4 cup quick-cooking tapioca
1 tablespoon freshly squeezed lemon juice
1/2 teaspoon ground cinnamon
1 tablespoon light or heavy cream
sugar to sprinkle on the pie (optional)

On a sheet of lightly floured wax paper, roll half the chilled pastry into a 12-inch circle and line a 9-inch pie pan with it, letting the edge hang over. Cover with plastic wrap and refrigerate while you make the filling. Preheat the oven to 425°.

Combine the peaches, currants, sugar, tapioca, lemon juice, and cinnamon in a large bowl. Set aside. On a sheet of wax paper, roll the other half of the pastry into an 11-inch circle. Turn the filling into the chilled shell and lightly moisten the outer rim with water. Lay the top pastry over the filling, pressing around the edge to seal. Trim the overhang to about 1/2 inch, then turn the overhang down and under, sculpting it into an upstanding ridge. Form a decorative edge if desired. Poke a few steam vents in the top pastry with the tines of a fork or a paring knife.

Brush the top of the pie sparingly with the cream. Sprinkle with a little sugar, if you like, then bake for 20 minutes. Lower the heat to 375° and bake for 45 more minutes, until the top of the pie is a rich golden brown. Transfer to a rack to cool. Serve warm or at room temperature.

VARIATION: *It isn't quite the same, but you can substitute raspberries for the currants. Cut back on the sugar by 1/4 cup.* ◆

# Logging Road Blackberry Pie

*Makes 8 servings*

In winter our favorite ski trail is an old logging road that, by late summer, produces wild blackberries like nobody's business. In a good year—and some years are better than others—I can't keep up with the berries, but I always try, this recipe being one of the quickest solutions. Nobody seems to mind the little blackberry seeds, but should you prefer to skip them, try either the Wild Blackberry Cream Pie (page 217) or the Blackberry Kahlua Cream Tart (page 234), both made with seedless blackberry puree. I like the All-American Pie Pastry (page 184) here.

1 9-inch unbaked pie shell (see note above), chilled

FILLING
5 cups (2¹/₂ pints) fresh ripe blackberries
³/₄ cup sugar
2¹/₂ tablespoons cornstarch
1 tablespoon freshly squeezed lemon juice
¹/₄ teaspoon freshly grated nutmeg

OAT TOPPING
¹/₂ cup unbleached flour
¹/₂ cup packed light brown sugar
¹/₃ cup rolled oats (not instant)
¹/₄ teaspoon ground cinnamon
pinch of salt
¹/₄ cup cold unsalted butter, cut into ¹/₄-inch pieces

Preheat the oven to 425°. To make the filling, combine all of the filling ingredients and let stand for 10 minutes. Turn the filling into the chilled shell and bake for 20 minutes. As soon as it starts baking, make the topping.

Mix the flour, brown sugar, oats, cinnamon, and salt in a bowl. Add the butter and cut or rub it in until you have gravellike crumbs. Cover and chill.

After the pie has baked for 20 minutes, pull the shelf out and spread the oat topping evenly over the pie. Reduce the heat to 350° and bake for about another 50 minutes, until the juices bubble thickly. (If the pie starts to bubble over, put it on a baking sheet.) Cool the pie on a rack for at least 1 hour before slicing. ♦

## Blackberry Picking

Blackberry season, for us, is a long summer comma, etched with deliberate pleasure and ritual. The expectation is half the fun, like Christmas in the dead of summer. As the season approaches, there are the frequent walks or bike rides to scout out favorite spots ("I *know* it's gonna be the *best* year yet, Pop, right?"). Recipe talk is as thick as the mosquitoes ("Why don't we make a lot of whipped cream, Pop, and stir in the berries!!"). We dream aloud of blackberry pies and cakes and cobblers as though they were old friends about to come visit for summer vacation.

When the big opening day finally arrives, there's a scramble for old yogurt containers. A couple of slits, and we serious pickers strap them to our belts: we know by now you need two free hands to do a good job. For the youngest of us, any old baggie or bucket will do: something else we know by now is when you're two or three or four, chances are slim any berries will make it past that bucket attached to your jaws. We don long sleeves and long pants.

Blackberry pickers are secretive, lest one accidentally divulge the whereabouts of a choice spot. So we sneak our way down to the old logging road, hush, hush, doing our best not to look like blackberry pickers, baggies flying and yogurt containers in tow. Once we're off the dirt road and onto the trail we feel safe, and the picking begins.

I like picking blackberries with my kids for the same reason that Christmas is a lot more fun since I've been a father: because the whole experience is magnified in the eyes of a child. When you pick blackberries with your kids, you never just run into a good spot. It's "Pop, I found *tons*!!" Blackberries off the bush never just taste good to a child; they're "the *best* blackberries in the *whole world*!" There's the other side of the coin too, of course: a thorn prick and it's "I think I'm *bleeding* to death, Pop!"

The pickings on opening day are never the greatest, of course: the berries are too small, underripe. It'll be several weeks yet before they reach that point where—anointed by warm summer rains and long days of sun—the berries just fall into your palm. But today nobody much cares, least of all the kids. Today we were out there fighting the brambles, and there were plenty of butterflies to chase. When the lightning began, we ducked into the woods and crouched in a gully, plastic bags pulled over our heads, a family of stranded Glad Bag aliens. A grouse scared the bejeezus out of us. The muffins will never taste better.

## Wild Blackberry Cream Pie

*Makes 8 servings*

We seem to have a high tolerance for little blackberry seeds in this family, so most of the blackberry pies we eat are the whole-berry type, like the previous one. Toward the end of the season, however, we do like to make this smooth-as-silk blackberry pie from strained blackberry puree. What you get is a really outrageous sort of blackberry custard in a crust. You can serve whole blackberries on the side of each piece or just make up a little extra puree to spoon on top. But that's not really necessary. I suggest either the Three-Grain Butter Pastry (page 193) or the Half-and-Half Pastry (page 185) for this pie.

1 9-inch pie shell (*see note above*), *partially baked* (*see page 200 for baking instructions*)

FILLING
2 cups ripe fresh blackberries
3 large eggs, at room temperature
1¹/₂ cups heavy cream
³/₄ cup sugar
1 teaspoon vanilla extract

Cool the pie shell on a rack and preheat the oven to 425° while you make the filling. Puree the blackberries in a blender or food processor. Pass the puree through a fine strainer to remove the seeds; you should have 1 to 1¹/₄ cups of puree left. Reserve.

Beat the eggs lightly, then stir in the cream, sugar, vanilla, and blackberry puree. Slowly pour the filling into the crust and bake for 10 minutes, then reduce the heat to 325° and bake for another 35 minutes. When done, the pie should jiggle all together, not ripple in waves. It's okay, however, if the very center is just a tad loose because it will finish cooking as it cools. Cool the pie thoroughly on a rack and then chill for several hours—loosely covered with foil—before serving. ◆

# Honey Pear Tarte Tatin

*Makes 8 servings*

I love everything about this upside-down pie, baked in a skillet—the wonderful flavor, the rustic appearance, and the speed and ease with which this can be assembled. It really is a safe bet for the pie-timid, because you essentially end up with a single-crust pie while bypassing some of the standard pie-making technicalities. I specify a 9- or 10-inch skillet here, but I have also used my 12-inch skillet; for that size, buy extra pears, double the amounts of butter and honey, and use almost all of the pastry instead of half of it.

*½ recipe Three-Grain Butter Pastry (page 193), chilled*

FILLING
*2 tablespoons unsalted butter*
*¼ cup honey*
*2 tablespoons packed light brown sugar*
*1 teaspoon vanilla extract*
*6 large ripe but firm pears, halved, cored, and peeled*

Preheat the oven to 400° as you make the filling. Melt the butter in a 9- or 10-inch cast-iron skillet over medium heat. Stir in the honey and brown sugar and bring to a low, frothing boil. Boil for several seconds, stirring constantly, then remove from the heat, stirring in the vanilla just as you do so.

Starting at the perimeter, arrange the pears in the skillet, rounded sides down and points toward the center. Put 2 halves in the center, pointing in opposite directions. If you have leftover pears, slice them and arrange them between the others, keeping everything reasonably neat and orderly.

On a lightly floured sheet of wax paper, roll the pastry into an 11- to 12-inch circle. Invert it over the pears, tucking the edge down between the side of the pan and the pears; don't worry if the crust looks rumpled—it will—because you won't even see it in the end. Poke a few steam vents in the crust with a fork. Bake for 40 minutes. Transfer the pan to a rack and cool for 10 minutes.

Run a knife around the edge, separating the crust from the pan, then put a large plate on top of the skillet. Using pot holders or oven mitts to protect your arms from hot juices, invert the pan; the tart should drop right onto the plate. Slice and serve with vanilla or coffee ice cream or whipped cream. I like to let this cool again for about 30 minutes before serving to crisp the crust.

VARIATION: *Try this made with quartered apples, the traditional tarte tatin filling, in place of the pears.* ◆

## Is It Done?

Knowing when a pie is done is an acquired skill and one worth honing, because it often spells the difference between pie bliss and the pie blues. The pies in this collection fall into only a few major categories, and the signs of doneness are pretty much consistent within each group.

*Double-Crust Fruit Pies:* There are two chief indicators here: the color of the top crust and the activity of the fruit juices (I almost always poke a steam vent in the valley below the outer ridge so I can see inside to check the juices). When the pie is done, the top crust usually will be well browned, even more so if it has been glazed with cream and/or sprinkled with sugar. In the latter case, it may even turn too brown before the filling is done, in which case you can cover the pie with a loose foil tent. As for the filling juices, they should be oozing thickly; if they're thin, the thickener hasn't done its job yet. Bake for at least 10 more minutes.

*Single-Crust Fruit Pies:* This type has some sort of crumb or crunchy topping or a lattice top instead of a top crust. The juice on such a pie should be thick when the pie is done, and it's easy to judge because it bubbles up through the topping. If the topping gets too brown before the juice is thick, cover with a foil tent.

*Custard Pies:* These are pies made with eggs, milk or cream, and sweetener. The timing for a custard pie is more crucial than for a fruit pie, which will suffer no great harm from overbaking. An overcooked custard pie, however, will be unpleasantly tough and grainy. Remove it from the oven when the center is still a bit wobbly but the rest of the pie seems set; the center will firm up as the pie cools.

*Translucent Pies:* Pecan pie is one example of a translucent pie, essentially a custard pie without milk or cream. The rule for custard pies applies here as well: the pie should be set, wobbly but not syrupy in the center (you can check it with a fork).

# Cherry Coconut Crumb Pie

*Makes 8 servings*

Cherries and coconut make a beautiful couple in this simple summer pie. I call for sweet cherries just because that's the only kind I can find here in New Hampshire. But from what I've read and heard, many people prefer sour cherries for pies; the pie recipes I've seen, using an equivalent amount of sour cherries, use about 1 cup of sugar, so adjust accordingly. Be sure not to use any more than 5 cups of cherries and to make a high rim on the pie shell, because this is very juicy. Almost any piecrust in this book will work fine here.

*1 9-inch unbaked pie shell, chilled*

FILLING
*5 cups (about 2¹⁄₂ pounds) quartered pitted sweet cherries (see note below)*
*¹⁄₂ cup sugar*
*juice of 1 lemon*
*2 tablespoons quick-cooking tapioca*
*1 teaspoon vanilla extract (optional)*

COCONUT CRUMB TOPPING
*¹⁄₂ cup unbleached flour*
*¹⁄₂ cup sugar*
*3 tablespoons cold unsalted butter, cut into ¹⁄₄-inch pieces*
*¹⁄₂ cup unsweetened shredded coconut (available at health food stores) or sweetened flaked coconut*

Preheat the oven to 425°. To make the filling, combine the cherries, sugar, lemon juice, tapioca, and vanilla. Turn the filling into the chilled pie shell, cover the top very loosely with foil (just lay it flat over the top), and bake for 20 minutes. As soon as that starts to bake, prepare the topping.

Mix the flour and sugar in a bowl. Add the butter and cut or rub it in until the mixture has a gravellike texture; all of the dry elements should be dampened by the butter. Lightly mix in the coconut with your hands. Refrigerate.

After 20 minutes, slide the pie out of the oven and spread the topping evenly over the top. Lower the heat to 350° and bake for 50 to 55 minutes more. If the topping starts to brown too much, either move the pie down to a lower rack or cover it loosely with foil. When the pie is done, you should see a good deal of thickish, bubbling juice around the edge. (If juice starts to leak over the sides, put the pie on a baking sheet.) Cool the pie on a rack. Slice and serve lukewarm or at room temperature.

NOTE: *To pit cherries by hand, score them along the circumference down to the pit, then pinch the halves off; messy, but not difficult. Or open up a paper clip into an S shape, stick it into the cherry at the stem end, and pop the pit out. Either of these methods keeps juice loss to a minimum, and once you get the hang of it, they're both very fast.* ◆

# Green Tomato Mincemeat Pie

*Makes 8 servings*

Green tomato pies are a country tradition in New England and beyond, anywhere cool temperatures rob ripe promise from the vine. This pie parlays adversity into advantage, with little more than a few spices and a splash of maple syrup (you *could* use all brown sugar or honey). What you get is something that tastes like mincemeat. A hearty pie, this is best served as a snack or after a light meal, with something hot to drink. My first choice here would be the Three-Grain Butter Pastry (page 193).

*1 recipe 9-inch double-crust pie pastry, chilled*

FILLING
*5 (approximately) medium-large green*
  *tomatoes*
*¹/₂ cup maple syrup*
*¹/₃ cup packed light brown sugar*
*¹/₂ cup chopped pitted dates*
*¹/₂ cup (about 2 ounces) chopped walnuts*
*1 tablespoon apple cider vinegar*
*¹/₄ teaspoon salt*
*¹/₄ teaspoon ground cinnamon*
*¹/₄ teaspoon ground allspice*
*¹/₄ teaspoon ground cloves*
*finely grated zest of 1 lemon*
*¹/₃ cup unbleached flour*

On a lightly floured sheet of wax paper, roll half the chilled pastry into a 12-inch circle and line a 9-inch pie pan with it, letting the edge hang over. Cover with plastic wrap and refrigerate while you make the filling. Preheat the oven to 425°.

Quarter the tomatoes and cut each quarter into ¹/₄-inch slices; measure 4 cups of tomatoes. Mix the tomatoes in a large bowl with the remaining filling ingredients.

On a sheet of wax paper, roll the remaining pastry into an 11-inch circle. Turn the filling into the chilled pie shell, then lightly moisten the rim of the shell with water. Lay the top pastry over the filling, pressing down around the rim to seal, then trim the overhang to about ¹/₂ inch. Turn the overhang down and under, sculpting it into an upstanding ridge. Form a decorative edge if desired. Poke a few steam vents in the top pastry with the tines of a fork or a paring knife.

Bake the pie for 20 minutes, reduce the heat to 375°, then bake for another 40 minutes, until the top is golden brown. Transfer the pie to a cooling rack and cool to lukewarm before serving.

NOTE: *If you want a shiny top crust, brush it with a little cream and sprinkle sugar over the top just before baking. For a slightly different pie, substitute some sliced apples for an equal amount of tomatoes.* ♦

# Sweet Potato Molasses Pie

*Makes 8 servings*

Sweet potato pies generally have a grainier, denser texture than pumpkin or squash pies because the flesh is more fibrous. This version is less sweet and darker than usual, from the molasses; if you want it sweeter, use all brown sugar. For Thanksgiving I often use all maple syrup as the sweetener, and that makes a superb pie too. I don't know why, but chilling the pie seems to give it a smoother consistency than serving it warm. In place of the Whole Wheat Press-In Nut Crust, you can use any other partially baked shell you like.

1 recipe Whole Wheat Press-In Nut Crust (page 202), partially baked

FILLING
1¼ cups mashed cooked sweet potatoes (see note below)
½ cup packed light brown sugar
¼ cup unsulphured molasses
1 cup light cream or milk
3 large eggs, lightly beaten
¼ cup unsalted butter, melted
1 teaspoon ground ginger
1 teaspoon ground cloves
1 teaspoon ground cinnamon
½ teaspoon freshly grated nutmeg
¼ teaspoon salt

Preheat the oven to 400° and make the filling as the nut crust cools on a rack.

In a large mixing bowl, whisk together the filling ingredients until well blended.

Scrape the filling into the shell—it will come right up to the top—and bake for 10 minutes. Then reduce the heat to 350° and bake for about another 25 to 30 minutes. When done, the top of the pie will have puffed a little, more so around the edges. Transfer the pie to a rack to cool. Serve with whipped cream or vanilla ice cream.

NOTE: *I don't think it makes a big difference whether you use boiled (peeled) sweet potatoes here or the flesh from baked sweet potatoes. Boiled potatoes probably lose some flavor, but frankly, with all the spices, you'll never taste the difference. But if you happen to have the oven on anyway, by all means bake them. For boiling you'll need about 4 to 5 medium potatoes; if you bake them, use a few extras, because some of the outer flesh always gets too dry to use. Mash the flesh briefly, by hand, because if you do it too much you draw out the stringy fibers.* ♦

# Crème Brûlée Pie

*Makes 10 servings*

They don't make 'em any better than this: a custard of incomparable richness with a caramelized brown sugar topping. Crème brûlée, you'll remember, was one of the premier desserts of the eighties after comfort foods came back in. Find the best fresh eggs you can, preferably from a local supplier; the flavor will be much fresher and the pie a good deal richer in color. You have to start this the day before you plan to serve it.

1 9-inch pie shell, partially baked (see page 200 for baking instructions); I like the Three-Grain Butter Pastry (page 193) best here

FILLING
5 large egg yolks
1/2 cup packed light brown sugar
1 1/2 cups light cream
1 cup heavy cream
1 teaspoon vanilla extract
an additional 1/4 cup packed light brown sugar for the top

Let the pie shell cool on a rack while you make the filling.

Put the egg yolks and 1/2 cup brown sugar in a medium bowl and blend with a wooden spoon; don't use a whisk, or you may make the custard grainy. Set aside. Preheat the oven to 325°.

Heat the creams in a small saucepan until very warm to the touch, then blend about one-third of the cream with the yolks. Slowly stir in the remaining heated cream, then the vanilla.

When the crust has cooled—do this next step right at the stove—pour the custard into the shell and place it in the oven; at the same time put a loaf pan of water on the rack also, to create a steamy environment. Bake for about 45 minutes, until the center is barely set. Cool thoroughly on a rack. Cover tightly with plastic wrap—creamy things act like a magnet for refrigerator smells—and chill overnight.

Just before you serve the pie, sieve the 1/4 cup brown sugar evenly over the pie. Run the pie under the broiler just until the sugar bubbles and melts, turning a caramel color; watch it like a hawk. (And if you blow it and char the sugar, just scrape it off and eat the pie.) Slice and serve. ♦

# Maple Banana Cream Pie

*Makes 8 servings*

Okay, so banana cream pie isn't exactly hip anymore (if it's hip you want, check out the Peaches and Cream Pie, page 225), but my better half—who grew up on allegedly legendary midwestern cream pies—swears they come no better than this. Case closed. One little New England touch we've added to this no-bake pie is to pan-glaze the bananas with maple syrup—not enough to cook them; they're in the pan for only a few seconds. But you can skip that business if you like and just put the banana slices directly into the shell without dousing them. And you can also slather whipped cream all over the top or serve it on the side.

1 9-inch Graham Cracker Crust pie shell
    (*page 198*), prebaked

FILLING
³/₄ cup packed light brown sugar
¹/₂ cup unbleached flour
pinch of salt
3 large egg yolks
2 cups milk
1 cup light cream
1 teaspoon vanilla extract
5 tablespoons unsalted butter
¹/₄ cup maple syrup
2 medium-size ripe but firm bananas, sliced
¹/₄ cup unsweetened shredded coconut
    (*available at health food stores*) or
    sweetened flaked coconut

As the pie shell cools, make the filling.

In a medium nonaluminum saucepan, whisk together the brown sugar, flour, and salt. Put the egg yolks in a mixing bowl and beat well with a whisk. Scald the milk and cream in another saucepan, then whisk a little of it into the egg yolks. Add the yolks to the dry mixture in the first saucepan and begin to cook over moderate heat, stirring pretty much constantly while you gradually add the remaining milk and cream.

When the mixture starts to boil, turn the heat down a little and cook, stirring, until quite thick, about 3 minutes; get your spoon into the bottom crease of the pan so it doesn't burn there. Take the pan off the heat and whisk in the vanilla and 3 tablespoons of the butter; add it several small pieces at a time, then wait until it melts before adding more. Press a piece of plastic wrap directly over the filling so it doesn't form a thick skin. Cool for 30 minutes while you prepare the bananas.

Over high heat, bring the maple syrup and the remaining 2 tablespoons of butter to a boil in a heavy skillet. Boil for 1 minute, then add the banana slices. Stir to coat well for about 15 seconds, then scrape the bananas and the gooey stuff left in the pan onto a big plate. Cool.

To assemble the pie, scrape the cooled bananas and juices into the shell, then ladle the filling over the top; it will be a very full pie. Let cool for 30 minutes, then sprinkle the coconut over the top. Cover very loosely with foil and refrigerate for at least 2 hours before serving. ◆

# Peaches and Cream Pie

*Makes 8 servings*

This would be a great menu item for one of those New Wave diners I hear are popping up in metropolitan areas, places where you can get oldies but goodies with a nouvelle twist, like burgers with salsa and BLTs with Belgian endive. Instead of the banana cream pie (delicious, but not New Wave enough) you could serve this no-bake, peach lover's fantasy. There are fresh peaches on the bottom and peach puree in the cream topping. Be sure to make this in the morning if you're going to serve it for dinner, because it needs plenty of time to chill.

*1 9-inch Graham Cracker Crust pie shell (page 198), prebaked*

FILLING
*²/₃ cup sugar*
*¹/₂ cup unbleached flour*
*pinch of salt*
*3 large egg yolks*
*4 large ripe peaches*
*2¹/₂ cups (approximately) light cream*
*1 teaspoon vanilla extract*
*3 tablespoons unsalted butter*
*freshly grated nutmeg to sprinkle on top*

Let the pie shell cool on a rack while you make the filling.

In a medium nonaluminum saucepan, whisk together the sugar, flour, and salt; do not heat. Put the egg yolks in a mixing bowl and beat well with a whisk. Peel and slice 2 of the peaches, dropping them right into a 2- or 4-cup measure. Pour enough cream into the cup to get an even 2-cup measurement. Pour the cream and peaches into a blender and puree. Pour the puree into another nonaluminum saucepan, add 1 more cup of light cream, and heat gently, just until hot to the touch. Remove from the heat.

Whisk a ladleful of the heated mixture into the egg yolks. Stir this into the saucepan with the dry ingredients and turn the heat on low. Gradually add the rest of the liquid, stirring almost constantly and slowly increasing the heat to medium.

When the mixture starts to boil, turn the heat down a little and cook, stirring, until quite thick, about 3 minutes; get your spoon into the bottom crease of the pan so it doesn't stick or burn there. Take the pan off the heat and whisk in the vanilla and then the butter, several small pieces at a time, waiting until it melts to add more. Press a piece of plastic wrap directly over the filling so it doesn't form a skin. Cool for 30 minutes.

After 30 minutes, assemble the pie. Peel and slice the remaining peaches, dropping the pieces directly into the pie shell; spread them evenly. Ladle the filling over the peaches. Let the pie cool at room temperature for 30 minutes, then cover loosely with a foil tent; it shouldn't touch the pie's surface. Refrigerate for at least 3 hours before serving. Dust with nutmeg just before slicing. ♦

# Chocolate Molasses Pecan Pie

*Makes 8 servings*

This pie, I'm afraid, is going to reveal my true revisionist colors. For the life of me, I can't look at a recipe—say, pecan pie—without wondering how it would taste with a little molasses, some chocolate, and a crumb topping, the alterations I've made here. How indeed? Very, very fine! The filling has the consistency of the richest, moistest brownie you can imagine. My favorite crust for this pie is the Three-Grain Butter Pastry (page 193); Karen, my wife, prefers the Half-and-Half Pastry (page 185). Excellent served warm, with vanilla ice cream—though I wouldn't turn down a piece at any temperature.

1 9-inch pie shell (see note above), partially baked (see page 200 for baking instructions)

FILLING
5 tablespoons unsalted butter
1/3 cup unsulphured molasses
3 ounces semisweet chocolate
2/3 cup packed light brown sugar
1 teaspoon vanilla extract
2/3 cup (about 3 ounces) pecan halves
3 large eggs, lightly beaten

TOPPING
3 tablespoons yellow cornmeal, preferably stone-ground
2 1/2 tablespoons packed light brown sugar
1 tablespoon unbleached flour
pinch of salt
2 1/2 tablespoons cold, unsalted butter, cut in 1/4-inch pieces
1/3 cup finely chopped pecans

Cool the pie shell on a rack and preheat the oven to 375° while you make the filling. In a large saucepan, heat the butter and molasses over medium heat until the liquid reaches a boil. Reduce the heat to very low and add the chocolate. Swirl the pan so the liquid runs over the chocolate, then just let the pan sit over very low heat for a minute. Whisk until smooth, then stir in the brown sugar. Heat for another minute, stirring, then remove from the heat and stir in the vanilla. Spread the pecans evenly in the pie shell.

Make the topping by combining the cornmeal, brown sugar, flour, and salt. Add the butter and rub it into the dry ingredients until you have a damp, crumbly mixture. Stir in the pecans and set aside.

Whisk the eggs into the saucepan, just until blended. Slowly pour the liquid over the pecans in the pie shell, scraping out the pan with a rubber spatula. Gently rap the pan on the counter to help the pecans rise, then spread the topping evenly over the top. Bake for 15 minutes, reduce the heat to 350°, and bake for another 15 to 20 minutes. When done, the pie will just be starting to puff and crack on top. The center may seem a little loose, but it shouldn't be soupy. Transfer to a rack to cool. Serve at any temperature except very hot. ◆

# Brown Sugar Yogurt Pie

*Makes 8 servings*

This is my adaptation of the old-fashioned American buttermilk pie. We buy a local made-on-the-farm brand of yogurt with the rich, delicious yogurt cream on top. (Our family has made a pact that the first of us to open the yogurt will stir the yogurt cream in instead of hogging it all, but like most of our other food pacts—at least those involving restraint—this one has proved pretty worthless.) This pie has a perfect balance of sweet and tart flavors, the brown sugar giving it a slight caramel touch; it tastes almost like a tart crème brûlée. We like it warm, but cold is everyone's favorite. Try this with the Three-Grain Butter Pastry (page 193).

1 9-inch pie shell (see note above), partially baked (see page 200 for baking instructions)

FILLING
1 cup packed light brown sugar
3 tablespoons unbleached flour
3 large eggs
1 large egg yolk
1 teaspoon vanilla extract
1¹/₂ cups plain yogurt
¹/₄ cup unsalted butter, melted and cooled

Cool the pie shell on a rack and preheat the oven to 350° while you make the filling.

Put the brown sugar and flour in a large mixing bowl and rub them together between your fingers until smooth, breaking up all the clumps. In a separate bowl, lightly beat the eggs and egg yolk. Whisk the eggs into the sugar along with the vanilla, yogurt, and melted butter until uniformly blended. Pour into the pie shell and bake for 35 to 40 minutes. When done, the pie will be slightly puffy and just a little wobbly in the center; shake it a little to see. If the surface moves in waves, give it 5 more minutes. Cool the pie on a rack. Refrigerate within 2 hours, loosely covered with foil. ◆

## Cottage Cheese Mint Lime Pie

*Makes 8 servings*

*H*ere's a creamy, honey-sweetened summer pie that can be whipped up in a flash. And because it calls for a graham cracker crust, there's no pastry to worry about. Make this early in the day so it has plenty of time to chill before dinner.

*1 9-inch unbaked Graham Cracker Crust pie shell (page 198)*

FILLING
*2 large eggs*
*1 large egg yolk*
*1/2 cup milk or light cream*
*1/2 cup warm honey*
*1 tablespoon freshly squeezed lime juice*
*finely grated zest of 1 lime*
*1/4 cup fresh mint leaves (not packed)*
*1 pound small- or large-curd cottage cheese*

Place the pie shell in the freezer to chill. Meanwhile, preheat the oven to 350° and make the filling.

In a medium mixing bowl, beat the eggs and egg yolks lightly and set aside. Gather the remaining ingredients and a blender in front of you. In 2 batches, puree the remaining ingredients in the blender, using roughly half of everything for each batch; it helps to put the more liquid ingredients into the blender first. (This can also be pureed all at once in a food processor.) Blend the pureed ingredients with the beaten eggs, then care-fully pour the filling into the graham cracker pie shell. Bake for approximately 35 minutes. When done, the pie will probably just be starting to puff around the edge and the filling should jiggle as a whole; the center shouldn't be soupy. Cool thoroughly on a rack, then cover loosely with foil and refrigerate for at least 3 hours before serving. ◆

# Chocolate Tofu Fudge Pie

*Makes 10 to 12 servings*

Tofu is soybean curd, low in fat and calories and somewhat bland, which makes it an excellent vehicle for the chocolate here, especially if you're watching your weight. The consistency of this filling is a little stiffer than mousse but close in flavor. There's no baking involved; just pour the filling into the crust and chill.

1 9-inch Graham Cracker Crust pie shell (page 198), prebaked

FILLING
3/4 *cup honey*
2 *tablespoons unsulphured molasses*
2 to 3 *ounces unsweetened chocolate (see note)*
1 *tablespoon instant coffee or espresso powder*
1 *teaspoon ground cinnamon*
1 *pound fresh tofu (the* soft *kind, if you have a choice)*
1/3 *cup milk*
1 *cup (4 to 5 ounces) toasted coarsely chopped walnuts*
1/4 to 1/3 *cup unsweetened shredded coconut (available in health food stores) or sweetened, flaked coconut*

Cool the pie shell on a rack while you make the filling.

Put the honey and molasses in a small saucepan and place over very low heat. Lay the chocolate on top of the honey. As the honey warms, swirl the pan so the heated honey runs over the chocolate. Add the powdered coffee or espresso and the cinnamon and whisk the mixture until smooth. Remove from the heat.

Put the tofu in a dish towel and twist to express some of the water; don't worry about getting every last drop. Assemble in front of you the tofu, chocolate mixture, milk, and a blender.

Put roughly half each of the tofu, chocolate mixture, and milk in the blender and puree until very smooth; you may have to turn the blender on and off and scrape down the sides with a rubber spatula. Pour the puree into a bowl and repeat for the remaining half of the ingredients. Blend both halves of the puree and fold in the walnuts. Scrape the filling into the pie shell and even it with a spoon. Chill, loosely covered with foil, for at least 3 hours before serving. For an attractive topping, sprinkle with the coconut before slicing.

NOTE: *The greater amount of chocolate (3 ounces) will make for a very intense chocolate flavor. It will be somewhat more mellow using the lesser amount.* ◆

Why is it that those American bakers who think nothing of knocking out a pie shrink at the thought of making a tart? One reason, I think, is that our veneration of French food gives tarts an aura of inaccessibility ("I couldn't make one of *those*—why, that's a *French* dish!"). This inaccessibility doesn't diminish, either, when one runs across pictures of tarts in magazines or books: the symmetry of apple slices arranged in precise rows or perfect circles of overlapping eggplant and tomatoes is confounding. Makes the inside of your average fruit or pot pie look like a demolition derby.

You can, of course, take tart making to extremes. But everyday tarts should be a source of fun and enjoyment, not intimidation. A tart, after all, is just an open-face pie, either sweet or savory. Tarts are inherently pretty, so you needn't go to a lot of trouble to make them look stunning.

Here, then, is a little collection of home-grown tart wisdom to get you rolling.

*Pans:* The typical tart pan has a removable bottom, so you can unveil the tart when you serve it (the tart, however, is always baked *in* the pan). The sizes range from just a few inches in diameter for individual tarts to about 11 inches. The sides are usually about 1 inch high. Most cookbooks call for 9-, 10-, or 11-inch pans. Compared to some pieces of baking equipment, tart pans are relatively inexpensive, so if you take up tart making in a big way it's worth it to buy a full range of sizes.

*Getting the Pastry in the Pan:* I am not, and never have been, a big fan of rolling the pastry onto the pin and unrolling it over the pan—a piece of advice I often see in baking books. Not only does it feel awkward, but if the pin accidentally drops and hits the sharp edge of the pan, you can slice your pastry up. Tart pastry—and pie pastry, for that matter—is stable enough to allow you to roll it out on lightly floured wax paper, invert it over the tart pan, peel the paper off, and gently tuck the pastry into the pan. Perhaps the most important thing to remember is *not to stretch the dough when you tuck the lower edge of the pastry into the pan.* Otherwise, when the shell bakes it will shrink and the top edge will pull down, leaving a low spot where filling can run out. To avoid stretching, pull up the pastry that's hanging over the edge so you have plenty of slack as you tuck. What I generally do with the overhang is just fold it over and press it into the side to beef up the edge; press the pastry into the flutes if your pan is fluted. If there's very little overhang, you can just push it down to a point even with the top rim of the pan. As you work your way around the pan, if you find that the upper edge of the dough is lower in spots than the side of the pan, lightly moisten that area with water and patch it with the excess you trim from another part of the pastry.

*Trimming the Upper Edge:* Generally the upper edge is trimmed flush with the top of the pan, either with a paring knife or by running a rolling pin over the top; I don't care for the latter method.

If you find that the upper edge has dropped and shrunk after the tart shell has been prebaked, that's a good indication you're stretching the dough as you put it in the pan and you run the risk—as I mentioned—that the filling will run over the side. If the problem persists, try this: take the overhanging dough and roll it back over the outside edge without trimming it off. Then, after the tart is fully baked, trim the edge flush with the top of the pan while the tart is still hot, using a sharp paring knife. That's somewhat unconventional, but it works.

*Lining the Shell:* Before you line the shell with foil, put it in the freezer for about 15 minutes to firm it up and stabilize it. Once the shell is very firm, tear off a 12-inch piece of foil and tuck it into the pastry, just like you tucked the pastry into the pan. Then pour a very thick layer of dried beans into the foil, enough

that they're easily supporting the side up to the top edge. (When you're done with the beans, cool them and store in a sealed jar for future use.)

*Prebaking the Shell:* Place the weighted shell in a preheated 400° oven and bake for 15 minutes. Remove the pan from the oven and very carefully lift the foil out of the pan with the beans still in it. At this point you will have to bake the shell further, either about 7 minutes (*partially baked,* if the tart will be filled and cooked longer); or 10 to 12 minutes (*fully baked,* if the tart isn't baked after it is filled). Before you put the tart shell back in the oven, pierce the bottom several times with a fork to discourage it from puffing up and not cooking properly. (After the shell is baked, if it's going back in the oven I always like to fill in those fork holes with a little flour putty, made with a teaspoon of flour and a few drops of water, to make a paste. I took up this practice after making several "leak tarts," where the custard actually ran out through the fork holes and all over the oven, once right before I had some friends over for dinner— "My, that's a mighty skimpy quiche there, Ken.")

*Cooling the Shell:* Once baked, just put the tart pan on a rack to cool before filling it.

# Apple-Applejack Tart

*Makes 8 to 10 servings*

The usual way to glaze a free-form apple tart such as this is with apricot preserves. One day I thought I'd try something a little different and soak the apple slices in maple syrup and applejack, then boil down the liquid left in the bowl and use that for a glaze. Then I got really carried away and served the tart slices with whipped cream and more applejack drizzled over the top; it was a big hit. In the end I was pleased with the way the applejack introduced a masculine balance to a dessert with an otherwise feminine personality (it looks like a flower blossom).

*⅓ cup maple syrup*

*⅓ cup applejack*

*4 large Golden Delicious apples*

*1 tablespoon unbleached flour*

*1 tablespoon sugar*

*1 recipe 10-inch Tart Pastry (page 201), chilled*

*1 tablespoon unsalted butter*

Get out a large cookie sheet, preferably not a dark one because this bakes for a long time and you don't want the bottom to scorch.

Pour the maple syrup and applejack into a large bowl and blend briefly with a whisk. Peel the apples, then cut them in half from top to bottom; remove the cores. Now, slice the apples the other way—across—into ¼-inch-thick slices, dropping them into the bowl of applejack and maple syrup as you work. Toss gently with your hands so the slices are saturated, then set aside for 15 minutes; preheat the oven to 425°. Meanwhile, mix the flour and sugar in a small bowl and set aside.

On a sheet of wax paper, roll the pastry into a large, wide oval, about 14 to 15 inches long; invert it onto the baking sheet. Sprinkle the flour/sugar mixture over the pastry, leaving about a 1-inch margin of uncovered dough all around. Drain the apples, reserving the liquid.

Now, using the smaller and any broken slices for the first (outer) row, make a ring of apple slices, just touching end to end, around the perimeter, leaving roughly a 1½-inch margin of dough at the edge. Continue to make rows in this manner, overlapping the rows slightly; the one you are working on should lean against the previous one. As you get toward the center, it will be more difficult to keep the rows overlapping in any logical arrangement, but if you change the angle and start overlapping them the long way you should get an attractive-looking center. Keep in mind that you are trying to simulate a flower blossom.

When all the apple slices have been used, fold the uncovered perimeter of dough over the outer edge of the apples, making sure you have a continuous lip of dough at the bottom edge. (In other words, if the dough rips in places as you fold it up—which is not unusual—just make sure you pinch the seam together so there's no gap for juice to run out on the sheet.) Put the tart in the oven.

Immediately pour the reserved applejack/maple liquid into a small saucepan and bring to a boil. Boil for about 1½ minutes, swirling the butter in at the end to melt it. Remove from the heat and set aside.

When the tart has baked for 15 minutes, slide it out and brush the apples heavily with the glaze. Reduce the heat to 400° and bake for another 45 to 55 minutes, brushing the tart with the glaze every 15 minutes. In the end the apples—and the bottom of the tart—will be well browned, and it isn't unusual for some of the tips of apple pieces to scorch ever so slightly, which really doesn't affect the overall flavor.

Slide the tart onto a rack and cool for at least 10 minutes before slicing into wedges. Serve with whipped cream and, if you like, sprinkle a little extra applejack over each piece. ◆

# Blackberry Kahlua Cream Tart

*Makes 10 servings*

This recipe has its roots in some milk shakes we once made with blackberries and Ben & Jerry's White Russian ice cream, because our local village store was out of vanilla. The shakes were great, so I reconstructed the flavors in this outrageous tart, suitable for a formal summer dessert. (Make this in a prebaked pie shell if you want a little less formality.) You cover the crust with a seedless blackberry puree and cover that with Kahlua-spiked whipped cream. Pretty simple, but quite stunning.

*1 10-inch Tart Pastry shell (page 201), fully baked (see page 230 for baking instructions)*

BLACKBERRY PUREE
*4 cups ripe fresh blackberries (save out a few if you want to decorate the top of the tart)*
*1/2 cup sugar*
*4 teaspoons cornstarch*
*grated zest of 1 lemon*

KAHLUA WHIPPED CREAM
*1 1/2 cups heavy cream*
*3 tablespoons confectioners' sugar*
*2 tablespoons Kahlua*

Cool the tart shell thoroughly on a rack. Transfer the shell to a large, flat plate or platter, cover with foil, and refrigerate.

To make the blackberry puree, process the blackberries in a blender or food processor until smooth. Strain the puree through a fine-mesh strainer, working and pushing it with a spoon so you end up with as much seedless puree as possible; you should be left with close to 2 cups of puree. Put the puree into a nonaluminum saucepan. Mix the sugar and cornstarch in a small bowl and stir it, along with the lemon zest, into the puree. Bring to a boil over medium heat, stirring often. Hold it at a low boil for 1 minute, stirring, then scrape it into a glass casserole or pie pan and place it in the fridge to cool. Once it has cooled, scrape it into the tart shell, evening it with a fork. Cover and refrigerate for at least 30 minutes. (The recipe can be made a couple of days ahead up to this point.)

When you are just about ready to assemble the tart, put the beaters and whipping cream bowl in the freezer. Once they're chilled, beat the cream until it almost holds soft peaks, then add the sugar and Kahlua. Beat until good and firm, but don't let it get grainy. Spread the whipped cream over the puree and arrange a few blackberries here and there if you saved some out. Slice and serve right away or hold in the fridge, covered, for up to several hours (it will hold beyond that, but it won't stay in tip-top shape). ◆

# Honey-Glazed Seckel Pear Tart

*Makes 8 servings*

Seckel pears are about half the size of the large ones you normally see in the market, and they have a reddish-brown skin. They're firm when ripe, and they hold their shape well, which is one reason I chose them for this free-form tart. A simpler tart you'll never find: just sprinkle flour and sugar in the shell, cover with halved pears, and glaze once while it bakes. I don't even bother to peel the pears since the skin is so thin, and the dark color looks good against the creamy pear interior when the tart is cut. Serve lightly sweetened whipped cream on the side. Good coffee is a must.

1 9-inch Tart Pastry shell (*page 201*),
    *partially baked (see page 230 for baking
    instructions)*

FILLING
*2 tablespoons sugar*
*1¹/₂ tablespoons unbleached flour*
*¹/₄ teaspoon ground ginger*
*¹/₄ teaspoon freshly grated nutmeg*
*8 to 10 (about 1¹/₂ pounds) Seckel pears,
    halved*
*2 tablespoons unsalted butter, softened*

HONEY GLAZE
*¹/₄ cup honey*
*2 tablespoons unsalted butter*
*1 tablespoon bourbon (optional)*

Cool the tart shell on a rack and preheat the oven to 375° while you make the filling. In a small bowl, mix the sugar, flour, and spices; set aside. Using an apple corer or a sharp paring knife, remove the cores from the pears, setting the pears aside on a plate as you work. To assemble the tart, spread the flour mixture evenly in the shell and lay the pear halves on top, flat side down; fit them in randomly and snugly. Smear the softened butter over the pears and bake for 40 minutes. Immediately put the honey and butter in a small saucepan.

When the tart has baked for 25 minutes, bring the honey and butter to a boil. Stir in the bourbon and quickly remove from the heat. Pull the oven shelf out and spoon half the glaze over the tart, basting each pear. Save the remaining glaze.

When the tart has baked for 40 minutes, remove from the oven and place on a rack. Cool for at least 15 minutes before slicing; this should be served warm. When serving, reheat the reserved glaze and spoon a little over each piece. ♦

# Cheesecake Fruit Tart

*Makes 10 servings*

I've always liked fruit cheesecakes, but I've never been wild about those gloppy canned fruit toppings that are the standard in so many diners and restaurants. This is much more to my taste—a thin layer of cheesecake in a tart shell, over which you can spread fruit preserves or fresh summer berries. Our favorite preserves and fruit spreads are made by a company called Sorrell Ridge, which uses a lot more fruit than most commercial brands, so the flavor is superior; its products are now widely available. Another advantage of this cheesecake is that because it's thinner, you can make, chill, and serve it the same day. Regular cheesecake almost always needs to be refrigerated overnight. My first choices for the preserves are apricot and peach, but use what you prefer.

1 9-inch Tart Pastry shell (*page 201*),
   *partially baked (see page 230 for baking
   instructions)*

FILLING
*6 ounces cream cheese, softened*
*¹/₃ cup sugar*
*1 large egg, at room temperature*
*2 teaspoons freshly squeezed lemon juice*
*finely grated zest of 1 lemon*
*¹/₂ teaspoon vanilla extract*
*¹/₂ cup heavy cream*

TOPPING
*1 10- or 12-ounce jar fruit preserves or fruit
   spread or about 1 pint fresh berries*

Cool the tart shell on a rack and preheat the oven to 350° while you make the filling.

Beat the cream cheese with an electric mixer until fluffy, gradually adding the sugar. Beat in the egg, lemon juice, lemon zest, and vanilla, then beat in the cream just until the mixture is smooth. Scrape the filling into the shell and bake for 20 to 25 minutes, just until set. Cool the tart in the pan on a rack to room temperature, then cover loosely and refrigerate for at least 1 hour.

If your preserves are very chunky, it is probably best—though not absolutely necessary—to press them through a fine sieve with the back of a wooden spoon. Do this directly into a bowl, then whisk in a teaspoon (or several) of water to get a somewhat looser, more spreadable consistency. Pour the fruit over the tart and spread it out evenly. Slice and serve or refrigerate first.

If you're using fresh berries, simply rinse them and spread them out on a layer of paper towels to blot up excess moisture. Then cover the tart with them or serve them spooned over individual slices. If you're using strawberries, halve them first or slice thinly and arrange on top. ◆

# Maple Pecan and Hazelnut Tart

*Makes 10 to 12 servings*

This tart has all the gooeyness that makes pecan pie a perennial favorite, but in a classier package; where one might serve pecan pie after a family dinner, this would be a good company dessert, holiday or gift tart. As rich as this is, better to serve it in modest portions, with strong coffee and maybe a little unsweetened whipped cream on the side. Very simple to make.

1 9-inch Tart Pastry shell (*page 201*),
   *partially baked (see page 230 for baking
   instructions)*

FILLING
1 cup (4 to 5 ounces) pecan halves
3/4 cup (about 4 ounces) hazelnuts
3 large eggs
1 cup maple syrup
1/2 cup packed light brown sugar
1/4 cup unsalted butter, melted
1 teaspoon vanilla extract

Cool the tart shell on a rack and preheat the oven to 350° while you make the filling.

Spread the pecans and hazelnuts on a baking sheet, in separate areas, and toast them in the oven for about 8 to 10 minutes, until the skins on the hazelnuts are quite dark. Set the pecans aside to cool, but put the hazelnuts in a tea towel, fold the towel over, and rub the nuts to get the skins off—or at least some of the skins; some will stay attached, but don't be concerned. Transfer the hazelnuts to a chopping board and chop them coarsely.

Put the remaining filling ingredients in a large bowl and beat with a whisk or an electric mixer until blended. Working right near the oven—so you don't have to walk far with this—spread the pecans and hazelnuts evenly in the shell. Slowly pour the liquid filling into the shell. (To minimize the nuts going every which way when you pour in the filling, hold a rubber spatula under the stream as you pour.) Using a fork, dunk all the nuts to coat them with liquid—they'll bob right up—at the same time spreading them out evenly in the shell.

Bake the tart at 350 degrees for 45 minutes, until somewhat puffed and set. Cool on a rack for at least 30 minutes before slicing. ♦

# Peach Preserves Macaroon Tart

*Makes 10 to 12 servings*

I love this tart, a flaky tart pastry covered with peach preserves and a coconut-almond topping. Since there's no filling to prepare and you don't have to pre-bake the pastry, you can assemble this very quickly and easily. Naturally you can use other preserves here—apricot is another favorite—or a blend of preserves. A rustic-looking free-form tart like this would look right at home in a flat, cloth-lined basket, cut into thin wedges. Eat out of hand, or for a more formal meal, serve with plate and fork.

*1 9-inch recipe Tart Pastry (page 201)*

TOPPING
*1 egg white*
*2 tablespoons sugar*
*³/₄ cup slivered almonds*
*¹/₂ cup unsweetened shredded coconut
 (available in health food stores) or
 sweetened flaked coconut*

FILLING
*1 cup peach preserves*

Chill the tart pastry and preheat the oven to 400° while you make the topping: Beat the egg white with the sugar, just until frothy. Stir in the almonds and coconut. Set aside.

When the pastry has chilled, roll it into a circle just slightly larger than 11 inches in diameter. Put a pie plate or some other 11-inch template on top of the dough and trim it with a paring knife into an even circle. Transfer the circle to a baking sheet.

Put the preserves in a bowl and stir briskly to loosen, then spread evenly on the circle of pastry, leaving a ³/₄-inch margin of uncovered dough around the edge. Spread the topping over the preserves, then fold the uncovered edge of dough up and over, leaning it against the filling; if the edge cracks when you're doing this, pinch it back together so the filling doesn't run out. Bake for 10 minutes, reduce the heat to 350°, and bake for another 30 minutes, covering the top loosely with foil during the last 15 minutes if it starts to get too brown. Slide the tart onto a rack to cool. Serve in thin slices, barely warm or at room temperature. ♦

## My Problem with Machines

I have a Stone Age attitude about kitchen machines in general, especially the big two that most other cooks and bakers rant and rave about: the food processor (I don't have one, but I've used it in professional kitchens) and the hefty KitchenAid mixer (I seldom use mine).

I learned to cook and bake without the benefit of these machines, and being a creature of habit, I tend to cling to ingrained ways. I like using a sharp knife, the way some carpenters enjoy using their hand planes or chisels. I like mixing bread doughs by hand; and for me it's just no big deal—and actually a bit of a pleasure—to spend 5 or 10 minutes kneading a dough by hand.

I know other good cooks who use these machines all the time, and probably if you own them, you'll know how to adapt these recipes to make full use of the machines. See the box on page 191 on piecrust in the food processor and page 63 for notes on using the dough hook of the mixer for kneading.

I also think that the kitchen machine craze—and the attendant change in recipe writing that assumes these machines—has spawned a nervousness among cooks, who start to view these devices as critical links in home cooking, gadgets without which their own cooking won't quite measure up. But the one critical link in home cooking is you, the cook, your approach to and involvement with your food. We already have enough machines that minimize our involvement with food. There's even a bread-making machine on the market now, into which you dump all your ingredients, hit a few buttons, and in a few hours you have a loaf of bread, without ever getting your hands dirty. Is this home baking when we simulate factory baking and move it into our homes? Progress? Perhaps. But progress has a voracious appetite, and what it consumes is never quite the same. Let's hope that progress never becomes the battle cry of home cooks.

# Pear Tart with Almond Cake Topping

*Makes 8 servings*

This is a simplified version of a tart I used to make often, something called Pear Tart Frangipani. Visually it was more breathtaking than this—the pear halves poked seductively out of the filling—but it got to be too much of a production after a while: poach the pears in wine, slice them thinly, make an apricot glaze. . . . My short-cut version uses unpoached chopped pears, and you pour the cake topping right over them, thus eliminating several time-consuming steps and in the process saving the bottle of wine, which you can now have with your dinner.

1 9-inch Tart Pastry shell (*page 201*),
  *partially baked (see page 230 for baking
  instructions)*

FILLING
2 cups (2 to 3 large) peeled, cored, and
  chopped ripe pears
1 tablespoon freshly squeezed lemon juice
¼ cup honey
3 tablespoons unbleached flour

ALMOND CAKE TOPPING
¼ cup unsalted butter, softened
1 large egg, at room temperature
½ teaspoon vanilla or almond extract
1 tablespoon unbleached flour
½ teaspoon baking powder
½ cup (2 ounces) almonds
¼ cup packed light brown sugar

Cool the tart shell on a rack and preheat the oven to 400° while you make the filling.

Mix all of the filling ingredients together in a bowl. When the tart shell has cooled, turn the filling into the shell, smooth it out, and put it in the oven. Immediately make the topping.

Using an electric mixer, cream the butter until fluffy. Beat in the egg and vanilla, then mix the flour and baking powder and beat them in. Put the almonds and brown sugar in a blender or food processor and grind to a fine consistency. Beat the almonds/brown sugar into the creamed mixture.

After the tart has baked for 20 minutes, pull it out of the oven and spread the topping evenly over the pears. Reduce the heat to 375° and bake for another 20 minutes, until nicely browned. Cool the tart in the pan on a rack for at least 15 minutes before serving. ◆

## Black Mission Fig Tart

*Makes 8 to 10 servings*

I have always wanted to make a fig tart, but all the recipes I've ever seen use fresh figs, which are about as rare in New Hampshire as snowless winters. So I just devised my own *dried* fig tart, using Black Mission figs, which have the softest skins. After the figs are cooked in wine and water, they're pureed and spread in the tart shell, then an almond cake topping is baked on top. This tart is superb, and I guarantee it's the classiest fig bar you've ever eaten. It takes a little time, but it's worth it. To make things easier, you can make the fig puree and/or the pastry the day before.

1 10-inch Tart Pastry shell (*page 201*), *fully baked (see page 230 for baking instructions)*

FILLING
1 1/4 *cups quartered dried Black Mission figs, stems cut off (about 6 ounces)*
1 1/2 *cups water*
1/2 *cup red wine (I like to use Zinfandel)*
1 *3- to 4-inch cinnamon stick*
1/4 *cup honey*

CAKE TOPPING
1 *recipe Almond Cake Topping (page 240)*

Cool the tart shell on a rack while you make the filling.

Put the filling ingredients in a medium saucepan and bring to a boil. Reduce to a very low boil, cover, and cook for about 40 minutes; during this cooking the figs will swell as they take on moisture, but they won't get mushy. Pour the contents of the pan into a bowl and cool. Remove the cinnamon stick.

While the figs are cooling, make up the almond cake topping and set it aside. Preheat the oven to 375°.

Once the figs have cooled, puree them and their juices in a blender or food processor. Spread this thick puree evenly in the tart shell and bake for 10 minutes. Slide the tart out and scrape the almond topping on top, quickly leveling it, as well as you can, with a fork. Bake for 20 minutes more, until the top is a deep golden brown. Cool the tart on a rack for at least 15 minutes before serving. ◆

# Toasted Pecan Honey Tart

*Makes 10 servings*

If you like sweet, rich desserts, you'll love this. It's so easy to make that you can have it in the oven in less than 10 minutes after the tart shell has baked.

1 9-inch Tart Pastry shell (*page 201*),
   partially baked (*see page 230 for baking*
   *instructions*)

FILLING
1¹/₂ cups (6 ounces) pecans
³/₄ cup honey
³/₄ cup heavy cream
2 tablespoons unsalted butter
1 teaspoon vanilla extract

Cool the tart shell on a rack and preheat the oven to 350° while you make the filling.

Spread the pecans in a single layer on a baking sheet and toast them in the oven for about 8 minutes, until lightly colored. Take them out and cool them on the sheet.

Put the honey, cream, and butter in a medium saucepan and gradually bring to a boil over medium-high heat. When it reaches a full boil, boil for 1 minute, then remove from the heat and stir in the pecans and vanilla. Scrape the mixture into the tart shell and spread the nuts out evenly. Bake for 25 minutes; the filling will have thickened and become a soft, candylike coating on the nuts. Slide the tart out of the pan and cool on a rack for 30 minutes before slicing. ♦

# CAKES

*M*y philosophy about cake making is this: if you need a pastry bag, I'm probably not interested. The fact that I'm already hedging—saying *probably* when I really mean just plain *not interested*—betrays the fact that I don't feel entirely comfortable with my admission. There is a side of me that would love to be the Larry Bird of pastry baggers, pumping out chocolate stars the way the Bird pumps in free throws. But to put it as plainly as possible, I feel like a total klutz with a pastry bag; I'm not patient enough, and the last I saw of my star tip—or was it a rose tip?—it was in the sandbox, looking like it had recently taken the path of greatest resistance through the lawn mower, which is probably just what happened. If that had been one of my bread pans, I would have been upset. But in this case I think it's just another sign from above to forget about cake decorating, at least for this lifetime.

Now that that's off my chest, let me tell you about the types of cakes I do like to make. They are, for the most part, the fringe cakes, the mavericks, the ones with the rough-hewn looks and killer taste. My home-style cakes aren't fussy. I don't even like to ice a cake if I can help it, and I don't use cake flour; the cakes I make work fine with unbleached flour. So, we have cheesecakes, always a consuming pleasure to a fellow who grew up cruising the diners of New Jersey, the cheesecake capital of the world. We have cakes made with fruits—cobblers (which are really a type of cake), holiday fruitcakes, and upside-down cakes (love those upside-down cakes). Not to mention pudding cakes and pound cakes. Always easy, and always good, these are everyday cakes, cakes anybody can make, right now, with little more than some basic pans, an electric mixer, and an oven.

If the cakes I like to make are short on decoration, they're long on pure pleasure, distinguished by their great flavors, the use of fresh ingredients, and a selection of whole grain flours. There are sugar cakes, but alternatives too, made with molasses, honey, and maple syrup. Whole wheat flour makes an appearance in some of my cakes. As with so many other baked goods, I think whole wheat flour adds character to cakes—not every cake, mind you—and I'm not too concerned if these aren't as downy-light as they might be when made with cake flour; what you sacrifice in lightness you gain back manyfold, in my opinion, in flavor and overall integrity, without losing an iota of across-the-board appeal. Of that this collection of simple, home-style cakes has plenty. ◆

## The Ultimate Baking Gift

What could be nicer than giving friends and family a tin of cookies or a great fruitcake for the holidays? Giving them baked goods year-round, that's what. Call it the Baked-Good-of-the-Month Club. Here's how it works.

Come Christmas you hand the lucky recipient a booklet of 12 coupons, one redeemable per month, for 12 outrageous baked things. You might write on the coupon what the baked thing will be, maybe just hint at it, or not commit yourself at all. Then, when each new month rolls around, you hand over the sticky buns, cheesecake, or yeast loaf of the month. Ideally you keep it seasonal—Triple Strawberry Cream Pie in spring, Raspberry Mint Muffins in the summer—and ideally you wouldn't fail to live up to your end of the deal; this isn't one of those clubs where you can cancel your commitment at any time. Be sure to keep it personal and make the recipients the sorts of things they like. (When in doubt, ask. I used to live under the false assumption that everybody would eat *my* fruitcake, just because I liked it, but I found out the hard way that wasn't the case.)

Please note that this amounts to a good deal of baking over the long run and should probably be reserved for somebody high on your shopping list, somebody you love dearly or hope to love dearly, and who'd really appreciate it.

# Honey Ginger Pound Cake

*Makes 2 medium or 3 smaller cakes*
*(roughly 20 to 24 servings)*

Having a homemade pound cake in the fridge—where it will last up to a week, tightly wrapped—is probably the best insurance against ever coming up short for an easy breakfast, snack, or dessert idea. You can serve a slice alone, of course, with hot coffee. But you can also top it with fresh berries, berries and whipped cream, yogurt, applesauce, ice cream, apple and other fruit butters, fruit compotes—you name it. This is what you would call our basic pound cake—with which we do all of the above and more—sweetened entirely with honey and enriched with whole wheat flour. Maybe it isn't as light as some pound cakes, but it isn't heavy either: it's just right, moist and even-textured, with a close grain and golden crumb. If you prefer, use smaller pans than the ones I specify; just make sure the batter comes two-thirds to three-quarters of the way up the sides of the pan. And for best results, I recommend using a mild-flavored honey, such as orange blossom. Otherwise the honey can be too intense.

1 cup (½ pound) unsalted butter, softened
1 cup honey, at room temperature
4 large eggs, at room temperature
1 teaspoon vanilla extract
grated zest of 1 lemon
2 to 3 tablespoons minced candied ginger
1¼ cups unbleached flour
1 cup whole wheat pastry flour
1 teaspoon baking powder
½ teaspoon salt
¼ teaspoon freshly grated nutmeg

Preheat the oven to 325° and butter 2 3¾-by-7¾-inch loaf pans or 3 smaller ones; don't use dark pans. Line them with buttered wax paper, buttered side out. Set aside.

Using an electric mixer, cream the butter and honey. Beat in the eggs, one at a time, beating well after each one. Mix in the vanilla, lemon zest, and candied ginger.

Sift the remaining ingredients into a bowl—including any pieces of bran that remain in the sifter—then fold them into the creamed mixture in stages; stop stirring as soon as the batter is blended. Divide the batter evenly between the loaf pans, then bake for 45 to 50 minutes, until a toothpick inserted in the center comes out clean. Cool the pans on a rack for 15 minutes, then lift out the cakes by the wax paper. Continue to cool the cakes on the rack, peeling off the paper while they are still warm. As soon as there's no trace of warmth left in the cakes, wrap them in plastic wrap and overwrap in foil. Store at room temperature for 2 to 3 days, but refrigerate for longer storage than that.

FREEZING: *If overwrapped in foil, this will freeze for up to two months. Thaw at room temperature, without unwrapping, before slicing.* ◆

# Dark and Moist Cranberry Nut Fruitcake

*Makes 1 large cake (16-20 servings)*

A variation of the Pumpkin Molasses Cake on page 250, this is unusually moist because it's made with fruit—raisins, cranberries, and dried apricots—that's been cooked in cider. I also use dates, but I precook them with the cider only if I can't find the soft Medjool dates at my local health food store. Dried cherries are also excellent in this classic cake for the late fall and early winter months, and it needs no embellishment other than mugs of dark, hot coffee or tea. This is the kind of filling, wholesome snack I like to pack in our fanny sacks when we go cross-country skiing.

1 cup fresh cranberries
1 cup dark raisins
¹/₂ cup chopped dried apricots
¹/₂ cup apple cider
1 modified recipe Pumpkin Molasses Cake
    (page 250), as outlined below
1 cup chopped pitted dates
1¹/₂ cups (about 7 ounces) chopped pecans
    and walnuts

Put the cranberries, raisins, apricots, and cider in a medium nonaluminum pot and bring to a boil. Reduce the heat, cover, and cook at a low boil for 5 minutes. Uncover and cook for about another 5 minutes, until the small amount of remaining liquid is a thick glaze. Scrape the contents of the pot onto a plate and cool to room temperature.

Meanwhile, preheat the oven to 350° and butter and flour a 9- or 10-inch tube or kugelhopf pan.

Prepare the Pumpkin Molasses Cake, making the following changes: Replace the pumpkin with ²/₃ cup milk; use ¹/₂ cup each of light brown sugar and molasses; in addition to the cinnamon and ginger, sift ¹/₂ teaspoon ground cloves and 1 teaspoon unsweetened cocoa powder with the dry ingredients. Also, omit the ¹/₂ cup raisins listed, because you're adding a cup already.

Once the batter is mixed, fold in the cooked fruit, the dates, and the nuts. Scrape the batter into the prepared pan and bake for about 55 minutes, until a tester inserted in the center comes out clean and the top of the cake feels springy to the touch.

Cool the cake in the pan on a rack for 10 minutes, then invert it onto a rack. (Note: if your cake isn't about level with the top of the pan, you should probably cut a cardboard template and slip it over the tube before you invert the pan. That way you're less likely to break up the cake if it clings to the pan. Simply make a cutout that will fit over the tube and slide down to touch the cake. Then turn the pan over, supporting the cardboard from below. Ease off on the support until the cake drops out.)

Cool the cake on the rack—you can leave it on the template if you want—then carefully transfer to a serving plate. Wrap the cake well to keep it from drying out. ♦

# *Ricotta Fruitcake*

*Makes 4 loaves (about 8 servings per loaf)*

One of my favorite gift cakes, this is a variation of the Ricotta Cheese Pound Cake on page 250. I've intentionally chosen light-colored fruits to keep the color scheme golden, but you can add darker fruit if you prefer. These fruits, however, do seem to have a particular affinity for the cake. As moist as this is, I've kept one in the fridge, wrapped in plastic wrap and overwrapped in foil, for more than a week and it was still in prime condition at that. The pans I specify are one of the common sizes available in the supermarket in disposable aluminum; but don't dispose of them when you're done.

*1 cup chopped candied pineapple*

*1 cup golden raisins*

*1 cup (4 to 5 ounces) coarsely chopped pecans*

*¹/₃ cup dark rum*

*1 modified recipe Ricotta Cheese Pound Cake (page 250), as outlined below*

*²/₃ cup unsweetened shredded coconut (available at health food stores) or sweetened flaked coconut*

*2 tablespoons unbleached flour*

At least an hour before baking, preferably longer, combine the candied pineapple, raisins, pecans, and rum in a mixing bowl. Stir, then cover, periodically stirring to saturate the mixture thoroughly. In the meantime, butter 4 3³/₄- by 7³/₄-inch loaf pans and line them with buttered wax paper, buttered side out, letting the paper come over the edge by about an inch so you can pull the cakes out easily later. Set aside. When you start to prepare the cake, preheat the oven to 350°.

Prepare the cake as usual, substituting 1 teaspoon ground ginger for the nutmeg. Mix the coconut with the dried fruit and rum, then mix in the 2 tablespoons flour. Fold the fruit mixture into the batter, then divide the batter evenly among the pans. Bake for 50 to 60 minutes, until a tester inserted in the center comes out clean. Cool the cakes in the pans on a rack for 10 minutes, then lift them out by the wax paper. Cool for another 30 minutes, then carefully peel off the wax paper. As soon as the cakes no longer feel warm, wrap them in plastic wrap and overwrap in foil. Store in a cool location in an airtight container.

FREEZING: *Overwrapped in foil, this will keep in the freezer for up to 2 months. Thaw at room temperature, unwrapped, before slicing.* ♦

## Ricotta Cheese Pound Cake

*Makes 1 large cake*

So rich and moist, this great cake has a texture almost like custard. Even though this cake is less rich than many other pound cake recipes, it's still far from dietetic. But the good news is, this one cake goes a long way; one time I cut this up for a Cub Scouts pack meeting (I'm the refreshment committee), and I must have gotten 30 respectable pieces out of it. This is the foundation for one of my favorite holiday cakes, the Ricotta Fruitcake on page 249.

1 cup (1/2 pound) unsalted butter, softened
2 cups packed light brown sugar
6 large eggs, at room temperature
2 teaspoons vanilla extract
finely grated zest of 2 lemons
2 cups unbleached flour
2 cups whole wheat pastry flour
1 tablespoon baking powder
1 teaspoon salt
1 teaspoon freshly grated nutmeg
1³/₄ cups milk or light cream
1 cup ricotta cheese

Preheat the oven to 350°; butter and lightly flour a 10-inch tube or bundt pan. In a large mixing bowl, cream the butter with an electric mixer, gradually beating in the brown sugar. Add the eggs, one at a time, beating well after each one. Beat in the vanilla and lemon zest.

Sift the flours, baking powder, salt, and nutmeg into another bowl, adding any pieces of bran that remain in the sifter; set aside. Puree the milk or cream and the ricotta cheese in a blender.

Stir the dry ingredients into the creamed mixture alternately with the milk/ricotta; do this in several stages, beginning and ending with the dry ingredients. Do not beat the batter. Distribute the batter evenly in the prepared pan, then bake for approximately 1 hour and 15 minutes; a tester inserted in the center should come out clean.

Cool the pan on a rack for 10 minutes, then invert it onto the rack and cool the cake for at least an hour before cutting. (Transfer the cake to a serving platter before you cut it; it will be more difficult if you cut the cake first.) ◆

## Pumpkin Molasses Cake with Maple Rum Glaze

*Makes 10 to 12 servings*

I do a lot with pumpkin, mainly because my friend Chris grows and sells them. This is the perfect cake to take to a Halloween party or make for your busy bees as a reward for helping to button up the house on some gorgeous fall weekend. Powdered sugar would be a pretty touch if you didn't want to bother with the sauce. But even that's not necessary to enjoy this soft, moist cake.

2 cups peeled, seeded, cubed pumpkin or ³/₄
    cup canned (see note below)
¹/₂ cup (¹/₄ pound) unsalted butter, softened
¹/₃ cup unsulphured molasses
²/₃ cup packed light brown sugar
3 large eggs, at room temperature
1 teaspoon vanilla extract
finely grated zest of 1 orange
2 cups unbleached flour
2 teaspoons baking powder
¹/₂ teaspoon baking soda
1 teaspoon salt
1 teaspoon ground ginger
1 teaspoon ground cinnamon
¹/₂ cup dark or golden raisins

GLAZE (optional)
2 tablespoons maple syrup
2 tablespoons heavy cream
2 teaspoons dark rum

Put the pumpkin in a large saucepan with plenty of lightly salted water. Bring to a low boil, cover, and cook for about 20 minutes, until very tender. Drain, cool, then puree in a blender, food processor, or food mill. Measure out ³/₄ cup and set aside. (If there's extra, save it for another use.) Preheat the oven to 350° and butter a 9-inch spring-form pan.

With an electric mixer, cream the butter in a large bowl, gradually adding the molasses and brown sugar. Beat in the eggs, one at a time, then the vanilla and orange zest.

Sift the flour, baking powder, baking soda, salt, and spices into a separate bowl. Stir half the dry mixture into the creamed, then fold in the measured pumpkin puree, followed by the rest of the dry ingredients; fold in the raisins.

Scrape the batter into the prepared pan and bake for 40 minutes, until the center is springy to the touch and a tester inserted in the center comes out clean. Cool the cake in the pan on a rack for 10 minutes before taking off the side. Cool at least 30 minutes before slicing. Serve with the maple rum glaze, if desired.

To make the glaze, bring the maple syrup, cream, and rum to a boil in a small saucepan. Boil for 1 minute, then remove from the heat. You can either spoon this over the whole cake while it is still hot so it sinks in; let it cool and become slightly thicker, then spread it on top of the cake with the back of a spoon; or cut pieces of cake, lay them on their side, and pour a spoonful of hot sauce over each piece.

NOTE: *You can, of course, opt for the canned pumpkin, but it is so easy to make your own puree that you should really try it. It is always nice to have extra on hand; it has been a favorite first food for our babies and a nice little item to throw into pancakes or muffins or to thicken winter soups with.* ♦

## Finding the Time to Bake

Quite often someone will say to me, "Oh, I'd love to bake more often, but who has the time to bake anymore?" And I can relate to that, as anyone with children can. With so many two-career families today, how *does* anybody find the time to bake nowadays?

Actually there are ways we can make more time to bake without sacrificing huge blocks of time each week. Here are some helpful tricks that might work for you.

♦ First, get your baking act organized. I used to be the world's biggest baking slob, a sin I paid for dearly in many useless hours searching for lost baking sheets and cinnamon that didn't exist. Believe me, baking is much more fun—and a heck of a lot faster—when

all the essentials are within arm's reach. (I go into organization in more detail on page 7.)

♦ Learn to prepare recipes in little steps. Most parents of young children I know can't find 30 or 40 minutes, undisturbed, to prepare a recipe. That's fine; take it slow. Cream the butter when you can; mix the dry ingredients later; find a few minutes to mix and shape or do whatever. So what if it takes you all day to bake a batch of cookies? You'll still have the satisfaction of baking something from scratch.

♦ With yeast baking, get really good at one or two breads. Familiarity,

when it comes to yeast breads, can be a real asset, especially if you're new to it. Learning a recipe well helps build your baking confidence. It lets you skim the recipe without getting bogged down in the details. Often, after a while, just referring to the ingredient list is enough. And you're never left wondering whether the dough is behaving as it should, since you already know it.

♦ This is a little tricky, but try to commit a few basic recipes to memory; that way you can just fly into a recipe without even referring to a book. Start with biscuits or muffins or something else you eat often.

♦ When you do bake, prepare multiple batches. A lot of the time involved in baking is just taking things out and putting them away. You can bypass that by bagging up the dry mix for biscuits, muffins, soda breads, and the like, then storing it in the freezer. When you're ready to bake, all that's left is to mix the liquid, blend, and bake. Be sure to mark the bags clearly with a permanent marker: "Dry Mix/ Whole Wheat Biscuits," for example.

♦ Finally, take advantage of weekends, when time is generally more available. Pick a day when you plan to be at home anyway and work on something fun and a little ambitious. Try to get the whole family involved if you can—maybe take a ride to a farm stand or farmers' market to buy fresh fruit. Then come home and make a big family pie or cobbler together. You'll be glad you did.

# Maple Banana Spice Cake with Coconut-Almond Topping

*Makes 9 servings*

One of our favorite fast cakes, this can be mixed in 5 minutes and ready to eat within the hour. There's a minimum of fat here, but the cake still tastes moist and rich, thanks to the banana, maple syrup, and whole wheat flour. The topping is optional, but the cake's kind of naked without it. Excellent with orange sherbet.

CAKE BATTER
*2 large eggs, at room temperature*
*³/₄ cup (about 2 medium-size) mashed very ripe banana*
*¹/₂ cup maple syrup*
*¹/₄ cup flavorless vegetable oil*
*1 teaspoon vanilla extract*
*³/₄ cup unbleached flour*
*³/₄ cup whole wheat flour*
*1 teaspoon baking powder*
*¹/₂ teaspoon baking soda*
*¹/₂ teaspoon salt*
*¹/₂ teaspoon ground cinnamon*
*¹/₂ teaspoon freshly grated nutmeg*
*¹/₂ teaspoon ground cloves*
*¹/₂ teaspoon ground ginger*

TOPPING
*2 tablespoons unsalted butter*
*2 tablespoons maple syrup*
*¹/₄ cup unsweetened shredded coconut*
*(available at health food stores) or sweetened flaked coconut*
*¹/₄ cup slivered or thinly sliced almonds*

Butter an 8-inch square cake pan and preheat the oven to 375° (350° if you're using glass, which I generally do for this recipe). Put the eggs, banana, maple syrup, oil, and vanilla into a mixing bowl and beat well with an electric mixer for 1 minute.

Into a separate bowl sift all the dry ingredients, adding any pieces of bran that remain in the sifter. Stir the dry ingredients into the wet mixture in 2 stages, just until uniformly blended. Scrape the batter into the pan.

Immediately make the topping: Melt the butter in a small saucepan, adding the maple syrup. When the butter is fully melted, stir in the coconut and almonds. Spoon the topping over the cake, then bake for 30 minutes, until the center is springy to the touch and a tester inserted in the center comes out clean. Cool on a rack for at least 20 minutes before slicing. ♦

# *Amalia's Maple Oat Cake*

*Makes 9 to 10 servings*

I've made a number of different oat cakes over the years, and this one is the best plain one I've come across. By plain I mean not frosted, but there's really nothing plain about the flavor, which is rich with walnuts, coconut, maple, and oats. This is a low, dense cake, and the texture becomes firm with age, but if you keep it covered it stays moist for several days. Great with coffee or maple walnut ice cream.

*1/2 cup (1/4 pound) unsalted butter, softened*
*1/2 cup packed light brown sugar*
*1/2 cup maple syrup, at room temperature*
*1 large egg, at room temperature*
*1 teaspoon vanilla extract*
*1 cup rolled oats* (not *instant*)
*1 cup unbleached flour*
*1 teaspoon baking powder*
*big pinch of salt*
*1/2 cup (2 ounces) finely chopped walnuts*
*1/2 cup unsweetened shredded coconut*
  *(available at health food stores) or*
  *sweetened flaked coconut*

Butter an 8-inch square baking pan or a 9- or 10-inch round cake pan. Preheat the oven to 350° (325° if you're using glass). In a medium mixing bowl, cream the butter and brown sugar with an electric mixer. Beat in the maple syrup, then the egg and vanilla, until soft and fluffy. Reserve.

Put the oats in a blender and process briefly, until you have a combination of finely and roughly cut oats. Transfer to a sifter and sift into a bowl with the unbleached flour, baking powder, and salt; add any oat pieces that were left in the sifter. Stir the dry ingredients into the creamed ones in 3 stages, then fold in the walnuts and coconut; do not beat the batter.

Scrape the batter into the prepared pan and even it out with a fork. Bake for 35 to 40 minutes, until the top is golden brown and offers a little resistance to light finger pressure. Cool in the pan on a rack. Slice and serve warm or at room temperature. ◆

## Lemon Cornmeal Cake with Boiled Honey Glaze

*Makes 1 large cake (12 to 14 servings)*

Here's an all-honey-sweetened cake with a pretty cornmeal-and-lemon-yellow interior. Sometimes I'm not crazy about a lot of honey in cakes, because the taste is overbearing, but in this case the honey blends in very naturally. At the end I put on a boiled honey glaze, which keeps everything nice and moist, but you can substitute a dusting of confectioners' sugar or leave it plain.

CAKE BATTER
1 cup honey
3/4 cup flavorless vegetable oil
3 large eggs
2 teaspoons vanilla extract
finely grated zest of 2 lemons
1 tablespoon freshly squeezed lemon juice
1 cup unbleached flour
3/4 cup yellow cornmeal, preferably stone-
  ground
1/2 cup whole wheat flour
1 teaspoon baking powder
1 teaspoon baking soda
1/2 teaspoon salt
1 cup unsweetened shredded coconut
  (available at health food stores) or
  sweetened flaked coconut
1/2 cup plain yogurt

BOILED HONEY GLAZE
1/4 cup honey
1 tablespoon unsalted butter
1 tablespoon freshly squeezed lemon juice

Preheat the oven to 350°. Grease and flour a 9- or 10-inch bundt or tube pan; if it has a dark, nonstick coating, set the oven temperature at 325°. Better to grease the pan with solid vegetable shortening than butter for this to keep the exterior of the cake from turning too dark.

In a large mixing bowl, beat the honey, oil, eggs, vanilla, lemon zest, and lemon juice with an electric mixer. Into a separate bowl, sift the unbleached flour, cornmeal, whole wheat flour, baking powder, baking soda, and salt; add any pieces of bran left in the sifter. Stir in the coconut. Stir half the dry ingredients into the liquid, then blend in the yogurt, then stir in the remaining dry ingredients until the batter is smooth; don't overbeat.

Pour the batter into the greased pan and bake for approximately 45 minutes. When done, the cake will be springy to the touch and a tester inserted in the center will come out clean. Let the pan cool on a rack for 10 minutes, then invert onto a large plate. As it cools, prepare the glaze.

Bring all of the glaze ingredients to a boil in a small saucepan. Boil for 30 seconds, then immediately remove from the heat. Let the glaze cool for 5 minutes, then spoon it all over the top of the still-warm cake; it will be rather runny. Serve the cake warm or at room temperature. ♦

## The Frugal Baker

From the very beginning, home cooks have held firmly to the values of economy and thrift. We as bakers can carry on with that tradition in our daily lives by watching for opportunities that will save us a few dimes here and there. Not that the savings will make or break us. It's more for our psychic balance sheet, the satisfaction that comes with knowing we're putting our resources to full use instead of squandering them. That said, here are some frugal baking habits up for adoption.

♦ Use butter wrappers to butter pans with. The best ones come from soft sticks of butter because more of the butter clings to the wrapper.

♦ Don't throw away egg washes you glaze yeast breads with. Use them in pancakes, waffles, for an omelet, or anywhere else you'd use an egg. Another option, if the bread recipe itself includes an egg, is to beat the egg before adding it to the dough and then reserve a teaspoon or so of it for the wash.

♦ Use potato cooking water in bread. It's a shame to throw out that good stuff.

♦ By the same token, incorporate leftover mashed potatoes or squash in your baked goods, particularly yeast breads.

♦ Make bread crumbs from stale bread. I just use a box grater for this and then toast them briefly in the oven on a baking sheet. Or just give your stale bread to the birds.

♦ Wash out empty honey and molasses jars with hot water. Put the lid on, shake it up, and use it as part of the liquid in yeast breads. Or loosen it by putting the entire jar in a saucepan of water set over low heat.

♦ Use up your pastry scraps (see page 196).

♦ If you have the storage space and the cash, and you bake a lot, buy in bulk. This way you always pay less for honey, flour, maple syrup, whatever. One other nice thing about buying in bulk: you aren't always running out of something.

# Karen's Winter Squash Chocolate Cake

*Makes 1 large cake (12 to 14 servings)*

Karen adapted this terrific cake from one of Marian Morash's recipes in *The Victory Garden Cookbook* (Knopf, 1982), one of our all-time favorite cookbooks. We really go crazy over this, and anybody who has ever been fortunate enough to arrive before we demolish the whole cake has either taken home the recipe or begged for seconds. This is a good cake to keep in mind when you're cooking squash in the fall and winter months; bake or boil extra, and you'll save time in the preparation. Canned pumpkin or squash will work fine too.

3¼ cups (1 medium) peeled, cubed winter squash or pumpkin or 1½ cups canned puree
1¼ cups honey
¼ pound unsweetened chocolate
2 cups whole wheat pastry flour
1 cup unbleached flour
2 teaspoons baking powder
2 teaspoons baking soda
1 tablespoon ground cinnamon
½ teaspoon ground ginger
½ teaspoon ground allspice
¼ teaspoon freshly grated nutmeg
¼ teaspoon ground cloves
1 teaspoon salt
1¼ cups flavorless vegetable oil
4 large eggs
1 cup (4 to 5 ounces) chopped walnuts

confectioners' sugar for dusting the cake (optional)

Put the squash or pumpkin cubes in a medium-size pot with enough lightly salted water to cover generously. Bring to a low boil and cover. Cook for about 20 minutes, until the squash is quite tender. Drain, then puree the squash in a blender or food processor; you should have about 1½ cups. Reserve.

Put ¼ cup of the honey in a small saucepan, lay the chocolate on top, and place over very low heat to melt the chocolate; swirl the pan from time to time to facilitate the melting. Remove from the heat when the chocolate is melted. Whisk to smooth, then set aside. Preheat the oven to 350° and butter a 10-inch bundt or tube pan.

Into a large mixing bowl, sift the flours, baking powder, baking soda, spices, and salt; include any bran left in the sifter. Using an electric mixer, beat the pureed squash, the remaining honey, the oil, and the eggs in a separate bowl. Stir the dry ingredients into the liquid just until smooth, folding in the walnuts on the last few strokes; don't overbeat the batter.

Put about one-third of the batter into the bowl you had the dry ingredients in and stir the melted chocolate into it. Spoon about half of the nonchocolate batter into the prepared pan, then about half the chocolate batter, the rest of the nonchocolate, and finally the rest of the chocolate. Don't worry if it looks all mottled and uneven in the pan; the layering isn't too important.

Bake the cake for approximately 60 minutes. When done, the cake will be springy to the touch and a tester inserted in the center should come out clean. Cool the pan on a rack for 10 minutes, then invert the cake onto a big plate. Let it cool until you can no longer resist. When thoroughly cool, you can dust the cake with confectioners' sugar if you like. Store in an airtight container or covered with foil.

FREEZING: *Overwrapped in foil, this will keep up to 2 months in the freezer. Thaw at room temperature, wrapped, before slicing.* ♦

## *Brownie Banana Upside-Down Cake*

*Makes 8 to 10 servings*

 ou might think this is pushing the boundaries of upside-down cake credibility, but this is one incredibly good cake: a topping of brown sugar–sweet bananas on top of the best brownie you've ever had. Even Karen, my wife, who rates cooked bananas right up there with going to the dentist on her list of favorite things in life, thinks this is sublime. The one drawback is, by the end of the second day the bananas are starting to get tired and discolored, as good an excuse as any to serve seconds.

FRUIT TOPPING
*4 to 5 medium-size bananas, just barely ripe
   (not starting to turn brown)
¼ cup unsalted butter
¾ cup packed light brown sugar
1 tablespoon dark rum (optional)*

CAKE BATTER
*¼ cup milk
¼ pound semisweet chocolate
½ cup (¼ pound) unsalted butter, softened
¾ cup sugar
2 large eggs, at room temperature
1 teaspoon vanilla extract
1 cup unbleached flour
¼ cup unsweetened cocoa powder
2 teaspoons baking powder
¼ teaspoon salt*

Generously butter a 9-inch round cake pan (or a 9-inch cast-iron skillet if that's all you have). To prepare the fruit topping, peel the bananas, then cut them in half lengthwise. Place them in the pan, flat side down, the curve of the banana following the curve of the pan; start on the outside, working your way in, keeping the bananas in tight concentric circles. You'll have to cut the bananas at some point to get a nice fit in the center. Set aside.

In a medium saucepan, melt the butter, adding the brown sugar as it begins to melt. Cook this mixture over medium-low heat, stirring, just until the sugar dissolves. If you're using the rum, stir it in a few moments before taking the mixture off the heat. Scrape this mixture over the bananas, spreading it around as evenly as possible. Set aside. Preheat the oven to 350°.

Now make the batter. Put the milk in a small saucepan and add the chocolate. Turn the heat to very low, periodically tilting the pan so the milk runs over the chocolate. When the chocolate is soft, whisk to smooth, then remove from the heat. Set aside.

*(continued)*

259

(*continued*)

Using an electric mixer, cream the butter and sugar in a large mixing bowl until light and fluffy. Beat in the eggs, one at a time, then the vanilla, and finally the melted chocolate.

Into a separate bowl, sift the remaining (dry) ingredients, stirring them into the creamed mixture in 3 stages; stop mixing as soon as they are blended and no dry streaks remain.

Scrape the cake batter over the bananas and smooth with a fork. Bake for 45 minutes. When done, the cake part will be cooked through—probe it with a fork—but may seem a little loose in the center, where the cake and topping meet. That's okay. Place the pan on a cooling rack for 1 minute, then put a large plate over the pan and, using pot holders, quickly invert. The cake should drop right onto the plate. Remove the pan. You may get a little moisture running around the side of the cake; that's fine. Any moisture slowly absorbs into the cake, giving it a fudge brownie quality. Wait at least 15 minutes before slicing. Very good with vanilla ice cream. ♦

## Yeasted Pear and Molasses Upside-Down Cake

*Makes 6 to 8 servings*

Big upside-down cake fan that I am, I couldn't help wondering how a yeasted version of upside-down cake would be. This is what I came up with, and I'm very happy to say that nothing was lost in the translation. Like any other yeasted item, the extra time involved with preparing this bestows it with an old-fashioned goodness you just can't find outside the home anymore. This is a good, grainy cake for a fall or winter weekend morning, to top off a big, mid-morning breakfast. Try this with apples sometime too.

CAKE BATTER
1/4 cup lukewarm water
1 1/4-ounce package (*about 1 tablespoon*) active dry yeast
1/2 cup sour cream
1/4 cup unsalted butter, melted
1/4 cup unsulphured molasses
1/4 cup packed light brown sugar
1 large egg
1 large egg yolk
1 teaspoon vanilla extract
1/2 cup rolled oats (not *instant*)
1 cup whole wheat flour
1/4 teaspoon salt
2/3 cup unbleached flour

FRUIT TOPPING
*3 tablespoons unsalted butter*
*⅓ cup packed light brown sugar*
*4 large pears (ripe but not too soft), peeled, halved, and cored*

To make the batter, pour the water into a small bowl and stir in the yeast. Set aside for 5 minutes to dissolve. Put the sour cream in a large mixing bowl and beat in the melted butter, molasses, brown sugar, egg, and egg yolk. Stir in the vanilla, rolled oats, and dissolved yeast. Cover and let sit for 5 minutes, then stir in the whole wheat flour, beating hard for 2 minutes. Cover with plastic wrap and set aside in a warm spot for 15 minutes.

After 15 minutes, add the salt and the unbleached flour, ⅓ cup at a time, beating hard by hand for about 1½ minutes after each addition. Cover the cake batter with plastic wrap and set aside in a warm spot.

Prepare the fruit topping. Melt the butter in a 10-inch cast-iron skillet over medium heat, adding the brown sugar as it melts. Stir until the mixture starts to boil. Boil briefly, stirring, then remove from the heat. Slice each pear half into quarters and arrange the slices in the pan, keeping most of them on the flat; they don't have to look perfect. If the pan is still very hot, give it a few minutes to cool down, then scrape the cake batter over the fruit and spread it out with a fork as evenly as you can. Cover with foil and put in a warm spot until the cake batter is doubled in bulk. When it appears nearly doubled, preheat the oven to 375°.

When the batter has fully doubled, bake the cake for 35 to 40 minutes, until well browned and the cake is cooked through. Cool for 2 minutes, then invert the cake onto a big plate, watching out for hot, dripping juices. If some pear slices stick to the pan, which is common, just pull them off and put them on the cake. And if you'd rather not bother inverting the cake at all, that's fine too. Serve hot or warm.  ♦

## Peach Oatmeal Upside-Down Cake

*Makes 8 to 10 servings*

This cake—glazed, bright yellow peaches on top of a honey-sweetened oatmeal cake—is both eye-catching and wholesome. For best results, use peaches that are ripe but not too soft.

FRUIT TOPPING

*3 tablespoons unsalted butter*
*1/3 cup packed light brown sugar*
*6 or 7 medium-size peaches*

BATTER

*6 tablespoons unsalted butter, softened*
*1/2 cup honey, at room temperature*
*2 large eggs, at room temperature*
*1/3 cup sour cream or plain yogurt*
*1 teaspoon vanilla extract*
*1 cup unbleached flour*
*1/2 cup oat flour (see note below)*
*1 teaspoon baking powder*
*1/2 teaspoon baking soda*
*1 teaspoon ground cinnamon*
*1/2 teaspoon salt*
*1/4 cup rolled oats (not instant)*
*1/4 cup milk, at room temperature*
*freshly grated nutmeg for dusting the cake*
   *(optional)*

To make the fruit topping, melt the butter and brown sugar in a 9- or 10-inch cast-iron skillet over medium heat, stirring with a wooden spoon; remove from the heat. Halve and peel the peaches, removing the pits. Lay them close together in the pan, flat side down. If you have to trim the last 1 or 2 halves to get a good fit, that's fine. Set aside and preheat the oven to 375°. Make the batter.

Using an electric mixer, beat the butter and honey in a mixing bowl until creamy. Beat in the eggs, one at a time, followed by the sour cream and vanilla. Into a separate bowl, sift the two kinds of flour with the baking powder, baking soda, cinnamon, and salt, including any oat flecks left in the sifter; stir in the rolled oats.

Stir half of the dry ingredients into the creamed mixture, then stir in the milk, then the rest of the dry, just until blended. (If the batter seems a bit dense, don't worry or attempt to thin it; this will compensate for the liquid the peaches will throw off.)

Cover the peaches with the batter, then bake for about 35 minutes, until the cake feels springy to the touch. Cool the cake in the pan for 5 minutes, then invert it onto a big plate; watch for hot dripping juices that could burn you (I like to wear oven mitts for this maneuver). Dust lightly with nutmeg if you like. Serve hot, warm, or at room temperature.

NOTE: *You can buy oat flour at a health food store or make your own by buzzing rolled oats (not instant) in the blender. Incidentally, this doesn't make a bad plain oat cake if that idea appeals to you. Just make the batter as above, increasing the milk to 1/3 cup. Bake in an 8-inch square pan for about 30 minutes.* ◆

# Pineapple Upside-Down Gingerbread Cake

*Makes 8 to 10 servings*

*H*ere's a dessert I'd been making mentally for a long time before I actually tried it, because this combination of gingerbread and pineapple just sounded so good. I'm happy to say that once I got around to it it tasted as good as it did in my imagination. Do use the fresh ginger if you can, because the flavor is so surprisingly fresh and alive. But even if you use ground ginger, it tastes just great. This is a good, filling dessert to follow a light meal.

FRUIT TOPPING

3 tablespoons unsalted butter

1/4 cup honey

2 tablespoons packed light brown sugar

7 canned pineapple slices, blotted dry on a
    paper towel

CAKE BATTER

2 large eggs, at room temperature

1/4 cup unsalted butter, melted and cooled

2/3 cup unsulphured molasses

1/3 cup honey

3 tablespoons (about 1 ounce) peeled, finely
    minced fresh ginger or 1 tablespoon ground
    ginger

1 cup unbleached flour

1 cup whole wheat pastry flour

1 teaspoon baking powder

1 teaspoon baking soda

1 teaspoon ground cinnamon

1/4 teaspoon ground cloves

1/4 teaspoon freshly grated nutmeg

1/4 teaspoon salt

1/8 teaspoon cayenne pepper (or less if kids
    will be eating this)

3/4 cup milk

Preheat the oven to 350°. To make the fruit topping, melt the butter in a 10-inch cast-iron skillet over medium-high heat. Before it's fully melted, stir in the honey and brown sugar and bring to a boil. Boil, stirring, for 30 seconds, then remove from the heat. Lay the pineapple slices in the pan, one in the center and 6 around it. Prepare the batter.

Beat the eggs in a mixing bowl using an electric mixer. Beat in the melted butter, molasses, honey, and ginger. Set aside. Into a separate bowl, sift the flours, baking powder, baking soda, spices, salt, and cayenne, including any pieces of bran left in the sifter.

Stir half the dry ingredients into the egg mixture, blend in the milk, then stir in the rest of the dry, just until smooth. Pour the batter over the pineapple slices, then bake the cake for 30 minutes. When done, the cake will have darkened a few shades and the top should feel slightly springy to the touch. Cool the pan on a rack for 2 minutes, then invert it onto a large plate; protect your hands and arms in case there's any dripping, hot liquid. Serve hot, warm, or at room temperature, with lightly sweetened whipped cream or vanilla ice cream. Cover leftovers loosely with foil. ◆

263

# Frangelico Cheesecake

*Makes 14 to 16 servings*

Frangelico (hazelnut liqueur) is one of our perennial holiday indulgences. In general we don't keep many liqueurs around—you can tie up a small fortune in that sort of thing—though after Thanksgiving we always have a bottle of Frangelico on hand, ready to pour for almost any flimsy excuse. So eventually the Frangelico ended up in the cheesecake, cheesecakes being in big demand around the holidays, and the idea proved so stellar that we added a hazelnut crust and some maple syrup as the sweetener. This makes one big creamy cake—an ideal contribution to any holiday get-together.

*1 recipe Whole Wheat Press-In Nut Crust (page 202), made with hazelnuts (see directions below)*

FILLING
*1¹⁄₂ pounds cream cheese, softened*
*¹⁄₂ cup sugar*
*¹⁄₃ cup maple syrup, at room temperature*
*¹⁄₂ teaspoon salt*
*3 large eggs, at room temperature*
*¹⁄₄ cup Frangelico*
*1 tablespoon freshly squeezed lemon juice*
*1 teaspoon vanilla extract*
*2¹⁄₂ cups sour cream, at room temperature*

Make the crust using at least half hazelnuts—the remainder can be pecans or almonds—toasted for 10 minutes in a 350° oven; keep the oven on. Lightly butter a 9-inch springform pan and press the crust into it and slightly up the side. Bake for 15 minutes, then cool on a rack. As it cools, make the filling.

In a large mixing bowl, beat the cream cheese until fluffy, gradually adding the sugar, maple syrup, and salt. Beat in the eggs, one at a time, followed by the Frangelico, lemon juice, and vanilla. Blend in the sour cream.

Scrape the filling into the pan and bake for 55 minutes. Transfer the cheesecake to a rack and cool thoroughly. Cover with foil or plastic wrap and chill overnight or for at least 6 hours. (Once this is in the fridge, take it out after an hour or so and either change the plastic wrap or foil or wipe off the condensation that inevitably ends up inside the wrapping; that way it won't drip onto the cake.)

When you're ready to serve this, remove the side of the pan and slice. If you like, you can press a whole hazelnut into the top of each piece and perhaps drizzle a teaspoon of Frangelico over it as well. ◆

# Fresh Mint Chocolate Cheesecake

*Makes 14 to 16 servings*

An abundance of mint in the garden—and if you have mint, there's always an abundance—can be a boon for bakers. Over the years, for instance, I've devised ways to use fresh mint in everything from pies to muffins, not to mention this creamy cheesecake, made with just a hint of chocolate. When the mint starts coming in in mid-May, this is usually the first recipe on my agenda. For an attractive presentation, decorate each piece with a small spray of mint leaves.

1 recipe Chocolate Graham Cracker Crust (*page 198*)

FILLING
1 cup fresh peppermint or spearmint leaves (not *packed*)
³/₄ cup light cream
1¹/₂ cups sugar
2 ounces semisweet chocolate
2 pounds cream cheese, softened
1 teaspoon vanilla extract
1¹/₂ cups sour cream
3 large eggs, at room temperature
1 large egg yolk, at room temperature

Pat the crust into the bottom of a 9-inch springform pan and place in the freezer. Preheat the oven to 350° and make the filling.

Put the mint leaves, ¹/₂ cup of the cream, and ¹/₄ cup of the sugar into a blender and puree briefly; try to leave some small flecks of mint so you can see them in the finished cake. Set aside. Put the remaining cream and the chocolate into a heavy saucepan and melt over the lowest possible heat; tilt the pan now and then so the cream runs over the top of the chocolate. Whisk to smooth, then set aside.

Using an electric mixer, beat the cream cheese and the remaining sugar until fluffy in texture, about 3 minutes. Beat in the pureed mixture, followed by the vanilla, the melted chocolate, and the sour cream. When smooth, beat in the eggs and egg yolk, just until blended. Scrape the mixture into the pan and bake for 55 to 60 minutes; the top of the cake will have risen and, perhaps, become very lightly browned in spots. Transfer the cake pan to a rack and cool completely. Cover loosely with wax paper and refrigerate for at least 6 hours before unmolding and slicing. I don't recommend freezing this cheesecake. ♦

# Spiced Pumpkin Cheesecake

*Makes 14 to 16 servings*

This tastes like pumpkin pie, only better and richer, if you can believe that. This recipe was written around a 15-ounce can of pureed (cold-pack) pumpkin. I actually prefer canned pumpkin here, because the moisture content is minimal and more predictable than home-pureed, which is liable to be watery and cause the cheesecake to weep. If you do use home-pureed pumpkin (or other winter squash), you might bake out some of the moisture first, putting the puree in a small, shallow baking dish, and substitute 2 more egg yolks for 1 of the whole eggs.

*1 recipe Graham Cracker Crust (page 198)*

FILLING
*1 pound cream cheese, softened*
*1 cup packed light brown sugar*
*1/3 cup sugar*
*2 teaspoons vanilla extract*
*2 large eggs, at room temperature*
*2 large egg yolks, at room temperature*
*pinch of salt*
*1 15-ounce can (about 1³/₄ cups) pureed pumpkin or squash*
*1 cup sour cream*
*1¹/₂ teaspoons ground cinnamon*
*1 teaspoon ground ginger*
*1 teaspoon ground cloves*

Prepare the crust and pat it into a 9-inch springform pan, pushing it just slightly up the sides. Freeze. Preheat the oven to 325°.

Using an electric mixer, cream the cream cheese, brown sugar, and sugar until light and fluffy, about 3 minutes. Beat in the vanilla, eggs—one at a time—and egg yolks. Add the remaining ingredients and beat for another 30 seconds. Pour the batter into the chilled pan and bake in the center of the oven for 1 hour. Carefully transfer the pan to a rack and cool for several hours. Cover the pan with wax paper and refrigerate overnight.

When ready to serve, carefully remove the side of the pan. Cut the cake with a knife that's just been run under hot water. To store leftovers, put the side of the pan back on and cover with foil. Store in the refrigerator. I don't recommend freezing this cheesecake. ◆

## Chocolate Raspberry Pudding Cake

*Makes 8 servings*

No one makes pudding cakes anymore, or so it seems. That's a shame, because it really is a good idea: not only do you get two desserts in one—the pudding and the cake—but there's no chance of textural difficulties, because the bottom is all gooey anyway. In this cake, patterned after one in Jeanne Lemlin's *Vegetarian Pleasures* (Knopf, 1986), I incorporate a seedless raspberry puree, which mysteriously combines with the chocolate to make a raspberry-chocolate pudding under a chocolate cake. Serve alone, with a little cream, or—best of all—with vanilla ice cream. This is *sweet*.

²/₃ cup milk

¹/₂ cup honey

2 tablespoons unsalted butter

1 teaspoon vanilla extract

1¹/₂ cups (a little less than 1 pint) fresh
   raspberries

1 cup water

2 tablespoons sugar

1¹/₄ cups unbleached flour

¹/₂ cup unsweetened cocoa powder

2 teaspoons baking powder

¹/₄ teaspoon salt

³/₄ cup packed light brown sugar

¹/₄ teaspoon ground cinnamon

Put the milk, honey, and butter in a small saucepan and heat gently for several minutes, just until the butter is melted. Pour into a small bowl and add the vanilla. Set aside to cool. Preheat the oven to 350°.

Meanwhile, puree the raspberries and water in a blender and strain through a fine strainer; work the mixture with a spoon to get out as much liquid as possible. Put the puree and sugar in a small saucepan and heat for several minutes to melt the sugar.

Sift the flour, ¹/₄ cup of the cocoa, the baking powder, and the salt into a medium mixing bowl. Make a well, then pour in the partially cooled milk/honey; whisk just until blended. Don't worry about beating out all the lumps. Spread this batter in an ungreased 8-inch square baking dish or 9-inch deep-dish pie pan, glass or ceramic.

Rub together the brown sugar, remaining cocoa, and cinnamon. Spread evenly over the batter. Slowly pour the hot raspberry puree over the cake. Bake for 35 minutes. Cool the cake on a rack for at least 5 minutes before serving; even then, be careful, because the pudding part stays hot for a while. ◆

## Little Nut and Seed Cakes

*Makes 2 small loaf cakes*
*(about 8 servings per cake)*

These unusual little cakes start with a base of ground, toasted sunflower seeds and whole wheat flour, then you fold in poppy seeds, pecans, and hazelnuts. All this weight keeps the cakes compact; the tops come out flat. Flavor is what counts, and these have plenty. Make these only for someone who's really into nuts and seeds.

*1/2 cup (2 ounces) hazelnuts*
*1/2 cup (2 ounces) pecans*
*1 cup raw hulled sunflower seeds*
*3/4 cup (approximately) whole wheat flour*
*2 teaspoons baking powder*
*3/4 teaspoon salt*
*2 tablespoons poppy seeds*
*2 large eggs, at room temperature*
*3/4 cup packed light brown sugar*
*1/4 cup unsalted butter, melted and partially*
  *cooled*
*1/3 cup milk*
*1 teaspoon vanilla extract*

Preheat the oven to 350° and butter 2 3½-by 7-inch loaf pans. Spread the hazelnuts and pecans on a baking sheet and toast them in the oven for about 7 minutes, until fragrant. Cool the nuts on a plate, then chop coarsely.

Put the sunflower seeds in a large, heavy skillet and toast them over medium heat, stirring almost continuously. When they're lightly browned, dump them onto a plate and spread them around to cool.

When the seeds have cooled, grind them to a fine meal in a blender or food processor; it's okay if you have a few remaining seeds in the meal. Measure out 1 cup, dump it in a bowl, then put the remainder in a 1-cup measure and add enough whole wheat flour to make 1 cup. Sift this second cup into the bowl with the baking powder and salt; anything that won't pass through the sifter should be dumped into the bowl too. Stir in the poppy seeds.

In a separate bowl, beat the remaining ingredients with an electric mixer. Stir the dry ingredients into the wet, in several stages, just until blended; fold in the chopped nuts. Divide the batter between the pans, then bake for 30 to 35 minutes, until the center is slightly firm to the touch. Cool the pans on a rack for 10 minutes, then invert the cakes onto the rack and let them cool, bottoms up. As soon as they are cool, wrap snugly in plastic wrap and foil to keep fresh.

FREEZING: *Overwrapped in foil, these will keep for up to 2 months in the freezer. Thaw at room temperature, wrapped, then slice.* ◆

# *Classic Wheaten Shortcake*

### *Makes 8 individual shortcakes*

Crisp on the outside, downy-soft within, this near-traditional shortcake is just about perfect. If you split these, still warm, and pile on the fresh strawberries and whipped cream, you'll wish that time could stand still. Remember, other summer fruit is great with shortcakes too: blackberries, blueberries, peaches, and raspberries.

*1¹/₂ cups unbleached flour*
*¹/₂ cup whole wheat flour*
*3 tablespoons sugar*
*2¹/₂ teaspoons baking powder*
*¹/₂ teaspoon baking soda*
*¹/₄ teaspoon salt*
*7 tablespoons cold unsalted butter, cut into small pieces*
*1 large egg*
*¹/₂ cup milk*
*¹/₄ cup sour cream*
*egg wash: 1 egg yolk beaten with 1 tablespoon milk*
*a little sugar to sprinkle on top*

Preheat the oven to 450° and lightly oil a large, heavy baking sheet. In a large bowl, mix the flours, sugar, baking powder, baking soda, and salt. Add the butter and cut it into the dry ingredients until the largest pieces of butter are no bigger than split peas. In a separate bowl, beat the egg lightly, then whisk in the milk and sour cream. Make a well in the dry ingredients and pour in the liquid. Stir just until the mixture pulls together in a shaggy mass; it may be dampish. Scrape it out onto a well-floured surface and knead very gently, with floured hands, for no more than 20 seconds, dusting the dough with flour to keep it from sticking to your hands and work surface.

Pat the dough to a thickness of ³/₄ inch, then cut circles with a 3-inch (or larger if you like) biscuit cutter or a glass. You will have to collect the scraps to cut the last biscuit or 2. Place the circles on the prepared sheet with a little space between them. Brush the rounds sparingly with the egg wash and sprinkle just a pinch of sugar on top of each. Bake for 13 to 15 minutes, turning the sheet around halfway through the baking. When done, the tops will be a deep golden and the bottoms just slightly more so. Transfer the shortcakes to a rack. Cool briefly, then split and serve with berries and whipped cream. ♦

# Lacy Oatmeal Shortcake

*Makes 5 to 6 servings*

This shortcake started out as a regular biscuit until my eight-year-old son, Ben, pointed out that its texture, fragile, flaky crust, and sweetness were more suited to a shortcake—to which I think I mumbled something like, "Ah, yes, son, of course, just about to say so myself." You'll love the pronounced oatmeal taste of these and the lacy look of the top crust. Strawberries and whipped cream have never had it so good.

*1¼ cups rolled oats (not* instant*)*
*1 cup unbleached flour*
*3 tablespoons packed light brown sugar*
*1 teaspoon salt*
*1 teaspoon baking soda*
*1 teaspoon baking powder*
*5 tablespoons cold unsalted butter, cut into*
  *¼-inch pieces*
*⅔ cup plain yogurt*
*1 tablespoon hot water*
*glaze: 1 tablespoon maple syrup melted with*
  *1 tablespoon unsalted butter (see note*
  *below)*

Preheat the oven to 400° and very lightly oil a heavy medium or large baking sheet. Put ¼ cup of the rolled oats into a large mixing bowl. Pour the remaining oats into a blender or food processor and process until they're reduced to a near-flour; it's fine if some larger flecks remain. Mix the processed oats with the whole ones, then stir in the unbleached flour, brown sugar, salt,

baking soda, and baking powder. Add the butter and cut it in until the mixture resembles a coarse meal.

Thin the yogurt with the tablespoon of hot water. Make a well in the dry ingredients, then add the liquid. Stir, from the center out, until the dough pulls together. Turn it out onto a floured surface and knead very gently for 1 minute, using sprinkles of flour to prevent the dough from sticking.

Using your hands, pat the dough on a floured surface to a thickness of ½ to ¾ inch. Cut into 3- to 4-inch rounds and place them, barely touching, on the prepared sheet. Reroll the scraps and cut them too. (This is not traditional for shortcake, but I sometimes like to pat the dough into a circle and cut the dough into wedges, reassembling the circle on the sheet.) Brush the top of the shortcake with the warm glaze, then bake for 20 minutes. When done, the tops will be golden brown and the bottoms even more so.

Transfer the shortcakes to a rack, cool briefly, then split them, using a sharp serrated knife. Top with fresh strawberries and lots of whipped cream.

NOTE: *Lacking maple syrup, you can simply brush the cakes with cream and sprinkle lightly with sugar.* ◆

## Pear Cobbler with Blue Cheese Biscuit Topping

*Makes 6 servings*

My guess is you will either love or hate this, depending on how you feel about blue cheese. I happen to love it, the not-too-sweet pears a natural mate for the savory biscuits. This is good hot, because the crust on the topping is at its maximum crustiness, but it's good lukewarm too; the flavors seem to be sharper. A spoonful of rich plain yogurt is the perfect sidekick here; whipped cream and ice cream are too sweet.

1 recipe Blue Cheese Cornmeal Biscuits
   (*page 33*)

FRUIT FILLING
6 (*about 3 pounds*) large ripe pears, peeled, cored, and sliced
1 cup fresh, nonpreservative apple cider
¼ cup sugar
1 tablespoon freshly squeezed lemon juice
1 tablespoon unbleached flour
1 tablespoon unsalted butter, cut into small pieces

Make up the biscuit recipe, but don't combine the dry and liquid ingredients. Preheat the oven to 400° and prepare the fruit filling.

Put the pears, cider, sugar, and lemon juice in a large nonaluminum pot. Bring to a boil over high heat, then reduce the heat to low. Cover and simmer for 5 minutes, then remove from the heat. Stir in the flour.

Mix up the biscuits and roll the dough on a sheet of wax paper into a 10-inch circle approximately ½ inch thick.

Carefully pour the pears and their liquid into a 10-inch nonaluminum deep-dish pie pan or baking pan. (This can also be made in a 7- by 11-inch casserole.) Cut the biscuits with a 2-inch biscuit cutter, keeping the cuts as close together as possible; you should get about 12 of them. Scatter the butter over the pears, then arrange the biscuits on top, barely touching. You'll probably be able to fit 9 around the outside and 3 in the center. (If you're using a rectangular casserole, arrange them in even rows.) Re-roll and cut the scraps if you need them. Otherwise, bake the leftovers separately.

Put the cobbler on a baking sheet and bake for 25 minutes, until the top is well browned and the fruit bubbles around the edge. Transfer the cobbler to a rack to cool. Serve hot or warm. ♦

# Cranberry Apple Cobbler

*Makes 8 servings*

Cobblers are one of the mainstays in our family, where the fruit filling and biscuit toppings are always changing with the seasons. Here's one we like so much it's liable to turn up any time of year (we always buy enough cranberries to freeze for year-round use). I put a little applesauce in the filling to help thicken up the juices without any other starch. The topping is sweet and soft, part whole wheat, with just an elusive accent of cardamom; we love cardamom and cranberries. If you like, the raisins can be omitted or replaced with chopped dried apricots.

FRUIT FILLING

3 cups (most of a 12-ounce bag) fresh
   cranberries
2 cups freshly squeezed orange juice
²/₃ cup sugar
2 large firm apples, peeled, cored, and
   coarsely chopped
¹/₃ cup applesauce
¹/₃ cup dark or golden raisins (optional)
finely grated zest of 1 orange

TOPPING

²/₃ cup whole wheat flour
²/₃ cup unbleached flour
¹/₃ cup packed light brown sugar
1¹/₂ teaspoons baking powder
¹/₂ teaspoon ground cardamom
¹/₂ teaspoon salt
5 tablespoons cold unsalted butter, cut into
   ¹/₄-inch pieces
1 large egg
¹/₃ cup plus 1 tablespoon milk

Prepare the fruit filling: Put the cranberries, orange juice, and sugar in a large non-aluminum pot. Bring to a boil over medium heat, stirring occasionally. Boil gently for 2 minutes, letting the skins pop and the fruit soften. Stir in the apples, applesauce, raisins, and orange zest. Cook for another minute, then remove from the heat.

Butter a shallow 8- by 12-inch casserole or baking dish, glass or ceramic, and set aside. Preheat the oven to 400°.

While the oven heats, prepare the topping: In a large bowl, mix the flours, brown sugar, baking powder, cardamom, and salt. Add the butter and cut it into the dry ingredients until only small, split pea-size pieces of butter remain. Beat the egg in a small mixing bowl, then blend in the milk. Make a well in the dry mixture, add the liquid, and blend the batter with a few deft strokes, just until mixed. Reserve. Pour the fruit from the pot into the casserole.

Take your mixing spoon and divide the batter, right in the bowl, into roughly equal quarters. Gently scoop half of each quarter on top of the fruit; you want to end up with

8 scoops of batter in 2 evenly spaced rows of 4. Bake the cobbler for 25 minutes, until the top is well browned and the biscuit topping is cooked through; probe it with a fork to check, expecting the topping to be moist where it meets the fruit. Remove the casserole to a rack and let cool for about 10 minutes before serving.

NOTE: *Like any cobbler, if you let this sit for much more than 30 minutes, the topping soaks up a lot of the juice from underneath. That's not the best way to eat this, in my opinion, but I can think of worse fates in life.* ◆

# Pan Pear Shortcake

*Makes 8 servings*

Here's an autumn shortcake you make up in one skillet and serve right from it. It's a very fast dessert, best eaten fairly hot, so I don't put this in the oven until we're almost ready for dessert, or breakfast, whatever the case may be; it takes only 20 minutes to bake. For breakfast I would serve this with plain yogurt. For dessert, try light cream or vanilla ice cream.

FRUIT

*3 tablespoons unsalted butter*
*1/4 cup packed light brown sugar*
*5 large pears, peeled, cored, and sliced*
*1/2 teaspoon ground cinnamon*

CAKE BATTER

*1 cup whole wheat flour*
*1 cup unbleached flour*
*1/4 cup packed light brown sugar*
*2 teaspoons baking powder*
*1/2 teaspoon baking soda*
*1/2 teaspoon salt*
*6 tablespoons cold unsalted butter, cut into small pieces*
*1 large egg*
*1/2 cup plain yogurt, buttermilk, or sour cream*
*1/2 cup milk*
*a little sugar to sprinkle on top*

Preheat the oven to 425°. To prepare the fruit, melt the butter in a 10-inch cast-iron skillet over medium heat. Add the brown sugar, increase the heat, and bring to a boil. Stir in the pears and cook, stirring occasionally, for 3 minutes. Remove from the heat and stir in the cinnamon. Prepare the cake batter.

Put the flours, brown sugar, baking powder, baking soda, and salt into a large mixing bowl. Add the butter and cut it in until the mixture resembles coarse crumbs. Set aside. In a separate bowl, beat the egg lightly, then whisk in the yogurt, buttermilk, or sour cream and milk. Set aside a tablespoon of this liquid.

Make a well in the dry mixture and stir in the liquid all at once, just until everything is dampened. Spoon the batter over the pears, trying to cover most of the surface. Lightly brush on the reserved egg liquid, then sprinkle the top with a little sugar. Bake for 20 minutes, then remove to a cooling rack. Serve within 10 minutes.

VARIATION: *This can also be served as an upside-down cake if you like; just invert the cake onto a big plate 5 minutes after it comes out of the oven. The reason I don't often do that is because one of this cake's most endearing qualities is the initial soft crunch on top of the cake. If you turn this upside down, you soon lose that because the steam from the cake softens it.* ◆

# Raspberry and Blueberry Shortcake Roll

*Makes 6 to 8 servings*

Essentially a rolled shortcake, this can be made with lots of different soft fruits and berries. The shortcake is rolled into a big rectangle, filled with the fruit, and sealed; it looks like a big calzone. In the baking the fruit softens up just enough to saturate the cake with sweet juices. Not at all hard to make, but you should try to prepare the dough ahead and give it as much time to chill as possible, which makes it easier to roll. We usually eat this for a weekend breakfast, but it also goes over big for dessert, with whipped cream.

*1 recipe Classic Wheaten Shortcake (page 269)*

FILLING

*2 cups (1 pint) fresh raspberries*

*1 cup fresh blueberries*

*3 tablespoons sugar*

*1 tablespoon unbleached flour*

*1/4 teaspoon ground cinnamon or freshly grated nutmeg*

*egg wash: 1 egg beaten with 1 tablespoon milk*

Prepare the dough as directed. After it is mixed, work in enough extra flour to get a kneadable dough. Knead the dough gently for 1 minute on a floured surface, then put it on a large sheet of plastic wrap. Flatten the dough into a rectangle about 3/4 inch thick; wrap, slide it onto a small baking sheet, and refrigerate for at least 30 minutes. In the meantime, lightly butter a large baking sheet.

When you are ready to proceed, preheat the oven to 400°. Rip off a sheet of wax paper about 18 inches long. Dust it generously with flour, then lay the dough on it. Dust the dough with flour and roll into an approximate 10- by 16-inch rectangle. Draw an imaginary line, lengthwise, down the center of the dough and scatter the berries just to one side of it in a long, reasonably neat row; leave about a 3/4-inch margin of dough outside the berries and at the ends. Mix the sugar, flour, and spice and sprinkle over the berries.

Brush a little water along the margin of the dough and then fold the uncovered half of the dough over the berries by picking up and flipping that half of the wax paper. Brush the excess flour off the dough. Line up the edges as well as you can, then pinch and curl slightly to seal. Pick up the wax paper by the ends and invert the roll onto the buttered sheet. Carefully peel off the wax paper.

Brush the entire surface with the egg wash and, if you like, sprinkle a little sugar on top. Bake for 30 minutes, until the top is nicely browned. Let cool for 5 to 10 minutes right on the sheet, then slice and serve.

VARIATIONS: *Use just about any mix of soft berries, some sliced peaches, plums, or other soft fruit.* ◆

## Apple and Pear Cheddar Cobbler

*Makes 8 servings*

The pleasure here is subtle, the whole effect understated: neither the fruit nor the Cheddar in the topping tries to crowd the other out. Someone who doesn't ordinarily go for sweets would probably go for this. It makes a great breakfast item, with a splash of plain yogurt.

*1 recipe Crusty Cheddar Biscuits (page 29)*

FILLING
*3 cups peeled, cored, and sliced apples (no more than 4 large ones)*
*2 cups peeled, cored, and sliced pears (no more than 3 large ones)*
*½ cup packed light brown sugar*
*1 tablespoon freshly squeezed lemon juice*
*1 teaspoon apple cider vinegar*

Prepare the biscuit dough as directed. On a sheet of plastic, flatten the dough into a rectangle about ¾ inch thick. Wrap it, then refrigerate while you prepare the filling. Preheat the oven to 400°.

Combine all of the filling ingredients in a mixing bowl, then turn them into a well-buttered 8- by 12-inch glass or ceramic baking dish.

Tear off a sheet of wax paper about 12 inches long and flour it. Put the dough on it, sprinkle lightly with flour, and roll it into a rectangle about the same size as the pan. Invert the dough over the fruit and peel off the wax paper. Bake for about 30 minutes, until the top is golden brown and crusty and the juices around the edge bubble vigorously. Serve soon.

NOTE: *I'd say there's an above-average proportion of topping to fruit here, but if you want to tilt the balance, put the fruit in a 9-inch deep-dish casserole and use only half the biscuit topping, cutting the rest as biscuits and baking them or freezing for later.* ◆

# Blueberry Plum Cobbler

*Makes 6 to 8 servings*

Here's a peach of a plum cobbler, one fine breakfast or summer dessert when blueberries and plums converge in the market. Don't feel bound by the exact proportions of fruit here; use a little more or less of the berries and plums, as you prefer. Since the fruit is on the sweet side, I like plain yogurt with this.

1 modified recipe Classic Wheaten Shortcake (page 269), as outlined below

FILLING
3 cups (about 6) sliced pitted plums
3 cups (1½ pints) blueberries
⅓ cup honey
⅓ cup sugar
juice of ½ lemon
finely grated zest of 1 lemon
1½ tablespoons quick-cooking tapioca
a little sugar to sprinkle on top (optional)

Preheat the oven to 425°. Put all of the filling ingredients in a large nonaluminum pot. Cook over medium heat for about 5 minutes, stirring occasionally, until the fruit has thrown off a lot of juice and you start to see a little boiling action. Pour the contents of the pan into an 8- by 12-inch casserole, preferably glass or enameled, and put it in the oven, while you prepare the shortcake.

Prepare the shortcake as directed, using an additional 2 tablespoons milk. Mix just until the dough pulls together in a dampish mass. Take the casserole out of the oven; if the juice reaches more than two-thirds up the sides, you should probably put a baking sheet under the pan to catch spills. Spoon golf ball-size globs of dough over the fruit in a random pattern; sprinkle the top with a little sugar if you like. Bake for 20 more minutes, until the fruit is good and bubbly and the top is deeply browned. Cool the cobbler on a rack for 10 minutes before serving. This is best if eaten within an hour.

NOTE: *A pinch of cinnamon or nutmeg is nice in the shortcake. Also, you could use all honey here for the sweetener; the flavor of the fruit is strong enough that the honey wouldn't be overpowering.* ◆

# Blueberry Coconut Crunch

*Makes about 8 servings*

This crunch is something like a crisp, only crunchier, since it has oats and coconut in the topping. There's a classic contrast here between the soft berries and the topping; the contrasting colors are pretty too. Sometimes I use lime juice in the fruit instead of lemon, since limes are often cheaper in the summer. Good with whipped cream, but butter pecan ice cream is even better.

FRUIT FILLING
*5 cups (about 2¹/₂ pints) fresh blueberries,
    rinsed and drained*
*¹/₃ cup honey*
*juice of ¹/₂ lemon or lime*
*1 teaspoon vanilla extract*
*1 tablespoon unbleached flour*

CRUNCH TOPPING
*1 cup unbleached flour*
*¹/₂ cup rolled oats (not instant)*
*²/₃ cup packed light brown sugar*
*¹/₄ teaspoon ground cinnamon*
*pinch of salt*
*¹/₂ cup (¹/₄ pound) cold unsalted butter, cut
    into small pieces*
*¹/₂ cup unsweetened shredded coconut
    (available at health food stores) or
    sweetened flaked coconut*

Preheat the oven to 350° and lavishly butter an 8- by 12-inch glass or ceramic casserole.

Set aside. Combine all the fruit filling ingredients and stir well. Set aside.

Prepare the crunch topping by mixing the flour, oats, brown sugar, cinnamon, and salt in a large bowl. Rub the butter into the dry mixture. When it is mostly gravellike—expect a few bigger clumps of butter—briefly rub in the coconut. Spread this as evenly as possible over the berries, breaking up the bigger clumps with your hands as you work. Bake for 45 minutes, until the fruit is quite bubbly and the topping is golden brown. Cool the pan on a rack for at least 10 minutes before serving. I think the flavors of this are best if it isn't served too hot; lukewarm is just about right. ♦

# Maple Pear Crisp

*Makes 6 servings*

It wasn't all that long ago that you could buy maple syrup for just a few dollars a gallon. Like everything else, however, the price has shot up, especially in the last few years following several poor crops. The best way to buy maple syrup, if you don't live in New England and have neighbors who sell it, is on a trip here. Many producers sell it right out of their homes, invariably announced on a handmade sign at the end of the driveway. You'll often get a better price if you buy directly from the producer. Cooking syrup—called either Grade B or C, depending on where you buy it—is the best buy, though purists are quick to point out that the flavor of the lower grades is more akin to caramel than genuine maple. In any case, when you do buy some, you'll have to try this easy, soft, and crunchy dessert, something we love to serve with coffee after a hearty mid-winter supper.

FRUIT FILLING
*½ cup maple syrup*
*½ vanilla bean (see note below)*
*1 tablespoon freshly squeezed lemon juice*
*5 cups (5 or 6 large) peeled, cored, thinly sliced pears*

TOPPING
*¾ cup unbleached flour*
*¼ cup yellow cornmeal, preferably stone-ground*
*¼ cup packed light brown sugar*
*pinch of salt*
*pinch of ground cinnamon*
*7 tablespoons cold unsalted butter*

Pour the maple syrup into a small saucepan and turn the heat to low. Slit the vanilla bean lengthwise and scrape the seeds into the maple syrup. Whisk in the lemon juice. When hot to the touch, remove the liquid from the heat and set aside.

Put the pear slices in a large bowl and pour the warm syrup over them. Let the pears steep for 15 minutes. In the meantime, preheat the oven to 350° and generously butter an 8- by 12-inch glass or ceramic baking dish.

Make the topping by mixing the flour, cornmeal, brown sugar, salt, and cinnamon in a bowl. Cut 5 tablespoons of the butter into pieces and rub or cut it into the dry ingredients until you have uniform gravel-like crumbs. Set aside.

Scrape the pears and their juice into the buttered dish and dot with the remaining butter. Spread the topping evenly over the pears, then bake for 30 to 35 minutes, until the top is golden brown and the juices bubble wildly. Cool on a rack for at least 10 minutes before serving.

NOTE: *If you don't have a vanilla bean, simply add ½ teaspoon vanilla extract to the syrup when it comes off the heat.* ♦

## High-Fiber Peach and Raspberry Crunch

*Makes 8 servings*

*D*esserts like this are just the thing—fast and easy—when you don't want to go to the extra work of making a pie. This one combines two summer favorites, peaches and raspberries, sweetens them lightly with honey, and finishes with a crunchy oat and oat bran topping. It comes from the oven tinged a pretty shade of raspberry-pink.

FRUIT FILLING
*4 cups (5 to 6 large) sliced peeled ripe*
*    peaches*
*2 cups (1 pint) fresh raspberries*
*⅓ cup honey*
*juice of ½ lemon*
*1½ tablespoons unbleached flour*

OAT TOPPING
*½ cup unbleached flour*
*½ cup rolled oats* (not *instant*)
*½ cup oat bran*
*½ cup packed light brown sugar*
*½ teaspoon freshly grated nutmeg*
*pinch of salt*
*6 tablespoons cold unsalted butter, cut into*
*    small pieces*

Preheat the oven to 350° and lavishly butter an 8- by 12-inch casserole, glass or ceramic. Mix together the filling ingredients and turn them into the baking dish. In a separate bowl, mix the dry topping ingredients. Add the butter and cut it in with a pastry blender or rub it in with your hands until you have a damp, coarse, crumbly meal. Spread this over the fruit and bake for 40 minutes, until the top is golden and the juices around the side of the pan bubble vigorously.

VARIATION: *If you like some other berry better than raspberries, use it.* ◆

# Lemon-Laced Apple Apricot Crisp

*Makes 5 servings*

*H*ere's a simple, fast dessert or break-fast with a generous amount of top-ping. It may seem like there's a lot of top-ping here for a 10-inch dish. In fact, I used to use less topping. But what I found is that human beings—even those of us who have told you in the very last breath that we're watching the amount of sugar and butter we consume—are beset by a type of strip-mining mentality in the face of a luscious crisp topping; we start excavating the top of the crisp that's left in the pan, before we've even finished the apples in our bowl. Serve with vanilla ice cream.

FRUIT FILLING
*5 large firm, tart apples, such as Granny
   Smith, peeled, cored, and thinly sliced
1 tablespoon freshly squeezed lemon juice
finely grated zest of 1 lemon
¼ cup chopped dried apricots, preferably
   unsulphured*

TOPPING
*1 cup unbleached flour
½ cup sugar
¼ cup packed light brown sugar
½ teaspoon ground cinnamon
¼ teaspoon salt
9 tablespoons cold unsalted butter, cut into
   ¼-inch pieces*

Preheat the oven to 375°. Generously butter a 10-inch deep-dish pie pan or shallow round casserole dish. In a large mixing bowl, toss the apples with the lemon juice, lemon zest, and apricots. Spread in the pre-pared pan, evening out the top.

Make the topping. In another large bowl, mix the flour, sugars, cinnamon, and salt. Add the butter and cut it in until all the butter is broken up and the mixture is start-ing to get clumpy. Spread the topping evenly over the fruit. Bake for about 40 minutes, until the topping is golden brown. Cool on a rack for 10 minutes before serv-ing. ◆

# COOKIES
# AND
# CRACKERS

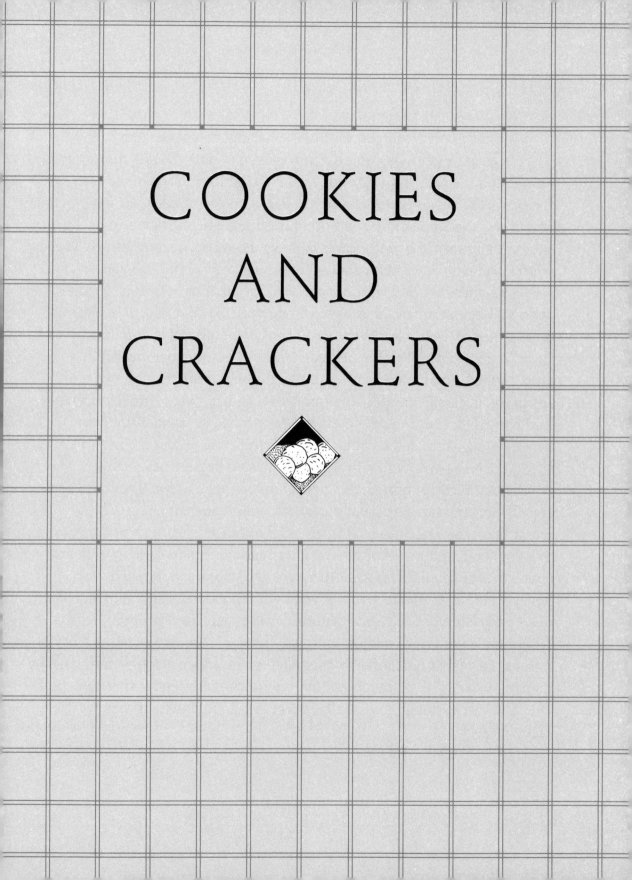

*O*f all the various categories of home baking, cookie making surely has the greatest following and the strongest tradition. Cookie making is so simple, and the gulf of quality between packaged and homemade is so easily discerned: there's just no way a home-baked cookie, made with fresh butter, brown sugar, chopped nuts, and other fresh ingredients, tastes anything like one made by machine, with lesser ingredients, weeks or months ago at plant #7563, and embalmed with enough preservatives to last 100 years.

Here, then, is a fat fistful of cookie recipes that have become tradition in our own home, the ones that have earned our collective stamp of approval because they deliver what every good cookie should: great homemade flavor, pure and simple. One or two are fancy, but the majority are simple drop, formed, and bar cookies, requiring nothing more than a bowl and spoon (or an electric mixer), a baking sheet, and an oven. And restraint, at least enough of it not to polish off an entire batch of cookies without remembering to stock the cookie jar, something we're dreadfully remiss about; the weak-willed should think about doubling recipes.

As you browse through this collection of cookies, you'll run into some ingredients you may not usually associate with cookie making. Whole wheat flour, for one. We use it freely in our cookies, steadfast in our resolve that the natural nuttiness of whole wheat endows many cookies with an abundance of flavor and nutrition. You'll find cookies sweetened with honey, some with maple syrup, several with molasses; you'll find a cookie made with leftover brown rice; another made with cashew butter; still others made with fresh and dried fruits. The cookie maker's craft is a flexible one; an awareness of alternative ingredients can broaden cookie horizons for modern cooks, who place a premium on purity, freshness, and imagination.

And that's enough said, really, because a good cookie speaks for itself. Enjoy these! ♦

## Whole Wheat Honey Butter Cookies

*Makes about 30 cookies*

This is our basic, all-whole-wheat butter cookie, very simple to make and incredibly good-tasting; it isn't uncommon for our family of six to finish the entire batch in one big binge (they're excellent warm) and still brood over the fact that we didn't double the recipe. The great flavor here depends on butter, naturally, but also on good, fresh whole wheat flour. If your flour has been sitting around more than 2 months and it hasn't been stored in the freezer (see page 10), it could well be rancid—smell it—and should be discarded.

> 1 cup (1/2 pound) unsalted butter, softened
> 2/3 cup honey, at room temperature
> 2 large eggs, at room temperature
> 1/2 teaspoon vanilla extract
> 2 1/3 cups whole wheat flour
> 1 teaspoon baking powder
> 1/2 teaspoon salt
> 1/2 teaspoon ground cinnamon
> a little sugar to roll the cookies in (optional)

Using an electric mixer, cream the butter and honey in a large mixing bowl until soft and creamy. Beat in the eggs, one at a time, then the vanilla. In a separate bowl, sift the whole wheat flour with the baking powder, salt, and cinnamon; include any bran that stays in the sifter. Stir the dry ingredients into the creamed mixture, about half at a time, just until thoroughly blended; don't beat the dough. Cover the dough and refrigerate for 30 minutes. Preheat the oven to 375° approximately 15 minutes before you are ready to bake the cookies.

Using floured hands, make balls of dough about 1 1/4 inches in diameter. Roll them in sugar if you like (or sugar mixed with a little cinnamon) and place the balls on ungreased cookie sheets, leaving a little room between them for expansion. You can leave the balls as is—in which case you'll have a rounded cookie—or flatten them just a little with the tines of a fork. Bake for 10 minutes, one sheet at a time. Cool for a minute on the sheet, then transfer the cookies to a rack to cool. Store in an airtight container. These are best eaten within a week. ♦

## Honey Wheat Oatmeal Cookies

*Makes about 24 cookies*

If you like the idea of a traditional cookie in a wholesome, grainy package, then make these. They're quite soft and chewy, and they're good keepers too.

*1/2 cup (1/4 pound) unsalted butter, softened*
*3/4 cup honey*
*1/4 cup unsulphured molasses*
*1 teaspoon vanilla extract*
*1 1/4 cups whole wheat flour*
*1 cup rolled oats (not instant)*
*1 teaspoon ground cinnamon*
*1/2 teaspoon salt*
*1/2 teaspoon baking soda*
*1 cup (4 to 5 ounces) coarsely chopped walnuts*
*1/2 cup dark raisins*

Preheat the oven to 350°. In a large mixing bowl, cream the butter, honey, molasses, and vanilla with an electric mixer. In a separate bowl, stir together the whole wheat flour, oats, cinnamon, salt, and baking soda and blend them into the creamed mixture. Stir in the walnuts and raisins. Let the dough sit for 10 minutes and, in the meantime, lightly butter 1 or 2 large baking sheets, preferably not dark ones.

Drop rounded tablespoonfuls of dough onto the buttered sheets, leaving about 3 inches between them. Bake, one sheet at a time, for 12 to 14 minutes. When done, the tops will still be a *little* soft and squishy to the touch and the edges will be a shade darker than the rest of the cookie. In general, however, the entire cookie will be on the dark side. Let them cool briefly on the sheet, then transfer them to a rack to cool. Store in a covered container. ♦

### Bread Crumbs

To make fine, dry whole grain bread crumbs, start with old ends of whole grain bread. I keep mine in bags in the freezer. Grate them on the big holes of a box grater. If they were in the freezer, grate them while they're still cold; they're easier to grate when firm. To make 1 1/2 cups fine crumbs, you'll need to put down a layer of crumb gratings about 1/4 inch thick on the bottom of a 12- by 18-inch baking sheet or jelly roll pan. Bake them in a 300° oven for about 30 minutes, stirring every 10 minutes. When they feel dry, take them out and cool them on the sheet. Pulverize them to a fine consistency in a blender or food processor or put them in a large plastic bag and run over them with a rolling pin.

# German Whole Grain Crumb Cookies

*Makes about 30 cookies*

One of the most unusual cookies I know of, this one has no leavening and uses fine bread crumbs for much of its bulk; frankly, I'm not sure why these are called German, but the German in me likes this setup—the gaiety of a holiday cookie seasoned with the practicality of plain bread crumbs. I make my own bread crumbs; I've never used prepared unseasoned bread crumbs here—have you ever read the ingredients on a can of "plain" bread crumbs?—because I can't imagine they'd taste the same. At the very least you'd want to leave the salt out of the recipe. Below are some notes on making your own fine bread crumbs. This is adapted from a recipe by Margaret Brindley of Milwaukee, Wisconsin.

1¹/₂ cups fine whole grain bread crumbs (see page 286)

1¹/₂ cups (about 6 ounces) finely chopped walnuts

²/₃ cup packed light brown sugar

¹/₃ cup sugar

1¹/₂ teaspoons ground cinnamon

¹/₂ teaspoon ground cloves

¹/₂ teaspoon freshly grated nutmeg

¹/₄ teaspoon ground cardamom

¹/₄ teaspoon salt

6 tablespoons unsalted butter, at room temperature, cut into ¹/₄-inch pieces

1 large egg, lightly beaten

¹/₄ cup unbleached flour

Preheat the oven to 350° and lightly butter a large baking sheet, preferably not a dark one. In a large mixing bowl, combine the bread crumbs, walnuts, sugars, spices, and salt. Rub them together with your hands to smooth, then add the butter and rub that in until the mixture has a coarse, uniform texture. Drizzle the egg over the top and work it in with your hands until you have a damp, gravelly texture. Sprinkle on the flour and work it in.

Using a tablespoon—preferably one on the deep side—as a mold, *pack* the dough into the spoon until it is level with the top plane of it. Pressing on one end of the cookie, carefully slide it out of the spoon and lay it on the sheet, flat side down; the cookie should hold together with no problem. (If you want to give these a sweet coating—they don't really need it—dip the spoon in sugar before molding each cookie.) Place the cookies on the sheet, almost touching; they don't spread.

Bake for 15 minutes, until the surface feels firm to the touch; it's fine if there is a little give beneath the firm surface. Cool the cookies on the sheet for 5 minutes, then transfer them to a rack to finish cooling. Store in an airtight container. ◆

# Michael and Wendy's Pecan Praline Sandies

*Makes about 48 cookies*

Michael and Wendy are Michael and Wendy London, an enormously talented baking duo in upstate New York who left New York City some years ago to open the renowned Mrs. London's Bakeshop in Saratoga, which they eventually gave up to specialize in making naturally leavened breads out of their country home/bakery. I call them from time to time to pick at their considerable baking knowledge. One year they were kind enough to send me this recipe when I was writing an article about favorite Christmas cookies from some of the best bakers in the country. These won't disappoint you.

1 cup plus 3 tablespoons (about 5 ounces)
   pecan halves
²/₃ cup sugar
2¹/₄ cups unbleached flour
1 cup (¹/₂ pound) unsalted butter, softened
¹/₂ cup plus 2 tablespoons confectioners' sugar
1¹/₂ teaspoons vanilla extract

Preheat the oven to 350°. Spread ¹/₂ cup of the pecan halves on an ungreased cookie sheet and toast them for 10 minutes, until crisp. Let them cool to room temperature and then transfer the nuts to a bowl. Grease the cookie sheet and turn off the oven.

In a heavy saucepan, cook the granulated sugar over moderate heat, stirring, until it begins to melt. Stop stirring and continue cooking until the caramel is a deep brown, about 6 minutes. Remove from the heat and stir in the toasted pecan halves until well coated. Quickly scrape this mixture (the praline) onto the greased cookie sheet and spread into a thin layer. Let cool to room temperature—about 15 minutes.

Break the praline into small chunks and grind to a powder in a food processor or blender. Add the remaining pecans and process until finely ground. Transfer to a medium bowl and toss with the flour.

In a large bowl, beat the butter until light and creamy. Beat in ¹/₂ cup of the confectioners' sugar and the vanilla until well blended. Gradually add the flour and nut mixture and mix well. Cover and refrigerate until cold but not hard, about 1 hour. Lightly butter 1 or 2 cookie sheets.

Preheat the oven to 350°. Shape the dough into 1-inch balls and gently roll each one to shape them into cocoons. Place the cookies about 2 inches apart on the sheet. Bake for 18 minutes, or until the edges begin to brown slightly. Let cool on the sheet for 2 minutes, then transfer to a wire rack and cool completely. Sift the remaining confectioners' sugar over the cookies. Store in an airtight container.  ◆

# Whole Wheat Walnut Chocolate Chip Cookies

*Makes about 36 cookies*

Here's a cookie for people who'd like to start eating healthier sweets but who, on the other hand, see no reason to rush into this sort of thing. The main difference between this cookie and others of its ilk is a full complement of whole wheat flour; this alone counts for at least a 30 percent guilt reduction factor over other chocolate chip cookies. Watch them very carefully in the last few minutes of baking so they don't overbrown.

1 cup (½ pound) unsalted butter, at room temperature
1½ cups packed light brown sugar
2 large eggs, at room temperature
1 teaspoon vanilla extract
2 cups whole wheat flour
¼ cup rolled oats (not *instant*)
1 teaspoon baking soda
½ teaspoon salt
1¼ cups semisweet chocolate chips
1 cup (4 to 5 ounces) coarsely chopped walnuts

Preheat the oven to 350°. In a medium mixing bowl, cream the butter with an electric mixer, adding the brown sugar as the butter gets soft. Beat in the eggs, one at a time, then the vanilla. In a separate bowl, stir together the whole wheat flour, oats, baking soda, and salt.

Add the dry ingredients to the creamed mixture in 3 stages, stirring just until blended after each. Stir in the chocolate chips and walnuts.

Using a tablespoon or soup spoon, drop slightly-smaller-than-golf-ball-size pieces of dough onto ungreased cookie sheets—preferably not dark ones—leaving about 3 inches between them. Bake for 12 to 14 minutes, one sheet at a time; remove from the oven when they have a slightly uneven, golden brown coloring. They may seem a little undercooked in the middle, but they'll firm up. Let them cool on the sheet for several minutes, then transfer by spatula to a cooling rack. Cool thoroughly before storing in an airtight container. ♦

# Brown Rice and Raisin Chewies

*Makes about 24 cookies*

Brown rice might seem like a weird cookie ingredient, but these taste anything but odd, something like a portable, crisper version of rice pudding. There's nothing wrong with cooking some brown rice to make these (½ cup rice in 1¼ cups water, simmered about 35 minutes), though the original idea was conceived during yet another attempt to blaze new leftover trails. Some of those trails I'd sooner forget; these are worth the detour.

*½ cup (¼ pound) unsalted butter, softened*
*1 cup packed light brown sugar*
*1 large egg, at room temperature*
*1 teaspoon vanilla extract*
*1¼ cups whole wheat flour*
*¼ cup rolled oats (not instant)*
*½ teaspoon baking soda*
*½ teaspoon ground cinnamon*
*¼ teaspoon salt*
*1 to 1¼ cups cooked brown rice, cooled*
*1 cup dark raisins*

Butter 1 or 2 cookie sheets, preferably not dark ones. Using an electric mixer, cream the butter and brown sugar in a medium mixing bowl. Add the egg and beat for another minute, until light in texture; add the vanilla before turning the mixer off.

In a separate bowl, combine the whole wheat flour, oats, baking soda, cinnamon, and salt. Stir the dry ingredients into the creamed mixture in several stages, stirring just to blend after each addition. Work in the rice and raisins until they're coated with and held in suspension by the dough. Cover the dough and refrigerate for 15 minutes. Preheat the oven to 350°.

Form balls of dough roughly 1¼ inches in diameter and place them on the sheets, leaving several inches between them for spreading. Flatten slightly with your fingers or a fork, then bake for 12 to 13 minutes. When done, the tops may still seem slightly soft to the touch, but they shouldn't feel like mush. Cool them on the sheet for several minutes, then transfer the cookies to a rack and finish cooling. Store in an airtight container. ♦

# Opal's Favorite Molasses Cookies

*Makes about 30 cookies*

Opal is my mother-in-law, and she can make Christmas cookies like you wouldn't believe. This is Opal's favorite molasses cookie, or at least our version of her favorite. We eliminated all the white sugar, went in a lot heavier on the molasses, and whole-wheated it to come up with a great dark, chewy cookie. I can't imagine you could do much better in a molasses cookie, whole grain or otherwise. You'll have a hard time stopping if you start eating these warm, off the sheet—but you wouldn't do that, would you?

*1/2 cup (1/4 pound) unsalted butter, softened*
*1/2 cup packed light brown sugar*
*3/4 cup unsulphured molasses*
*1 large egg, at room temperature*
*2 cups whole wheat flour*
*2 teaspoons baking soda*
*1/2 teaspoon salt*
*1 teaspoon ground cinnamon*
*1/2 teaspoon ground cloves*
*1/2 teaspoon ground ginger*

In a large mixing bowl, cream the butter and brown sugar. Beat in the molasses and egg. In a separate bowl, stir together the remaining ingredients and blend them into the creamed mixture about a third at a time; do not beat. Cover and chill the dough for at least 4 hours, preferably overnight. (See note below.)

When you plan to bake the cookies, preheat the oven to 350° and butter 2 large baking sheets, preferably not dark ones. Spoon up the chilled dough, shaping it into balls approximately 1 1/4 inches in diameter. Place the balls on the prepared sheet, leaving about 3 inches between them; they'll spread. Bake for 13 to 15 minutes, until the tops are slightly resistant to light finger pressure. Cool the sheet on a rack for 5 minutes, then remove the cookies from the sheet and let them cool on the rack. Store in an airtight container.

NOTE: *If you're in a hurry, you can skip the chilling of the dough here, but you get a more attractive, more shapely cookie when it is chilled first. If not chilled, don't try to form balls; just spoon the dough onto the sheet.* ◆

Talking about baking with kids, notice how the mind automatically flashes that Norman Rockwellian scene across our interior image screen: of some kindly white-haired matron, carefully instructing her young charge, who looks on with rapt patience, in the art of dropping cookie dough onto a baking sheet.

Well, maybe. But as the father of four youngsters, experience tells me there is often a yawning gulf—full of distractions, burned cookies, and shattered expectations—between our impression of baking with kids and the reality. I bring this up, not to rain on anyone's party but with the conviction that baking with kids—if you are equipped with some fair warnings and sound advice—can be a great, fun way to build family ties, as it has been for me and mine. Not everybody comes to the table as equals on this count. My mate, Karen, can bake with a kitchen full of kids with the equanimity of a saint, dispensing smiles and compliments like a politician at a fund-raiser. I, on the other hand, always have to keep reminding myself that a little flour on the floor isn't the end of the world, but I'm mellowing slowly, with age.

The first thing to realize is that kids and adults come to baking with different agendas. *You* may decide to bake something to please your family, fulfill a creative urge, fill in a few hours on a rainy day, or have a little fun; *kids* just want to have fun. I can tell you for a fact that my son, Ben, would sooner see me empty a 5-pound bag of flour on my head while doing my wildest Bruce Springsteen imitation than listen to some insipid speech on the merits of proper kneading. *You* want to bake with some semblance of law and order. *Kids* couldn't give a hoot about whether you add ingre-dients in the right order. *They'd* rather break an extra-large egg into each of your spice jars. So in this respect, baking with kids is the art of compromise, of balancing your child's natural impulses with your own sense of order, so there's something good to eat in the end.

That said, here are seven rules to get you baking, happily, with your kids.

1. Pick a good time. A bad time is when your child is tired or hungry. Get these basics behind you, and chances are everything will work out well. Tired kids probably won't be able to pay attention, and hungry ones are cranky and forever eating cookie dough. If your child is tired, sometimes you can bribe him into a nap by promising to make cookies when he wakes up. And make sure you're in a good mood too, so you can keep your humor. Otherwise nobody is going to have fun.

2. Read the recipe over before you begin. This is very important because you can pinpoint specific jobs for your child in advance. Look for tasks that are equal to your child's abilities. Measuring and adding flour—say, to bread dough—is always an easy thing for a wide age range of youngsters. Buttering pans is another. Sifting too. For children over the age of about five, opening the oven door—with direct supervision—is a real privilege.

   The other advantage to reading the recipe over first—which you should always do anyway—is that you'll know what to expect; you can keep up the pace if you're familiar with the territory. Break your stride, and kids get bored. That's when the eggs start going into the spice jars. Take the phone off the hook.

3. Once you've read the recipe, prep all your ingredients before you start mixing. Get out the baking powder, the flour, the vanilla; preheat the oven; pull out the pans and sheets. Again, this is to keep the pace moving, which you can't do if you have to keep referring to the printed page for information.

4. Once you do start mixing, be verbal and very clear about what the child should and shouldn't do. I find, with my own kids, that they work on the principle that if they haven't been told *not* to do something, it's okay to do it. ("But Pop, you never *said* not to shape little balls of dough and stick them in your typewriter while your back was turned.") Often I find it helps to say something like "The next thing we'll be doing is beating the butter, but please don't do anything until I've told you what to do next." That way they have something solid to look forward to.

5. Praise and be positive. This isn't always easy, because there are lots of opportunities for little mistakes to be made. Try to bite your tongue when they're innocent mistakes; most can be remedied without too much fuss. Take every opportunity to frame your comments in a positive light. Say things like "I really liked the way you creamed the molasses and butter," "You put just the right amount of spice in these cookies," and "I think Spot looks very cute with cookie dough in his ears, but let's keep it on the cookie sheet, dear." We're practicing the art of home baking in the fullest sense if we use it to help build our children's self-esteem; that's what it's really all about.

6. Don't place too much emphasis on looks. Realize anything a child helps you make is likely to *look* like a child made it. I must confess, this used to be a little problem for me, because I like things to look attractive, especially if I'm planning to serve them to guests. (I've had more fingerprints in pies than the FBI has in its files.) I eventually learned just to give over a portion of bread dough or cookie batter or whatever and let the kids shape it the way they want; we're all happier that way. And the kids really get a charge out of having a jarful of cookies or a loaf of bread they made entirely on their own.

7. Put safety first. This is a big issue with me because I cook a lot at home with little kids around; I see all sorts of accidents waiting to happen.

   One big thing is just to keep the kids back from the stove, especially the youngest ones. Anything can fall off the burners or splash out of pans unexpectedly. And the surfaces of your stove can get hot enough to do some serious damage if a little one grabs it or falls against it.

   Knives are also potentially very dangerous. I advise washing sharp knives and putting them out of harm's way as soon as you are finished with them. If you do leave them on the counter, put them way at the back edge so they can't be swept off the surface accidentally.

   Be careful with kitchen machines. This is hard, because kids are so naturally curious about them; mine love to run the mixers. I don't disallow this, but I watch like a hawk, don't let the kids crowd around, and really lay down the law when I have to. Watch for electrical cords hanging off counters that some little person might yank on.

## Fresh and Candied Ginger Lace Cookies

*Makes about 50 cookies*

Here's a different kind of ginger cookie, one that uses both fresh and candied ginger, accented by fresh lemon zest. These cookies are delicious and well worth the extra trouble of mincing the gingers, which takes only a minute. They come out as very thin wafers, only about $1/8$ inch thick, with a lacy look and crisp texture. There's plenty here to stuff a lot of stockings.

*3/4 cup (6 ounces) unsalted butter, softened*
*3/4 cup packed light brown sugar*
*1/4 cup unsulphured molasses*
*1 large egg, at room temperature*
*1/2 teaspoon vanilla extract*
*finely grated zest of 1 lemon*
*2 tablespoons finely minced candied ginger*
*2 tablespoons finely minced peeled fresh
  ginger*
*1 cup unbleached flour*
*2/3 cup whole wheat flour*
*2 teaspoons baking soda*
*1/2 teaspoon ground cloves*
*1/2 teaspoon ground cinnamon*

Preheat the oven to 300° and lightly butter 1 or 2 large cookie sheets, preferably not dark ones. In a large mixing bowl, cream the butter and brown sugar with an electric mixer for 2 minutes. Beat in the molasses, then the egg, vanilla, lemon zest, and gingers.

Mix the flours, baking soda, and spices in a separate bowl, then stir them into the creamed ingredients in 2 stages. Drop rounded teaspoons of dough onto the baking sheets, leaving about 3 inches between them; these spread. Bake, one sheet at a time, for 15 to 18 minutes, until fairly well browned. Cool for no more than 2 minutes on the sheet, then transfer the cookies to a rack to finish cooling. Store in an airtight container. ♦

# Maple Hazelnut Cookies

*Makes about 30 cookies*

The hazelnut/maple compatibility is one of the worst-kept secrets in New England cooking circles, something I found out when I was invited to judge a maple dessert cooking contest in Vermont. Present were chefs from all over Vermont, and of the 30 or so I swear half of them had brought hazelnut somethings: tortes, pies, cakes, puddings, sticky buns, tarts—you name it. For a few years afterward I was a bit tepid about the two together, but I finally regained my enthusiasm with this cookie. The nuttiness of the whole wheat flour here works nicely with the hazelnut flavor.

*1/2 cup (1/4 pound) unsalted butter, softened*
*1 cup maple syrup, at room temperature*
*1/2 teaspoon instant espresso or coffee powder*
*1 teaspoon vanilla or almond extract*
*1 3/4 cups whole wheat flour*
*1 teaspoon baking powder*
*1/2 teaspoon salt*
*1/2 cup (2 ounces) hazelnuts, toasted and
    skins removed (see page 237 for
    information about toasting hazelnuts)*
*1/2 cup rolled oats (not instant)*

Preheat the oven to 350° (see note below) and lightly butter 1 or 2 large cookie sheets, preferably not dark ones. Using an electric mixer, cream the butter and maple syrup until smooth and fluffy. Beat in the espresso or coffee powder and the vanilla or almond extract.

Mix together the whole wheat flour, baking powder, and salt. Stir it into the creamed mixture in 3 stages. Put the hazelnuts and oats in a blender or food processor and grind to a fine consistency. Stir this into the dough until evenly blended.

With floured hands, make balls of dough about 1 1/4 inches in diameter. Place them on the sheets about 3 inches apart, flattening them slightly with your fingers. Bake, one sheet at a time, for 13 to 14 minutes, until the tops offer some resistance to gentle finger pressure. Cool on the sheet for several minutes, then transfer the cookies to a rack to cool. Store in an airtight container.

NOTE: *Instead of preheating the oven at this point, you can wait and give the dough some time to chill, which will make it easier to handle—not a tremendous amount, but some. Another option is not to roll the dough but just drop it from a teaspoon. You don't get uniform-looking cookies this way, but if that doesn't bother you, it doesn't bother me either.* ◆

# Three-Nut Cookies

*Makes about 36 cookies*

The cream cheese gives these soft cookies a slight tartness, and the honey helps to prevent their cakelike texture from drying out. If, like me, you don't have a food processor, you can use your blender to grind the nuts: mix them together and process in 3 batches, stopping the blender often to fluff up the nuts. (I use the handle of a wooden spoon, and I stick it way down in there; if you find that most of the batch is finely chopped, but you still have a few big nuts left, stop and dump out what you have, then sift your hands through and pull out any big pieces and chop them by hand. This way you won't overprocess the nuts.)

*²/₃ cup (about 3 ounces) almonds*

*²/₃ cup (about 3 ounces) hazelnuts*

*²/₃ cup (about 3 ounces) pecans*

*a few extra whole nuts to press into the tops*

*¹/₂ cup (¹/₄ pound) unsalted butter, at room temperature*

*¹/₄ pound cream cheese, at room temperature*

*¹/₂ cup honey*

*¹/₂ cup packed light brown sugar*

*1 large egg, at room temperature*

*1 teaspoon vanilla or almond extract*

*1²/₃ cups unbleached flour*

*1 teaspoon baking powder*

*¹/₂ teaspoon salt*

Preheat the oven to 350° and lightly butter 2 large cookie sheets. (If you have some extra time, however, this dough handles more easily—and the finished cookies look more symmetrical—if you can let the dough chill for 30 or so minutes, in which case don't preheat the oven yet.) Mix the nuts in a bowl, then finely grind them in a food processor or blender (see note above). Set aside.

In a medium mixing bowl, cream the butter and cream cheese with an electric mixer. Add the honey, brown sugar, egg, and vanilla and continue to beat until smooth and light in texture. Mix the flour, baking powder, and salt and stir into the creamed mixture; blend in the nuts, stirring just until evenly blended. If you have the time, cover and chill the dough for at least 30 minutes. Preheat the oven 15 minutes before you plan to bake these.

If the dough isn't chilled and you don't want to get your hands all messy, drop tablespoonfuls of dough onto the prepared sheets, leaving 2 inches between them. If it is chilled, gently roll balls slightly larger than 1 inch with floured hands, placing them about 2 inches apart on the sheets. Gently press a whole almond or hazelnut or a pecan half into the top of each, at the same time flattening the cookie a little. (Get any hazelnuts way down in there; the skins get dark very quickly.) Bake, one sheet at a time, for 13 to 15 minutes, until the tops are ever-so-lightly tanned and the bottoms are lightly browned. Cool the cookies on the sheet for several minutes, then transfer them to a rack to finish cooling. Immediately store in an airtight container.

NOTE: *If you like, you can lightly toast the nuts first, for a more pronounced flavor (see page 237 for toasting instructions).* ◆

# Honey Cranberry Softies

*Makes 40 to 48 cookies*

I like the idea of cranberries in a cookie; they add a festive touch and keep the cookies moist. And this *is* a moist, soft cookie, best eaten the same day (though I've never seen anybody turn down a day-old one). This is adapted from a recipe sent to me by Mavis Diment, a home cook from Marcus, Iowa.

3/4 cup honey
1/4 cup flavorless vegetable oil
1 large egg
1 teaspoon vanilla extract
finely grated zest of 1 orange
1 1/2 cups whole wheat flour
1/2 teaspoon baking soda
1/8 teaspoon salt
1 teaspoon ground cinnamon
1/2 teaspoon ground allspice
1/8 teaspoon ground cloves
1 cup chopped fresh cranberries
1/2 cup (2 ounces) chopped walnuts

Preheat the oven to 375° and lightly butter 1 or 2 large cookie sheets, preferably not dark ones. In a medium bowl, beat or vigorously whisk the honey, oil, and egg; add the vanilla and orange zest.

In a separate bowl, mix the whole wheat flour, baking soda, salt, and spices. Stir the dry ingredients into the liquid until thoroughly blended, then fold in the cranberries and walnuts. Drop rounded teaspoonfuls of dough onto the sheets, leaving about 2 inches between them. Bake one sheet at a time for 12 to 13 minutes, until the cookies offer just a little resistance to gentle finger pressure. Cool on the sheets for 5 minutes, then transfer to a rack to finish cooling. ♦

297

## Double Chocolate Chip Mint Cookies

*Makes about 30 cookies*

Here's decadence, laced with lots of fresh mint from the garden. Spearmint and peppermint both have an intense mint flavor and work well here, but other types of mint can be used too. These would be a big hit at any summer food gathering, family reunion, or picnic. Tip: gardening friends will want this recipe.

*¼ pound semisweet chocolate*
*½ cup (¼ pound) unsalted butter, softened*
*¾ cup plus 1 teaspoon packed light brown sugar*
*1 large egg*
*1 teaspoon vanilla extract*
*¾ cup fresh mint leaves (not packed)*
*1 cup unbleached flour*
*¾ teaspoon baking soda*
*½ teaspoon salt*
*1 cup chocolate chips*

Preheat the oven to 350° and lightly butter 1 or 2 large baking sheets, preferably not dark ones. Using a double boiler or a saucepan set over a pan of simmering water, melt the chocolate. Remove from the heat and whisk until smooth. Cool.

In a large mixing bowl, cream the butter with an electric mixer. Add the ¾ cup brown sugar and beat for 1 minute, then beat in the egg and vanilla until light in texture, about another minute. Blend in the melted chocolate.

Mix the remaining teaspoon of brown sugar with the mint leaves and mince them, using either a sharp knife or a food processor. Stir into the creamed mixture. In a separate bowl, mix the unbleached flour, baking soda, and salt. Stir the dry ingredients into the creamed mixture in 3 stages, just until blended. Fold in the chocolate chips.

Drop slightly mounded tablespoons of dough onto the cookie sheet, leaving about 3 inches between them. Bake, one sheet at a time, for about 13 minutes; the tops will still be soft to the touch, but don't worry because they'll firm up. Remove the sheet to a rack and cool for several minutes, then transfer the cookies to the rack to finish cooling. Store leftovers in a sealed container. ◆

# Toasted Sunflower Seed Cookies

*Makes about 36 cookies*

*H*ere are wholesome, virtuous cookies, invented by Karen, my wife, whose baking tends to be more wholesome and virtuous than my own. You can tell right away that they were invented by a busy mom; no fussy techniques are involved, there's no butter to soften—it's pretty much low-maintenance cookie making. These taste rich, but not in a butter-rich sense (there's no butter in these). It's the sort of richness you associate with whole grains, seeds, and other natural ingredients.

2 cups raw hulled sunflower seeds
1¹⁄₂ cups whole wheat flour
¹⁄₂ cup rolled oats (not *instant*)
1 teaspoon ground cinnamon
¹⁄₄ teaspoon ground cloves
³⁄₄ teaspoon salt
¹⁄₂ teaspoon baking soda
¹⁄₂ cup flavorless vegetable oil
¹⁄₂ cup honey
¹⁄₂ cup unsulphured molasses
2 tablespoons plain yogurt or sour cream
1 large egg
1 teaspoon vanilla extract
¹⁄₂ cup dark raisins

Put the seeds in a large, heavy skillet—I like cast iron for this—and turn the heat to high. Toast the seeds, stirring very often, for several minutes; you'll hear the seeds start to pop. Turn the heat down to medium and continue to toast and stir for a total of about 10 minutes, until the seeds are a rich golden brown. Transfer to a plate to cool.

While the seeds cool, mix the whole wheat flour, oats, cinnamon, cloves, salt, and baking soda in a large bowl. In a separate bowl, beat the oil, honey, molasses, yogurt, egg, and vanilla with an electric mixer. Reserve.

Put 1¹⁄₂ cups of the toasted seeds in a blender or food processor and grind to a coarse meal; if you're using a blender, you may have to start and stop it and stir them around so they all get ground. Mix both the ground and whole seeds in with the dry ingredients.

Make a well in the dry ingredients and pour in the liquid. Stir, just to blend, then fold in the raisins. Let the dough rest for 15 minutes while you preheat the oven to 350° and lightly butter 1 or 2 large cookie sheets.

Drop mounded tablespoonfuls of dough onto the buttered sheets, leaving several inches between them. Bake, one sheet at a time, for about 12 minutes. When done, the tops of the cookies will offer just slight resistance to gentle finger pressure; they shouldn't be squishy-soft. Let them cool on the sheet for several minutes, then transfer the cookies to a rack to cool. Store in an airtight container. These are best eaten within 3 days. ◆

# Sesame Seed Lemon Drop Cookies

*Makes about 30 cookies*

Like the previous cookie, these are made with toasted ground seeds. They're very soft, for the first few hours especially, and very lemony; the lemon and sesame are great together.

1 cup toasted sesame seeds (*see note below*)
1¹/₂ cups whole wheat flour
²/₃ cup unbleached flour
¹/₂ cup yellow cornmeal, preferably stone-ground
¹/₂ teaspoon salt
¹/₂ teaspoon baking soda
1 cup honey
¹/₂ cup flavorless vegetable oil
¹/₄ cup plain yogurt
¹/₄ cup freshly squeezed lemon juice (*from 1 large lemon*)
finely grated zest of 1 lemon

Put ³/₄ cup of the toasted sesame seeds in a blender and grind to a coarse flour consistency; you may have to stop the blender and stir them down once or twice so they all get ground. In a large bowl, mix the remaining whole seeds, the ground seeds, flours, cornmeal, salt, and soda.

In a separate bowl, whisk together the remaining ingredients. Make a well in the dry ingredients, add the liquid, and stir to blend. Let the dough sit for 15 minutes while you preheat the oven to 350° and lightly butter 1 or 2 large cookie sheets.

Drop slightly mounded tablespoonfuls of dough onto the sheets, leaving about 3 inches between them. Bake, one sheet at a time, for 12 minutes. When done, the tops of the cookies will feel fairly firm to the touch and the bottom edge, where it meets the pan, will be starting to turn golden. Cool on the sheet for several minutes, then transfer the cookies to a rack to cool. Store in an airtight container. These are best eaten within several days.

NOTE: *If you can't buy toasted sesame seeds, toast your own, following the procedure in the preceding recipe for toasting sunflower seeds, but reduce the total toasting time to about 6 minutes.* ◆

## Banana Coconut Cookies

*Makes about 30 cookies*

Here's a soft cookie with a fresh banana flavor, spiffed up with coconut and pecans. The taste is just right; even chocolate chips don't do anything for these, if you can believe that.

*½ cup (¼ pound) unsalted butter, softened*
*¾ cup honey*
*1 large egg, at room temperature*
*1½ teaspoons vanilla extract*
*1 large very ripe banana, mashed*
*1 cup unbleached flour*
*¾ cup whole wheat flour*
*2 teaspoons baking powder*
*½ teaspoon salt*
*½ teaspoon ground cinnamon*
*¼ teaspoon ground allspice*
*¾ cup unsweetened shredded coconut*
  *(available at health food stores) or*
  *sweetened flaked coconut*
*½ cup (about 2 ounces) chopped pecans*

Preheat the oven to 350° and lightly butter 1 or 2 large cookie sheets, preferably not dark ones. In a large bowl, cream the butter and honey with an electric mixer. Beat in the egg, vanilla, and banana.

In a separate bowl, mix the remaining ingredients, stirring them into the creamed mixture in 2 or 3 stages. Let the dough sit for a few minutes, then drop slightly mounded tablespoonfuls onto the sheets, leaving about 3 inches between them. Bake, one sheet at a time, for 12 to 13 minutes, until the tops take on an ever-so-slight bit of browning here and there; the tops should also offer some resistance to gentle finger pressure. Cool the cookies on the sheet for several minutes, then transfer them to a rack to finish cooling. Store in an airtight container. They are best eaten within 3 days. ◆

# Easy Carob Drop Cookies

*Makes about 30 cookies*

These are really amazingly good for cookies that (1) have no butter or eggs, (2) use all whole wheat flour, and (3) can be made in just minutes. They're chewy and moist with rich, deep flavor. I like them with mostly maple, the way I do it here, though in fact *all* maple would be wonderful. Another good mix of sweeteners would be ⅓ cup molasses and ⅔ cup honey. Very highly recommended.

*½ cup flavorless vegetable oil*
*¾ cup maple syrup*
*¼ cup unsulphured molasses*
*2 tablespoons sour cream*
*1½ teaspoons vanilla extract*
*2 cups whole wheat flour*
*2 tablespoons carob powder (or unsweetened cocoa powder, if you aren't a carob fan)*
*1 teaspoon baking powder*
*1 teaspoon salt*
*1 cup unsweetened shredded coconut (available at health food stores) or sweetened flaked coconut*
*1 cup (4 to 5 ounces) chopped walnuts*
*½ cup dark raisins*

Preheat the oven to 350° and lightly butter 1 or 2 large cookie sheets, preferably not dark ones. In a medium mixing bowl, briskly whisk together the oil, maple syrup, molasses, sour cream, and vanilla. In a separate bowl, mix the whole wheat flour, carob powder, baking powder, and salt. Stir in the coconut. Gradually stir the dry ingredients into the liquid until blended. Stir in the walnuts and raisins.

Drop mounded tablespoonfuls of dough onto the prepared sheets and bake, one sheet at a time, for 15 minutes. The tops of the cookies should just barely be browning, and they'll feel semifirm to the touch. Cool the sheet on a rack for several minutes, then transfer the cookies to the rack and cool. Store in an airtight container. ♦

# The Art of Not Measuring

Baking is a science and an art predicated on precise measurements and equations: you take so much flour, this much salt, X amount of butter, mix it all together, and here's what you get. And because success in baking often does hinge on formulas, especially in the ratio of flour to liquid, the smart baker knows that to tamper is to risk a baking disaster.

There are times, however, when not measuring ingredients or only sort of measuring them makes perfectly good sense, generally because the ingredient in question isn't critical to a recipe's success. Not measuring, in these cases, is a good idea because (1) it can save you time in recipe preparation and (2) it helps to develop your commonsense instincts as a cook, building confidence in the bargain.

For example, let's take pizza. The basic recipe in this book calls for 3 cups of grated cheese. Now, let's say your measuring cup is buried under a ton of dirty dishes, the kids are gnawing on each other because they're so hungry, and your spouse was last seen heading north on the interstate in a red Corvette. Are you going to dig out the measuring cup and wash it at a time like this? Of course not. Instead, you try to visualize what 3 cups of cheese looks like and then you start grating like mad. And if you're off ½ cup or even a whole cup, well, the only damage done is you have an extra-gooey or perhaps a slightly spartan pizza to eat.

Or maybe you need 1 cup of chopped onions for a quiche. Why measure it? You'll only have to wash the measuring cup later. Instead, try to visualize the volume. Check yourself from time to time. Learn what 1 cup of chopped onions looks like on your cutting board; 1 cup of chopped peppers or celery looks the same (only greener).

In the same way that you can judge a cup of onions by the amount of space they take up on your cutting board, there are other "built-in" measures at your disposal. When you grate that cheese for the pizza, and it comes up to the center of the box grater, find out how much cheese you have. If it equals 2 cups, file that information away in your head for future reference. How many raisins or nuts can you hold in a loose handful? One-third cup? Then forever after 3 handfuls will make a cup for you. What does a teaspoon of salt look like in your cupped palm? A half teaspoon?

I'm not proposing complete abolition of measurements; leavenings—such as baking powder and baking soda, for instance—should be measured with accuracy for best results. I'm merely suggesting that there's a measure of leeway in many recipes and that such awareness can make home baking more enjoyable for you.

# Tahini Aniseed Cookies

*Makes about 36 cookies*

Tahini is sesame seed paste, with a texture like thin peanut butter. In baking it acts somewhat like butter, adding not only richness but also a sesame flavor that speaks well for itself and even more eloquently—I think—alongside whole wheat; you'll see what I mean when you make these. You have 3 options for baking them: plain or rolled in coconut or toasted sesame seeds.

*½ cup tahini*
*¼ cup unsalted butter, softened*
*¾ cup honey or maple syrup*
*1 large egg*
*1 teaspoon vanilla extract*
*2 teaspoons finely grated orange zest*
*2 cups whole wheat flour*
*2½ teaspoons crushed aniseed (crush whole seeds with a rolling pin between sheets of wax paper)*
*1 teaspoon baking powder*
*½ teaspoon salt*

Preheat the oven to 350° and lightly butter 1 or 2 large baking sheets, preferably not dark ones. Using an electric mixer, beat the tahini, butter, and honey or maple syrup for about 2 minutes, until well blended. Beat in the egg, vanilla, and orange zest.

In a separate bowl, stir together the whole wheat flour, crushed aniseed, baking powder, and salt. Stir half the dry mixture into the creamed mixture, just to blend, then work in the remaining dry mixture; do not beat the dough.

Form the dough into small balls, roughly 1¼ inches in diameter, and place them about 2 inches apart on the prepared sheets. Using a fork, press the balls down gently to a thickness of about ¼ inch. Bake, one sheet at a time, for 10 minutes; the bottoms will just be beginning to brown. Cool for several minutes on the cookie sheet, then transfer by spatula to a rack to finish cooling. Store in an airtight container. ♦

## Apple Apricot Spice Cookies

*Makes about 24 cookies*

Here's a delicious, cakey cookie, sweetened mainly with apple butter and a little honey. Try to find unsulphured apricots if you can; a local health food store will probably carry them. You'll be surprised at how much better they taste than the more common sulphured variety. You get a truer apricot flavor. Recipe tinkerers be forewarned: I've already tried adding nuts and other dried fruits to "improve" these, with little luck. Also, this isn't the type of cookie that improves with age, so eat them as fresh as possible. That shouldn't be a problem.

1/2 cup (1/4 pound) unsalted butter, softened
1/2 cup apple butter (see note below); if spiced, reduce the overall amount of spice listed below
1/3 cup honey
1 large egg
1 teaspoon vanilla extract
finely grated zest of 1 orange
3/4 cup unbleached flour
1/2 cup whole wheat flour
1 teaspoon baking powder
1/2 teaspoon ground cinnamon
1/4 teaspoon ground cloves
1/4 teaspoon salt
1 1/2 cups chopped dried apricots, preferably unsulphured

Preheat the oven to 350°. In a medium mixing bowl, cream the butter, apple butter, and honey with an electric mixer. Beat in the egg, vanilla, and orange zest.

In a separate bowl, sift the flours, baking powder, spices, and salt. Stir half the dry ingredients into the creamed mixture, just to blend, then stir in the rest of the dry mixture; add any bran flakes that are left in the sifter. On the last few strokes, fold in the apricots. Lightly butter 1 or 2 large cookie sheets, preferably not dark ones.

Drop tablespoonfuls of dough onto the sheets, keeping them about 2 inches apart. Bake, one sheet at a time, for about 12 minutes. When done, the tops should be just slightly resistant to light finger pressure. Cool the cookies briefly on the sheet, then transfer them to a rack to finish cooling. These are excellent warm.

NOTE: *This is one of several recipes using apple butter. Either use a good store-bought brand or try my homemade recipe on page 306.* ◆

## Making Apple Butter

Every fall we end up with tons of apples, a few bought but the majority bestowed on us by our friends, who—in the pursuit of a carefree but marginal existence—pick apples annually here in New Hampshire and neighboring Vermont.

One way we cope with apple abundance is by making apple butter, essentially a thick, smooth applesauce and a great item to spread on breads and to bake with; see "apple butter" in the index. The process is simple: peel and core the apples, cook them in a little water or cider, and cook further—unsupervised, in the oven—with a little spice and sweetener. For extended storage you can put this up in small canning jars, but we often finish it quickly enough that it just goes in the fridge.

Specifically, peel, core, and thickly slice 5 pounds of apples; I've never worried too much about variety, and it doesn't seem to matter. If you want to save money, and you live near an apple orchard, see if you can buy "drops," apples that have been picked from the ground, or seconds, those with blemishes.

Put the apples in a large nonaluminum pot with 2 cups of apple cider or water and the juice of half a lemon. Bring to a boil, reduce the heat to low, and cover. Cook for about 30 minutes, stirring occasionally, until the apples have turned to mush; it's okay if there are a few big chunks here and there that haven't quite mushed. Remove from the heat and cool briefly.

Now you have to smooth the fruit out. I use a little Foley food mill, but other methods work just as well: a food processor, a little gadget you can get at some hardware stores called a Squeezo, or one of those big conical sieves with a wooden pusher. Don't use a blender, because it makes the fruit too fluffy.

Process the fruit and transfer to a bowl. Stir in ½ teaspoon ground cinnamon and ½ cup sweetener of your choice: sugar, brown sugar, honey, or maple syrup. Plain sugar will give you the purest apple flavor; honey and maple syrup will impart their own flavors. Turn the fruit into a 9- by 13-inch nonaluminum baking dish and cook in a 350° oven for about 1½ hours, stirring occasionally so it cooks evenly and doesn't form a skin. When done, it will be reduced by about half. Cool in the pan.

The last step, if you want to put this up, is to pack your apple butter in sterilized jars and process for 10 minutes in a boiling water bath. I think half-pint jars are best, because then you can share this with your friends. For the details of processing in a boiling water bath, refer to a good canning book.

# *Cashew Butter Chocolate Chip Cookies*

*Makes about 30 cookies*

Cashew butter is peanut butter's upscale cousin and can be had, for a price, at most any health food store. Watch the timing on these cookies: they reach a point at the end when they start to spread and the surface cracks. That's the clue that they're almost done. One could, I suppose, make a case for dropping the chocolate chips so as not to sacrifice the cashew flavor. But then, I believe a little sacrifice now and then is good for everyone. An excellent cookie.

³/₄ cup cashew butter
¹/₂ cup (¹/₄ pound) unsalted butter, softened
1¹/₄ cups packed light brown sugar
1 large egg
1 teaspoon vanilla extract
1 cup whole wheat flour
²/₃ cup unbleached flour
1 teaspoon baking soda
¹/₄ teaspoon salt
1 cup (4 to 5 ounces) chopped roasted
   cashews
³/₄ cup semisweet chocolate chips

Preheat the oven to 350°. Lightly butter 1 or 2 large cookie sheets, preferably not dark ones. Set aside.

In a large mixing bowl, cream the cashew butter, butter, brown sugar, egg, and vanilla with an electric mixer. In a separate bowl, mix the flours, baking soda, and salt. Stir the dry ingredients into the creamed mixture, in 3 stages, just until blended. Mix in the cashews and chocolate chips.

Using your hands, form balls of dough approximately 1¹/₂ inches in diameter and place them on the cookie sheet, leaving at least 3 inches between them. Bake on the center rack for 12 to 14 minutes. They're done just at the point when the surface starts to crack and the cookie has spread out somewhat but before the tops start to brown; a tiny bit of top browning is okay, however. Don't be concerned that the top surface feels squishy to the touch. Remove the sheet to a cooling rack and cool them on the sheet for several minutes before transferring the cookies to the rack. Cool thoroughly, then store in an airtight container. ◆

# Peanut Butter Honey Date Cookies

*Makes about 36 cookies*

Instead of dates, you could use raisins here. These have a soft, moist interior, and they stay like that for days. Always a big hit with the kids.

*½ cup (¼ pound) unsalted butter, softened*
*½ cup honey*
*½ cup packed light brown sugar*
*1 large egg, at room temperature*
*1 cup peanut butter, preferably freshly ground*
*1 teaspoon vanilla extract*
*1 cup unbleached flour*
*¾ cup whole wheat flour*
*1 teaspoon baking soda*
*½ teaspoon salt (¼ teaspoon if the peanut butter is salted)*
*1 cup chopped pitted dates (see note below)*

Preheat the oven to 350°. In a large mixing bowl, cream the butter and honey with an electric mixer. One at a time, beat in the brown sugar, egg, peanut butter, and vanilla, mixing until light and fluffy. In a separate bowl, mix the flours, baking soda, and salt. Add the dry ingredients to the creamed mixture, in 3 stages, blending until smooth. Fold in the dates.

Drop slightly rounded tablespoonfuls of dough onto ungreased baking sheets. Bake, one sheet at a time, for about 12 minutes, until the tops are beginning to get brown. Don't worry if they give way under gentle finger pressure; they'll firm up as they cool. Cool the pan on a rack for a minute or 2, then transfer the cookies to the rack to finish cooling. Store in an airtight container.

NOTE: *If you have whole pitted dates that seem to be on the dry side, put them in a little bowl and pour on enough very hot water to cover. Let sit for 5 minutes, drain, and blot dry on a paper towel. Dust the dates lightly with flour, chop, then fold them into the batter.* ◆

# Nut-Crusted Preserve Tarts

*Makes 12 small tarts*

This is the type of tart or cookie that I have no inclination to make at all, except around the holidays, when I have a total change of heart. Then these formal-looking pieces of cookie architecture fit right in with the festivities. They're just perfect for a party; I like to arrange them on a little rectangular platter, in rows, each row with a different filling. (I also like to use fruit butters as well as preserves.) Sounds a little fussy, I realize, to line the muffin cups with wax paper strips, but don't be tempted to skip that step; you might get a few out intact without them, but you're taking a big gamble.

1 recipe *Whole Wheat Press-In Nut Crust* (*page 202*)
1 cup (*approximately*) (*1 10- or 12-ounce jar*) *fruit preserves or fruit butter*

Refrigerate the nut crust, preheat the oven to 350°, and butter 12 muffin cups. Tear off 2 sheets of wax paper about 6 inches long and cut them into strips 6 inches long and almost as wide as the bottom of your muffin cups, probably about 1½ inches. Lightly butter one side of each strip.

Take the strips and line each cup with one, buttered side facing out; the strips should go down one side of the cup, across the bottom (centered), and up the other side, so you end up with a roughly equal overhang on each side. (The purpose of the strips is to lift the tart shells out of the cups without damaging them.)

Run your fingers through the nut crust to loosen it up. Then, using a measuring cup, scoop a level ¼ cup (not packed) of the nut crust into each cup. Press the dough firmly into the cups, sculpting it into a shallow dish; if you make the sides too high and thin, they will tend to crumble, when you're either removing the shells from the cups or filling them. Bake for 15 minutes.

Place the muffin pan(s) on a rack to cool. After about 15 minutes the shells should be firm enough to pull out by the wax paper tabs; try one. If it still seems too soft, cool a little longer. Cool the nut shells on a rack, then peel off the wax paper strips.

When you're ready to assemble these, stir the preserves briskly to loosen them up. (If you want to get fancy, stir a few teaspoonfuls of compatible fruit liqueur into the preserves.) Spoon a tablespoon of the preserves into each nut shell.

These are best stored in a shallow box, with a foil (or the original) cover, with some sort of padding—such as paper muffin cup liners—so they don't slide around and bump one another. Crumpled-up paper towels on the bottom work well. Don't put anything on top of them or the preserves will stick. Store in a cool spot. ♦

## Whole Wheat Carob Cutout Cookies

*Makes about 36 cookies (depending on size)*

*H*ere's an alternative-style cookie, with all the flavor and goodness of a classic butter cookie. We love the dark color because it adds a handsome contrasting tone to a plate or boxful of other holiday cookies. Carob powder—sometimes called carob flour—is a caffeine-free product ground from the carob pod or locust bean. It has a faint, chocolaty flavor—fainter, I'm afraid, than a lot of carob converts would have you believe—so it is a good replacement for people, especially kids, who are sensitive to the caffeine in cocoa products. You can, however, substitute unsweetened cocoa powder for the carob powder.

*1 cup (¹/₂ pound) unsalted butter, softened*
*³/₄ cup packed brown sugar*
*¹/₄ cup unsulphured molasses*
*1 large egg*
*1 teaspoon vanilla extract*
*2 cups whole wheat flour*
*¹/₂ cup unbleached flour*
*¹/₄ cup carob powder*
*¹/₂ teaspoon baking soda*
*¹/₄ teaspoon salt*

In a large mixing bowl, cream the butter, brown sugar, and molasses. Beat in the egg and vanilla. In a separate bowl, sift together the remaining ingredients. (If the carob is clumpy, and it often is, you should rub it through the sifter.)

Using a wooden spoon, stir the dry ingredients, about a third at a time, into the creamed mixture. Stop mixing as soon as they're incorporated. Scrape the dough out onto a floured surface and form it into a ball with floured hands. Divide it in half and put each half onto a large sheet of plastic wrap. Flatten to about ¹/₂ inch thick, then wrap snugly in the plastic. Refrigerate for at least 2 hours, preferably overnight.

When you're ready to roll the dough, preheat the oven to 350°. Lightly oil 2 large cookie sheets; it's best not to use dark sheets. On a floured surface or lightly floured sheet of wax paper, roll the dough about ¹/₈ to ¹/₄ inch thick. Cut into any shapes you like and place them on the prepared sheets, leaving a little room between them. Bake, one sheet at a time, for 10 to 13 minutes. When done, the tops will dimple under gentle finger pressure, but they shouldn't squish down. Cool for a minute on the sheet, then transfer the cookies to a rack to finish cooling. These will keep well, stored in an airtight container.

NOTE: *This dough can be refrigerated, well wrapped, for several days. If overwrapped in foil, it can be frozen for several months. Thaw in the refrigerator and roll as usual.* ♦

# *Whole Wheat Shortbread*

*Makes 10 pieces*

Almost everybody likes shortbread. All that butter and the great crumbly texture are pretty much irresistible, especially with a cup of tea or coffee. This shortbread is easy to make, though in time you'll discover little things that make it perfect to your own taste, like a particular pan to bake it in, the precise amount of time it takes to bake, the color it turns when done. I bake mine in a 9-inch springform pan, which makes it on the thin side, and that's the way I like it. If you want to make it a little thicker, use an 8-inch springform or a 9-inch tin pie pan and bake it a little longer. But I do think the thinner you go, the better texture you get. This is based on the recipe in Helen Witty's *Fancy Pantry* (Workman, 1986), one of the friendliest and best-informed cookbooks I have.

> 1 cup whole wheat flour (finely ground is best)
> 1/3 cup confectioners' sugar
> 2 tablespoons cornstarch
> big pinch of salt
> 1/2 cup (1/4 pound) unsalted butter, softened a little
> 1 teaspoon vanilla extract

Preheat the oven to 325° and lightly butter the bottom of a 9-inch springform pan. Sift the flour, confectioners' sugar, cornstarch, and salt into a medium bowl. If any bran flakes remain in the sifter, add them to the dry ingredients. Cream the butter in a separate bowl, adding the vanilla before you turn the mixer off. Add the dry ingredients to the butter in 3 stages, stirring just to blend after each addition.

Flour your hands lightly—you'll have to do this periodically—and press the dough evenly into the prepared pan. (You may find that it helps to take off the side of the pan; put it back on before you bake.) If you are having trouble getting it even, and the warmth of your hands is making the dough too soft, just put the whole thing in the freezer for a few minutes to firm it up.

Once the dough is pretty even, lay a ruler across the top of the pan to use as a guide while you cut the shortbread into 10 wedges. Run a sharp knife down along the edge of the ruler, poking the dough to make deep indentations, keeping them a little apart. Next run a rubber spatula down the inside edge, all around, just to push the dough out from the side a tad. Bake the shortbread for about 40 minutes. The entire surface will darken a few shades, with the only noticeably darker area at the very perimeter. Undo the side of the pan and cool the shortbread on the pan's bottom on a rack. While the shortbread is still warm, finish the cuts with a sharp paring knife, but don't move the pieces until they've cooled. For storage, wrap pieces individually in plastic wrap. Wrap and cushion very well if you plan to mail shortbread. ♦

# Spiced Cornmeal Shortbread

*Makes 10 pieces*

Less traditional than the previous whole wheat shortbread—which itself is less traditional than classic shortbread—this has a grittier texture, because of the cornmeal, and a festive hand with the spice. A selection of the two shortbreads, individually wrapped pieces in a pretty tin, would be a thoughtful holiday food gift.

*½ cup whole wheat flour (finely ground is best)*

*½ cup unbleached flour*

*¼ cup yellow cornmeal, preferably stone-ground*

*⅓ cup confectioners' sugar*

*2 tablespoons cornstarch*

*¼ teaspoon ground ginger*

*¼ teaspoon ground cloves*

*¼ teaspoon ground cinnamon*

*pinch of salt*

*½ cup (¼ pound) unsalted butter, softened a little*

*1 tablespoon unsulphured molasses*

*1 teaspoon vanilla extract*

Preheat the oven to 325° and lightly butter the bottom of a 9-inch springform pan. Sift the dry ingredients into a medium mixing bowl. Cream the butter and molasses in a separate mixing bowl, adding the vanilla before you turn the mixer off. Add the dry ingredients to the butter in 3 stages, stirring just to blend after each addition.

Keeping your hands lightly floured, press the dough evenly into the springform pan; it may help to take off the side of the pan, but put it back on before baking. If the dough starts to get too soft from the heat of your hands, put the whole pan in the freezer for a few minutes, then proceed.

Once the dough is even, lay a ruler across the top of the pan to use as a guide while you score the shortbread. Run a sharp knife down along the edge of the ruler, poking the dough to make deep score marks; keep the marks a little apart. (You can also do this freehand, with a fork, but the pieces probably won't come out as even.) Next, run a rubber spatula down the inside edge, all around, just to push the dough out from the side a little. Bake for 35 minutes. The surface will darken a shade, with the edges a little darker. Undo the side of the pan and cool the shortbread on the pan's bottom on a rack. While the shortbread is still warm, finish the cuts with a sharp paring knife, but don't move the pieces until they're cool. To store, wrap pieces individually in plastic wrap. Wrap and cushion very well if you plan to ship the shortbread. ◆

# Ben's Carob Mint Brownies

*Makes 12 brownies*

These brownies are a concession to my son, Ben, who would have preferred candy cane pieces in his brownies, but whose old man—Scrooge that he is—made him settle for peppermint oil. They're very moist, tender, and soft, use mostly whole wheat flour, and are sweetened with honey. I put chocolate chips in them too, even though carob chips would seem to be the logical choice; the fact is, even though I like baking with carob powder, carob chips don't do anything for me. But if you like them, by all means use them.

½ cup (¼ pound) unsalted butter, softened

1 cup honey

2 large eggs, at room temperature

1 teaspoon vanilla extract

⅛ teaspoon peppermint oil (available at health food stores and herb shops)

¾ cup whole wheat flour

¼ cup unbleached flour

½ cup carob powder or unsweetened cocoa powder

½ teaspoon baking powder

¼ teaspoon salt

¼ cup milk

½ cup (about 2 ounces) chopped walnuts or pecans

½ cup semisweet chocolate chips

Butter an 8- or 9-inch square pan, glass or metal, and preheat the oven to 350° (325° if you're using glass). In a mixing bowl, cream the butter and honey with an electric mixer, beating until fluffy. Beat in the eggs, vanilla, and peppermint oil.

Sift the flours, carob powder, baking powder, and salt into a separate bowl, including any bran that's left in the sifter; carob powder is often clumpy, and you may have to rub it through the sieve.

Stir half the dry ingredients into the creamed mixture, blend in the milk, then whisk in the remaining dry ingredients, just until the batter is smooth. Fold in the nuts and chocolate chips. Bake for 35 to 40 minutes, until the brownies pull away from the sides of the pan and the top darkens a shade. When you press the top, they'll offer a little resistance, but not too much. Cool the brownies in the pan on a rack. Cut when thoroughly cooled. ◆

# Date-Apple Bars

*Makes 16 or more bars*

These triple-layer bars have a nut crust, a honey-sweetened date and apple filling, and a little more of the nut crust sprinkled over the top. My preference here is for the soft, moist Medjool dates I buy at our local health food store, but lacking those, use any other variety that's available.

*1 recipe Whole Wheat Press-In Nut Crust (page 202)*

FILLING
*1 large Golden Delicious or other cooking apple, peeled, cored, and coarsely chopped*
*2 cups chopped pitted dates*
*³/₄ cup water or cider*
*¹/₄ cup honey*
*a few gratings of lemon zest*
*¹/₄ teaspoon ground cinnamon*

Press all but 1 cup of the crust into an 8-inch square baking pan, glass or metal; refrigerate both the crust and the reserved cup.

To make the filling, put the apple, dates, and water or cider into a medium non-aluminum saucepan. Bring to a boil, reduce the heat, and simmer, stirring occasionally, for 5 minutes. Uncover and cook for about another 5 minutes, until the remaining liquid forms a thick glaze. Scrape the fruit mixture into a large bowl, then stir in the honey, lemon zest, and cinnamon. As that cools, preheat the oven to 375° (350° if you're using glass).

When the date mixture has cooled to about body temperature, spread it evenly over the refrigerated crust. Sprinkle the reserved nut crust evenly over the top, rubbing it between your fingers to break up any big clumps. Using a fork, very gently embed the crumbs into the filling; don't push them way down—just enough to set them.

Bake for 40 minutes, then cool thoroughly on a rack. They'll cut more easily if you refrigerate them first. ◆

# Dark Fudge Molasses Bars

*Makes 16 or more servings*

I love bars like these, where you save out some of the bottom crust and use it as a topping. Here we have a pecan-graham cracker base and a chocolate filling made with unsweetened chocolate melted in honey and molasses. That's blended with cream cheese, so you get a cheesecakelike filling, only a good deal firmer when it has been chilled. Because they're so dense, you can stack the pieces on a plate, pyramid style, for an attractive table presentation without fear of damage.

CRUST

- ³/₄ cup (*about 6 whole crackers*) *graham cracker crumbs*
- ²/₃ cup (*about 3 ounces*) *finely chopped pecans*
- ²/₃ cup *unbleached flour*
- ¹/₂ cup *packed light brown sugar*
- ¹/₂ cup (*¹/₄ pound*) *unsalted butter, slightly chilled and cut into small pieces*

FILLING

- ¹/₄ cup *honey*
- ¹/₄ cup *unsulphured molasses*
- 2 ounces *unsweetened chocolate*
- ¹/₂ pound *cream cheese, softened*
- 1 large *egg*
- 1 teaspoon *vanilla extract*
- 1 teaspoon *instant coffee or espresso powder or instant coffee substitute, such as Postum*

Butter an 8-inch square baking pan—I like glass here—and preheat the oven to 350° (325° if you're using glass). To make the crust, combine the graham cracker crumbs, pecans, flour, and brown sugar in a mixing bowl. Add the butter and cut it in with a pastry blender or rub it in with your fingers until you have damp, gravellike crumbs. Refrigerate 1 cup of this mixture and firmly pat the rest into the pan, pushing it ever so slightly up the sides. Bake for 15 minutes, then set aside on a rack.

To make the filling, gently heat the honey and molasses in a small saucepan. Add the chocolate and swirl the pan so the heated liquid flows over the chocolate. As soon as the chocolate has melted, whisk to smooth, then scrape the mixture onto a plate and cool to room temperature; to hasten the process, put it in the fridge.

Using an electric mixer, beat the cream cheese and egg until fluffy. Add the vanilla, instant coffee, and cooled chocolate. Beat until smooth, then scrape the filling over the crust. Evenly spread the reserved crumbs over the filling and lightly push on them with a fork to level the top.

Bake for approximately 35 minutes, until the surface is puffed and set. Cool on a rack to room temperature, then cover and refrigerate for several hours before slicing.

NOTE: *If you aren't crazy about molasses, use all honey instead of the combination. The bars will be sweeter.* ♦

## Coconut Almond Bars

*Makes 16 small bars*

*I* wanted to call these Almond Joy. Actually, these are almost like candy because they're so gooey and sweet and good. Cut them into small bars. Dense and firm, they ship well.

CRUST

*¹/₂ cup whole wheat flour*
*¹/₂ cup unbleached flour*
*¹/₂ cup packed light brown sugar*
*¹/₂ cup (¹/₄ pound) unsalted butter, at room temperature, cut into ¹/₄-inch pieces*

TOPPING

*¹/₂ cup packed light brown sugar*
*2 tablespoons unbleached flour*
*¹/₂ teaspoon baking powder*
*¹/₄ teaspoon ground cinnamon or freshly grated nutmeg*
*2 large eggs, lightly beaten*
*1 teaspoon vanilla or almond extract*
*³/₄ cup (about ¹/₄ pound) slivered almonds*
*³/₄ cup unsweetened shredded coconut (available at health food stores) or sweetened flaked coconut*

Preheat the oven to 300°. In a medium mixing bowl, mix the flours and brown sugar, rubbing them in your hands to smooth. Add the butter and cut it in with a pastry blender until you have a gravelly mixture that's starting to clump together. Spread it around in an 8- or 8¹/₂-inch square baking pan—I recommend glass—then press it in as evenly as you can, pushing it very slightly up the sides. Bake for 40 minutes, then cool on a rack for at least 30 minutes. Increase the heat to 350°.

As the crust cools, prepare the topping. Mix the brown sugar, flour, baking powder, and spice in a medium bowl, rubbing with your hands to take out the lumps. Add the eggs and vanilla and whisk them in until smooth. Fold in the almonds and coconut. Pour the filling over the crust and smooth it out. Bake for 25 minutes, until the topping has puffed up and turned a golden brown. Cool thoroughly on a rack before cutting into 2-inch square bars. Store in an airtight container. ♦

## Men Who Bake, Women Who Love Them

My first male baking model was my dad. Dad almost never cooked, but for some reason he had this thing for homemade apple pie. I can remember walking into the kitchen at some odd hour of the weekend and there he'd be, rolling out his pie pastry on a piece of wax paper, streaks of flour smeared across his forehead, a balding Pillsbury warrior. Of all the images I have of my father from my childhood days, this has always been one of the most vivid. Dad never made a big deal of his pies, showed them off, or collected recipes; that wasn't his style. In fact, I think he just used the recipe on the Crisco can. What mattered to him was the quiet act of doing something he found fulfilling and relishing—I suspect—something almost totally unrelated to the never-ending obligations of raising seven children. That and the fact that he loved homemade apple pie.

I think my dad may have felt a little uncomfortable in his occasional baking role. Maybe he felt men shouldn't make pies or that making pies was frivolous; even today, when the division between a man's and woman's work is fuzzier than ever, a guy could feel those kinds of feelings pretty easily. We men, after all, are only human, and we tend to act in accordance with the male tradition: strong, tough, the breadwinner, not the bread baker. We'll change the oil, mow the lawn, and man the grill, but home baking, somehow, doesn't fit the image. You don't see flour companies sponsoring ads with bunches of big, brawny guys punching the air, hootin' and hollerin' over a great batch of cookies.

From my own perspective as a family man, I like the time I spend in the kitchen. It puts me on the front line of fatherhood, where—with practice—one can learn patience, empathy, tolerance, and many other things you would have needed a lot less of had you remained single. Being there, as an active participant, keeps me close to my kids at a time in their young lives when almost every day brings some new treasure to savor: first steps, primitive three-word sentences, the excitement of a new dress or haircut. Yeah, those are just little things, but for a parent they're warm, sweet little things you can't buy or retrieve after the fact. No, it isn't always easy being in the geographic center of our home. It does get awfully hectic at times because youngsters tend to congregate where their parents are and compete for their attention; one's patience can wear thin. But that's to be expected. You get better. I think my baking and ongoing position in the kitchen also reinforce a lesson we've always tried to get across to the kids: that we all contribute what we can to the common cause. Nothing could make the point more clearly to kids than a fresh loaf of bread, a plate of cookies, or a warm pie.

So, guys, if you have any inclination at all to try your hand at home baking, by all means do it. You have more to gain from it than you think. Just pick something that sounds good and easy and go for it and don't feel discouraged if it doesn't come out perfect the first time. You'll catch on. And when you finally do pull that perfect loaf from the oven, all dark and crusty and smelling seductively of amber fields, and the wife sidles up next to you and whispers sweetly in your ear about what a great baker you are, you'll banish forever the thought that a man's place isn't in the kitchen.

## Cranberry Apricot Bars

*Makes 16 small bars*

Everybody loves a fruit bar like this, in a packed lunch, as an afternoon snack, or with coffee after dinner. These have a chewy brown sugar, oatmeal, and whole wheat crust—a little of which is pressed into the top to give them an attractive finish. The fruit filling is honey-sweetened, laced with cloves and lemon zest. A tin of these would brighten the holidays for a close friend, the mail carrier, or your favorite serviceman.

CRUST

*³/₄ cup unbleached flour*
*¹/₂ cup whole wheat flour*
*¹/₃ cup rolled oats* (not *instant*)
*¹/₂ cup packed light brown sugar*
*big pinch of salt*
*7 tablespoons unsalted butter, at room temperature*
*¹/₃ cup finely chopped walnuts (almost 2 ounces)*

FRUIT FILLING

*2 cups fresh cranberries*
*³/₄ cup water*
*1¹/₄ cups chopped dried apricots*
*¹/₂ cup honey*
*finely grated zest of ¹/₂ lemon*
*¹/₄ teaspoon ground cloves*

Select an 8- or 8¹/₂-inch square baking pan; I like glass for this and most other bar cookies. Preheat the oven to 325° (300° if you're using glass).

Make the crust. Put the flours, oats, brown sugar, and salt in a mixing bowl and toss with your hands to mix. Add the soft butter and work it in with your hands or a pastry blender until the mixture is damp and clumpy. Set aside ²/₃ cup (not packed) of this mixture in a small bowl and add the walnuts to it. Reserve. Press the unreserved portion into the ungreased pan and bake for 30 minutes. Cool on a rack.

Meanwhile, make the filling: Put the cranberries and water into a medium non-aluminum pot. Bring to a boil over high heat, cover, and reduce the heat to medium. Cook for about 3 or 4 minutes; the skins will pop, and it will start to thicken. Add the remaining ingredients and cook at a gentle boil, uncovered, for 3 to 4 minutes more, long enough to become visibly thicker but still quite moist. Scrape into a large bowl and cool to body temperature. Increase the oven temperature to 350° (325° if you're using glass).

Scrape the cooled filling over the crust and spread it evenly. Rub the walnuts into the damp flour mixture you added them to, then spread this topping evenly over the fruit. Press it very gently into the fruit. Bake for 25 minutes. Remove the pan to a rack and let cool completely before slicing into 2-inch square bars. For longer-term storage, and especially if you're sending these in the mail, wrap each one individually in plastic wrap. ♦

## Cookie Craft

—If your cookies tend to burn on the bottom, you can remedy that problem by "double-panning." Just put the pan inside of a second one of the same size, to create a thin, protective air layer between the two of them. If you're using flat sheets, use pennies for spacers between the sheets.

—For even baking, don't bake more than one sheet of cookies at a time, unless the sheets fit on one shelf, with at least 2 inches of space between the sides of the pans and the oven walls. Unless otherwise indicated, bake cookies on the center rack of the oven. Turn the sheets 180 degrees midway through the baking.

—Generally, cookies should cool just briefly—a minute or two—on the sheet, to firm them up before transferring to a cooling rack.

—Store cookies as soon as they have cooled. Most cookies will keep at least 4 days in the cookie jar, at room temperature. For longer storage you can refrigerate or freeze them, individually wrapped. Frozen cookies will remain in good condition for up to 2 months.

# Honey Bran Crackers

*Makes 20 to 30 crackers*

A graham-type cracker, these are thicker than some, rugged in appearance with a crumbly texture but a firm bite. Not fancy, but good-tasting and homey. Let the kids do some of the cutting; this is a real kid cracker.

1¹/₂ cups unbleached flour

³/₄ cup whole wheat flour

³/₄ cup wheat bran

1 teaspoon baking powder

1 teaspoon ground cinnamon

¹/₂ teaspoon unsweetened cocoa powder

¹/₂ teaspoon salt

¹/₂ cup honey

¹/₄ cup unsalted butter, melted and partially cooled

1 large egg

Preheat the oven to 350° and get out 2 large baking sheets, preferably not dark ones. Into a large mixing bowl, sift the dry ingredients; dump in any bran left in the sifter. In a separate bowl, whisk together the honey, melted butter, and egg.

Make a well in the dry ingredients and stir in the liquid, working the dough with your wooden spoon until it coheres. Knead the dough 5 or so times in the bowl, then let it rest, covered, for 5 minutes.

Working with half the dough at a time, roll it into a square or rectangle ¹/₈ inch thick on a sheet of lightly floured wax paper. Lightly flour your pin and the dough, if needed, to prevent sticking. Using a sharp knife, cut the dough into squares or rectangles or other shapes; the size is up to you. Slide a dough scraper or spatula under the crackers and transfer each one individually to the baking sheets, leaving just a little room between them. Bake, one sheet at a time, for 12 to 15 minutes. When done, the edges will just be starting to brown and the bottoms should be golden brown. Transfer the crackers to a rack to cool. Store in an airtight container. ♦

# Oatmeal Shortbread Crackers

*Makes 20 to 25 crackers*

Something like graham crackers; in these the fat comes from the cream, giving them a finished texture much like shortbread. So they're almost more like cookies than crackers. Great with a glass of milk.

*1 cup oat flour*
*1 cup unbleached flour*
*1/3 cup packed light brown sugar*
*1 teaspoon baking powder*
*1/2 teaspoon salt*
*3/4 cup (perhaps a little more) heavy cream*

Put the flours, brown sugar, baking powder, and salt in a medium bowl and rub with your hands to blend; rub out any clumps of sugar. Make a well in the dry ingredients and stir in most of the cream. Stir well, working in more cream if it is clear the dough is too dry to cohere. When the dough pulls together, knead it once or twice—on a floured surface if it's a bit damp. Divide the dough in half and shape each half into a rectangle about 1/2 inch thick. Wrap them in plastic wrap and refrigerate for at least 30 minutes.

When you're ready to roll the dough, preheat the oven to 350°. Working with one piece of dough at a time, roll the dough on a piece of lightly floured wax paper into a rectangle about 1/8 inch thick. Cut crackers of any size you wish, then transfer them to an ungreased baking sheet, preferably not a dark one, to keep the bottoms from getting too dark. Bake for approximately 15 minutes, until ever so slightly shaded gold; be careful not to overbake. Transfer the crackers to a rack to cool, then store in an airtight container. ♦

At the risk of sounding like a perfect nerd, I like to make crackers, a sentiment I share with one of this country's first commercial cracker makers, an ex–ship's captain by the name of Josiah Bent. Captain Bent, in his seagoing days, had come to loathe one of the common shipboard biscuits of his time, an unleavened loaf of flour and water called *hardtack*. Also known as ship biscuit, this compact loaf was well suited to long ocean voyages but had all the edible appeal of a Ping-Pong paddle.

So Bent—on a hunch that what this country needed was a better cracker—took to his Milton, Massachusetts, kitchen in 1801 and soon emerged with several successful recipes for thin, crisp wafers. He called them crackers, according to an account in the corporate history of Nabisco, probably because of the noise they made when eaten. Bent traveled from town to town, selling his crackers from his saddlebags, while his wife and kids did the baking.

If you've ever rolled a piecrust, you've already mastered the most difficult part of making crackers. The following collection of cracker wisdom should smooth the way for you.

♦ If you have to roll the dough in a small area (and even if you don't), it's easier to divide the dough in half or thirds first and work in smaller batches. Keep your rolling area uncluttered.

♦ Don't bully the dough with your rolling pin, or you'll end up with the cracker maker's version of the iron-on decal. Use authoritative but gentle strokes with your pin.

♦ Keep your surface lightly floured or roll directly onto a sheet of wax paper.

♦ Cut your crackers any way you please. Part of the charm of homemade crackers is their roughness, so I can't see getting carried away with special cutters and a lot of precision. I generally just roll a big rectangle, mentally divide up the dough, then do my best samurai routine with a sharp knife. A pastry jagger or ravioli cutter makes a pretty edge.

♦ It's a good idea to prick your crackers with a fork before baking; it helps to keep them flat on the sheet.
As for baking:

♦ Turn the sheet 180° halfway through, for even baking.

♦ Make a first check, several minutes before they're supposed to be done, scouting for potential early finishers; pull those off the sheet and bake the rest longer.

♦ With experience you'll be able to tell at a glance when a cracker is done. The perfect look varies from cracker to cracker, but you usually want a golden brown bottom and just-beginning-to-brown edges.

# *Vegetable-Flecked Semolina Crackers*

*Makes 12 crackers*

Because I have so many gardening friends, I really wanted to come up with a cracker that evoked the garden, one that would be a fitting gift for the green thumbs who supply me with so many of my raw materials. This stunningly pictur-esque cracker is what I came up with: a big, thin, golden wafer streaked with shards of grated carrot, bits of onion, sun-dried toma-toes, and dried mushrooms. For a simple but special gift basket, divide these between two plastic bags—slightly blown up, so there's a little air cushion—and tuck them in a basket with a bottle of wine, a cheese or two, and some unblemished pears. Just a nice, homemade soup and these crackers would be a great present too.

*1 medium-size carrot, peeled*
*2 tablespoons finely minced onion*
*2 tablespoons finely minced dried mushrooms*
*1 tablespoon finely minced sun-dried tomatoes (not oil-packed)*
*2 teaspoons dried basil*
*²/₃ cup unbleached flour*
*²/₃ cup semolina flour*
*2 tablespoons finely grated fresh Parmesan cheese*
*1 teaspoon baking powder*
*³/₄ teaspoon salt*
*¹/₃ cup plus 1 tablespoon water*
*2 tablespoons good-quality olive oil*

Preheat the oven to 250° and get out a large baking sheet. Tear off a piece of wax paper the length of the baking sheet and line the sheet with it. Grate the carrot right onto it, using the larger, not the smallest, holes. Spread the gratings evenly on the sheet, then sprinkle the minced onion over them. Place the sheet in the oven for 30 minutes to dry the vegetables out.

Cool the vegetables on the sheet, then scrape them into a medium bowl. Add the dried mushrooms, dried tomatoes, and basil and mix with your fingers. Dump the flours, Parmesan cheese, baking powder, and salt on top of the other ingredients and mix well. Make a well in the center, then pour the wa-ter and oil into the well. Mix with a wooden spoon until the dough coheres, then knead in the bowl for about 1 minute; a squeezing type of kneading may be easiest with such a small piece of dough. Roll the dough into a thick rope between your palms and wrap in plastic wrap; refrigerate for 15 minutes. In the meantime, preheat the oven to 350° and get out 1 or 2 large cookie sheets.

After its rest, cut the dough into 12 equal pieces. Working with one piece at a time—keep the others covered—roll the dough into a ball between your palms. Place it on a sheet of lightly floured wax paper and roll into a 4- to 5-inch circle. Place the circles of dough on the sheet—they can touch be-cause they won't spread—and bake, one sheet at a time, for about 15 to 18 minutes. When done, they'll be golden, but don't let them overcook and turn too brown or the flavor will suffer a good deal. Cool the crackers directly on a rack before storing in an airtight container. ♦

## Cracked Wheat Wafers

*Makes 20 to 30 crackers*

Here's a basic wheat cracker, speckled with cracked wheat. I specify *fine* cracked wheat, which is simply cracked wheat I've put through the blender, then sifted to remove the big, hard pieces. This isn't absolutely necessary, though it's highly recommended if you value your teeth. An easy cracker to customize with your choice of seeds on top or herbs in the dough.

> 1¹/₃ cups unbleached flour
> ²/₃ cup whole wheat flour
> ¹/₃ cup fine *cracked wheat (see note above)*
> ¹/₂ teaspoon baking powder
> ¹/₂ teaspoon salt
> ¹/₄ cup cold unsalted butter or vegetable shortening (or a combination)
> 1 large egg
> ¹/₂ cup cold water
> egg wash: 1 egg white beaten with 1 teaspoon water (optional)

In a large bowl, mix the flours, cracked wheat, baking powder, and salt. Add the butter and cut it in until the mixture resembles coarse meal; the fat will be broken into very tiny pieces. Lightly beat the egg and water in a small bowl, make a well in the dry mixture, and stir in the liquid just until the dough coheres. If it seems a little on the damp side, add a few shakes of flour. Knead the dough once or twice in the bowl, then flatten it into a thick disk and wrap in plastic wrap. Refrigerate for about 15 minutes while you preheat the oven to 375°.

On a lightly floured surface or a long sheet of wax paper, roll the dough a little less than ¹/₈ inch thick; use shakes of flour on top of the dough too so the pin doesn't stick. Cut the crackers however you please and transfer to ungreased cookie sheets. If you like, glaze lightly with the egg wash and sprinkle with seeds and salt. Bake, one sheet at a time, for about 20 minutes; the tops should be crisp and the edges a light golden brown. Transfer the crackers to a rack and cool thoroughly before storing in a sealed container. ◆

# Cornmeal Cheddar Crackers

*Makes 20 to 30 crackers*

We love these crackers; they're great for parties. What works well is to divide the dough in thirds and then roll circles, cutting the crackers into pielike wedges. You serve them on a big platter, surrounding a bowl of guacamole to dip into. Have a little salsa on the side. Great with other spicy dips too.

1 cup unbleached flour
1/4 cup whole wheat flour
3/4 cup yellow cornmeal, preferably stone-ground
1/2 teaspoon salt
1/2 teaspoon baking powder
1/4 teaspoon cayenne pepper
1 cup (about 3 ounces) grated sharp Cheddar cheese
1 large egg
1/4 cup flavorless vegetable oil
1/4 cup water

In a large bowl, mix the flours, cornmeal, salt, baking powder, and cayenne; stir in the Cheddar. Lightly beat the egg, oil, and water in a separate bowl. Make a well in the dry ingredients and stir in the liquid just until the dough coheres. Give the dough a shake of flour and knead it once or twice in the bowl. Flatten it into a thick disk, wrap in plastic wrap, and refrigerate for 15 minutes.

Preheat the oven to 375° while the dough chills.

On a lightly floured surface or long sheet of wax paper, roll the dough a little less than 1/8 inch thick; closer to 1/16 inch is actually better. Dust the top of the dough, if necessary, to keep your pin from sticking. Cut the crackers any way you like, then transfer to ungreased cookie sheets. Bake, one sheet at a time, for 15 to 20 minutes, depending on thickness (longer for thicker crackers); when done, they'll be nicely browned around the edges. Transfer the crackers to a rack and cool thoroughly before storing in a sealed container. ♦

## Drop Me a Line, or When Bad Things Happen to Good Bakers

Having spent a number of years developing recipes, cooking daily at home, and writing recipe pieces for magazines, I can say with some certainty that there are times when— for any number of reasons—recipes don't turn out. No one likes to admit that in public, but it's true. I may have tested something to death, fine-tuned a recipe to perfection, only for you to follow my instructions and, in the final analysis, decide the recipe hasn't worked for you. And baking recipes—because you're often dealing with precise measures, flours that vary in moisture content and composition, and leavenings with limited life spans—seem more prone to glitches than other types of recipes.

I hope any baking you do from this book will be trouble-free, and by all rights it should be: the recipes herein have been thoroughly tested, a lot of them four, five, and six times. In writing the recipes I've always tried to anticipate possible questions and to let you know how something will look or feel at various stages of preparation.

But just in case something does go wrong, I want to hear about it (in the nicest words you can use; nasty letters have a way of getting lost around here). Just explain, as briefly as possible, what recipe you had trouble with and what the trouble was; for instance, you made the Cashew Butter Chocolate Chip Cookies, and they drooled off the baking sheet and made a big mess on the oven floor. Then I'll write back and ask as many intelligent-sounding questions as I can think of, like "Did you remember to add the flour?" Maybe the problem was the pan you used or the type of flour; maybe your leavening is deceased—between the two of us, we should be able to figure it out.

And while you're waiting for my answer, don't lose heart, because it's probably something simple. Anyway, send your letters to me in care of my publisher—with a self-addressed stamped envelope—and they'll be forwarded to me and I'll be happy to answer.

# Metric Conversion Chart

## CONVERSIONS OF QUARTS TO LITERS

| *Quarts (qt)* | *Liters (L)* |
|---|---|
| 1 qt | 1 L* |
| 1 1/2 qt | 1 1/2 L |
| 2 qt | 2 L |
| 2 1/2 qt | 2 1/2 L |
| 3 qt | 2 3/4 L |
| 4 qt | 3 3/4 L |
| 5 qt | 4 3/4 L |
| 6 qt | 5 1/2 L |
| 7 qt | 6 1/2 L |
| 8 qt | 7 1/2 L |
| 9 qt | 8 1/2 L |
| 10 qt | 9 1/2 L |

* Approximate. To convert quarts to liters, multiply number of quarts by 0.95.

## CONVERSIONS OF OUNCES TO GRAMS

| *Ounces (oz)* | *Grams (g)* |
|---|---|
| 1 oz | 30 g* |
| 2 oz | 60 g |
| 3 oz | 85 g |
| 4 oz | 115 g |
| 5 oz | 140 g |
| 6 oz | 180 g |
| 7 oz | 200 g |
| 8 oz | 225 g |
| 9 oz | 250 g |
| 10 oz | 285 g |
| 11 oz | 300 g |
| 12 oz | 340 g |
| 13 oz | 370 g |
| 14 oz | 400 g |
| 15 oz | 425 g |
| 16 oz | 450 g |
| 20 oz | 570 g |
| 24 oz | 680 g |
| 28 oz | 790 g |
| 32 oz | 900 g |

* Approximate. To convert ounces to grams, multiply number of ounces by 28.35.

## CONVERSIONS OF POUNDS TO GRAMS AND KILOGRAMS

| *Pounds (lb)* | *Grams (g); kilograms (kg)* |
|---|---|
| 1 lb | 450 g* |
| 1 1/4 lb | 565 g |
| 1 1/2 lb | 675 g |
| 1 3/4 lb | 800 g |
| 2 lb | 900 g |
| 2 1/2 lb | 1,125 g; 1 1/4 kg |
| 3 lb | 1,350 g |
| 3 1/2 lb | 1,500 g; 1 1/2 kg |
| 4 lb | 1,800 g |
| 4 1/2 lb | 2 kg |
| 5 lb | 2 1/4 kg |
| 5 1/2 lb | 2 1/2 kg |
| 6 lb | 2 1/4 kg |
| 6 1/2 lb | 3 kg |
| 7 lb | 3 1/4 kg |
| 7 1/2 lb | 3 1/2 kg |
| 8 lb | 3 3/4 kg |
| 9 lb | 4 kg |
| 10 lb | 4 1/2 kg |

* Approximate. To convert pounds into kilograms, multiply number of pounds by 453.6

## CONVERSIONS OF FAHRENHEIT TO CELSIUS

| *Fahrenheit* | *Celsius* |
|---|---|
| 170°F | 77°C |
| 180°F | 82°C |
| 190°F | 88°C |
| 200°F | 95°C |
| 225°F | 110°C |
| 250°F | 120°C |
| 300°F | 150°C |
| 325°F | 165°C |
| 350°F | 180°C |
| 375°F | 190°C |
| 400°F | 205°C |
| 425°F | 220°C |
| 450°F | 230°C |
| 475°F | 245°C |
| 500°F | 260°C |
| 525°F | 275°C |
| 550°F | 290°C |

* Approximate. To convert Fahrenheit to Celsius. subtract 32, multiply by 5, then divide by 9

## CONVERSION OF INCHES TO CENTIMETERS

| *Inches (in)* | *Centimeters (cm)* |
|---|---|
| $^1/_{16}$ in | $^1/_4$ cm* |
| $^1/_8$ in | $^1/_2$ cm |
| $^1/_2$ in | $1^1/_2$ cm |
| $^3/_4$ in | 2 cm |
| 1 in | $2^1/_2$ cm |
| $1^1/_2$ in | 4 cm |
| 2 in | 5 cm |
| $2^1/_2$ in | $6^1/_2$ cm |
| 3 in | 8 cm |
| $3^1/_2$ in | 9 cm |
| 4 in | 10 cm |
| $4^1/_4$ in | $11^1/_2$ cm |
| 5 in | 13 cm |
| $5^1/_2$ in | 14 cm |
| 6 in | 15 cm |
| $6^1/_2$ in | $16^1/_2$ cm |
| 7 in | 18 cm |
| $7^1/_2$ in | 19 cm |
| 8 in | 20 cm |
| $8^1/_2$ in | $21^1/_2$ cm |
| 9 in | 23 cm |
| $9^1/_2$ in | 24 cm |
| 10 in | 25 cm |
| 11 in | 28 cm |
| 12 in | 30 cm |
| 13 in | 33 cm |
| 14 in | 35 cm |
| 15 in | 38 cm |
| 16 in | 41 cm |
| 17 in | 43 cm |
| 18 in | 46 cm |
| 19 in | 48 cm |
| 20 in | 51 cm |
| 21 in | 53 cm |
| 22 in | 56 cm |
| 23 in | 58 cm |
| 24 in | 61 cm |
| 25 in | $63^1/_2$ cm |
| 30 in | 76 cm |
| 35 in | 89 cm |
| 40 in | 102 cm |
| 45 in | 114 cm |
| 50 in | 127 cm |

* Approximate. To convert inches to centimeters, multiply number of inches by 2.54.

# Index